BEING
CONSCIOUSNESS
BLISS

BEING
CONSCIOUSNESS
BLISS

A SEEKER'S GUIDE

Astrid Fitzgerald

Lindisfarne Books

Lindisfarne Books
P.O. Box 799
Great Barrington, MA 01230
www.lindisfarne.org

Interior book design by Sherry Williams/Oxygen Design
Production: Tilman Reitzle

Library of Congress Cataloging-in-Publication Data

Fitzgerald, Astrid, 1938–
  Being consciousness bliss : a seeker's guide / Astrid Fitzgerald.
      p. cm.
Includes bibliographical references.
  ISBN 0-9701097-8-4
  1. Spiritual life. I. Title.
  BL624 .F542 2001
  299'.935—dc21
                            2001029186

10 9 8 7 6 5 4 3 2 1

This book is dedicated to the One Self

CONTENTS

PART ONE
IN SEARCH OF THE SELF

PART TWO
THE VOICE OF THE SELF:
EXCERPTS FROM THE PERENNIAL PHILOSOPHY

PART THREE
UNCOVERING THE SELF

EXERCISES

About This Book

LIKE ANY ENDEAVOR, the book started as an idea — a "seed-form." It underwent many changes, took on a life of its own, and in a way had its own "spiritual evolution." It was at first to be a compilation of aphorisms representing the essence of the great Wisdom tradition — a primer or companion for the spiritual seeker, the kind of book I wished I had for occasional reflection or daily inspiration. But it soon became obvious that the seed-form contained more than was first anticipated.

As I began to reread sacred texts, scriptures, and hymns I had studied in the past, I was once again moved by the illuminating power of the Word and was nourished and reminded of the great truths of the ages — the wisdom of the Perennial Philosophy. This somehow fueled both my energy and the seed-form. I realized that while the sacred truths can stimulate our higher aspirations, they alone are not enough to help us along the path of Self-knowledge. We need the guidance of those who have walked to the end of the path, especially if for some reason we have to go it alone or choose to go it alone. We have to know what is involved, and we have to understand the fundamental principles underlying the traditions that lead to Self-knowledge.

As I studied my favorite texts, I came across the book that had inspired my own inquiry into the nature of human existence. It was Aldous Huxley's *Perennial Philosophy* — a masterpiece on the mysticism of the East and West that was my first contact with true philosophy and fired my then-dormant love of truth. Huxley framed the quotations, consisting mostly of empirical observations, poetic and pithy statements of truth and of direct experiences of the divine, with his own brilliant insights. The book was a true revelation for me, as it continues to be for many.

I searched for other texts in the tradition of the *Perennial Philosophy* and gathered an enormous amount of material from the treasure-trove of ancient Eastern texts, Western philosophers, and thinkers and mystics of all ages. I discovered the unity of vision underlying many of the wisdom teachings, philosophies, and schools of thought, but I also became aware of the subtle yet fundamental differences between monistic and dualistic beliefs, between the unified vision of God as manifestation and the dualistic view of God versus the world, and the critical differences in the paths based on these philosophies.

As the idea took form, the compendium of aphorisms grew into a guide for the seeker. I was glad to find that I did not need to go afar to conduct my research. An extensive library of ancient and modern philosophical texts, dating back to the beginning of my own continuing search and of the relentless study and inquiry of my husband, the writer Richard Geldard, lay right at my fingertips, in our combined library of the Great Books and the many new texts, commentaries, and miscellanies.

In my search for meaningful quotations and sources for a practical system of Self-recovery, I felt discouraged more than once as I kept getting lost in a wilderness of meaning — of too many conflicting theories and too much information. Reluctantly I had to let go of much wonderful material I had collected and discard many different tangents.

It became clear at some point that I could not merely lay out a smorgasbord of infinite possibilities for the seeker without using discrimination, one of the most important faculties in the search for truth. I realized that in order to make choices I had to have some basic understanding of the fundamental truths and beliefs that inform the many different paths to Self-knowledge. If I was to draw out some useful systems from this vast body of sacred teachings, the individual principles of the systems had to support each other. They had to be complementary rather than contradictory.

The aim of all spiritual work is to enlighten — to bring light and also to make lighter, as in having less weight — and to uncover the essential nature of the Self rather than to add or superimpose anything extraneous. Too much information, even truthful information, runs the risk of simply adding more layers. So I began the process of discarding what was not essential. My criteria for including material was, first, that I had to understand it, at least on some level; second, that I could relate it to experience, at least to a certain degree; that it was not, as far as I could see, tainted with ordinary belief and opinion, colored by time and place, or based on idle curiosity; and third, that it could be integrated into a more unified vision.

Just as we find out on the spiritual journey, that the word is not the truth until it is actualized in being and that wisdom is not true wisdom until it is lived, I realized the book was not complete until it showed in a practical way how to live the knowledge. To be a useful guide it had to go beyond theory and at least point to a way of using the great principles to shed our ignorance and grow into our own true nature. Here I was able to draw from thirty years of experience on the spiritual path. Part Three contains some of the most essential knowledge and practical information for the discovery of the true Self, as well as the disciplines necessary for the unfoldment of the higher faculties. It is by no means comprehensive, but I believe it will provide a solid beginning for anyone with the desire to embark on the journey of Self-knowledge. Enjoy!

Acknowledgments

I WISH TO EXPRESS MY GRATITUDE to all those sages, mystics, and scholars who have expressed, preserved, and revitalized the wisdom of the ages. In particular I wish to acknowledge the guidance and inspiration of H.H. Shantanand Saraswati, Shankaracharya of Jyotir Math in northern India, and to express my deep gratitude for the wealth of knowledge gathered from His Holiness's talks and answers to questions, graciously made available by the Study Society, London.

I wish to thank my family and all my friends on the path for their insights and support over many year. Deep appreciation goes to my husband, the writer Richard Geldard, for his encouragement and insightful editorial comments during the writing of this book. I also want to thank Susan Lipsey for reading the manuscript and sharing her wisdom. Finally, I wish to express my gratitude to Christopher Bamford of Lindisfarne Books for seeing the possibilities in the early stages of this project and to my editor, Richard Smoley, for his thoughtful and consummate editing.

INTRODUCTION

It is because we don't know Who we are, because we are unaware that the Kingdom of Heaven is within us, that we behave in the generally silly, the often insane, the sometimes criminal ways that are so characteristically human. We are saved, we are liberated and enlightened, by perceiving the hitherto unperceived good that is already within us, by returning to our eternal Ground and remaining where, without knowing it, we have always been.

OVER FIFTY-FIVE YEARS AFTER Aldous Huxley wrote those wise words in his beautiful anthology *The Perennial Philosophy*, published in 1944, there has been no notable change in our behavior. We are still teetering on a precarious balance. While some areas of human existence have improved, others have gotten much worse. For the most part we still do not know who we are or what our purpose is; we are still asleep individually and collectively. We spend a great deal of time immersed in a hypnotic trance that has us believing that somehow things will improve, that somebody will do something about the predicament we are in, and that in the end we will somehow survive despite our wrongdoing.

There are many changes afoot at the turn of the millennium — a general rethinking, reshuffling, and searching for new paradigms and new solutions to old problems. Much of this activity is in reaction to the frenetic way of life to which we have condemned ourselves. Millions in the Western world are changing lifestyles, careers, and professions. Many are looking for the simplicity of alternative lifestyles, while the very hardy and ecologically minded are "getting off the grid." Although all of this searching for a saner existence may look like a positive trend, in reality we are still headed in the same direction. We are still on the same train; we have just changed compartments. We are on the same linear track of thinking, being, and acting. We may be somewhat more content for the time being with a little more happiness and a little more leisure time, but we are still asleep. We don't know who we are or what our true potential is.

Although there currently seems to be an increased readiness to give up some of our materialistic excesses, as a whole we are still clinging to an outdated mechanistic worldview perpetuated by our education and social conditioning. Although even science is telling us that mind and consciousness are everywhere and that the unseen is far, far greater than the seen, we act as if this were not the case. We have not changed our thinking, nor have we integrated such knowledge into our waking consciousness.

Why would we want to hold on to this kind of thinking when it no longer serves either the individual or humanity? Because we are attached to it. We are the slaves of our conditioning, our desires, and our technology. We have an insatiable passion for "more" of the physical kind — pleasure, comfort, gadgets, information — and we believe we cannot live without these things. Why do we expect so little from life? Because we don't know who we are, as Huxley said. We are ignorant of our true nature. And we do not know what we are here for. We have forgotten our true purpose.

We have tried many ways of escaping from our personal and social ills. Yet we approach our problems from the perspective of matter, from the outside; we concentrate on the symptoms and try to fix them rather than treating the cause. But time is running out. We are a menace to the planet. We are harming the delicate balance of life and our own mental and physical health. We have to stop thinking that we can fix things on the physical level. We have to refrain from endless intellectualizing about problems and solutions and instead give our minds to the *understanding* of a few principles, and then turn these into effective action and wise solutions. We have to realize that "right thinking" begets "right action," as the Eastern tradition puts it.

Right thinking and right action have everything to do with knowing who we are. The world out there is a reflection of our thinking and our beliefs. If we can "return to our eternal Ground" and discover our true nature, then changes in the world will necessarily follow. When we find out who we are individually and what the purpose of human life really is, we free ourselves of ignorance and the bondage of material thinking and existence. It becomes easy to let go of the "needs" and "musts" of ordinary thinking and living. We then become open to a creative way of being in the world that is based on an understanding of universal principles and yet remains infinitely tolerant of the particular, inviting many diverse views and ideals. As we begin to see the hidden unity of human vision, we also delight in the diversity of expression of the creative force as it take a stand and effects constructive change.

THE AIM OF HUMAN LIFE is to know who we are — to realize our Self, our true nature, and our identity with the Universal Self, the one Reality. There is no other aim, say the voices of the Perennial Philosophy from the ancient Vedic sages to present-day mystics and lovers of eternal truths. The great masters have told us that the "kingdom of heaven is within you"; that our true nature is *sat-chit-ananda,* or being, consciousness, and bliss; that "thy Self is thy true teacher"; and that "the Atman, the experiencer, is pure consciousness." These statements are not just poetic or abstract ideas, but in fact confirm our experiences as we explore our true being. We have all experienced the "eternal now" or "that which *is,*" however briefly. We have all had heightened states of consciousness when we were acutely aware and alive. We all remember specific moments of real happiness or even bliss — a state of pure being, untainted by name or place or circumstance. Such memories never fade, because we have made a connection with reality. The rest of the time we are asleep as we go about our daily chores, often physically and mentally disconnected from the task at hand.

Since we have forgotten who we are, we first need to be reminded of our true nature; then we have to verify the great truths for ourselves and realize them in our own being. We need to know a few necessary truths about our purpose and about the means to liberation. We need to be convinced that Self-realization is our first duty here and that our calling is secondary and serves the latter in manifesting a greater power — a conscious unfolding of universal Self. We need to find a teaching that speaks to us clearly and directly and that will most perfectly harmonize our inner and outer lives.

The love of truth and wisdom is an innate desire in every one of us. Where it has been smothered, it may be fanned alive by inner aspiration or simply by hearing words of wisdom. We are most privileged to be able to have access to the great sacred library, the lovingly preserved Wisdom tradition, to satisfy our desire for truth. As we explore our own nature and the nature of existence, we will realize that creation is in fact a school of higher learning. Everything in it is imbued with meaning, symbols, and signs, if we but open our hearts and minds to them. We are invited to enjoy this creation and creatively participate in it. As we continually learn, see, and understand and put these truths to the test, we become wiser, happier, more conscious and alive. Discovery becomes a way of life, and life becomes interesting once again. We will learn from everything and realize that whatever is in front of us is our teacher, be it a child, a companion, a guru, a challenge, a task, or an inner reaction.

Our innate love of the good, of beauty and harmony, will surface as we are reminded of our true calling. We develop a taste for quiet enjoyment and self-reflection. We prefer peace over agitation. We are freer to give and to love. We notice a change of values and a marked decrease in worldly desires. We tread more lightly on the surface of the earth and leave less physical and mental residue in our wake. As our lives become simpler, they also become more joyous. These benefits are not the aim of the search for truth, but as by-products they are not to be despised and can be seen as the outer proof that the inner work is progressing. As we realize who we *are*, that which we are *not* will dissolve and with it all our illusions and attendant miseries.

When the inward journey, the "return to our eternal Ground," is undertaken by the many — as seems to be a real possibility at this time — we will not only be liberated but most likely saved as a species. Some of us may actually live to see and enjoy a renaissance of the Spirit. As we become aware of the "good that is already within us," we will also perceive a positive transformation of the world around us and note the dissolution of our mind-made problems and disasters. We will see clearly that they were caused by ignorance of our true nature and of the laws of nature.

As these problems dissolve, we will have the leisure to come together and consciously build a new world. Our search for truth might then give birth to a convergence of science, philosophy, culture, and art. Such a unified vision will in turn inform the use of technology and energy and form a basis for a wiser, happier, and more creative way of life. We will no longer be at the mercy of our unconscious deeds but will act prudently and responsibly towards each other and toward creation. We will have the time and aspiration to nurture, honor, and celebrate that which is eternal — our true Self — and in doing that we will not harm our planet, but will instead enjoy this precious creation, this magnificent playground of the Self.

As this new awakening of Spirit takes hold, we will come to understand that consciousness does not arise from matter or our body, but that everything we perceive — our bodies and the whole creation — appears in consciousness. Our sciences will confirm quantitatively what the ancient sages knew through introspection. The arts will find new forms and ways to celebrate the flowering of Spirit, of consciousness and knowledge, and will express not only the truly unique but also the truly universal in both man and nature. As we gain a wider view, we will respect and recognize the unity behind all the great truths and wisdom teachings, and a new, fresh, and living philosophy will emerge — one that reflects both the ancient and the new, as well as the emergent realities of a greater unfolding of consciousness. We may once again affirm that whatever lives is animated by the force of the one universal Self and that whatever we see is held in universal consciousness.

PART ONE

IN SEARCH
OF
THE SELF

ONE
WHERE WE FIND OURSELVES

WE SPEND OUR DAYS in a world of a myriad of external and manmade influences. We seek to subdue nature, just as our ancestors did, but we have gone too far in trying to control the natural course of our external world. Now we are faced with a new dilemma — managing the consequences of our actions.

We exert so much energy in trying to change our environment because we believe that in the end we will have the leisure to enjoy more comfort, more pleasure, more fun. We have built ourselves beautiful homes, universities, sports arenas, and temples to culture and pleasure, all in an effort to make ourselves happier, more beautiful, and more cultivated.

We have created a tremendous amount of labor-saving machinery to avoid the drudgeries of life and to acquire the leisure we desire. Every day we are dazzled by new inventions that we harness in the hope of making pleasure and comfort permanent conditions. We have become extremely mobile and can travel faster than the speed of sound. Communication of information is virtually instantaneous. We send telescopes into deep space and are awed by the images they send back, affording us glimpses into the beginning of time. We explore, we conquer, we acquire, we produce, and we try to do it faster than anyone else in order to compete and win in the global economy. Our heroes are the ones who win: the athletes with the best records, the entrepreneurs with the most money.

Our belief in progress remains unshakable even when confronted with the consequences of our excesses. Even our humanitarian beliefs are rooted in the idea of progress on the material level. We hold tenaciously to the conviction that by concerted effort we can improve our condition — we can "make things better" politically, economically, environmentally. When we fail to see positive results — more happiness, more leisure, a better life — we try harder to change the external world. We throw more money at our "problems" — physical and mental health, the educational system, the ailing environment.

At the 1992 World Economic Forum in Davos, Switzerland, Vaclav Havel, then-president of Czechoslovakia, expressed his concern with our incapacity to deal with our problems despite an unprecedented amount of information: "We are looking for new scientific recipes, new ideologies, new control systems, new institutions, new instruments to eliminate the dreadful consequences of our previous recipes, ideologies, control systems, institutions, and instruments. We treat the fatal consequences of technology as though they were a technical defect that could be remedied by technology alone." In other words, we are looking to eliminate our problems through the same kind of thinking that caused them in the first place.

When will we concede that our arrogant belief in material progress is not working for us? What is wrong with the picture we have painted? Are we becoming better human beings? Are we happier? Or are we merely moving in a vicious circle of providing and consuming more and more material goods to assuage our ever-increasing physical and emotional needs, thereby giving more power to a belief system that is itself the source of our problems?

We find ourselves in the midst of plenty, and yet there is an increasing sense of malaise and doom and of being at the mercy of the economic and technological machinery we have set into motion. We are sick of the noxious fumes, dissatisfied and overwhelmed by the ever-increasing clutter of daily life. Most of all we feel cheated by our inability to enjoy a balanced and happy life. The wealthy few have taken to the hills and pastures to enjoy country life. But the life of this modern gentry is supported by every convenience, and their privacy is guaranteed by sophisticated electronic devices.

Some, in need of something spiritual, have become adherents of New Age movements. Others have joined megachurches or gone back to traditional religion, which for many fulfills a need for a communal experience and for social life outside the home and office. At best these institutions serve as arbiters of ethical standards and preservers of family values, and also enable the individual to prac-tice altruism through humanitarian activities. Unfortunately their emphasis is on form, custom, and convention — not exactly a model we can easily integrate into our lives or align with our postmodern worldview. Moreover the dichotomy between organized religion, which emphasizes doing good works and loving and helping one another, and the marketplace, which condones stealing, deceiving, and outdoing competitors and coworkers in the name of progress, creates a tremen-dous rift in the individual psyche. As a result we are fragmented and disturbed in our being, a condition which is reflected back to us in our circles of family, community, and humankind at large.

One of our problems lies in the fact that there is no consistency in our feel-ings, thoughts, and actions. This inconsistency creates an ambiguity that we see in every facet of our lives. Deception has crept into the very fabric of contemporary language, with its fondness for paradox and words with contradictory meanings. Often the use of such verbiage is purposeful and intentional; it is designed to confuse, corrupt, and adulterate, harming communication and human relations in general. Ambiguity and deception contribute to the bewilderment of our children and to the difficulties in our families, befuddling our educational ideals, our polit-ical issues, and our national goals. Such deception can even produce violent outcomes when national leaders make use of it in their dealings with other nations, resulting in terror and war.

How can we make any sense out of this manmade conundrum? We cannot fix our mistaken philosophies or beliefs by national decree. We cannot change society by applying measures from the outside. All our laws and regulations, as we see on a daily basis, are not helping to make life more joyful and healthful for the majority. Nor have they made the slightest difference in the lives of those in need. Political repres-sion may be able to change the beliefs and behavior of society — but only for a short time. And as we have seen in the failures of totalitarian regimes, the long-term effects of such approaches are devastating to the human spirit.

In our commitment to improving life through material means alone, we created an imbalance not only in nature but in our own being. Sri Aurobindo, the eminent

Indian sage and philosopher, looking at our present situation, concludes that "the West has concentrated more and more on the world, on the dealings of mind and life with our material existence, on our mastery over it, on the perfection of mind and life and some fulfillment of the human being here: latterly this has gone so far as the denial of the Spirit and even the enthronement of matter as the sole reality."

We only know a very brief history of humankind. We know little about our heritage and ancient cultures; the traces of our ancestors have been all but erased. Our natural sciences provide us with glimpses into human evolution, but these are chiefly limited to the physical stages of development. When we look to interpretive anthropology, we gain a somewhat larger view of our past: the fragments of ancient cultures — the remains of colossal architecture, magnificent arts and crafts, mysterious artifacts and tools — not only give us an appreciation for their creators' accomplishments, but also suggest their level of consciousness. Even so we are left wondering. We can marvel at the brilliance of the consciousness that informed the builders of the pyramids and ancient temples, but we can never enter into the consciousness of our ancestors. We will probably never know exactly what they thought or what moved them to action.

Nevertheless when we look back at the fragmentary evidence, we can trace, if somewhat uncertainly, the evolution of consciousness, which seems to wax and wane in different eras. When we look from a distance at the periods of flowering and periods of darkness in human history, it becomes clear that these fluctuations reflect the state of consciousness of our ancestors. From this larger view we can see that mankind is somehow instrumental in the evolution of consciousness in creation. The sages tell us that we are, willingly or not, knowingly or not, the instruments for the greater unfolding of Spirit on earth and that we are perfectly suited to the task since we partake of both Spirit and matter. They tell us that we are spiritual beings in earthly bodies, not just the by-products of biological evolution or, as some would have it, a cosmic accident.

The expression of consciousness takes many forms, from the earliest stages of almost purely intuitive articulation to the mostly intellectual interpretations of the present. Some of the earliest cultures, documented in the Vedas, expressed their cosmological worldviews through a symbolic language articulated in myth, poetry, art, and dance. During the Middle Ages, this ancient, unified view shifted to a more dualistic one. Art and poetry was no longer in celebration of the universal, but was separated into the secular and the profane.

In more recent history we have seen a shift in social consciousness from the community or state to the individual, from national or cultural identity to the private citizen. The individual has taken center stage against a backdrop of multicultural diversity. We celebrate individual achievement and excellence. We strongly believe in the rights and freedoms of the individual and guarantee them by our laws. We value our power of revolt, cherish our freedom to progress, and assert our right to self-fulfillment and self-expression. Our humanistic causes and civil rights movements attest to our strong defense of our freedoms. Our culture is defined by diversity of expression in highly individualistic works of art and literature. But with a few exceptions, most art forms are based on a personal vision and are purely profane. The artist has little concern with universal ideas, with God or cosmos.

We are dazzled by our intellectual capacity, which has disclosed the wonders of nature to us, and well we should be. We find great delight in our physical achievements and explore new and thrilling ways to express our joy in motion and test the human spirit and endurance. We love our modern gadgetry and conveniences, many of which do serve us well. In their rightful place, these achievements are useful and even wonderful. However, when they come to constitute the sole reason for living, we are not winning but losing. When we are totally dependent on the perfect functioning of technology, we are in trouble.

When we ignore our true nature and fail to inquire into the meaning of our presence here on this planet, we eventually become bewildered and disenchanted. The prevailing reductionistic view has dethroned the spiritual man from his unique position and potential and reduced him to biological man. Ralph Waldo Emerson spoke of the consequences of such confusion when he wrote:

> *There are two laws discrete*
> *Not reconciled —*
> *Law for man, and law for thing;*
> *The last builds town and fleet,*
> *But it runs wild,*
> *And doth the man unking.*

The reductionistic stance has ignored the subtle difference between these laws and places man under what Emerson calls the "law for thing." As such he is regulated by the mechanistic worldview and judged according to its laws, the criteria being how well he fits into the modern machinery of production and consumption or how quickly he can adapt to the new demands of the information and service industries. In other words, he is rewarded according to how well he fits into the picture of the "useful member of society" and the "gainfully employed citizen." The subtle "law for man" no longer regulates this modern man: consideration of the spiritual nature of the human being is missing.

We do not need to deny our great technological achievements or the advances and discoveries of science, but we need to acknowledge once again our spiritual nature. We have seen the consequences of the denial of Spirit in the serious harm to our mental and physical well-being and to our environment. We do not need to agree on political issues, moral standards, religious and philosophical questions, or individual lifestyles. These are individual choices of no great consequence in the larger scheme of things; they are not the essence of the "law of man," just ripples on the surface of society. The "law of man" pertains to that which is common to all of us: our true nature, our mind, our consciousness, and our divine origin. When we acknowledge our spiritual nature and find wisdom in our own hearts, the seeming problems of society will dissolve. Our excesses will diminish, and the harm they have caused will be dealt with in the light of truth. When we come to realize our immense potential and our true purpose in life, we will no longer live by the "law for thing" or lend our power to a materialistic mass consciousness. We will aspire to an ideal of a higher nature, which we all hold in common deep within our hearts.

Our present stage of human development, sometimes referred to as the stage of individuation, has seen its negative aspects in the selfish pursuits of the "me generation" and its positive aspects in individual achievements and individual rights and freedoms. This stage may well have reached its culmination. Our discontent indicates that we are no longer happy with the status quo. We seem to be yearning for another kind of freedom, another way of being in the world.

What lies before us is in our hands. We still have a chance to determine our future, and as individuals we have the freedom to stop believing in our limitations and in reductionistic views. By not giving power to materialistic concerns and systems, we can help dismantle the precarious constructs of modern existence. We can each take a leap individually, and when enough people take this leap, we will collectively and consciously create a new reality that just might precipitate the next flowering of human evolution. All we need to do is want this reality and envision it, and then open up to our infinite potential.

We need to reconsider our existence in the light of this acknowledgment of universal consciousness and of the interconnectedness and preciousness of all life. We need to rethink our way of being in the world in the light of the universality of mind and consciousness and consider how science and technology can be the servants of this new reality. Most importantly, we need to embody this greater consciousness in ourselves and project it into our surroundings to create a new world.

The inquiry into existence and consciousness which has fueled philosophy since the beginning will be substantiated by enlightened scientific research. This common understanding will bring about a true synthesis of philosophy, science, and art. This knowledge will take root in the individual first and eventually will expand into collective consciousness to make itself felt in daily life. This development will bring about the consistency and cohesion we are now so utterly lacking in our obsession with specialization and departmentalization.

We do not actually have a choice of whether to join this evolution of human consciousness or not: we are in the midst of it. We do, however, have a choice whether or not to consciously, actively, and creatively take part in it. The urgency is evident: our health and that of our planet depend on our willingness to participate in the unfolding of consciousness and acknowledgment of our spiritual nature. It is through the advancement of Spirit in the world that the healing of the individual and society can begin. The challenge is formidable, and our intent has to be rooted in the love of truth and a desire for simplicity and a more introspective and joyful existence. Then will we serve the greater good according to our own nature, each doing what he or she loves most.

*

TWO

THE INDIVIDUAL CONDITION

O UR SOCIAL CONDITIONING begins at a very tender age, and, as research suggests, even before birth. As its ability to perceive develops, the fetus responds to sounds heard through the womb. At birth the child hears the voice of its mother and family members, and soon enough experiences the full din of modern life. These sounds have a profound effect on the soul, mind, and body. As we grow, our senses are subject to a continuous stream of impressions and influences. We have no control over this acculturation or over the external influences which insinuate themselves and create our persona. We are, quite literally, receivers picking up sounds, digits, bits of information from all around us — from generations of senders.

The process of conditioning goes on in adult life, depositing layer upon layer of beliefs and opinions into the psyche from home, school, church, peers, morality, education, and the media. Then, as parents, we in turn pass this social conditioning on to our children. Even if we found the acculturation process painful, we dutifully pass on this social armor to the next generation as if it were a precious heirloom.

Later on in life, we claim this accumulation of influences, regarding the conditioning and schooling as "my knowledge," "my point of view," and "my vision." We hardly ever stop to question this process or to consider how rarely we have a truly fresh or original thought. If we were to look for a truly creative thought or act or work of art — one that is not based wholly on the stale influences of the past — we would find that these are the rare exceptions in our time and that the articulations of true genius are equally rare.

As adults, we have a strong conviction that we are in control of our lives, that we are doing what we want to be doing, and that we are succeeding at it. We prove our reason for existence in our achievements as documented in impressive résumés. We engage in ceaseless activity of work and play. Our well-traveled Filofaxes attest to our notability, and our busy schedules give us the feeling of being an important cog in the world of progress and success — the comforting nod of "having arrived." Then we get to enjoy our dessert by spending our hard-earned money on the luxuries of life, on entertainment, on personal trainers and gurus. The art of perfecting the body has been elevated to a veritable cult to which we sacrifice time and energy. We count on the seemingly unlimited potential of medical engineering to keep us young and vital. We regard physical stress as an inevitable result of modern life; sometimes we even value mental stress and anxiety for their stimulating effects on the adrenal glands, giving us stamina and a competitive edge.

Our internal lives are equally busy. Our minds are engaged in a continuous stream of internal commentary, considering likes and dislikes, weighing actions and their consequences, perusing the past, and projecting the future. We may be dimly aware of the silent battle between heart and mind, between conscience and desire, but we do not stop and pay heed to it. We are not even puzzled when the outcome of our actions bears no resemblance to our plans and dreams, when there is no consistency between intent and goal. Deaf to the murmurings of our inner being, we keep on imagining that we are pursuing our heart's desire. We have learned to deny the truth and ignore our lack of real satisfaction and happiness.

We rarely stop to question this paltry way of being in the world, but rather we accept the tenets of a society that considers incessant activity and materialistic extraversion as a normal condition. Even when health research points to a connection between this frantic pace and our increasingly precarious state of health, we give it but a fleeting glance and dismiss it all too quickly as too esoteric or impractical.

We believe that we do not have time to think or consider. We are reluctant to turn our minds inward and just sit and reflect for fear that those around us will wonder what is wrong with us. Wanting to fit in, we rarely question the status quo. In order to question we would have to be aware of ourselves and the world around us. Then we would see that we have becomes slaves of a lifestyle that requires incessant activity to satisfy our material needs and desires. If we were awake, we would see that we are caught in a machinery in which we automatically participate, acting and reacting, desiring and acquiring, oscillating between pain and pleasure. Pleasure never truly satisfies but always calls for more, while in turn the procurement of pleasure demands more and more material wealth and hence more activity. There is no peace of mind, no quiet enjoyment of the present moment and the wonder of existence. When we are caught up in the surfaces of material life, we are unaware of our own being, whose very nature is stillness and happiness. We are, as it were, clinging to the circumference of a gigantic spinning wheel, mesmerized by its motion, holding on for dear life, unaware of the still point at the hub.

If we could wake up for a moment from this waking sleep and observe ourselves objectively, we would realize that all our inner conversations, our endless evaluating, planning, categorizing, criticizing go on by themselves and that we have no control over them. We would realize that we are not truly masters of ourselves, that our being is fragmented, our intent fickle and our attention scattered. We would see that we go about our daily life in a hypnotic trance in which we never feel quite alive or connected to our tasks or to those around us. We would realize that what lies at the core of all our acquisitiveness is in fact our birthright — our natural inborn desire for love, happiness, and peace. But in our ignorance of our spiritual nature, we seek to satisfy these innate natural desires by material means and settle for the banal: loveless relationships of convenience, passing pleasures and distractions, and the attempt to secure peace of mind by amassing financial wealth. We think we need more *because* there is no deep and lasting satisfaction in these temporal pursuits.

What keeps us asleep is our reductionistic stance — our belief in the supremacy of matter as well as our tendency to identify with everything we perceive. Dazzled by the appearances of things, we identify with whatever our senses grasp — the whole world of visible forms, particularly our own physicality. Because we have forgotten our true nature, the false ego assumes authority, identifying with body, mind, and senses and its objects of desire. In addition, we would like our life to last forever. While there is nothing wrong with this desire, the ego wants to claim this immortality for itself, and so we unwittingly become bound by time, form, and the body.

When we are not awake, there is no permanent "I," because the false ego is a master at disguises and assumes many different personalities. While it assumes great power, in fact it is ignorant and mechanical. In this state, the mind and reason succumb to the sensual world. The faculties of mind lag behind the senses and are subject to the desires these evoke; thus we become hopelessly enmeshed in attractions and can only react.

In our ignorance, we believe that this permanent entity we call "I" is willing, doing, thinking, and deciding what happens in our lives, when in fact the false ego is affected by external events and influences and is only able to react in a mechanical, conditioned way. We view ourselves as separate — "me against the world" — and we react accordingly, and live as if on a lonely island. Even when we are a member of a larger circle such as a family, community, or nation, the false ego maintains its sense of separateness, satisfying different needs of its conflicting personalities. We identify with these many personalities, with their peculiar attitudes, and we become very attached to them. These illusions would be quite humorous if they were not the cause of our unhappiness, suffering, and fears.

In fact all our fears and suffering are caused by our attachments to what we consider to be "me" and "mine" and the illusion that results when we claim "I am the body," "I am the doer," "I am the thinker." Fears are fueled by our imaginings about loss of life, loss of control over the body, emotions, and mind. Attachment to the body results in our preoccupation with physical needs. Attachment to doing leads us to a concern with results as well as to a preoccupation with past and future actions. Our attachment to personal beliefs creates that intolerance and stress we so often encounter in human relationships. Our mindless adherence to collective beliefs about creed or origin results in the ugliness of racial hatred. When we feel different and separate, we not only bring unhappiness to ourselves but export this ignorance into the world in the form of fear, hatred, dissent, and even war.

When, in a moment of great danger or grace, we are hurled out of our mechanical state and are given a glimpse of a different reality, for that brief moment we experience total freedom from our conditioning and self-imposed limitations. Time and space expand; we accomplish the impossible or are stunned into awed silence. In retrospect, we marvel at the experience and remember that we were looking from a higher perspective, where the necessary knowledge was simply available. These glimpses provide opportunities to escape our illusion and to wake up. But we cannot wait for these rare moments. We *can,* through conscious efforts, undo the wrong functioning of our instrument and step out of our conditioned and mechanical state. We *can* taste freedom from habitual negative thinking, from being subject to external influences, and from simply reacting to sensual stimuli. We *can* wake up from our slumber and know who we are and what our glorious potential is.

Our first step is to know that we are asleep. We have to truthfully assess our condition and observe that much of what we consider to be "our" life and "our" doing simply happens to us. Only when we accept the fact that we cannot *do* and hardly ever truly *are* do we have a chance to wake up.

We live our lives in a very horizontal manner and are largely unaware of our possibility to move in another direction — vertically. The large majority of humans beings live in two states of consciousness only: sleep and waking sleep. There is, however, a third level, which P.D. Ouspensky calls *self-consciousness,* in which an individual can know the full truth about himself, as well as a fourth level called *objective consciousness,* in which an individual may know reality — the full truth about everything. In our present state, we can know very little about this latter state, which is of a very refined nature. But the third level is definitely within our reach with the help of those who have gone before.

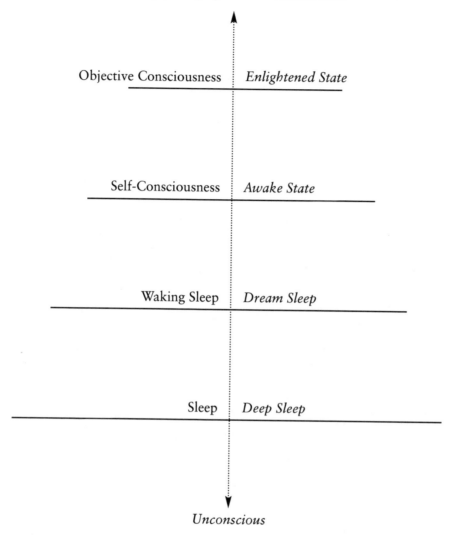

Figure 1. States of consciousness in the terms of
P.D. Ouspensky (left) and the Vedanta (right).

Fortunately we are the inheritors of the greatest wisdom of all ages —
the revelations of the ancient seers and avatars, the visions of the yogis and mystics
— all those great beings who have lived the "examined life" and gone on the quest
to awaken from slumber. They realized their true nature and grew into their full
stature as human beings and became liberated from suffering. By their observations
and methods they have shown the way.

This path to higher consciousness may rightly be called a science of the Spirit,
because it is verifiable, step by step and moment by moment, though self-observation,
study, inquiry, and certain disciplines that lead to direct experience of a higher reality.
The quest for Self-knowledge and the love of truth is as ancient as humanity. In fact
it dwells in the heart of each one of us and is our proper activity here on earth.

THREE
EXISTENTIAL CRISIS

WE OFTEN BELIEVE THAT WE are collectively progressing; that the world will be a better place in the future when we have more social and economic justice for all; that the discoveries of science will make life easier and longer; and that there will be more leisure time in order to have more and more time for pleasure. As long as we treasure this view, which is based on belief and wishful thinking, then we can function with a reasonable amount of contentment and contribute our share to this ultimate ideal. When no disharmony disturbs this ideal picture, we have no desire to go on the quest for Self-knowledge, since we are totally unconscious of our higher purpose.

If, however, we look at our situation in a moment of awakening, we might get a glimpse of the futility of being nothing more than a little screw in the big machine of the postmodern technological age. In the light of truth, we recognize that our state of existence is one of perpetual forgetfulness and illusion. We become perplexed and distraught or depressed. A crisis may befall us. We may disguise its spiritual nature by calling it a midlife crisis, career crisis, an identity crisis, or by some other name. The symptoms may vary from a general malaise or ill health to mild depression. If unheeded, it may evolve into more serious pathological states, such as severe depression or total fragmentation of the psyche. If we are conscious of our predicament, we try to find some help and, if we are fortunate, may even get some temporary relief from our symptoms.

The cause of the crisis, however, is seldom addressed. A second or third shock is often needed to rouse us. Sometimes an impulse to wake up comes from external events, from simple everyday things, from a book or the company we keep. Or we may recognize suddenly that there is no meaning in our lives and then go out in search of it. We try everything. We look to do something meaningful and creative. We may take drawing or pottery classes, join clubs and churches, or give time and energy to "good" causes.

For most of us, life has its unremarkable ups and downs. We accept the blows and duck and punch back; we fall flat on our faces and manage to struggle to our feet again. We dismiss the mishaps by saying "That's life" and muddle along as well as we can. But we feel somewhat deprived and shortchanged. Our affairs and relationships remain in a state of unresolved discord — rather like a cold war. We accept compromise as a rule of thumb and sacrifice the light of truth for the sake of temporary peace.

But this quiet desperation is precarious, and our peace treaties are easily upset. Sudden hardships, illness, and the loss of a loved one can easily throw us over the edge. Grief can quickly turn to despair, and we may pray for oblivion or even extinction. This "dark night of the soul" is very profound and was seen by the medieval mystics as a descent into hell. The desolation and despondency may be so immensely acute that total inertia overtakes us and we have no strength left to get out of the darkness. We feel separate, alone, and dislocated from our very self. Yet this shattering of the sense of self is seen by some seekers as an act of grace. The false ego has lost its grip.

In our destitute state, we are given a glimpse into the darkness, the shadow side of our psyche and the absence of the light of truth and consciousness. The struggle to reintegrate ourselves into a new and greater harmony is the beginning of wisdom and the beginning of our spiritual work. The greater the depth of the dark night of the soul, the greater the yearning for change and the desire for truth.

Some individuals experience a milder but more persistent crisis. Not content with the prevalent view or with living life on the surface, they are aware of the disharmony in their existence. Their intuition tells them that there is more to know and that there is a more harmonious way of being and enjoying this magnificent creation. Their state of consciousness is already expanded through their personal efforts to transcend a banal existence. Through their struggle to escape ignorance and by direct experience of their true nature, they have acquired certainty.

Such individuals often gain wisdom from the hard knocks of life and the agony of defeat. They have come to the point where they want to assume greater responsibility and find their "rightful place and proper duty," as Emerson would say. The idea of a personal God no longer serves them. They are seeking to integrate their relative knowledge with their inner knowing.

Some are spurred on by dim memories of having been happy once. Some want to recapture their peak experiences, flashes of higher consciousness, and glimpses into the true nature of things. They search for the means to bring about the integration of their knowledge, consciousness, and being.

In his book *The Life of the Soul,* Georg Kühlewind, the eminent proponent of spiritual psychology, explains how the disease of consciousness familiar to us today arises from the decay of the higher cognitive potential which he calls supraconsciousness. He says: "For if matter, and not the word, is the fundamental reality, then man cannot know himself in reality as soul and as spirit. If he does not become aware of his spiritual being, his Logos-essence, then he is not free and can solve neither his psychological nor spiritual nor material problems: as an unfree being he can solve nothing at all, he can do nothing; everything happens to him. This threatens his entire existence."

When, by grace or wisdom, we become conscious that our existence is threatened, we have already entered the quest and are ready for the next step. We have already met one of the prerequisites of the search for a higher order, which is either a thoroughly reasoned conclusion through the intellect or a direct experience of our true nature which confirms that we are more than meets the eye and that we are in fact a unique synthesis of the infinite and the finite.

On the path of Self-inquiry, we need not rely on belief or accept any dogma until we *feel* it to be the truth in our innermost being and we *know* a higher reality and a higher state of consciousness by our own experience. Then we can stand firm in our conviction, and our certainty will provide a ground upon which to stand.

Our desire for truth will propel us forward in our search for higher knowledge and for practical wisdom. It will give us the power of introspection and lead us to good company in form of books and kindred souls; some may be directed to a school of thought or a teacher. All we need to do at first is intend to wake up and put ourselves in the stream of the infinite Spirit.

FOUR
THE AUTHORITY OF IGNORANCE

WHAT IS IGNORANCE? The Eastern tradition would quite simply answer that ignorance is not understanding our own true nature and that we suffer because we are ignorant of our own nature. In the West we use the word *ignorance* to denote the lack of knowledge or intelligence, but more often the lack of education and learning. There is, however, a deeper meaning to this word.

Ignorance is not the opposite of knowledge. Although the dictionary definition of the word *ignorance* is "the state or fact of being ignorant," when we look at the verb "to ignore," meaning "to disregard," we see that it implies a willed and conscious act. It is the esoteric meaning of this word — and the original meaning of words and language in general — that we are concerned with in our quest to uncover truth. In this book the word "ignorance" will be used in its esoteric meaning — in the sense of "ignorance of what is," that is, "the state of ignoring reality."

The fact that we had to resort to this little exercise to define the meaning of a common word points quite poignantly to the pernicious nature of ignorance. Ignorance and confusion seep into our language, or rather result from our imprecision in expression, which in turn reflects the state of our undisciplined minds and our level of ignorance.

We should not be surprised, for example, that what we call teaching today consists of administering education to our children. We presume their ignorance and treat them like receptacles into which we pour information to be stored and retrieved at a later date when they become "useful citizens." When we reflect on the etymology of the word "education," however, we are reminded of the true meaning of education: the word *educate* comes from the Latin *educare*, which means "to draw out," strongly suggesting that there is something within the child that can be drawn out. Ignorance in our language hides the fact that within ourselves lies hidden all knowledge, and that education, when truly understood, is the means to draw out this hidden knowing, the strengths, talents, and unlimited potential of every human being.

Nor should we be surprised at the confusion that has arisen at every level of society when we look at the degeneration of our language, in which many words have taken on the opposite meaning of their original ones. New words with ambiguous meanings have entered into our vocabulary, along with others having a barely disguised intent to deceive. For example, the paradoxical composite word "build-down" in reference to our arsenal of weapons of destruction seems to be consciously coined to mislead and to confuse the issues.

A cloud of ignorance hovers over our lives, our affairs, our thinking and being. This cloud is heavier and darker than ever before in the history of mankind. It arises from education, conditioning, and imitation, and is maintained by holding on to the past, to our imaginings and self-deception. We allow the cloud to form by the power of our convictions and beliefs, which arose from this cloud in the first place. Beliefs change over the centuries — we no longer give credence to omens or to the wrath of nature gods — but they are promptly replaced with new superstitions and cults.

Our minds are implanted with ideas, concepts, and information, inseminated with opinions, ideologies, and theories, and impregnated with cravings, desires, and needs by electronic, vocal, subliminal, and other means — a process that is happening faster and more insidiously than every before. The eminent scientist Lewis Thomas touches on this concern when he says, "The human brain is the most public organ on the face of the earth, open to everything, sending messages to everything.... Virtually all the business is the direct result of thinking that has already occurred in other minds. We pass thoughts around, so compulsively and with such speed that the brains of mankind often appear, functionally, to be undergoing fusion."

W HEN WE INDISCRIMINATELY SUBJECT OUR MINDS to this bombardment as if they were inert receptacles for information, and we give credence to these messages, we are giving up our authority to the powers that be. We are thereby contributing to the density of the cloud of ignorance. We give authority and power to ignorance every time we choose to *ignore* what is really going on in our relationships, our families, our schools, our society, in our government, and more tragically within ourselves. Our lives have become so busy and complicated that we choose to delegate our decisions, our responsibilities, and our very psyches to the experts. We have been led to believe that the experts can cure all ills, so we send our children to psychiatrists, take our ailing marriages and families to group therapists, our monetary problems to financial advisers, and our disputes to lawyers.

There is hardly an aspect of modern life that does not have a corresponding arbiter, nor is there a branch of government that is not run without the consent of advisers. We still live under the illusion that somehow in this democratic country the rights and wishes of the individual are represented by our elected officials who use their best judgment. But in fact much is shunted onto the shoulders of experts, interns, and researchers; what is worse, even the most crucial decisions in the highest office depend on the opinions of these unknown and unelected advisers.

The cloud of ignorance casts a darkness over our institutions of higher learning, which cultivate a disbelief in anything that cannot be perceived and verified with the five senses or by the scientific method. Obviously there is nothing wrong with science in its own right, which is simply the systematic exploration of nature. Such research magnifies our sight and our powers, enriches our lives, heals our bodies, and can even enhance our spiritual vision. What is dangerous, however, is, that its methods of controlled experiments have overwhelmed every facet of human endeavor, including philosophy, religion, and education and are reflected in literature, thought, and the culture at large. The "hermeneutics of suspicion" has become the accepted stance of modern inquiry. This outgrowth of science — generally referred to as "scientism" — is the dangerous perversion which adds sulphurous fumes to our cloud of ignorance. Its practice has assumed overwhelming authority and has entered the mainstream mindset.

Scientism comes with a hidden agenda, adding two amendments to the precepts of pure science. It presupposes, first, that science is not only reliable but is the most reliable method available to reveal reality, and, second, that material things are the most important things. It is this constricted reasoning that has shed a darkness over the human spirit, from which it is hard to escape and realize our true potential.

Philosophy in our institutions of learning is no longer a dialectic inquiry into the essence and nature of man and the universe, the nature and purpose of existence, and what can be established as true or not true. Rather the discourse reveals a preoccupation with semantics, form, and presentation, and aims to dazzle the audience as an intellectual tour de force. Philosophy has become a sport. This perversion of the practice of philosophy has become hopelessly entangled in vain exercises of validation and disputation of theories and beliefs, and has very little to do with the love of wisdom — the true and original meaning of the word "philosophy."

This perverted form of inquiry reaches into our courts, where the criteria is not to get at the truth of an incident but rather focuses on procedure, form, and semantics. Untruths and lies are fine as long as they are couched well. The criminal gets away if his counsel is better at the game of semantics — of who is allowed to say what and how — and at covering and muddling the facts than the prosecution.

These proceedings are then covered by the media, the experts, and the spin doctors — the other authorities in whom we trust and to whom we delegate responsibility. They tell us how to think about the judge's performance, how and why the prosecution did or said what they did, and why the jury reached the verdict they did. Thus the plot thickens: we now have a spin upon a spin upon a spin, and we in our ignorance call this rehash "news" and accept the media's elegant presentations as the facts of what is going on in the world.

The authority of ignorance clouds our upbringing as well. When we are small, parents and teachers keep us in a narrow line of behavior and an even narrower spectrum of perception, and we in turn pass our mental inhibitions on to our children. We cannot know ourselves or meet the living present until we break down this stale conditioning based on the past and fed by imagination, identification, and self-deception. This is the gloomy side of the picture — the bad news.

The good news is that this authority of ignorance deals in surfaces and in procedures. It is ugly and insidious, but in fact has no reality of its own. It is a manmade construct, an illusion, and therefore cannot permanently affect the human spirit or change *what is*. It can only for a time cover the human condition with a blanket of arrogance, ill will, and violence. When we stop giving collective power to this cloud of ignorance and withdraw the authority we have lent to it, it will dissipate without delay.

When we reassume responsibility, we will once again be able to shape a world we want to live in. We still have a chance to undo the web of illusion of materialism and once again understand the full meaning of the words of the Greek philosopher Heraclitus: "Eyes and ears are bad witnesses, especially if we have souls that do not understand their language." When we change our minds, we will be able to correct the effects of wrong thinking and heal the ills it has caused. Through "right thinking" (to use a Buddhist phrase), and through knowledge of our true Self, we may avert our own extinction and instead contribute to a new climate in which the human spirit comes first and in which genius can flourish. We will be able to articulate a new vision that will foster a renaissance of human greatness — a fresh, magnificent, and harmonious synthesis of philosophy, science, and art.

As individuals endowed with the powers of self-reflection, intelligence, and reason, we have the ability and responsibility to dispel our self-deception right here and right now. We do not have to succumb to the authority of ignorance, nor do we have to live in this collective twilight one moment longer. We do not have time to

await the arrival of a messiah, of mysterious forces from outer space, or of a philoso-
pher-king, nor do we have the luxury to dream of a kinder, gentler nation.

We are free to make a choice and to take charge of our lives. We can come out
from under the cloud of ignorance, step into the light of knowledge, and join the
many that are on the path of self-recovery and self-determination. The path is
getting wider, and the number of seekers is rapidly increasing. These trailblazers have
already discovered that ignorance has no real existence and therefore no real power.
When we come to know that for a fact and realize it — that is, *make it real* — in our
minds, hearts, and deeds, we will weaken the power of ignorance and let the light of
truth shine upon our human affairs.

*

FIVE

FIRST STEPS ON THE QUEST

WHEN WE COME TO THE POINT in our lives when we begin to question the status quo and when our yearning for something real and meaningful can no longer be appeased, there is a natural hiatus — a brief pause. This is a propitious gap in which we realize that something needs to happen. We decide that we want to take steps to remedy our predicament.

We reach this crossroads from many different directions. We may have come through the wilderness of meaning; we may have passed through an arid plane of spiritual starvation, or we may have been flooded by grace and blessed with glimpses of a higher order. Some want to be rescued from a life of misery, from illness and grief, or even from the slumber of relative happiness. Or we may have had a moment of clarity in the jungle of worldliness and realized that we don't like what we see. We are ready for change and long to stand on higher ground and find the secret source of our being.

When John the Baptist came out of the wilderness, he said: "Make way and *repent*" — a word that in the original Greek of the New Testament means "turn around." To *turn around* is a drastic action and suggests much more than just changing our ways to some degree. Waking up from our sleep — our immersion in the world of matter — requires a drastic change of thinking.

First, we take a little time to reconnoiter — to clearly see where we are. Then we take the steps to clear away the most immediate obstacles. To give ourselves strength and sustenance on the quest, we make a conscious decision that will not be altered. We pledge to find our way back to our true Self, to serve that one Self, and thereby to gain knowledge of our divine nature. This decision is the beginning of the quest.

In order to know anything, we have to ask questions. But not just any questions. Only a fool wants to know "why?": "Why is it that … ?" These questions most often arise from idle curiosity and cannot be answered in the tradition of true philosophy. Rather we must ask, "What am I?" "What is the essence of humanity, nature, the universe?" "What is being and what is existence?" "What is being versus becoming?" We may address these questions to ourselves or to others, perhaps to one who has tread the path or to the great texts of the Perennial Philosophy.

The concern of the Perennial Philosophy has always been to point to the unity of metaphysical truth in all teachings as revealed in ancient texts and scriptures and to reformulate the age-old dictums: to know thyself, to know God, to know the nature of the universe, and to know our place in the creation. Although as seekers, we look to the wisdom of the ancient seers and masters, we have to ask and find, each in his or her own way, the answers hidden in our own hearts and souls. No one else can do it for us. No one else can *know* for us.

It is said that we can only phrase a question to which we already know the answer in the depth of our minds and hearts, and this holds especially true when speaking of spiritual knowledge. This suggests that we have knowledge of the highest nature within ourselves, as Heraclitus affirmed when he said, "I searched myself." Eastern philosophy goes a step further and asserts that we have the system of Self-knowledge and Self-Realization — the means to return to our own true nature — within ourselves. We have eloquent testimony to this assertion in the spontaneous outpourings of the mystics and lovers of truth and in the lives of the great teachers, avatars, and yogis. The poetry and literature composed by the sages of past and present acquaint us with the struggles, the aspirations, the pitfalls and, above all, the joys of the journey inward. These devout seekers reveal to us the great knowledge they attained and the states of higher consciousness they enjoyed through intense self-reflection and self-inquiry.

Only a few souls in each century, however, have the purity of heart and discipline of mind for this solo ascent. For most of us, help along the journey is a necessity, since, to begin with, we have forgotten how to ask questions. We are most blessed in this time and place to have available many of the great teachings and systems dating back to the dawn of mankind. Sacred texts, guarded in antiquity with great secrecy and passed on only to the worthiest of disciples, are now in print and within reach of anyone with a desire for knowledge. We can choose from innumerable translations of this ancient wisdom from the Egyptian, Chinese, and Indian traditions, from the thought of the Greek philosophers, from the writings and fragments of Heraclitus, Pythagoras, Hermes Trismegistus, and Plato, and the teachings of the great avatars — Krishna, Jesus, Buddha, Ramakrishna, and the eminent scholar and reformer Shankara. Contemporary seekers are indeed fortunate to have access to this wealth of sacred knowledge.

Each one of us will no doubt soon find the text and language with which he or she finds a soul connection. We must be drawn to the truth like a bee to the nectar, and we must love it with the passion of the lover. Although there is only one truth and one reality, there are hundreds of different formulations of the experience of reality and hundreds of different voices expressing the moment of revelation. We are naturally drawn to one expression or another, to the words that illumine our particular minds and reverberate in our hearts. But the expression has to resonate with the individual. There is no use in milking a text for meaning when it leaves us thirsting for revelation. It is a waste of time to struggle with certain scriptures if they don't give us the "aha" experience. Rather we would do better to find and then sing in unison with the voices that have the right pitch to lift us and carry us to a higher plateau. As we gain new insights into ourselves and as our view of the nature of existence expands, we will yearn for still finer food with which to nourish our being.

The first steps, as we all know, are often the hardest. Many doubts surface: the many impermanent "I"'s feel threatened by the lack of attention and question the veracity of our new interest. We may feel "special" or "alone" and wonder if we are the only ones attempting the spiritual journey. Suddenly we find find many obstacles, maybe even a minefield. The going gets rocky. We question our sanity. Our friends, seeing a change in our tastes and pursuits, may think we are becoming unhinged. Despite all the seeming adversities, we must not lose heart. Before long we will get a second wind. Our doubts will be replaced by certainty gained from a new insight or a direct experience, from observation of the simple things of life, from the whisperings of nature, or from good company — a kindred spirit, the right book, a group, or a teacher.

Sooner or later we come to the realization that the quest for Self-knowledge is not some special journey for the privileged few, a pleasant pastime, or an escape from mundane existence. We will understand that our life here on earth *is* the spiritual quest and that our particular incarnation is a very special privilege. We are all here on the quest, whether we know it or not. But it is far better to take each step consciously and joyfully in the light of knowledge than to be buffeted by every wind.

We are not alone in our quest. Those that have gone before are here and now in spirit, in consciousness, and in knowledge. The path is well-trodden and our trust is justified, when, in the words of the sages, we see that "at each step, there stands waiting that which is propitious to that step."

⁜

SIX

LANGUAGE AND MEANING

IF WE ARE TO UNDERSTAND EACH OTHER, we have to have a common language. If we wish to understand the language of the Spirit, we must study and penetrate the true and original meaning of certain key words, concepts, and phrases. Unfortunately, in our present-day, utilitarian English language there remain only faint traces of the original essence of words. We discover that the language is quite impoverished, especially when we wish to express the subtleties of spiritual meaning and the ideas behind certain words or figures of speech. Worse yet, many words relating to spiritual ideas and experience have degenerated into having the opposite connotation. Thus words such as "reality," "spirit," "mind," "intuition," "compensation," "self-reliance," and "responsibility" are used indiscriminately and have long lost their deeper meaning — a meaning which, no more than a hundred years ago, was understood by many and held great significance for the student of metaphysics.

To add to our daily confusion, new words are entering our vocabulary every day. These newly coined terms, usually relating to a specific field of science, information, and technology, arise out of the need to name a product, a concept, or an image. Hence they are descriptive and the result is a word which is an image of an image or a figure of speech which is a trope of a trope. Rarely is this new verbiage based on an idea or essence in the true sense of these terms. Our language has further degenerated as a result of the popular and unfortunate misuse of nouns as verbs. We also commonly adopt phrases, expressions, and expletives arising from street language and popular entertainment and welcome them into our homes and conversation. They may be amusing on the surface, but they insidiously contribute (to use such popular parlance) to the "dumbing down" of our language.

In order to understand philosophical discourse and ancient spiritual precepts, we have to divest ourselves of dead, utilitarian, and materialistic language and rediscover a purer means of expression. We once again need to address meaning and essence and dig deeply into the origin of each word. For example: the word "philosophy" as commonly used today refers to a corpus of doctrines, to academic categories, or various sets of ideals, ideas, or opinions, as in the phrase "His philosophy is that ... " The verb "to philosophize" has taken on a negative connotation and is generally used in the sense of "to speculate." The original meaning of the word "philosophy" (from the Greek words *philein*, "to love," and *sophia*, "wisdom") is "love of truth" or "love of wisdom" — a far cry from its present usage.

The language of the Perennial Philosophy has been called the only perfectly intelligible language. As seekers, we must learn this language once again and become familiar with the semantics and concepts of real philosophy. Without this deeper knowledge of meaning, the wisdom contained in the vast discourse of the Perennial Philosophy and the literature of the Wisdom tradition will remain hidden or at best obscure.

Even armed with this deeper understanding of words, we have to acknowledge that language is a very limited means of communication, especially when we are speaking about Self-Realization, the nature of the Self, universal principles, and the Absolute. "Truth" and "reality" are, after all, just words; the essence behind these words can only be *experienced*. Words are especially inadequate when they describe anything that does not fall within the realm of time and space. Just as quantum physics has had to invent a new jargon to explain and describe subatomic events, metaphysics uses a special language to hint at spiritual events, such as the experience of "One Consciousness" or "One Mind." Yet it remains difficult, if not impossible, to capture and communicate the essence of such an experience in relative terms. The only way to truly *know* the full measure of such expressions is to enter the same level of consciousness in which the revelation was perceived.

Some of the purest and simplest expressions of spiritual wisdom come down to us from seers and mystics who, through austerities and disciplines, have purified their souls and have brought their hearts, minds, and bodies into perfect balance. They have perceived reality, have seen the abyss, and have enjoyed bliss, and then celebrated their bounty in inspired hymns, poems, and prose. The beauty and clarity of these verses have the power to illumine our consciousness. We need their words until we can realize truth for ourselves.

We already have conceded that semantics cannot describe the ultimate reality, and yet language, however inadequate, is necessary to communicate the means to attain truth and to describe specific steps on the spiritual quest. At first this language may seem quite technical. But we need to be as clear and precise as possible. For example we need to establish that whenever "self" is written in lower case, it refers to the small self or ego; whenever we speak of "the Self" capitalized, we mean by it the higher Self — the true nature of the human being.

In many philosophical writings, the word "man" refers to mankind, and not to any distinction of gender. The English word "man" is related to the Sanskrit root *man,* which means "to think" and which is also the root of *manas* or "mind." Hence man the thinker, or man as thinker. It is useful on the quest to imbue the word "man" once again with its original and splendid meaning and to blithely ignore issues of gender and political correctness. In metaphysics, the capitalized word "Man" is often used to refer to humankind in a context of "the ideal man" or "universal man," and so we shall use it in this work.

We find in the Vedas, the *Yoga Sutras* of the Indian sage Patanjali, and the many systems of enlightenment not only the means and tools for our own quest, but also a language that is beautiful, precise, and full of light. Sanskrit is the language of the Spirit. It is for this reason that even modern philosophers such as René Guénon, Ananda K. Coomaraswamy, and Paul Brunton insisted on its use to more clearly express the subtleties of higher knowledge and the rewards of their philosophical inquiry.

Sanskrit, unlike other languages, is not an evolved language; it was consciously conceived and perfected by the intellectual genius of the ancient seers. The word *Sams-krta* means "perfected" or "refined." The Sanskrit script is called *Devanagari,* from *deva,* "God," and *nagara,* "city," or writing of the "divine city." Each sound of the alphabet has mantric power and is said to consist of both an inaudible and audible element. The inaudible or subtle sound, known as *sabda,* contains the real meaning, and the audible sound, called *dhvani,* is its instrument of outward expression. These sounds are said to be indestructible. Every word can be reduced to a verb root known as *dhatu*, a seed-sound that never changes and is expressive of an action either related to being or becoming. Each word and each sound have a power or *shakti* to convey the sense, which is inseparably related to the sound.

It is said that AUM or OM is the first sound and that out of this vibration arose the whole creation — the manifestation of Brahman or the Absolute. Hence the sacred teachings and scriptures tell us that Brahman or God is the Word (or *mantra*) and the Creation is the meaning of the Word (or *sabda*). In a lucid and highly recommended text on Sanskrit and its amazing symbolical significance entitled *The Language of the Gods,* Judith M. Tyberg writes, "Actually the universe was sung into being according to the Veda: '*Vageva visva bhuvanani jajne.*' Vag (vach), the 'Logos' or the 'Divine Word' or the 'Divine Mother of Sound,' became all the worlds. *Vach* is the creative Word, the dynamic principle of Creation which manifests its *artha* or meaning. The word and its meaning are nothing without one another, just as Sun and sunlight, fire and heat have no absolutely separate existence."

As expounded by the three great grammarians, Patanjali, Panini, and Katyayana, Sanskrit contains within its grammar, its rules, and symbolic and mantric power the key to higher knowledge. The study of the language and the sacred knowledge that informs it provide the student with a clear path to Self-knowledge. We do not have to become Sanskrit scholars in order to appreciate the beauty and purity of this magnificent living legacy. A modest familiarity with Sanskrit and some of its most commonly used terms will open our perception to a beautiful and harmonious order and give us a new appreciation for language and the meaning of words, even in English.

For example, the Sanskrit word *atman* — the Divine Self in man or the Infinite Divine — comes from the verb *at*, "to breathe." The English word "atmosphere" is related to this beautiful word; hence a metaphysical reading of the substance surrounding our planet is "the sphere of the *atman*." We speak, for example, of a congenial place as "having a great atmosphere" — the intangible substance created over time by the presence of happy people. The German word *atmen*, which means "to breathe," is even closer to the Sanskrit.

The beauty of Sanskrit lies in the fact that essence and meaning are conveyed simultaneously and that the sounds *do* what they *mean*. Moreover the use of Sanskrit terms such as *ahamkara* (sense of individual self, ego-sense), *buddhi* (discrimination, judgment, higher reason, intelligence), *chitta* (consciousness, self-aware force of existence), and *manas* (discursive mind, sense mind) provide us with the precision and clarity required when we begin to study specific inner faculties of the mind and observe the workings of our instrument. Such precise distinctions and terms relating to the human mind are either simply lacking in modern language or mislead the understanding because the language has been corrupted. Thus psychology, for example, sums up our inner world as the "human psyche," a term we do not question because it suggests an unknown and unknowable entity — a mysterious, undifferentiated lump. At best, psychology distinguishes between the conscious and the subconscious, and additionally in some cases between the subconscious and the collective unconscious.

Scientific research has provided us with new information relating to the functioning of the various centers in the brain, and new conclusions are being drawn about multiple intelligences. This research, which is confined to the physical realm, does not take into account the subtle and causal bodies of the human being. Very often the words "mind" and "brain" are used interchangeably, which only adds to the confusion. Individuals who are seeking to understand the metaphysical nature of their instruments will not be satisfied with these materialistic conclusions.

In recent years the study of consciousness has taken great leaps. Many professional conferences around the world attest to a resurgence of an interest in the mysterious nature of consciousness. Experiments prove that human consciousness, in the form of directed attention, can influence events on the other side of the planet. In this endeavor the language of philosophy and science have begun to merge and what might be emerging from this research is a new metaphysics. The ancient dictums "all is consciousness" and "consciousness is everywhere" are about to be proven and might someday come to be expressed in a mathematical formula.

THE VEDAS PROCLAIM THAT OUR true nature is *sat-chit-ananda* or being-consciousness-bliss. Even a little study of the individual Sanskrit words will provide us with the tools to penetrate this and many other statements. By observing the workings of our subtle instrument, we can then confirm the meaning of these Vedic concepts and see, for example, how *manas* receives impressions and categorizes, how *buddhi* discerns and knows, and how *chitta* remembers and reflects. As these terms become more familiar, we will experience their illuminating quality in our understanding and enjoy the immediate effect their pure sounds have on the organ of mind. The words actually contain knowledge within them, and the subtle meaning of the statement is transported through the subtle vibrations of the pure sounds, penetrating the inner organs of mind, the senses, and the body. The intent of a Sanskrit invocation conjoins with the aspiration of mind and heart and thereby transforms the state of being of the seeker. When we experience the power of these words, we will learn to appreciate the value and beauty of Sanskrit in the quest for Self-knowledge. A glossary of Sanskrit terms is provided in the back of this book. It is intended to serve for clarification while reading the book, but may also be used as a text for study and reflection.

Our current English language is encumbered by misuse and overuse, by materialism, sarcasm, and inaccuracies (we do not mean what we say). But it is not too late to reverse this trend and to refine our individual expression and by so doing to, as it were, "spiritualize" the language again. The philosopher Martin Heidegger once said that "Language is the house of Being." We most certainly need this "house" to nurture our humanity and our spiritual essence. We need it for survival as much as we need air, food, and shelter. Language is our most precious domicile, and the refinement of language can elevate our existence, education, and culture.

The refinement of voice and speech is the most direct way to refine thought. When we consider language even for a moment, we will stand in awe of this immense gift, realizing that language is a miracle, just as life is a miracle. We might reflect on the miraculous mechanics of language: Words are uttered. They then travel as vibrations through the atmosphere and exert an impression on the ear. The mind-body mechanism of the listener transforms the incoming impressions into experiences of consciousness and instantaneously reconstitutes them into meaning. More often than not, the listener understands the meaning. And we take this amazing miracle for granted.

Richard Geldard, in his book *Remembering Heraclitus,* says, "Language is a self-reflective instrument. When we speak our thoughts, the thoughts return to us as formed understanding, heard by our own minds and judged true or not in the crucible of our powers of discrimination. Without language, in other words, meaning (*telos*) cannot be found. Without such meaning, we are absent in existence, having no presence. We simply pass through, like mayflies, in a day."

It is not easy to completely avoid the intrusion of sounds and messages clamoring for our attention every day. But we can make use of our faculty of discrimination as well as of another gift, commonly referred to as free will. In spiritual terms, we would say that we have a choice (if we are awake enough) and that we have a faculty within us that has the power "to intend." We can choose to listen to the banal and commonplace and slumber on, or we can choose to listen to the loftiest of truths and let their meaning enlighten our understanding and expand our consciousness. It is our choice.

The language of the Perennial Philosophy is pure and intentionally simple. It seeks to make truth known and to shed light and clarity where there is darkness and doubt; it endeavors to make explicit what is implicit; it marvels at the wonder of life as it seeks to explain the mystery of human existence. When the language does not manage to inspire the contemporary seeker, it may well be that it is outmoded and that we need to reformulate the ancient truths to meet the needs of this particular time and place.

SEVEN
SEARCH FOR A TEACHING

WHEN WE REALIZE that the kind of lasting joy and peace and the freedom from fear and anxiety we are looking for cannot be found in the pursuit of sensory pleasure or in the world of competition and success, we begin to look for something to nourish our insistent craving for what is missing in our existence — something less tangible, something beyond ordinary everyday consciousness, and yet within our reach.

Among the many seekers, there are those few blessed souls in whom some aspects of the personality, psyche, or mind are already highly developed. Their certainty of vision and conviction of a higher calling attracts them to a teaching, or rather the teaching is drawn to them. They feel immediately comfortable with the precepts of a particular path or system, and their memory of truth just needs a tiny jolt. They have a sense of "having known it before" or "having done this work before," and it feels like "coming home."

Then there are those who seek and seek, and travel great distances to achieve extraordinary experiences or to find a guru on a mountaintop, only to be unceremoniously turned away. Yet upon their return, they discover the words of wisdom they had been so eager to find right there on their own bookshelf. They realize that what in the past they had considered as just so many empty words or abstract ideas is now leaping off the page and illuminating their comprehension of sacred truths. The self-same words are now falling on fertile ground — on an open heart and open mind. The sacred teachings are only revealed to those have "eyes to see and ears to hear" and who approach them with simplicity and humility.

And then there are many seekers (and their numbers are growing each day) who are attempting to still their craving for meaning but get lost in the woods of endless possibilities. They stumble around endlessly, uncertain of their direction. They have followed a few leads and have grown discouraged by too many dead ends.

The multiplicity of spiritual offerings has never been more astounding — from weekend workshops for instant Self-Realization to vision quests in the wilderness to rigorous Zen retreats, from intimate garage churches to the new megachurches. We are living in an age of religious pluralism. Within each faith, there are many splinter groups, and within the larger denominations there are innumerable movements, each with a personal mission to reform these bodies from within.

More than ever, seekers will need to exercise their intelligence and discrimination in order not to be enticed by "quick-fix" guarantees, New Age mix-and-match approaches, so-called "prophecies" and "revelations." They will need to steer clear of the new religious hybrids that have cropped up to fit every taste, lifestyle, and pocketbook. It is also wise to be skeptical of religions that promise to "empower" the individual by some external means or supernatural force. It is far better to trust a teaching that has its basis in universal laws, that points the way to the realization of our own nature, and that provides a method for finding the Supreme Self, which is unlimited being, knowledge, and bliss.

To many seekers the process of finding the right teaching can be lengthy and confusing. How do we discriminate between the eternal truths and bogus forms of instant salvation? How do we discern between the real and the unreal? How do we find a teaching that is right for us?

To begin, let us define what a true teaching is. The principles of the great wisdom teachings have traditionally conformed to a few important characteristics. First, they must be lawful at every level, from the minute to the cosmic, and they must be constant; that is, they must be as true now as they were in 3000 B.C. Secondly, they must be based on intuition or revelation — a direct experience of reality — rather than on theory, belief, or dogma. Furthermore, they should teach that the ultimate goal is attainable by anyone who gives his or her heart and soul to it and that truth or reality can be known by anyone willing to tread the path of Self-inquiry. Finally, these teachings should stress that Self-Realization or cosmic consciousness is possible while in this body, not at some future time in heaven above, and that the bliss this affords is beyond measure, exceeding all pleasures known to earthly existence.

There are many other subtle criteria by which we can recognize the truthfulness of a teaching. A true teaching is nondual, acknowledging the unity between the Universal Self and the individual Self. It does not require adherence to beliefs, but asks aspirants to investigate their own nature and inquire into the nature of the universe in a detached and scientific way. It does not dictate ritual or behavior, but rather suggests disciplines that gently remove the obstructions that keep us from realizing our divine nature. It teaches that we are ultimately responsible for our lives, that we are the creators of our own destiny and that whatever we encounter is our *dharma* — a word that refers not only to our rightful duty, but also to the law that governs all our deeds and leads us back to our own true nature. A true teaching also gives us the wisdom to realize that whatever happens in any given moment is intimately connected with our thoughts and feelings and that whatever we see is a projection of our state of mind in that moment. It should be added that a true teaching is not financially expensive.

Similarly, true teachers meet the same kinds of criteria. They are tolerant of the many paths that lead to freedom and never claim exclusivity for their own methods. They never impose their beliefs or tell anybody how to conduct his or her life, but rather gently guide by their simple presence of *being* — by their embodiment of wisdom, love, and knowledge. Additionally, they are nonjudgmental, completely accepting of the faults of others, and yet live their own lives according to the highest principles. In short, they are living symbols of the highest ideals and virtues — purity, intelligence, and compassion — and, most importantly, they are full of humor, happiness, and delight.

There are many paths that lead to enlightenment, and there are many methods that lead to freedom from suffering. The forms sometimes vary considerably from one path to another, but the goal remains universal and constant. The sages have discovered that there is only one eternal truth — that which *is*. We all have the potential to realize this for ourselves. The eternal truth is One, but has been expressed in a profusion of ways since the dawn of mankind to meet the needs of time and place.

Many of the Christian mystics soared high above the prevalent dualistic views of their time and sung of their ecstasies and bliss in the union with the divine. Theirs was the path of devotion or *bhakti* yoga, as it is called in the Eastern tradition. Many seekers have embraced *jnana* yoga, the path of wisdom, by reflecting on the eternal truths and cosmic laws and thus have reached the ultimate goal through their intellect and higher reason. Still others have chosen the practice of karma yoga — the path of selfless action.

A number of different paths or yogas focus on the development of specific aspects of the human psyche or inner organs of mind, while others tend towards the acquisitions of certain higher powers. Some of the yogas, such as *hatha, tantra, mantra,* and *laya* yoga, seek to arrive at higher states of consciousness by perfecting the physical and mental bodies through various practices and austerities. The highest form of these is *kundalini* yoga, which seeks to attain *samadhi* by union with Shiva by bringing mind and body into complete harmony.

Most of these ancient yogas were designed for the spiritually ambitious disciples and ascetics, who desired to renounce the world, conquer their bodies, and attain immortality. They are of another age and another state of consciousness and are therefore not very useful or practical for the contemporary spiritual seeker. What may seem like a simple matter, the practice of breath control, for example, may in fact be harmful unless it is guided by a supremely qualified teacher. In the past, a yogi would not have been initiated into the practice of *kundalini* yoga until he had shown his worthiness, undergone great austerities, and endured a process of purification.

ULTIMATELY, A TEACHING HAS TO BE practical and not merely an abstract philosophy or intellectual exercise. If it is not applicable to daily life, it is probably not totally truthful or universal. We would not be able to verify it in action and we would soon abandon it. We need a teaching for our time and our needs and for our harmonious development on all levels — knowing, being, and doing. Unless we *live* our newly acquired intuitions and apply this higher knowledge in our daily lives, we will not become whole or free or happy. Unless it can freely flow in action, knowledge will remain dead and theoretical and will eventually turn sour. If development is too lofty, our feet will not be able to touch the ground. If it is too physical, the emotions and intellect cannot soar.

The environment and the world in which we live is our laboratory, our testing ground. A true teaching affirms the creation and the enjoyment of life — the interaction of matter and spirit — and celebrates our conscious human participation in the manifestation of beauty, truth, and genius.

As "rational" contemporary seekers fully engaged in life, we are searching for a practical, nondogmatic, and universal teaching that can point the way to Self-inquiry and Self-Realization. Our search often ends when we find a teaching or a system loosely referred to as "the way of the householder" — a philosophy of living, substantiated by the teachings of the perennial Wisdom tradition, that can lead to an understanding of our true nature and the development of our full potential. Nor does it rule out the possibility of Self-Realization in this life. Today many individuals and groups are engaged in the way of the householder, also known as "the Fourth Way" in the teachings of P.D. Ouspensky and G.I. Gurdjieff. This approach is concerned with inner development within the ordinary conditions of life.

We are very fortunate to have access to many different models for Self-Realization that are as useful today as they were in ancient times and which can easily be adapted for the modern householder. It is within our reach, for example, to arrive at a beautiful synthesis of wisdom and practicality when we live our lives based on an integration of *jnana, bhakti,* and karma yoga — the paths of knowledge, devotion, and action. As we will see later, such an approach ensures the harmonious and simultaneous expansion of all three centers of the human instrument: the head, heart, and hand, that is, our capacities of knowing, being, and doing.

Many contemporary seekers are not content with being told to simply believe in some dogma or religion, adhere to some vague moral values, and muddle through. It seems that at this stage of evolution and individuation, we want to comprehend the reasons for ourselves and not follow blindly. We not only insist on the right to know everything there is to know about any given subject in our material world, but have a need to expand and explore our inner world — our spiritual essence and knowledge. We are willing to consider a teaching we can investigate for ourselves — a philosophy that is applicable to daily life and verifiable through observation of our own faculties.

We know a true teaching of Self-knowledge by its fruits. If we become freer, happier, less judgmental, more accomplished in our vocations, and more loving in our relationships, we must be on the right path. Once we find this treasure we have no need to search and shop around any more. Then we must not delay any longer and begin the Work of our spiritual quest. *Now* is the only time in which true seekers function and have their being.

With intelligence, discrimination, heart, and soul, we begin our quest and trust that we will meet with the right conditions. As the Vedic scriptures say, "Step by step, word by word, action by action, at each step, word, or action, there stands waiting that which is propitious to that step, word, or action."

In other words, we acknowledge that whatever we meet in our daily lives *is* our *dharma* — our path — and that it is propitious for our unfoldment. Our life in a sense *is* our *dharma,* so our "duty," or the role we play on this earthly plane, provides us with the experiences we need to grow into our true nature and the knowledge of our Self.

*

EIGHT
EXISTENCE AND CONSCIOUSNESS

I F WE CONSIDER LIFE ON THIS EARTH solely as a physical manifestation, regarding the universe as a blind mechanical mass powered by chemical reactions and biological proliferation, we might well wonder, "What is the purpose of this furious activity?" Some people maintain that our existence here is mere accident and that there is no greater meaning to life or any higher reason for existence.

We tend to believe in the sole reality of matter because our senses feed us with a continuous stream of impressions that our minds process into a perception of a solid exterior reality. We thrive on this input and experience great comfort in the never-ceasing flow of sensory information, which lets us know that we are alive and well. We know from research that when human beings are deprived of sensory stimulation for any length of time, perception is altered and circadian rhythms disturbed; in some cases, a gradual disintegration of the personality has been observed.

We are hardly aware that our whole lives revolve around the senses. Yet we treasure our senses and love the objects they perceive. We enjoy the sense of comfort we feel when we stand on a solid floor, sit in a comfortable chair, or lie in a fragrant meadow. We feel pleasure when we smell freshly baked bread, taste a fine wine, breathe the ocean breeze, or listen to a great symphony. We derive a sense of well-being from all this sensory input. Even the memory of a pleasant event or the recollection of a beautiful sight will bring about a physical reaction of ease and pleasure.

All this reenforces our trust in the senses and our belief in the phenomenal world as something outside ourselves. Yet we know from science that, for example, there is no such thing as local or permanent color in nature. When we "see" an object as red, blue, or yellow, we are interpreting the stimulation of the retina in response to the refraction of light from the surface of the chemical or mineral particles that we call pigments.

We also know from research that when perception is altered by drugs or pathological chemical changes in the brain, the experience of the phenomenal world changes drastically. Higher levels of experience, such as clairvoyance, can also change our view of "normal perception." We know from reports of higher states of consciousness and mystical experiences that phenomenal reality as we generally accept it tends to disappear altogether. Emerson's observation in his essay "Nature" addresses this point: "If Reason be stimulated to more earnest vision, outlines and surfaces become transparent, and are no longer seen; causes and spirits are seen through them. The best moments of life are these delicious awakenings of the higher powers, and the reverential withdrawing of nature before its God."

Although science has altered our perception of the solidity of matter, we go on living as if matter mattered. Although both science and mysticism have shattered the illusion of time and space, we have not absorbed these insights into our thinking or integrated them into our everyday consciousness. At most, some of us might manage to hold the concept of relativity in mind, but only for a brief time.

Attempts in physics and mathematics to discover the fundamental laws of nature suggest that physical reality is a nonlocal process that lies outside of the space-time continuum and derives from something beyond space and time. As we "see" deeper into the subatomic realm, it gets curiouser and curiouser! Here the law of cause and effect is no longer apparent; here randomness and simultaneity rule; here mind affects matter; here there are no divisions. At the quantum mechanical level, only energy and information exist, and our bodies are nothing more than a localized disturbance in the larger quantum field that is the universe.

Another mind-boggling discovery is that a vacuum in the space of a thimble contains more energy than all the stars in our galaxy. In the world of quantum mechanics, power and size exist in an inverse relationship. And yet we remain fooled by surfaces and we have not yet found a way to integrate this knowledge into our collective consciousness. Einstein said that everything has changed except our way of thinking. We cling to the notion that somehow evolution has its origin in matter, when in fact what we see "out there" is but the end result of what takes place in the invisible subtle world and derives from the causal world. We rarely consider that nature, including our bodies, is inert without the presence of the life force and the force of consciousness. We rarely reflect on the fact that it is by the light of consciousness behind mind and perception that we apprehend at all.

EVERYTHING WE SEE, ALL OF CREATION, consists merely of phenomena that have their origin in the noumenon. But the two are not separate in reality. We may find that the unified field currently sought by science is just another designation for the pure consciousness of metaphysics. Quantum physics seems to be on the verge of "proving" the existence of pure consciousness, sometimes referred to as "the field of pure potentiality" or "the creative principle," which exists everywhere in the universe, as it does in every human being. The cause, however, will most likely remain elusive to science, since our perception is not yet attuned to this level, and our present state of mind does not penetrate the dimensions of space, time, and causation.

But we know from many accounts, ancient and contemporary, that it is possible to experience higher states of consciousness. We all have the potential to taste the "delicious awakenings" of the higher faculties and participate in the unfoldment of the Spirit. In his essay "Involution and Evolution," Sri Aurobindo says, "Life itself is only a colored vehicle, physical birth a convenience for the greater and greater births of the Spirit.... The spiritual process of evolution is then in some sense a creation, but a self-creation, not a making of what never was, but a bringing out of what was implicit in the Being."

The Upanishads declare that all this universe is *maya* — the web of illusion — offering the image of the spider who spins his web out of himself and then uses this self-made structure as his world. This suggests that *maya* exists in our collective consciousness, but has no absolute existence. The Vedas teach that the whole creation and everything we behold is held in our own *prakriti* or Nature. The Buddha taught that "All is Mind." Advaita — the nondual philosophy of consciousness — declares that "One alone" exists. This "One" is both noumenon and phenomenon and manifests itself in multiplicity as many different forms. Advaita propounds that there is only one consciousness. Human beings have their lives in this consciousness and by it cognize and experience the various aspects of consciousness, which are information, awareness, knowledge, and wisdom.

Paul Brunton, one of this century's most dynamic spiritual thinkers, who successfully synthesized Eastern and Western ideas, clarifies our understanding of consciousness and mind in his voluminous notebooks. He writes:

> *The individual mind presents the world-image to itself through and in its own consciousness. If this were all the truth then it would be quite proper to call the experience a private one. But because the individual mind is rooted in and inseparable from the universal mind, it is only a part of the truth. Man's world-thought is held within and enclosed by God's thought.... Our idea of the external world is caused partly by the energies of our own mind and partly by the energies of the World-Mind. It is not caused by a separate material thing acting on our sense organs.... It is a generative idea. Here is a whole philosophy congealed into a single phrase: the world is an idea.*

Eastern teachings propound that the Creative Principle — the Absolute — is everywhere; everything begins in the Absolute, is sustained by the Absolute, and returns to the Absolute. Yet another principle states that all actions take place in the mind. These ancient truths are universal and manifest at every level of the creation. The Creative Principle is a point, a void beyond time and space that expands by the force of the Logos, the will or desire to become manifest in time and space. This same Creative Principle — that "unmoving from which all movement comes" — lies hidden in the center of every human being.

According to the Vedas, the outward thrust of the Creative Principle into manifestation proceeds in a lawful manner from pure consciousness through the causal, subtle, and sensory worlds. This emanation is also said to reflect the proper ordering of the human being:

Absolute
purusha (conscious noumenon)
prakriti (unconscious noumenon)
mahat (supreme intellect, consciousness)
atman (individual Self)
buddhi (intellect)
ahamkara (ego consciousness)
chitta (memory, perception)
manas (mind, thinking)
The senses and sense objects

As we go about our human affairs, we get lost in phenomena and are totally unaware of the grand design. In our ignorance, we believe in an inverse order of existence: we literally get the whole picture backwards. This is quite evident from the fact that we expend most of our energy tending to the material world, devoting little time to the development of our minds and almost totally neglecting the care of our spiritual nature.

The Creative Principle or Void is beyond time and space, without limit or bounds. Pure potentiality is everywhere, yet rests coiled up and hidden, a principle that may be confirmed by the latest discoveries in astrophysics, which have led to the conclusion that space contains invisible matter that is far more abundant than visible matter. This "dark matter" also corresponds beautifully to the ancient Eastern concept of *avyakta prakriti* — unmanifest nature — as well as to Vedic references to "the unseen remainder."

The ancient sages reveal the splendor of their seemingly unlimited knowledge about the nature of existence, when they declare in the *Eesha Upanishad,* "That is perfect. This is perfect. Perfect comes from perfect. Take perfect from perfect, the remainder is perfect."

If we fully understood the meaning of this essential truth, we would have no need to look to further elucidations. Many of the commentaries on the Upanishads agree that *That* refers to pure consciousness or Brahman and *This* refers to the creation or conditioned Brahman. In its simplicity, this poetic statement is not only full of beauty and wisdom but seems to describe the universe as a hologram, a view advanced by several modern physicists.

When we look at a different translation of the same verse by Swami Gambhirananda, the statement becomes even more illuminating:

> That is infinite, and this is infinite. [This] infinite (conditioned Brahman) proceeds from [that] infinite (Supreme Brahman). (Then through knowledge), taking the infinite of the infinite (conditioned Brahman), it remains as the infinite (unconditioned Brahman) alone.

In its universality, the statement also describes the properties of the Golden Mean proportion and can be used to demonstrate this enigmatic mathematical/geometrical principle. The Golden Mean proportion (whose mathematical symbol is the Greek letter ϕ or phi) has fascinated philosophers and architects from the Egyptians to Pythagoras to Plato, who in the *Timaeus* elaborates on the relationship between the regular solids (three-dimensional forms relating to the phi proportion) and the elements. This proportion has also inspired the builders of the Gothic cathedrals, the artists and thinkers of the Renaissance, and architects and artists of the present day.

The Golden Mean proportions appear everywhere in organic and inorganic matter, in the structure of the human body, and even throughout the intergalactic worlds. These "divine proportions," as they are known, in combination with the Fibonacci numbers,* can be found in our solar system, in growth patterns of flora and fauna, in viruses, and in DNA. The Golden Mean spiral is most evident in the patterning of seeds in the center of a sunflower, in the shell of the nautilus, in vortices, and in galactic formations. It may well be the matrix underlying the outward thrust of the ever-expanding universe. All this suggests that human beings are intimately linked with this law of Unity and regeneration. We might thus consider the expanding Golden Mean spiral as a symbol of the lawful evolution of human consciousness and its inward movement as a sacred symbol of the return of the individual to the source of being.

---

* Fibonacci series are a set of numbers in which each number is the sum of the two previous ones: 1, 2, 3, 5, 8, 13, etc. Any number divided by the following one approximates 0.618, and any number divided by the previous one approximates 1.618 ad infinitum, these being a mathematical expression of phi or the Golden Mean.

A recent finding by the eminent scientist Roger Penrose proposes that the Fibonacci numbers may underlie the cellular structures, mainly the microtubules, of every cell in the human body. This leads to the conclusion that consciousness is present throughout the body. It may well be that these minute "structures" reflecting the phi proportion represent the link between quantum mechanics and classical physics and therefore give shape to our consciousness.

The Golden Mean or Phi proportion can be illustrated in a line asymmetrically divided. It is the only proportional division possible with *two terms,* in which the smaller term has the same proportion to the larger term as the larger term has to the whole (see fig. 2). This asymmetrical division is what makes dynamic expansion possible. Robert Lawlor, the author of *Sacred Geometry: Philosophy and Practice,* puts it as follows:

> In a sense, the Golden Proportion can be considered as suprarational or transcendent. It is actually the first issue of Oneness, the only possible creative duality within unity. It is the most intimate relationship, one might say, that proportional existence — the universe — can have with unity, the primal or first division of One.... An asymmetrical division is needed in order to create the dynamics necessary for progression and extension from the unity. Therefore the ɸ proportion is the perfect division of unity: it is creative, yet the entire proportional universe that results from it relates back to it and is literally contained within it, since no term of the original division steps, as it were, outside of a direct rapport with the initial division of unity.

Thus the Golden Mean rectangle demonstrates geometrically and symbolically what the verse from the Upanishad states poetically and philosophically: when we take a perfect square which represents *This* or the visible universe which is the manifestation of the Fullness of the Absolute from the Golden Mean rectangle which represents *That* or the Supreme Brahman, or pure consciousness, what remains is another perfect rectangle. The integrity of the proportion remains the same: *the remainder is perfect.* In other words, the manifestation of the universe does not affect or diminish in any way the Infinite or Brahman.

In his book *The Life Divine,* Sri Aurobindo says it best: "As the poet, artist, or musician when he creates does really nothing but develop some potentiality in his unmanifested self into a form of manifestation, and as the thinker, statesman, mechanist only bring out into a shape of things that which lay hidden in themselves, was themselves, is still themselves when it is cast into form, so is it with the world and the Eternal. All creation or becoming is nothing but this self-manifestation."

The question "what is existence?" will probably never be fully answered by science with its reliance on the senses and sense-enhancing instrumentation. We are slowly beginning to realize that the information we receive through ordinary perception may not give us an accurate view of reality or at least not the whole picture. Some are beginning to explore new paradigms within their fields. Others have found ways and means to explore a vast universe within ourselves.

We can turn our inquiry inward and address our higher nature. We have a direct line to "higher authority." We can refer our inquiry further up the line — bypassing the discursive mind, evaluations based on the dead past, or stale emotions stored in memory — to the highest principle in us, the Self, or that which alone is real. Here in the light of consciousness resides the higher intellect or higher reason and all knowledge.

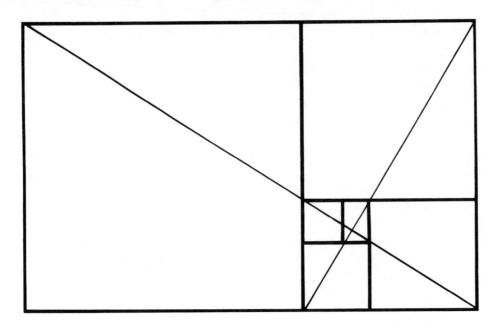

The Golden Mean Proportion. Whether adding or subtracting a perfect square, the remainder is always a Golden Mean rectangle.

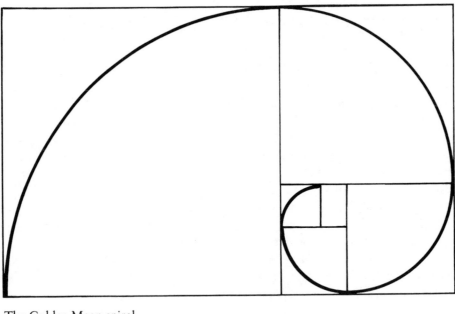

The Golden Mean spiral.

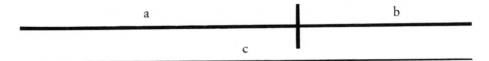

The line divided: (b:a) is the same as (a:c)

Figure 2. Development of the Golden Mean.

The sages teach that union with the Self is attainable to those who desire it. While we lack an intimate connection with reality, with the one Self, a small act of faith is required to bridge the gap until such time that we experience it for ourselves. We also need to hypothesize for the time being that an evolution of consciousness is a real possibility. We are told by the Wisdom tradition that in this expanded state of human consciousness — the "objective consciousness" of P.D. Ouspensky, the "pure Reason" of Plato or the "freedom from ignorance" of the Vedas — it is possible to know everything fully about everything and apprehend the world as it is. The sages saw this search for truth as the highest form of inquiry.

The reductive modern idea of a fortuitous accident propelled by a blind force hurtling through space in an endless orbit does not hold up in light of many recent scientific discoveries in physics and the study of consciousness. Whether science explains existence in terms of energy, randomness, chaos, waves, particles, or some other concepts, all these seeming "realities" or matrices exist simultaneously on one level or another, conjuring up a magnificent and eternal differentiation manifesting as the invisible and visible substance we call the universe, nature, and life. But these tendencies are just the observable phenomena of the interaction of "information" and energy and represent but a few glorious and extraordinary facets of the One Perfection, the One Intelligence, and the One Consciousness that lies behind them.

We do not need to deliberate about the existence of a Supreme Intelligence or look for verification of it outside ourselves. The reductive view of life simply does not hold up in the light of simple observation of our own human instrument, which is itself a matrix of the universe — a marvel of differentiation. The evidence of a higher Intelligence may be objectively experienced in our own being as "the Witness," "the observer," or "that which is looking." The Witness is beyond thinking, evaluating, and considering, beyond feeling, beyond the body and the senses.

By turning our inquiry inward, we gain knowledge of our own nature as well as the nature of the universe. When we dive more deeply into our being, as in meditation, the supreme Intelligence reveals itself in the full spectrum of its essence, which is pure existence, pure consciousness, and pure bliss. We know and feel in that moment our true Self, whose nature is *sat-chit-ananda*.

The mystery of life, like the concept of eternity, cannot be pondered by the ordinary mind; it always eludes us and defies definition. The reason for existence has been contemplated by all great thinkers. We are told by the sages that the aim of the eternal play that is life is to experience itself — to know Self-delight or bliss.

We can view our existence here on this plane as an expression of the supreme Intelligence through which we participate in the advancement of the evolution of consciousness. The individual Self, through reflection and introspection, gains knowledge of the nature of reality; by its power to intend and create, it collaborates in the eternal play, while the Supreme Self, resting in Self-delight, manifests itself through infinite expansion and limitless differentiation.

*

NINE
OUR TRUE NATURE

HUMAN BEINGS HAVE ASKED the questions "what am I?" and "who am I?" for thousands of years. These questions, which inquire into the essence of our being, have been answered in a thousand different ways and by just as many different means — in the East predominantly through Self-inquiry, reflection, and revelation, and in the West through intellect, reason, and discourse. Eastern philosophy answers the question almost unanimously when it states that we are the Self. The *Eesha-Upanishad* expresses the omnipresence of the Self in exalted words of revelation: "The Self is everywhere, without a body, without a shape, whole, pure, wise, all-knowing, far-shining, self-depending, all-transcending," while Emerson, through reflection and reason, arrived at the following truth: "In yourself is the law of all nature...in yourself slumbers the whole of Reason; it is for you to know all; it is for you to dare all."

We all have an inherent desire to know the truth and to know ourselves and to seek perfection, but often we are diverted, and instead of looking within, we look to satisfy these desires in the world of things. We do not recognize them as "inner needs" — as desires of the soul. Instead we forget who we are and live from personality and opinion.

We all come into the world with a wish to live, to be happy, and to be loved, and we want these things to last forever. These desires, manifesting at the elementary level of instinct alone, can achieve nothing higher than keeping the species going; in other words, they are mechanical and unconscious. If, on the other hand, these desires power our emotional or intellectual centers, we are reaching higher in an attempt to realize our ideals. On these levels we achieve happiness through successes in life; we find love in family and friends and comfort in the enjoyment of a good life. But since we want these things to last forever — and they don't — we experience sorrow and disease. When we are asleep, that is, unaware of our true nature, and express these desires in a relative and materialistic way, we experience but a faint glimmer of their potentiality.

As long as our lives conform to our modest expectations of happiness, love, and comfort, we tend not to ask the deeper questions or to embark on the quest of Self-inquiry. As long as we get an occasional fix of satisfaction and pleasure, we are willing to do our share, playing among surfaces and appearances. But because we want to hold on to life, happiness, love, and the expectations and acquisitions that go along with them and secure them for eternity, we set ourselves up for a complicated no-win situation. We now have to protect "our" life, "our" happiness, and "our" acquisitions. Fear sets in. We are afraid of losing life, happiness, and love and all the material things and pleasures associated with them. This fear of loss will not let us truly enjoy this relative happiness.

All along we are dimly aware of an undercurrent of wanting more. This desire for "more," felt as secret stirrings of the heart or as faint whisperings of the intuition, is nothing other than the memory of a more perfect love and joy and the recognition of a more perfect order. Unfortunately these gentle intuitions are often drowned out by the shrill din of materialism and the world of duties.

We can temporarily silence the questioning heart and mind and attend to the details of our daily existence until a louder cry for true knowledge is heard. This awakening, whether prompted by grace or by the hard knocks of life, is cause for rejoicing.

When the body is sick, we get medical advice and take healing medicine. We know that sickness and malfunctions of the body arise from an overload of toxic substances, which throw the body out of balance. When the psyche is out of balance from an overload of unhealthy substances — wrong thinking, wrong attitudes, compulsions, and attachments — we also need to give it the proper medicine, which is the sweet nectar of sacred truths and the bliss arising from the experience of our true nature. We need to remind ourselves of the divine order — our healthful state.

Many of the sacred texts and hymns that have come down to us through the ages are accounts of direct experience of the Self — revelations of the divine, ecstatic outpourings of spiritual aspirants who in a flash realized their identity with Brahman or the Godhead. An ancient Vedic sage inspired by his rapture proclaims: "Hear, ye children of Immortal Bliss.... I have found the Ancient One, who is beyond all darkness, all delusion."

Other sacred truths were established through discourse and Self-inquiry. The masters asked their disciples: "Who art thou?" and after reflection, they answered "*Tat tvam asi*" — "That thou art." (*That,* here, refers to the infinite, indescribable divine.)

The Vedas teach that *atman* — the Divine Self — is our true nature and that it is knowable through experience. The nature of the *atman* is said to be *sat-chit-ananda* or being-consciousness-bliss. *Sat-chit-ananda* is the pure state of *atman* or Brahman, or the individual Self and the Universal Self, and is the first emanation of the Creative Principle — the source of all manifestation. *Sat-chit-ananda* describes the triple divine worlds as well as those of the individual Self, *sat* being the supreme Godhead or *purusha* ("Person") or substance of being, *chit* being the light of consciousness, active force, and knowledge, and *ananda* being supreme bliss, love, or delight. The entire manifest universe is said to be based on *chit* or consciousness. This suggests that the whole universe, everything in it, animate and inanimate, is based on consciousness and held in our own *prakriti* or nature. The Upanishads tell us quite simply and beautifully that "everything exists in name and shape only."

The Vedic teachings state that out of the great *mahat* — the supreme intellect or the stuff of consciousness — arises *ahamkara* — the individual limited consciousness. This in turn gives rise to the *gunas*, the primordial qualities, which give birth to *manas* (mind), the senses, and the *tanmatras* — the subtle states of the elements. All forms arise from combinations of these five subtle elements — ether, air, fire, water, and earth — which are orchestrated by the forces of nature and spun into the web of *maya*, the beautiful illusion of endless forms and stupendous varieties of patterns.

What has all this to do, we might ask, with understanding ourselves and finding happiness here and now?

The ancient sages knew, as we too are slowly coming to realize, that we cannot philosophize about the nature of Man without taking into account the nature of consciousness and that we cannot know who we are without considering the nature of the Supreme Intelligence; we cannot know the laws of human nature without looking at the cosmic matrix. We cannot aspire without comprehending something of the purpose of creation. So when we learn from the wise that the aim of creation is bliss, we know that Man is not excluded from this universal truth and conclude that our purpose here too is to realize this bliss.

Another reason to study these ancient concepts is that they hold the key for our return to the Absolute, to our source. The pattern by which Divine Intelligence manifests in nature, taken in reverse order, provides the means for our return. Our *prakriti* or nature, our individual manifestation in the world, holds within it the system by which we find our way back to our source of being.

The cosmic forces arising out of *prakriti* are called the three *gunas* or qualities — *sattva, rajas,* and *tamas,* and they are the cause of the first differentiation in Creation. The etymology of the Sanskrit word *guna* suggests "rope"; thus the *guna* has a binding quality. These three qualities bind the manifest universe together, from the atom to the galaxies, and they account for the magnificent diversity of forms and creatures. Everything in Creation is a result of the interplay of these forces, and all nature is subject to them. The effects of the *gunas* are observable and can be felt as a particular predominance of the qualities of *sattva, rajas,* or *tamas* in an event, an action, and the nature of a human being, and in our state of mind and emotions.

The word *sattva* comes from the Sanskrit root *sat,* "being" (from *as,* "to be"). It is the force of equilibrium and can be seen in the qualities of purity, harmony, light, and knowledge. It is "intelligence-stuff" and corresponds in science to the force of the proton. *Rajas* is from the Sanskrit verb-root *raj,* "to glow," "to be excited." It is the universal force of energy and motion, attraction and repulsion and can be observed in our own nature in activity, passion, effort, and desire. It is "energy-stuff" and corresponds to the force of the electron. *Tamas* comes from the root *tam,* "to perish," "to grow sad." It is the force of inertia, the quality of darkness, inaction, ignorance, and death. This is "mass-stuff" or matter and loosely corresponds to the force of the neutron. In the *Timaeus* Plato also speaks of three forces — *eros, thanatos,* and *dike* (passion or love, death or decay, and justice or order) — to which the human soul responds. Plato's three forces show a close correspondence with the Eastern concepts of *rajas, tamas,* and *sattva* respectively.

These *gunas* or qualities are present at every level of existence in the state of Becoming. It is said that when the gunas are in perfect balance, the creation is not manifest. Only Brahman or the state of pure being is without qualities. At the cosmic level the *gunas* create and sustain all forms and give rise to *maya* — the cosmic illusion. The Sanskrit word *maya* means "that which is measured" (from the root *ma,* "to measure," "to give form," "to limit"). *Maya* is said to be an inevitable result of manifestation. Everything in manifestation suffers some kind of distortion. At the individual level *maya* is the cause of ignorance or the distortion of our perception of reality. The sages tell us that everything changeable is subject to this illusion, which is the fabric of the veil that hides the Absolute.

The divine *maya,* the universe, can be seen as the "becoming" of the divine — the outpouring of Brahman measured in time and space, the substance of which is Divine Love. We are swimming in Divine Love, but rarely are we aware of our good fortune.

In our present state of consciousness, we see the world as physical, we are tricked by the magic of light and motion, by the illusion of space, time, and causality, by the glamour of surface and form, and we take these changing conditions to be real. But we are told by the wise that the phenomenal creation has no existence separate from Brahman, or (to use scientific jargon) that the visible universe and everything in it are an epiphenomenon. This statement is universal. It is true at every level, at the level of both the supreme Self and the individual Self.

We are totally dependent on and interconnected with the One Existence — the One Supreme Being, manifesting in the eternal becoming. We cannot consider our true nature or ponder the nature of consciousness except in the context of the One. We cannot study the human being as a separate entity, as science has tried to do. Our sense of separateness is but an illusion. If we want to find the truth, we must look at the fabric of this marvelous miracle called life and, in the knowledge of the One Self and the One Consciousness, pull out some threads and examine them a little more closely.

In the state of ordinary human consciousness, *maya* creates the illusion of separate existence. This duality — "me versus them" — is the cause of all strife, competition, and fear. But it doesn't end there. *Maya* also has us believe that we are our bodies, our minds, and our feelings, and that we are the doers of our actions. *Maya* is the cause of sleep and forgetfulness.

We are diminished when we forget our true nature and settle for a tiny share of what we are. We are denying ourselves our birthright — the enjoyment of the One Consciousness and everything in it. Brahman is in no way diminished by becoming — by manifesting in creation. In the same way, *atman* — the Self in man — is in no way diminished by the illusion of *maya*. The Self is pure consciousness and remains unchanged by its experiences and acts, but we humans are fooled by the effects of the *gunas* and *maya*. We identify with becoming and thus lose sight of our divine heritage.

THE SAGES TEACH THAT WE have to rise above the gunas and thus gain freedom from *maya*. This freedom is not achieved on the material level by escaping the world, nor by giving up our worldly treasures. Rather it is achieved, to use Emerson's words, by "the escape from all false ties." By ridding ourselves from the bondage of false beliefs, attachments, and identification with not-Self, we once again regain knowledge of our true Self and in the process become freer and more divine.

In an essay on joy, Aldous Huxley compares the universal attributes of *sat-chit-ananda* to the "three fruits of the spirit," which, according to St. Paul, are peace, love, and joy. Huxley says that "Peace [*sat*] is the manifestation of unified being. Love [*chit*] is the mode of divine knowledge. And bliss, the concomitant of perfection, is the same as joy." These three fruits of the spirit — peace, love, and joy, or being, knowledge, and bliss — are what we are continually seeking. But because we want them for ourselves, they forever elude us, and because we seek for them in the physical and mental worlds, they cause agitation, unhappiness, and misery.

The physical world is in fact the smallest world. It is encompassed and interpenetrated by a much larger subtle world, and these two worlds are again encompassed and interpenetrated by the causal world, and so on (see fig. 3).

When we are asleep, our consciousness encompasses only the physical and subtle worlds — the body and the mind. We may become vaguely aware of the causal — the shadowy body that carries past tendencies; we may even be annoyed by its insistent compulsions. When we wake up to the spiritual world, we become conscious of the true nature of our Self and the Self in everyone. On the next plane there is no sense of otherness or individual existence — the individual Self merges with the Supreme Self. The highest plane is that of full absorption and union with Paramatman. The *atman* is without limits, and it is free; it is only our false beliefs that keep us imprisoned in a small world of our own.

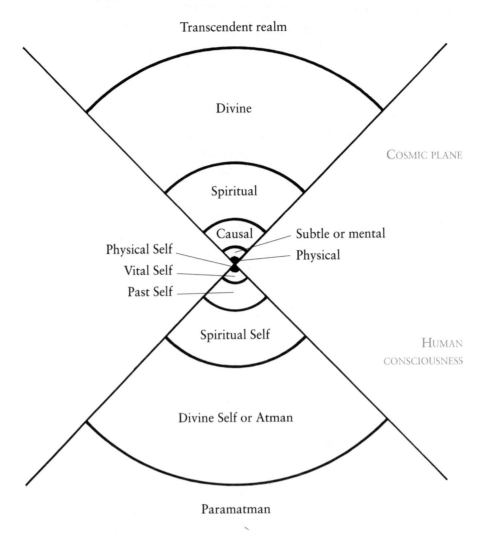

Figure 3. Cosmic planes compared to the levels of human consciousness.

The visible physical world, which we take to be the realest and most substantial of all the worlds, is in fact only a small facet of a much vaster reality. It is, so to speak, the end product of consciousness or the outward expression of Spirit and has no life of its own. Our bodies are such an outward expression. We are not that expression — we are not the finite body oscillating in the ocean of infinite consciousness, but rather we are the luminous *purusha* — the Spirit, the eternal Witness, the passive spectator — of *prakriti*, the world of name and shape.

Our Self is unchanging, eternal, birthless and deathless, free, and divine. When we realize fully that we are *sat-chit-ananda*, we will be completely and permanently absorbed in bliss. In the meantime we can at least have a small taste of the bliss of our higher Self and dispel our ignorance by reflecting on the great sacred truths. We are not here to live a life of drudgery and misery. We are here to enjoy. We are here to realize bliss.

We have the tools to uncover our most precious gifts — the higher emotion and intellect that serve as channels to the divine. The "work" to uncover our true nature is "done" by the Self. We can only know the Self and its attributes — being, consciousness, and bliss — through the experience of our Self; there is no other experiencer.

The reflective attributes of the Self are observable in our instrument even in everyday life. Thus in the manifest world of the conditioned individual, *sat* is that which exists and manifests as beingness or substance; we all experience *sat* in the feeling "I am." *Chit* is consciousness, and is experienced as knowledge and self-awareness. It varies greatly in the individual, and its functioning (as individual consciousness) depends on its purity. In ordinary life *ananda* is felt as happiness and love; this force vibrates through the human instrument, harmonizing mind and body and healing every cell. Through the force of *ananda* we experience pleasure in play and work. *Ananda* is the force behind love and devotion. In ordinary thinking, we attribute the pleasure we experience in love to the object. We attribute the love we feel to the person in front of us, but the reality is that bliss and love are inside us — are our nature — and do not come from the world. The Self loves the Self; bliss wants to merge with bliss.

Chit, consciousness, is the force that powers our desire for truth, Self-reflection, and Self-knowledge. It is the light behind the thought; it is conscious discrimination and makes us aware of our discontent with relative knowledge, relative existence, and relative happiness. It is the force that makes us aware of the One and leaves us yearning for the One — for the experience of our own true Self.

We can only love and value what we truly know and what is familiar to us; so we have to come to know Atman and experience *sat-chit-ananda* for ourselves. When we experience but a drop of the ocean of love and bliss of the Absolute, our being is transformed and we can take some of it back into the relative world. We develop a taste for this pure and free state, untouched by good and evil, and will aspire to dive deeper and deeper into our own Self. We will begin to prefer the stillness to the restless considerings of the ego, the feeling of oneness to that of separate existence, the experience of eternity to the hypnotic trance of time and space.

We speak of attaining freedom, enlightenment, and perfection. In reality we cannot *attain* any of these, since our Self is already free, illumined, and perfect. The only thing we can "work" towards is the removal of illusion. One of the many ways to find and know our true Self is to undo our mental constructs and social conditioning and thus leave behind what we are not. The perfect tool for the removal of illusion is within ourselves: the faculty known as *buddhi* or discrimination.

In his *Essays on the Gita,* Sri Aurobindo speaks from intimate knowledge and experience when he tells us, "This Self is our self-existent being. It is not limited by our personal existence. It is the same in all existences, pervasive, equal to all things, supporting the whole universal action with its infinity, but unlimited by all that is finite, unmodified by the changings of Nature and personality. When this Self is revealed within us, when we feel its peace and stillness, we can grow into that; we can transfer the poise of our soul from its lower immergence in Nature and draw it back into the Self."

TEN

THE HUMAN INSTRUMENT

THE HUMAN INSTRUMENT has been studied from the outside and the inside for thousands of years. It has been probed, dissected, and studied by science — anatomy, anthropology, physics, psychology — and it has been observed and reasoned and speculated upon by philosophy and religion. We are presented on a daily basis with new scientific findings, with bits and pieces of information and knowledge relating to the workings of the body and brain.

Much of the scientific research into our bodies and psyches is in response to our dismal state of physical and mental health; hence the concern is almost exclusively with disease and distress — the pathological state of our instrument. Very little emphasis is bestowed on the proper functioning and healthy state of our physical instrument and even less on the study of the proper functioning of the mind and psyche. Since the spiritual component of the human instrument is unprovable by scientific method and will probably remain so, it falls outside the interest of such research and is therefore often ignored altogether. Hence we are presented with a false picture, one that is heavily weighted towards the physical.

Nonetheless if we are to understand and heal our instrument, we have to take into consideration the entire mechanism — the body, the mind, the soul — the physical, mental, and spiritual person, or, as the Eastern tradition has it, the gross, subtle, and causal bodies —and we have to study the hierarchical order of these three bodies. If we are to understand how we perceive the world and how we interrelate with the universe, we need to have some knowledge of the proper working of our psyche.

Metaphysics provides us with many frameworks with which we can begin the study of the proper alignment of our instrument. One of these considers the ways in which we experience the world around us: that is, intellectually, emotionally, and in action. Each of these different modes of experience resonate in a particular "center" in the body. There are three basic centers, traditionally attributed to the head (the intellect, or the seat of knowing), the heart (the emotions, or the seat of being), and the abdomen (the active/instinctive, or the seat of doing). As we shall see in more detail in Part Three, this seemingly simple model provides us with a beautiful tool for self-observation. We will begin to appreciate that the most useful knowledge is that which is verifiable through our own powers of discrimination and perception.

When we begin to investigate our instrument, we might at first marvel at the more obvious attributes, such as the dexterity of the physical body with its inherent and learned functions. We might be struck by the mystery of self-awareness, creative thought, and the miracle of life itself. And then, at some point of awakening, we stand in awe and wonder of the wisdom and the intelligence behind the design of our being and our human instrument. We realize then that we humans are uniquely gifted. We are the only creatures endowed with *buddhi,* or discrimination, and the power to intend and create.

We usually refer to the power of intention as "free will" — a concept that leads to much confusion. The notion of free will as it is commonly understood is an illusion on many levels: free will does not exist at all for human beings who are asleep. When we are asleep, when we are not in the present, we act from compulsion and mistake these actions for free will. When we begin to wake up and observe, we see that we have access to a gap — a split-second of choice (another, more appropriate word for the concept of "free will") in any thought, feeling, or action. In this gap, which is beyond time and space, is the power of true intent, of choice and creativity. Here lies the potential — in combination with heightened *buddhi* or discrimination — for going against compulsion and the forces of nature. In the completely awakened being, the intent springs from the Creative Principle, untouched by ego or past conditioning, and this pure creative power manifests its intent in time and space.

We are also unique among all creatures both in that we are incomplete in our present state of ordinary consciousness and in that we have within ourselves a system for spiritual evolution. Not only are we endowed with a mind, a personality, and a physical body, but we are enveloped with a more intangible soul-nature and are crowned by the Atman or the Divine Self. These are the gifts that will aid us in our evolution and serve as our tools for outward expression. They also serve as the means for our ascent into the divine. The dictionary definition of the Sanskrit word for "evolution" — *pravitti* — is "unfolding of what is within or what is latent." Thus spiritual evolution is an unfolding of our implicit potential into the explicit — the here and now — in accordance with the desire of the spiritualizing force within us — a force that exercises its will upon our existence, whether we are aware of it or not.

In order to study our instrument in terms of its evolutionary possibility, we must look beyond our physical, mental and spiritual bodies and study the cosmic view — the macrocosm and microcosm. Here again, we are greatly indebted to Sri Aurobindo and his insight into the nature of the divine and Man and to his revelatory interpretation of the great Eastern wisdom tradition. Fig. 4 is a simplified rendering based on his writings.

Although this diagram shows a hierarchical order of being and consciousness beyond our common perception, it is well within our capacity to appreciate the beauty and love in this supreme design. When contemplating this divine outpouring, this creative unfolding into matter, or stepping down of energy, we have to keep in mind that, although it shows an explicit outward movement from the Divine into Man, from consciousness into matter, it is in reality all one and it all takes place in the eternal now.

We have the special task of carrying out the Divine Will and are compelled to obey this higher power whether we are aware of it or not. The laws that regulate the universe — cause and effect, attraction and repulsion, involution and evolution — also regulate the life of Man and the pulse of our existence. But we have the power to transcend our earthly nature and to realize our higher calling and eventually to return to our Divine Source. Through the perfecting of our higher faculties, we can rise above the forces of *prakriti.*

The more we become aware of the Divine Will, the easier our task becomes in the here and now in manifesting our true nature in the world and growing into our true Self. We have been given magnificent tools for expressing ourselves, and we are free to put them to any use we desire, whether for self-aggrandizement, for acquiring

	MACROCOSM	
Divine	*Brahman*	God
	Paramatman	The Self Beyond

	MICROCOSM	
Divine Consciousness	*Sat*	Reality, Pure Being
	Chit	Consciousness
	Ananda	Bliss
Divine Will, Power, and Knowledge	*Vijnana-Purusha*	Supermind and Knowledge
	Jiva-Atman	Spirit, Self
Man	*Antaratman* or *Purusha*	Soul, Psyche, God-Spark, Son of God
Psyche	*Chaitya-Purusha*	Psychic Being, Soul, Nature in Evolution
Inner Organs	*Ahamkara*	Ego Consciousness, Personal Outer Self (formed by Nature)
	Anna-Purusha	Physical Being
	Prana-Purusha	Vital Being
	Manah-Purusha	Mental Being

Fig. 4. Macrocosm and microcosm in the system of Sri Aurobindo.

supernatural powers, for humanitarian and altruistic pursuits, or for selfless action in the service of the One Self and the return to our source of being.

Our special human powers — self-awareness, love, creativity, compassion, discrimination, aspiration, and intent — suggest a greater purpose, and they will not easily be ignored. They invite us gently but insistently to a higher exertion. It is through the conscious and prudent use of these powers that we can best express our highest calling in the world. It is through effort that we develop and expand our faculties, and it is by perfecting them that we ascend to the divine.

LET US LOOK MORE CLOSELY at our earthly vehicle and our special endowments. We have already considered the *jiva-atman* (the Spirit or Self in all) — our true, pure invisible being, whose existence is light, self-concentrated force, and self-delight. It is surrounded by three bodies, the physical, the subtle, and the causal. They are in fact all one and interpenetrate each other. The subtle body is an emanation of the causal, while the physical body is an emanation of both the subtle and the causal. The human body is formed of matter, food, the vital force, the psyche, and the mind; the latter two serve as a bridge between matter and soul, between becoming and being.

The *antaratman,* also known as *purusha* (soul or inner Self), is spirit entering birth; it is the conscious projection of spirit for the purpose of evolution. It is here to express itself in creation, gathering the essence of all the experiences and developing higher perception, which eventually leads to full realization.

The force of creation then enters the *chaitya-purusha* — another name for soul or the psychic being (*chaitya* means "consciousness"; *purusha* means "person"). Through this power we aspire to Divine Truth. The "consciousness-person" — our Psychic Being — is said to unify the embodied existence.

These different expressions of consciousness are not knowable in the unawakened state. However, this ancient system of knowledge has been refined and tested over thousands of years and we must assume that it is more than an elegant solution to the human dilemma — that it is based on higher experience and revelation.

So far we have been looking at all the unseen energies that flow into the human being. We now come to a level of inquiry that we can more easily validate through observation, namely the mind-body mechanism. This instrument of knowledge consists of *manas, buddhi, chitta* and *ahamkara* and the senses. It is the only instrument of knowledge available to man. The Self uses this "machinery" to experience the world and to gain knowledge through this experience. H.H. Shantanand Saraswati says that "Knowledge is the material of consciousness and it is available all the time and at every place. This is experienced in two ways as *aham* ('I am') or *idam* ('this is' or 'that is'). All knowledge which is composed of these two types of experiences can be had only through [this] machinery supplied to all beings."

In order to truly understand our instrument of experience, we have to make use of the precise terminology of the East. Western post-Freudian psychology does not make such clear distinctions; its human psyche is an ill-defined abyss with conscious and subconscious drives, instincts, reflexes, and biological programming. The mental functions for reasoning, thinking, and logical analysis are equated with the simple capacity for problem solving, and, to add to the confusion, these terms are used interchangeably. The physical brain is studied as a separate entity, and the mind is often set aside as that part about which we can know nothing. This modern model of the human psyche has an ego at its center; it may or may not acknowledge the possibility of a soul.

True philosophy, on the other hand, says that it is through reason that we can gain knowledge. Eastern thought informs us that all the tools for inner and outer knowledge are within ourselves. The individual faculties are contained in our *antahkarana* — the internal organ of thought, feeling, and conscience. The term is sometimes used to denote the "individual soul," and in some systems it is synonymous with *prakriti* — the nature of the individual soul.

The *antahkarana* (from *antah,* "within," and *karana,* "acting") is our "inner instrument." It is our individual power of expression — that part we generally refer to in the West as the human psyche. It is our small share of the universal causal body, which is very large. The human causal body is said to be a combination of the light of the Atman and the *antahkarana.*

The *antahkarana* is the medium within us through which the mind, the emotions, and the senses all receive their respective powers to function just like the different parts of a machine. The functioning differs greatly from being to being and from situation to situation, and this difference is due to the balance of the three *gunas.* When there is unity of heart, mind, and activity, it is a clear sign that *sattva* rules the individual. The heart is then full of love, the mind still, and the senses under control. Actions flow naturally, spreading cheer and good will. When there is ignorance, disharmony, and agitation, the individual is under the spell of *tamas* and *rajas.*

The *antahkarana,* according to the Vedanta, is the seat of the Atman, and it is through this inner organ of mind that the Paramatman — the universal Self — manifests in the individual. In other words, it is the *antahkarana* which separates the individual Self from the universal Self. All our feelings, desires, thoughts, and intellectual processes arise out of this nucleus. Anything that results in action arises from it. After a feeling or thought has unfurled into manifestation, it again merges into this realm of infinite potential. It is the beginning and end of all feeling and thinking. We can verify this process when, in a moment of action, we see that "everything takes place in mind only." For this revelation to happen, the *antahkarana* has to be pure and free, the Self the master, and the mind and body perfectly aligned in one-pointed attention to the task at hand.

It is in the *antahkarana* that the *aham* makes itself known in the pure feeling of "I am." *Aham* is the observer or the "eye" which sees. But this eye cannot see itself. It can only see *idam* — the phenomenal world — by means of its subtle body, which is composed of *buddhi, chitta, manas,* and the senses. We might say then, that in order to experience itself and know itself, the *aham* needs the *idam.*

The *antahkarana* — our internal "machine" — is composed of four elements: *ahamkara* — the concept of individuality, experienced as the feeling of "I"; the *chitta* — the storehouse of memory and knowledge; *buddhi* — intelligence, discrimination, and decision; and *manas* — the mind or organ of thought, which stores information and data. These four functions have different speeds and work just like different gears in a machine. Some of them may be observed by perceptive self-inquiry as they manifest in the subtle body. On the causal level the four elements of *antahkarana* are joined together as a unity; hence in reality there is no division in *antahkarana.* It is through this organ that Divine Will or grace from the Paramatman manifests and enters into the subtle and physical levels of Man.

The *antahkarana* can only transmit the light and grace of the Paramatman when it is pure. It acts like a window; when it is clean, the sunlight can enter without any special invitation; when it is dirty the light cannot penetrate it. Similarly, when the *antahkarana* is dense and dull through ignorance, the grace of the Paramatman cannot shine through the being.

Let us look at the elements which make up the *antahkarana* more closely:

Ahamkara (from *aham,* "I," and *kara,* "action") in its pure state is the "feeling of existence" and is said to reside in the head. In ordinary consciousness it is experienced as the "sense of individuality," the feeling of a separate "I." *Ahamkara* lends its power to the personal outer self — the persona — which makes its mark in the world, and it creates the incentive to duty and ambition. In the undeveloped human being, the sense of "I" is very changeable and is always dual in its perspective: "me versus the world." This feeling of duality powers all thoughts and actions, resulting in all forms of egotism. This separate "I" or ego identifies with the physical being, the vital force, and mind. In the enlightened human, the pure *ahamkara* is identified or identical with *atman,* the Divine Self.

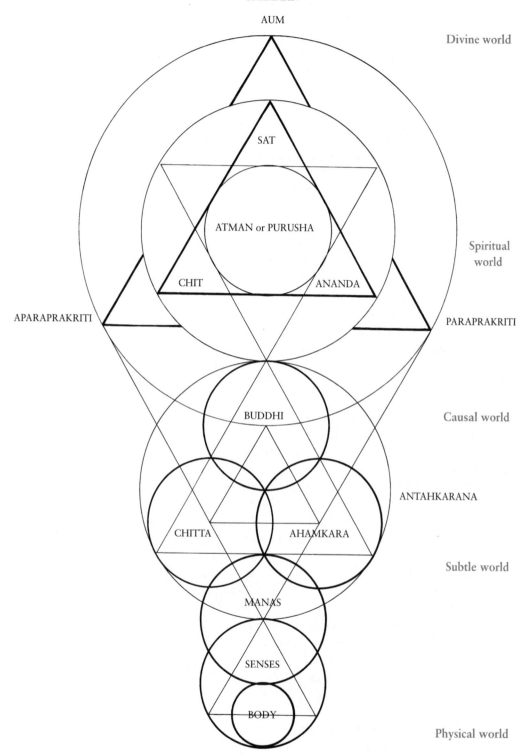

Figure 5. The human/divine makeup in the light of traditional knowledge. The senses present their objects to manas. Manas presents them to ahamkara and chitta, which present them to buddhi, which in turn presents them to Atman, who alone experiences. Manas—when under control—becomes the perfect vehicle of buddhi and enlightened buddhi the perfect vehicle of Atman.

Chitta (from *chit,* "to think, cogitate") is experienced in the heart and body. It is a partial and fluctuating reflection of pure Divine Consciousness in the human being. The *chitta* gathers and stores all experiences and individual memories. In the enlightened being, *chitta* reflects the light of truth. Here is the fountain of unlimited consciousness; the more we draw from it, the more becomes available. *Chitta* is the faculty that is purified by spiritual discipline until it becomes untainted and reflects the light of pure consciousness. We speak of the necessity of a "pure heart" as we ascend into the Light. The *chitta* of a pure human being is full of knowledge, thoughts, and ideals of the highest order. The *chitta* of an impure individual is filled with the darkness of ignorance, false knowledge, and evil thoughts.

Buddhi (from *budh,* "to know") is said to reside in the head. It is a gift that is unique to humankind. When this faculty is fully developed, it is referred to in various traditions as "higher reason," "higher intellect" or "illumined mind." It is often likened to a mother who warns of impending dangers and bad influences. The word *buddhi* in its more pragmatic sense refers to judgment, discrimination, choice, or discernment. We speak of it as "the still, small voice" of conscience, which addresses us in specific terms about right or wrong, good and bad. On the other hand, conscience varies from one individual to another. Quite often what we call conscience is, upon closer scrutiny, nothing more than the fear of punishment.

We make use of the power of *buddhi* in everyday life when we use judgment, when we are weighing the appropriateness of this or that or choosing between one thing or another. *Buddhi,* however, has a higher calling. When it is honed by frequent study of sacred truths and by reflection on the nature of Self, it becomes the perfect instrument for inner evolution — a sharp sword that severs the fetters of attachments. *Buddhi* is in close proximity to the Atman and receives its light, which is the light of consciousness. It is therefore our most precious and powerful tool. We can use this power for transformation or for the benefit of the ego. To make the *buddhi* pure, all we really need to do is love truth more than untruth and to love the true Self more than the ego. When, in a moment of grace, the veil of ignorance falls, all divisions vanish: there is only One Self, and the observer and the observed, *aham* and *idam,* are known to be one and the same.

Manas (from *man,* "to think") is related to "mind" in its largest sense — the thinking principle. In its widest sense it refers to all mental powers, including intelligence, perception, and understanding. In its philosophical sense *manas* is the organ through which thoughts enter and through which the objects of sense affect the soul. *Manas* partakes of all three worlds: gross, subtle, and causal.

Since it is intimately linked to the organs of perception, *manas* is felt in the head, heart, and body. *Manas* has the ability to turn inward and engage in thinking, questioning, classifying, and imagining, or it can turn outward and engage in perceiving through contact with the five senses and their objects. Thus it can experience the physical world and interact with it.

Manas is both the faculty that gets us into trouble and the means for getting us out of trouble. A mind disciplined by the practice of concentration performs its proper duty and becomes the servant of the Self and the doorkeeper to the *antahkarana.* But the mental chatter that goes on continually in the undisciplined mind, and over which there is no control in the ordinary state of consciousness, has little to do with the proper function of *manas.* It is in fact a pathological state due to misappropriation of one center by another. In the healthy state the mind is still until it is called into action by the master — the Self.

The force that works through the *antahkarana* is *prakriti* — the individual being or *jiva*. When our nature is pure through good intentions, thoughts, and actions, the *antahkarana* will function perfectly. All the subtle powers — *ahamkara, chitta, buddhi,* and *manas* — will work in unison, both in our worldly expression and duties and in our ascent towards the divine. When the faculties are perfected and pure, they reflect oneness with Paramatman. The individual Self and the universal Self create a bond. Light flows from the words and actions of such individuals. Their actions are neutral, without motive or claim; they are free of attachments and have no fear of loss; their attention in any endeavor is full of consciousness, knowledge, and love.

However, when through ignorance we claim these special powers as our own and we identify our sense of "I" with any of them, they become the Five Veils of Illusion, also known as the *koshas*. These five *koshas* arise from the intake of food, air, and impressions, from the lack of true knowledge and discrimination, and from negative emotions. (In Part Three of this book we will consider these veils in more detail.)

The Vedas teach that there are three obstacles that prevent the inner organ of mind from functioning properly. The first is perversity or willfulness, which entices the individual to do the opposite of what the conscience would have him do. The second obstacle is uncontrolled discursive thinking, circling thoughts and imaginings. The third is "grasping," which causes the feeling part of the mind to cling to any object of interest. These impediments to the proper functioning of our psyche have their consequences in the mind-body mechanism, which becomes knotted with tensions, crazed with uncontrolled imagining, and riddled with guilt and anger. Scientific research points to the connection between negative thinking and the eventual depression of the immune function, ending in illness. It has also been observed that negative memories are stored throughout the body. Sooner or later, when fed by stress and anxiety, they will take their toll. Conversely, it has also been shown that joy, laughter, and happiness have a positive effect.

MANY SPIRITUAL EXERCISES such as yoga and meditation are designed to bring about a balance of mind and body, particularly to balance the right and left hemispheres of the forebrain. We generally think of the left hemisphere, which contains the complex speech centers, as the outward-looking part of the mind, and the quieter right hemisphere, believed to be the seat of intuition and creativity, as the inward-looking part. We associate the former with verbal skills and masculinity, and the latter with creativity and femininity. Whether these centers are more dominant in one gender or another is a moot point. The fact remains that left-brain dominance creates an imbalance in the human being, in society, and in the environment. It contributes to our preoccupation with the material world and to the lack of understanding of our inner selves. We have seen the negative effects of a predominantly patriarchal culture concerned with "becoming": acquiring, consuming, conquering, winning. What is neglected is "being" — the quiet enjoyment of our true nature.

There is no clear line between the subtle or mental body and the physical body. The mind-body mechanism is intricately intermeshed. We are still pondering the elusive mystery of the connection between the subtle and the gross, the mind and brain, consciousness and matter. Maybe the link is intangible and we will never be able to put a finger on it. It is much more likely, however, that where science leaves off is where spiritual work begins. At any rate scientific research suggests that mind and consciousness pervade the physical body. Such findings contribute to our knowledge of the human instrument and help in closing the rift between natural science and metaphysics.

The mind-body mechanism is graced with exquisite organs of perception which are perfectly attuned to experiencing the outer world and creatively interacting with it. According to both Eastern and Western wisdom teachings, each one of the senses arises from the subtle aspect of one of the five elements: ether or space, air, fire, water, and earth. This knowledge is not just metaphorical, but can easily be comprehended by intuition and observation. Thus sound arises out of ether, touch out of air, sight out of fire, taste out of water, and smell out of earth. These subtle states of perception correspond to the five physical sense organs: ears, skin, eyes, tongue, and nose. In addition, the Eastern tradition also speaks of physical mechanisms, which it calls the five "organs of conation or volition": the hands, feet, speech, and the excretory and reproductive functions.

The physical body is what we are most familiar and most identified with. But it is only one of many tools that the Atman uses for its interaction with matter. It is, so to speak, the end-product of spirit, and as such its functioning reflects the health of the *antahkarana* and of the soul of the individual being. The ancients knew that disease of the body can be traced to wrong thinking and wrong feeling in the subtle body and devised methods for the healing of both the subtle and physical bodies. Some were even adept at the difficult task of healing illness that has its origin in the causal body.

Our interactions with the world are colored by our individual *prakriti* and our *antahkarana*. Whatever we experience, whatever we do is subject to the distortion which *prakriti* imposes and which is dependent on the condition of light available to our individual soul.

Spiritual work is nothing other than the removal of the distortion of reality, the cleansing of our perception, and the letting go of what is untrue. There are many paths that lead to realization of the true Self. The models we are studying are not the one and only ones. There are many systems that can serve us in the quest for Self-knowledge, and we have to find the most propitious one for our own nature. We have to keep in mind that systematized knowledge is composed of concepts and ideas that point towards truth — they are not the truth, they are not reality.

Higher knowledge only comes in flashes. It is revealed through Divine Grace to a few great souls, or it is acquired through fervent aspiration and devotion by those who have perfected their instrument through purification and discrimination. Their luminous observations provide us with a vantage point from which to start our own quest and with the tools we need for the accomplishment of any action, including Self-realization.

❖

ELEVEN

THE FULLY REALIZED BEING

SINCE IN OUR PRESENT STATE we cannot have any idea what it is like to be "fully realized," "perfected," or "liberated," we have to look to those great gurus, teachers, and avatars who have shown the meaning of perfection in their lives and taught the ways to attain it. Although the expression differs from teaching to teaching and is adapted to meet the needs of time and place, they all speak of the one important truth — a truth that defines the meaning of our existence and the goal to be achieved: "Realize God in this life." All the great masters point to this ideal and, in their infinite wisdom and love, they spell out how it is to be realized. In one way or another, they tell us that the ultimate way to liberation is through purity of heart, discrimination, and divine grace.

When Jesus said, "Be ye perfect, even as your Father in heaven is perfect," he was telling us that we should aspire to be perfect here and now in this life. He did not say "be somewhat perfect," that is, just relatively perfect or ethical, as this passage is often interpreted, but rather "be ye *perfect*," as the Father is perfect. Although no systematized knowledge has come down to us based on the teaching of Jesus, the content of these words suggest that this was an inner teaching, revealing the knowledge that leads to perfection to "those with ears to hear"; for example, "Blessed are the pure in heart, for they shall see God," "I am the way" and "I am the Light." All the events between his birth on this plane and his transcendence of death clearly show the stages of development and, as we shall see, are in fact a loving demonstration of the path to full realization.

Truth, reality, and the means to realization are formulated in many different traditions. Thus in the language of the *Theologia Germanica,* we learn that "union belongeth to such as are perfect…[and is brought to pass]…by pureness of heart." In the language of the Upanishads, we are taught, "Blessed is he who realizes God in this life." We are sternly forewarned as the verse continues: "If not, it is his greatest calamity." From the teachings of Shri Dada we learn that "the only object of the ego of man, the seat of the 'I,' is to realize its identity with God. It is in this school of the world to learn this one lesson: to forget its limitations and actively to realize its oneness with all."

Sri Ramakrishna beautifully clarifies the way to realization when he says: "Only when his heart becomes purified through the practice of spiritual disciplines does a man attain to wisdom. He then becomes convinced of the existence of God through realizing Him in his own soul. There is, however, something greater than this attainment. To become convinced that fire lies hidden in the wood is one thing, but greater is it to light the fire, cook food, and satisfy one's hunger."

This suggests not only that we have the potential to realize the divine within but that we can aspire to make it gloriously manifest by using its "fire" — the force of consciousness and love — wisely and creatively for the benefit of all sentient beings. Sri Ramakrishna goes on to say: "He indeed has attained the supreme illumination who not only realizes the presence of God, but who knows Him as both Personal and Impersonal, who loves Him intensely, talks to Him, partakes of His bliss. Such an illumined soul realizes the bliss of God while he is absorbed in meditation, attaining oneness with the indivisible, impersonal Being; and he realizes the same bliss as he comes to normal consciousness and sees this universe as a manifestation of that Being and a divine Play."

WHAT DOES IT MEAN to be perfect and free? Shankara, the great exponent of Advaita Yoga, explains it in his interpretation of the Vedas: "Knowing the Self as within and without, in things stable and moving — discerning this through the Self, through its comprehending all things — putting off every disguise, and recognizing no division, standing firm through the perfect Self — such a one is free."

The perfected ones know fully and permanently within their being, heart, and mind that, in the words of the *Eesha Upanishad*, "whatever lives is full of the Lord." They have fully realized — made real — in themselves this glorious truth.

The opening verses of the *Eesha Upanishad* are said to contain the essence of all knowledge and the means to the achievement of bliss:

> *Whatever lives is full of the Lord. Claim nothing; enjoy, do not covet His property.*
> *Then hope for a hundred years of life doing your duty. No other way can prevent deeds from clinging, proud as you are of your human life.*
> *They that deny the Self, return after death to a godless birth, blind, enveloped in darkness.*
> *The Self is one. Unmoving, it moves faster than the mind. The senses lag, but Self runs ahead. Unmoving, it outruns pursuit. Out of Self comes the breath that is the life of all things...*
> *Of a certainty the man who can see all creatures in himself, himself in all creatures, knows no sorrow.*

The first sentence — "Whatever lives is full of the Lord" — defines the nature of reality (*sat*), or the essence of our existence. The second sentence — "Claim nothing; enjoy, do not covet His property" — defines consciousness (*chit*), or the substance — His property — in which life has its abode. The next verse defines bliss (*ananda*) or goal of existence, and elaborates on the enjoyment of life and the attainment of wisdom: "Then hope for a hundred years of life doing your duty. No other way can prevent deeds from clinging, proud as you are of your human life." Then we are given assurance of freedom: "Of a certainty the man who can see all creatures in himself, himself in all creatures, knows no sorrow."

Fully realized human beings know that whatever they see, the creation and all creatures in it, are the outward expression of the divine — the One Reality. They experience no separation between the seer and the seen. They know their very own nature to be *sat-chit-ananda*. Having subdued the personal ego, they experience no duality; having surrendered their attachments and claims, they experience no fear. They are free to fully enjoy the blessings of creation, life, and their own particular duties and gifts, but do not desire to possess any of these. They see the One Self everywhere and experience themselves as one with it; they dwell in Self-delight, and, although acting in the world, they are free from the fetters of action, from suffering, and delusion. Their personality and being are completely integrated and harmonious; they show absolute consistency in their thoughts, feelings, and actions. Although living in the world, they are imperturbable, knowing themselves to be the actors in a play and simply and joyfully watching the unfolding of the drama. Their spiritualized individuality or *ahamkara* now stands for the Atman, the One Self, who takes its rightful place as the master, and their minds and bodies take their place as the perfect servants of the Self. Their individual consciousness remains rooted in universal consciousness. Their *antahkarana* is pure and completely integrated and perfected. Their *buddhi* and *chitta* are pure and reflect the light of the Atman.

Fully realized ones have attained the state of pure being, all-knowing, and desireless action and are unaffected by the laws of the *gunas*. They have transcended time, space, and causality. They have achieved "divine sight" or what is sometimes known as "cosmic consciousness." They are born anew into another state of consciousness — a transcendental state that is beyond the senses, beyond ordinary laws, and beyond the three ordinary states of waking, dreaming, and dreamless sleep. In the terminology of the Vedas, they have reached *turiya* — the fourth state of consciousness, also called higher *samadhi*.

Their discrimination between *aham* and *idam* — being and becoming, the real and the unreal in the realm of existence — is perfected and certain. Yet they also know that in reality there is just one eternal being-becoming. Their love is unconditional and their compassion is unlimited. They have no fear of death, having experienced the reality of the sacred truth that "there is neither birth nor death." They see no evil, having realized that evil has no separate existence, they see only divine justice, beauty, and goodness. They obey or rather are in accord with Divine Will. Having renounced all personal will, they stand under one law and become conscious co-creators, manifesting Divine Will and using its power for the benefit of all sentient beings. They watch the eternal becoming with utter joy and detachment.

Perfected beings radiate love and peace to all who come in contact with them. Their actions arise in Divine Love, are sustained by Divine Love, and return to Divine Love. They embody the perfection of the nature of Atman, which is *sat-chit-ananda,* whether they are meditating, teaching, or carrying out their daily duties. They have reached the state of pure being, consciousness, and bliss and have thus fulfilled the true purpose of human life. When liberation is complete and their bodies have grown old, they consciously choose a propitious time for their departure and blissfully let go of their earthly abode. There is no change in consciousness, only a merging into a greater ocean of bliss, into the light of the Paramatman.

Many seekers have reached liberation through devotion and renunciation, others through reason and knowledge. Many have realized themselves through discipline and selfless action, yet others by purification, grace, or proximity to a holy man or avatar. There are many accounts of instant realization at the moment of a touch, a sight, or a sound. The *Srimad Bhagavatam* ("The Wisdom of God"), one of the most beloved of Eastern scriptures, records Narada's moment of realization in his own words: "While I was thus living in the society of these holy men, my heart was purified. These sages were always singing the glory and praise of the Lord; I used to hear them, and thus in my heart grew great love for the Lord, and I became devoted to Him. One day the sages, because of their love for me, initiated me into the sacred mysteries of wisdom. The veil of ignorance was removed from me, and I knew my real Self as divine."

Few of us find ourselves in the company of great sages and avatars, so instant realization is hardly an imminent possibility. However, we know from their teachings that realization is possible — in time, in this earthly life, or in a future life — for anyone who aspires to this goal and is willing to do the work. Realization cannot be rushed or forced; we cannot flex some secret spiritual muscle. By the same token, it cannot be delayed, or we will have missed a most precious opportunity; we will have lived in vain. "Immortality," says Emerson, "will come to such as are fit for it, and he who would be a great soul in future must be a great soul now." We really have no choice, except to begin now and from where we are, just as thousands of seekers have done in the past.

One of the many ways leading to the one goal is the Nyaya Ladder, which even today provides us with a useful paradigm. In a concise and clear form it depicts the spiritual journey from the first longing for liberation to the final step of full realization. It is also said to be a "ladder of Being through Knowledge."

This seven-step ladder is part of Nyaya, one of the six main systems of Hindu thought. Nyaya, a realistic philosophy based on logic, was originated by a sage who later became known as Gautama the Nyaya (not to be confused with the Buddha Gautama). The Sanskrit word *nyaya* comes from the root *ni-i,* which means "to go back," hence an original or logical statement or axiom, which suggests a "going back" to our true nature and further back to our absolute nature.

Let us consider the seven steps or stages of development:

1. *Subheksha*. Longing, auspicious desire.
The beginning of the quest. The seeker has a longing for liberation and has already done good actions and followed disciplines. He is ready for inquiry into his true Self. The arising of good desire and good intention leads to the next step.

2. *Suvicharna*. Good reflection, good thoughts, investigation.
The act of investigation of all the knowledge the seeker has gathered while searching for liberation. He comes to a decision by reasoning and proceeds without doubt in his mind, fortified in his intention on the quest.

3. *Tanumansha*. Lessening of outward mental movements.
Through righteous living, discipline, and practice of meditation, the seeker has experienced unity between the Self and the universal Self. He begins to *know* himself. His being, mind, and body are being transformed by the influence of *sattva*. Grace enters in form of true knowledge or of the presence of a teacher.

4. *Sattvapatti*. The dawn of the true Self.
Doubts and illusion cease, and the seeker begins to comprehend his Self as it really is. Outside impressions no longer have any power over him. The sensory world loses its grip, and he is carried by the "pull of the Way." His will and confidence grow stronger. *Sattva* predominates his being, and he is more interested in spiritual work than in mundane pursuits. He experiences an increase in Divine love.

5. *Asaushakti*. Loss of attachments.
In the light of regular experience of the seeker's true Self, attachments to the mental and physical body fade away. There is no more identification with false notions, atti-

tudes, or possessions. He is beginning to see himself and the world as they truly are and is able to see the reality and essence of everything. He sees the cause and effect of things together as one. He begins to discover that he and the outside world are in fact one and the same.

6. *Padartha bhavan*. Absence of duality.
The aspirant realizes the existence of the Supreme Self in everything. He sees that everything is Paramatman. The pull of the exterior world is almost gone, and he comes closer to pure consciousness.

7. *Turiya*. Liberation. Full Realization.
The Self becomes one with Paramatman. He knows himself and knows all there is to know about everything. He is one and perfect with right action, right thoughts, right feeling.

At the moment of realization the aspirant joins in the chorus of the illumined ones who proclaimed in the sacred verses of the Upanishads: "The Self is one....The Self is everywhere, without a body, without a shape, whole, pure, wise, all knowing, far shining, self-depending, all transcending; in the eternal procession assigning to every period its proper duty." And with profound knowing, he cries out, "Lord of all. I myself am He."

The *Mandukya Upanishad* describes the final state of consciousness, or rather hints at the undescribable nature of this state: "*Turiya* is not that which is conscious of the subjective world, nor that which is conscious of the objective world, nor that which is conscious of both, nor that which is a mass of all sentiency, nor that which is simple consciousness, nor that which is insentient. It is unseen by the senses, not related to anything, incomprehensible to the mind, uninferrable, unthinkable, indescribable, essentially of the nature of consciousness constituting the Self alone, negation of all phenomena, the Peaceful, all-bliss, and the non-dual." A simplified version of the same statement reads: "The fourth condition of the Self [*turiya*] corresponds to Om as One, indivisible Word.... The world disappears in Him.... Om is nothing but Self.... He who understands, with the help of his personal self, merges himself into the impersonal Self; He who understands."

In the state of *turiya* human beings are said to become *purusha* or the "divine person." Their spirit joins with the consciousness of the universal soul, sometimes referred to as the oversoul or supraconsciousness, and forms an inseparable bond with it. *Purusha* is said to be beyond qualifications. The sages who have attempted to define its mysterious nature have arrived at the following qualities, or rather nonqualities: *purusha* is without cause, being the ultimate cause of all; it is eternal, beyond time; all-pervading, not pervaded by anything; unsupported, yet supporting everything; independent, not governed by any law; beyond the three *gunas;* beyond reason (although it is found through reason); unique, singular, the seed of all; all-conscious; inactive (although it alone acts); beyond gender (although it generates everything); united, without any parts.

This permanent merging into the universal soul is not to be confused with a temporary union — the vision of the mystic, the rapture of the saint, or the feeling of unity of the meditator — which are but temporary glimpses of another reality and vary from person to person according to their traditions and beliefs. In contrast, when spiritual seekers reach *samadhi* — the state of illumination or at-one-ment with spirit — their lives change and their entire being is transformed. In the words of the Upanishads, "all the knots of the heart are unloosed and all doubts cease to exist."

The sages tell us that there are two kinds of *samadhi*: the lower or *savikalpa* and the higher or *nirvikalpa*. In *savikalpa* an aspirant may have the experience of union with the divine, with One Mind or One Consciousness, but the sense of "I," however faint, is still present. In this state one or more of the various aspects of the personal divine are realized — God the Beloved, God the Mother, or God the Creator. The memory of this state is carried back into ordinary consciousness and is never forgotten. But *samadhi* is not yet permanent. The last shadow of duality remains: "I" and God, the lover and the beloved. The transformation of attention into the object of attention is not complete.

The higher form of *samadhi, nirvikalpa,* is the state of consciousness in which the "I" no longer exists and the individual Atman has merged with the Paramatman — the universal Self or impersonal God. This is the state of complete cessation of thoughts, impressions, and memories. This complete absorption is achieved through the discipline of concentration and meditation. Meister Eckhart speaks eloquently about the difference of the two kinds of experience: "When I still stood in my first cause, there I had no God and was cause of myself. There I willed nothing, I desired nothing, for I was a pure Being in delight of the truth. There I stood, free of God and of all things. But when I took leave from this state and received my created being, then I had a God."

Samadhi has been communicated directly from master to disciple and, as we know from many accounts in the scriptures, by the great avatars — incarnations of different aspects of the divine — to their devotees. This power of direct illumination was most evident in the great divine incarnations of Krishna, Buddha, Jesus, and, more recently, Ramakrishna. Unlike avatars, human beings are said to remain the "servants" or "children" of the divine even after they have merged with it. They may choose to come back into physical existence to help others attain to the Supreme. However, they remain distinct from avatars, who incarnate to fulfill Divine Will in creation and to carry out a specific duty or a special mission, such as inspiring the next step in the spiritual evolution of mankind. Avatars come in times of great need or danger — when materialism is rampant and darkness overshadows human affairs — and show the path to realization.

EACH AVATAR REVEALS A DIFFERENT ASPECT of the lawful and harmonious evolution of the human being. The Hindu avatar Rama is said to have awakened the *sattva guna;* Krishna revealed the joy and blessings of attaining to the supreme mind; Buddha awakened the heart of compassion; Christ revealed the power of love, charity, and sacrifice; the Virgin Mary embodied compassion and motherhood; while Ramakrishna pointed to the unity of all the different paths leading to God. They have all come here to help us evolve into the Spirit and to bring us the gifts of wisdom, knowledge, consciousness, joy, and love. At the beginning of the third millennium, there are said to be many avatars on this planet, each working towards a specific goal — some in the public domain, others in seclusion. They are here to help and are not asking for recognition.

Avatars do not need our adulation, nor do they want to be idolized, as has been done in the past. When we idolize them, we create a distance and stand in awe. Captivated by their outer personality, we miss the essence of their inner teaching.

When we adore rather than emulate them, we have misunderstood their mission. Then we ourselves are not aspiring to Self-realization. We are not *living* their teaching; remaining ignorant, we fail to fulfill our true purpose.

The mysteries, the inner teachings of the divine incarnations, were often taught only to the chosen few, the inner circle. But this knowledge is now being rediscovered by the many and is available to those who are willing to penetrate the deeper meaning of the great wisdom tradition. Institutionalized religion as we know it now is a human invention, and as such it runs down and calcifies. Eternal truth, however, stands aloof and firm. Divinely inspired knowledge, as declared by the great sages, will not calcify or become contaminated, although it may have to be reinterpreted to meet new needs, as was done by Shankara and more recently by Sri Aurobindo. The consciousness, knowledge, and love of the divine incarnations are always at hand, and their gifts are available here and now. Their force is palpable to those who are open to its influx.

Self-realization seems like a far-off reality for most of us, with our busy lives. Why would we even want to begin the ascent? Why engage in this seemingly endless and difficult work? The fact is that the rewards far outweigh the difficulties of living in darkness and ignorance. There is great joy in the first stirrings of aspiration and good intention which lead us to the inquiry of Self-knowledge. There is great wonder in finding out what we really are; it is most interesting, most mysterious, and most challenging.

There are many small increments of enlightenment along the way as beneficent thoughts replace negative ones and good actions supplant mindless activity. We enjoy greater harmony, poise, and peace — the fruits of study, discipline, and meditation. We become free of suffering and anguish as we discover that we really lack nothing, but in fact "have it all" in the knowledge of our true Self. Fear loosens its grip as we let go of attachments and realize that the Self is one and complete and that we have nothing to lose. Anger and rage can no longer overpower us, as the false ego is displaced from center stage. We become more magnanimous in calamity and can see a situation from many angles. Our values change automatically and we are no longer subject to the vagaries of the sensory world. All along the way we are showered with grace and our doubts vanish. As we have more and more glimpses of the unity of being, identification with the body and its faculties fades and we are lifted to greater and greater freedom.

Soon we realize that the work is really not too difficult. We only need to take a step at a time — aspire and practice, aspire and practice. At some point we are simply carried along. As the force of *sattva* increases in our being and the forces of *rajas* and *tamas* decrease, we are no longer subject to the *asura-gunas* — the "ungodly qualities" related to the state of becoming: egotism, bondage, ignorance, conceit, impurity, hate, deceit, arrogance, desire, anger, possessiveness, and pride.

The bounty we reap on the path is naturally expressed in acts of love and compassion, and we in turn enjoy the fruits of our actions in the qualities they bestow on us. According to St. Paul, these are love, joy, peace, endurance, gentleness, goodness, faith, meekness, temperance. Emerson defined the godly qualities as "Truth, Love, Justice, Freedom, and Power" and concluded that to the extent to which we partake of these qualities do we become God. The Buddhist tradition characterizes them as compassion, liberality, truth, purity, gentleness, peace, joyousness, saintliness, and self-control. They are the natural traits of an enlightened being. We may enjoy any or all of these qualities, as well as some other, unexpected benefits or supernatural powers — the aspects of *shakti*. These are said to include the glory of wealth, power of absolute will, dwelling in perpetual song of praise, goodness and perfect service, cosmic knowledge, and perfect detachment.

But we need not worry just yet about these powers, about anything remote or otherworldly. Along the way we content ourselves with small increments of bliss and the gradual recovery of our true stature, a stronger character, a more peaceful mind and heart, a more refined taste, and more perfect actions. As we aspire to pure being, our nature is also transformed.

Henry David Thoreau once said, "I have never yet met a man who was quite awake. How could I have looked him in the face?" This statement betrays great awe at the immensity of our true potential and at least some knowledge of what "waking up" means. The fortunate ones who have looked into the face of a fully realized human being have come back to tell us that "I saw my Self" or "she is full of light and love" or "he *is* stillness." What they saw is in fact their own reflection — their true nature or *sat-chit-ananda*. What they describe is the state of pure being and the reflection in consciousness of the pure light of the Paramatman.

*

TWELVE
THE PATH

W<small>E ALL KNOW FROM EXPERIENCE</small> that we cannot be a better person, a more loving individual, let alone a fully realized being, simply by intention alone. Spiritual seeking is a commendable activity in and of itself; it brings many rewards such as greater clarity, peace of mind, and serenity, and keeps us from mindless and destructive pursuits. But spiritual seeking that is undisciplined and aimless will not bring any improvements to our condition, nor will it be truly rewarding.

Seeking and aspiration need to be guided in the right direction. We need to know where we are going, how to get there, and what the goal is. We need to know what Emerson called the "necessary truths." We need every helping hand we can get to guide us along the path, in whatever form it takes: a system, a yoga, a guru, or a teacher. There is a distance to be forded; there are many steps between fragmentation and unity, between the personal and impersonal, between egocentric being and cosmocentric being. Belief is one of the "helping hands"; so is conviction; so is aspiration; devotion to a guru or deity is yet another. All of these, however, when seen in the light of truth, are but stages on the path to enlightenment. "Whenever spiritual seeking becomes an all-absorbing passion of our soul," said Emerson, "we are inevitably released from all doctrine and creed-bound beliefs and are brought face to face with the great cosmic, universal, and all-abiding truth." He may have been speaking of a specific instant of enlightenment, but we can see this also as a perfect description of the gradual release of beliefs, dogmas, ideals, and laws on the path to Self-knowledge.

At the beginning of the path, we are subject to many external influences, such as the laws of nature and those of man; we cling to rituals, creeds, and opinion. As we move up and gain self-reliance (to use an Emersonian term) external influences lose their power over us, we become more universal — we stand under a higher law and live according to universal principles. Still higher up, as we realize our true nature, we are released from all belief, all manmade laws, and all of nature's laws. Belief is replaced by complete knowing and understanding. A person who has reached this point understands (stands under) the One — the One Law, the One Will — or, in Emerson's words, the "all-abiding truth."

As we already know, there are many methods leading to perfection and many paths to enlightenment. On the surface they may seem quite disparate in form and method and terminology. Some rely on tradition with its ritual and devotional practices; others are more austere and rely on discipline and reason alone. Some emphasize renunciation and yet others seclusion. But as the paths ascend and reach the top of the mountain, they all merge and display their essential unity. The goal is the same, only the semantics are different: Self-Realization, liberation, *turiya,* enlightenment, unity with the Godhead, merging into the infinite, or supraconsciousness. All these words describe the merging with the one reality. But they are just words and as such are inadequate in describing the undescribable, the unfathomable, the mysterious and unnameable One.

To this day there are thousands of monasteries and ashrams around the world where spiritual work is the order of the day — a full-time job and an all-absorbing activity. These souls are on the fast track of spiritual enlightenment. As householders, we cannot emulate their abandonment of all worldly concerns. On the contrary, we find ourselves in the circumstances that are most propitious for our own spiritual development, for the lawful unfolding of our soul. Our duties are *here,* wherever we find ourselves. We need not abandon them in order to pursue the path of enlightenment. The way of the householder is in the world and through the world, through our particular functions, natures, and talents.

Rather than giving up the world, we seek to integrate our ordinary personality with our soul nature. As householders, we explore, express, and fulfill our purpose here. By doing our duty perfectly, and by perfecting our instrument, we grow in wisdom and insight, and by putting these into practice, we naturally ascend the path to Self-knowledge.

We need not change our lives or interrupt the lives of those around us. Positive changes will simply occur as a result of our growth and understanding. All we need to do is shift the focus of our attention from material reality to spiritual reality, from undue concerns with matter to the love of truth. The change takes place in the mind and in the consciousness.

The right path to follow for each one of us is the one that does not create conflict between our external life and our dedication to the "examined life." These two must be compatible, or else we will abandon the quest within a very brief time. We need not give up the comforts and joys of life, but we will realize that simplicity and even a measure of austerity will contribute to harmony and serenity.

IN ORDER TO START ON ANY JOURNEY, we have to begin where we are and we have to have a means of journeying — a map, a vehicle, and fuel. We also have to have a goal in mind as well as a sense of direction. On the spiritual journey, "where we are" is the given facts — our lot in life, our present state of consciousness, the condition of our instrument. All these together are determined by past action and comprise our *dharma* — our duty in life — which is the perfect place to begin. The "map" and "vehicle" are our chosen means: the teaching or method suited to our temperament and our way of life. The "fuel" is our desire for knowledge, our aspiration, and our innate love of truth, as well as the spiritual force known in the East as *tapas.* The "sense of direction" is the conviction, certainty, and knowledge of the aim we need on the path, without which we get lost. By maintaining a strong sense of direction, our spiritual path, which is also our *dharma,* becomes easy. The "goal" is the perfection of our true potential — both in life and in Spirit. The ultimate goal is Self-Realization.

Let us look at the "map" and "vehicle" — a specific means or system of Self-Realization. We are looking for a system that is in harmony with modern life and will bring about an integration of our entire being and does not require extreme practices. The threefold path or the way of action, devotion, and knowledge, also known as *trimarga* (from *tri,* "three," and *marga,* "path"), fulfills these requirements. It is a synthesis of three different paths or yogas that in the past were practiced separately and according to caste. Karma yoga is the path by which union with God is achieved through action; *bhakti* yoga brings about union with God through love and devotion; in *jnana* yoga, union with God is achieved through wisdom. Sri Ramakrishna and Swami Vivekananda were both followers and exponents of this threefold path of dedicated action, love, and wisdom as expounded in the *Bhagavad Gita* — the "Holy Song."

Through karma yoga (from the root *kri*, "to act"), the path of selfless dedicated action, we surrender and dedicate all actions to the Supreme Self and to the Self in all. Through inner renunciation, we gain equanimity; as we give up all claims to deeds, persons, and things. We rise above duality of pleasure/pain, like/dislike, love/hate, good/bad, elation/despair. Through attention in action and purity of thought, we free ourselves of past impressions, attachments, and impurities and create no further karma. Through this purification and concentration, we develop our higher Will. The highest aim of karma yoga is to attain unity of the individual soul with the Divine Will.

Through *bhakti* yoga (from *bhaj*, "to love"), the way of devotion to a deity or contemplation of the universal Self, we destroy the effects of karma — egotism and clinging to life. We increase devotion and love of truth through good company, chanting, remembering the Paramatman, and meditating on the divine qualities. The highest aim of *bhakti* yoga is Divine love.

Through *jnana* yoga (from *jna*, "to know") and the practice of purification, concentration, and inquiry into the God within, we develop discrimination and remove ignorance. Through the study of the scriptures and metaphysics and through reflection and meditation on Paramatman, we aim to know, see, and embody the divine. Realization is attained through Divine Wisdom and through the union of Atman with Paramatman. The highest aim of *jnana* yoga is to become the divine — *sat-chit-ananda*.

In more practical terms, through selfless, neutral action we are released from bondage of past and present deeds and gain equanimity and harmony in all our endeavors. Through devotion to the One Self, we are released from the petty concerns of ego, and we develop our higher emotions, creative imagination, and love of truth, beauty, and the good. Through discrimination we are released from ignorance and gain higher wisdom, higher reason, and inner vision — the very faculties by which we know ourselves and the universal Self. We develop what are known as the "Six Excellences": tranquillity, control of the senses, renunciation, endurance, concentration, and yearning for liberation.

All three paths are methods of liberation from ignorance and duality, and all three paths aim at union of the individual Self with universal Self. It is in fact impossible to walk on one path only. Intellectuals are devotional in that they *love* knowledge; it was a spark of devotion that prompted them to seek the truth. Devotional individuals must in turn have some knowledge of what they seek. Individuals on the way of action are obedient to a higher will that presupposes knowledge of the Supreme Self; their dedication of all their actions to the Self is pure devotion. These three paths, along with the practice of meditation, complement and support each other and foster the harmonious development of the whole human being — knowing, being, and doing. They are therefore most suited to the modern seeker who is fully engaged in life. This of course does not mean that individual seekers should not engage in any one specific path most suited to their nature. *Jnana* yoga, the path of wisdom, is said by many to be the best, while just as many claim the way of devotion to be the ultimate. As the debate goes on, a balanced approach seems to be a good course of action.

It is said that true knowledge can only come from those who have *realized* this knowledge in themselves and who speak from experience. It is for this reason that we look again and again to the masters, those pure and wise souls who are true teachers. One of these, Sri Aurobindo, points to the mutually dependent and integrated aspects of the three yogas of the *Bhagavad Gita*. He says in *The Synthesis of Yoga*: "By way of this integral knowledge we arrive at the unity of the aims set before themselves by the three paths of knowledge, works, and devotion. Knowledge aims at the realization of true self-existence, works at the realization of the divine conscious-will that secretly governs all works, devotion at the realization of the bliss which enjoys as the lover all beings and all existences — *Sat, Chit-Tapas,* and *Ananda.* Each therefore aims at possessing *Sachchidananda* through one or other aspect of his triune divine nature."

Tapas (from *tap,* "to burn, to shine") means warmth or heat and refers to the fiery energy produced by austerity, discipline, or suffering. It is produced when *rajas,* the force of passion and ego-striving, is transformed through spiritual aspiration into creative Divine power. This force powers all spiritual aspiration and all longing for liberation; it is the "fuel" we spoke of in our metaphor of the journey. As the force grows in intensity, it manifests as boundless energy, spiritual strength, and in some individuals as special powers.

There is yet another system called *raja* yoga (*raja* means "king," from *raj,* "to reign, to illuminate"), also known as the "king of yogas." On this path, aspirants gain control over their minds and bodies through certain disciplines; thereby they gain knowledge of that which is beyond mind and unite with it. They attain identity with truth or *samadhi* through the practice of concentration, contemplation, and meditation — one practice leading to the next.

THE *YOGA SUTRAS* OF PATANJALI — a reformulation of the teachings of the Upanishads — describe the steps that lead to union with the Supreme. This system of practices and spiritual disciplines is another ancient and yet relevant model for Self-inquiry, each individual step serving as a guidepost along the path.

There are many translations and elaborations of Patanjali's terse aphorisms, known as *sutras* (a Sanskrit word loosely translated as "threads"). One of these texts outlines the "Eight Steps to Enlightenment" — a rigorous system of spiritual disciplines designed for hardy and fearless souls who, with an experienced guide and dauntless aspiration, reached *samadhi* through control and stilling of the mind. These various methods — self-control, religious observance, physical postures, breath control, withdrawal of senses, concentration, meditation — are based on observation and investigation. They might be called a scientific approach to spiritual development.

These steps, which are said to include all possible psychological experiences, are as follows:

1. *Yama.* A firm determination to live a life dedicated to Truth.
The five resolutions are harmlessness; truthfulness in speech and action; honesty; sublimation of all lower drives; lack of greed; lack of seeking of reward.

2. *Niyama.* Moderation in mind and body as a means of leading life towards truth. The five methods are: cleanliness of body and mind; contentment; critical examination of the senses; study of physics, metaphysics, and the nature of the psyche;

realization of the oneness of individual existence with universal existence; complete self-surrender.

3. *Asana*. Physical exercise for the purpose of refining the mind and body to study truth.

4. *Pranayama*. The control of energy and breath.

5. *Pratyahara*. Sublimation of lower psychic energy for higher purposes.

6. *Dharana*. Fixation of attention on a particular object or idea with the aim of steadying the mind.

7. *Dhyana*. Continuous meditation and focusing attention on a particular spiritual object or idea.

8. *Samadhi*. Transformation of attention into object of attention.

In summation, *yama* relates to moral virtues, niyama to regular study of spiritual knowledge. *Asana, pranayama,* and *pratyahara* relate to the acquisition of powers for the transformation of lower into higher energies. *Dharana* relates to concentration, *dhyana* to meditation, and *samadhi* to absorption. The first five are external; the last three are internal.

With the introduction of meditation into the West, we acquired the privilege of skipping a few of the steps. Steps three, four, and five are no longer regarded as necessary or useful. These steps may in fact lead to spiritual materialism in those who see the acquisition of powers as an end in itself and use them for selfish purposes and profit. Regular practice of meditation automatically regulates all the vital and hormonal processes and thus also takes care of steps three and four — *asana* and *pranayama*. It also transforms lower energy into higher energy at step five (*pratyahara*) by the control of mind and withdrawal of the senses. In some ways meditation also takes care of steps one and two with its power to refine body, mind, and spirit. This is why the sages tell us that meditation is the "easy way" to enlightenment, especially in this time and age.

These principles and systems have been tested through the ages. They are no longer hidden, but are totally accessible to anyone willing to search. They should serve the harmonious unfolding of our true nature. If they do not bring about a flowering of our whole being, knowing, and doing, they are either not right for us or else they are being used in a rigid and uncreative manner that will burden us with rules rather than free us. In Part Three these disciplines will be reformulated to meet our present needs. As we practice them and see their effects in our lives, we will begin to appreciate the importance of such guides.

PART TWO

THE VOICE

OF

THE SELF

EXCERPTS FROM
THE PERENNIAL PHILOSOPHY

INTRODUCTION

O NE OF THE GREAT JOYS on the spiritual quest is finding a voice that speaks directly to our innermost being in familiar tones. We feel no resistance or skepticism towards this voice. The truth of the words are like an arrow that hits the target straight on. The voice stills the mind as it answers our questions and confirms our conclusions and is absorbed into our heart, where it refreshes our whole being. When we are sincere, our searching quite often and quite naturally takes us to the right place. The perfect book we need on our quest appears just in time to aid in the continuing unfolding of our being. We also find great joy in the diversity of the voices of truth and delight in the comparative study of ancient and new sources and of Eastern and Western philosophy. Our minds are stimulated by the discovery of the deep connectedness of all true philosophy and all true teachings.

We find the strains of the Perennial Philosophy at the center of all great inner teachings. The similarities among the great religions lies not in their outward forms but in their common source of inner knowledge. They share a common philosophy based on a few principles established by divine inspiration and human aspiration and intuition. The Perennial Philosophy is not a doctrine or a religion or a belief. Rather it attempts, through a few universal principles expressed in terse aphorisms, to shed light and understanding on the nature of the ultimate reality. Such statements point to the unity beyond multiplicity: to the source of light, to infinite love and peace, to One Consciousness, to One Mind. They point to the correspondences between macrocosm and microcosm and the hierarchial order in the universe and in Man, and finally they elaborate on how Man may realize the ultimate Reality.

Having assumed there is an ultimate truth, we may ask, "What is truth?" The sages tell us that it is "that which always was, is, and always will be," that "the truth is within our own hearts," that "truth and love are ultimately one and the same," and that they both lead the aspirant to the same goal. We are all looking for our true identity, which is *sat-chit-ananda,* or being-consciousness-bliss. Whether we are aware of it or not, we are all in search of truth, and the search takes many forms. The scientists, in their exploration of the minutest forms of matter and the immensity of deep space; the poets and artists, in tapping into their deepest emotions and intuitions; the explorers and athletes, in testing the strength of their character and endurance; the thinkers, in delving deeply into the recesses of reason and intellect; even the lovers of pleasure, in their relentless pursuit of experience, are all seeking for truth in their own way.

One of the speediest and most powerful ways to absorb truth and dispel ignorance is the ancient spiritual practice of reading, reciting, chanting, and reflecting on the great spiritual truths. Some of these practices — especially chanting — are finding a new following in our time. The power of the word sets in motion a vibration that reverberates in our hearts and minds and transforms our whole being. It not only strengthens our dedication to the truth and our aspiration for the work but also sharpens our discrimination and memory.

As the light of truth floods our being, darkness is dispelled. This is a constructive approach to realization, and in it there are no prohibitions. As lovers of truth, we need not worry about sin and evil or concern ourselves with unconscious desires or dark, deeply embedded tendencies. We cannot willfully empty our minds of their murky contents. But we can pour crystal-clear water — the ambrosia of spiritual truths — into our minds and souls and flush out the debris of falsehood, ignorance, and misery. By reflecting on eternal truths, we make full use of our faculties, including the restless discursive mind, and thus keep it from engaging in useless inner conversations.

As seekers of truth on the threefold path of *bhakti,* karma, and *jnana* yoga, we approach the words of wisdom with our whole being. However, since we all have a predilection to one particular approach or another — devotion, action, or knowledge — some may want to make use of these words in a devotional way, by chanting hymns and reciting verses, thereby increasing their love of truth. Others may wish to use the scriptures in their practical aspect, by remembrance of truth in dedicated selfless action as they serve the truth in all. Still others may emphasize the intellectual aspect, reflecting and contemplating as they develop discrimination and come to know the truth.

Above all, the great spiritual truths have the power to reawaken the memory of our true essence. By reflecting on the great texts from the Vedas, the Upanishads, the Sutras, the *Bhagavad Gita,* the scriptures and texts of Advaita philosophy and by saturating our minds with the wisdom of such mystics and philosophers as Heraclitus, Plato, the Buddha, Patanjali, and Jesus, we gain a taste for the transcendent, enjoy occasional glimpses of Unity, and gradually attain an intuitive understanding of truth.

With the daily company of the great books of wisdom, we enjoy a decrease in brain chatter, compulsive talking, bad habits, excitability, negativity, and misery. Studying them will also lead to observable positive benefits, increasing mental power, strength of character, serenity, creativity, inspiration, enthusiasm, lightness of being, and joy.

*

1
CREATION AND THE NATURE
OF THE COSMOS

In the beginning this world was merely nonbeing. It was existent. It developed. It turned into an egg. It lay for the period of a year. It was split asunder. One of the two eggshells parts became silver, one gold. That which was of silver is the earth. That which was of gold is the sky. What was the outer membrane is cloud and mist. What were the veins are the rivers. What was the fluid within is ocean. Now what was born therefrom is yonder sun.
   —*Chandogya Upanishad*

In the beginning was the Word, and the Word was with God, and the Word was God. The same was in the beginning with God. All things were made by him; and without him was not any thing made that was made. In him was life; and the life was the light of men. And the light shineth in darkness; and the darkness comprehended it not.... That was the true light, which lighteth every man that cometh into the world.
   —John 1:1–5,9

For God's Word, who is all-accomplishing and fecund and creative, went forth, and flinging himself upon the water, which was a thing of fecund nature, made the water pregnant....
   For [the world] has over it as ruler the creative Word of the Master of all. That Word is, next after Him, the supreme Power, a Power ungenerated, boundless, that has stooped forth from Him; and the Word presides over and governs the things that have been made through him.
   —Hermes Trismegistus

How does God "create" the universe? Since in the beginning God alone is, there is no second substance that can be used for such "creation." God is forced to use his own substance for the purpose. God is Infinite Mind, so he uses mental power — Imagination — working on mental substance — Thought — to produce the result which appears to us as the universe.
   —Paul Brunton

God the Father had such delight in himself that he called forth the whole creation through the divine Word. And then the divine creation pleased God, too, and every creature that God lovingly touched, God took in divine arms. Oh, what great delight you have in your work!

 —Hildegard of Bingen

This whole body [of the cosmos], in which all bodies are contained, is filled with soul; soul is filled with mind; and mind is filled with God. Soul fills the whole body within, and encompasses it without, giving life to the universe; without, it gives life to this great and perfect living creature, and within, to all the living creatures. In heaven above, souls persist in sameness; on earth below, it changes as things come into being.

 —Hermes Trismegistus

Then was not nonexistent nor existent: there was no realm of air, no sky beyond it.
What covered it, and where? And what gave shelter? Was water there, unfathomed
 depth of water?

Death was not then, nor was there aught immortal: no sign was there, the day's and
 night's divider.
That one thing, breathless, breathed by its own nature: apart from it was nothing
 whatsoever.

Darkness there was: at first concealed in darkness, this All was indiscriminated
 chaos.
All that existed then was void and formless: by the great power of warmth was born
 that unit.
Thereafter rose desire in the beginning. Desire, the primal seed and germ of spirit.
Sages who searched with their heart's thought discovered the existent's kinship in the
 nonexistent.

Transversely was their severing line extended; what was above it then, and what
 below it?
There were begetters, there were mighty forces, free action here and energy up
 yonder.

Who verily knows and who can here declare it, whence it was born and whence
 comes this creation?
The gods are later than this world's production. Who knows, then,
 whence it first came into being?

He, the first origin of this creation, whether he formed it all or did not form it,
Whose eye controls this world in highest heaven, he verily knows it, or perhaps he
 knows not.

 —*Rig-Veda*

While the world lay yet submerged beneath the ocean, God lay brooding on Ananta, king of the serpents, as Ananta floated upon the waters. God was resting, with eyes closed, but His consciousness was fully awake. He was completely merged in the bliss of His own Self.

As the time of creation drew nigh, God felt a stir within His being, and there issued forth from the center of His person a full-blown Lotus. Its luminosity was dazzling, and the whole ocean was lighted by its splendor.

Within this Lotus were all the materials for creation. God Himself was absorbed within it, and became its innermost being.

Immediately Brahma came forth from the Lotus, and, seating himself upon it, turned his head in all directions to see whether any other beings were present. Hence he is called the four-faced Brahma.

Brahma did not recognize himself, and had no recollection of his previous creations. Thereupon he became restless, and a desire for knowledge rose within his heart. Looking about him and seeing in the external world no hope for the fulfillment of his desires, he sought in meditation for the knowledge which he realized must be within himself, and at last he found the Truth, and God Himself, within his own heart. He then saw God everywhere and felt blest indeed.

Then God spoke to him, saying: "O Brahma, I command thee: again create the world, as thou hast often done in times past....Whatsoever is to be created is already within Me....Creation is only the projection into form of that which already exists."

During this time a strong wind had arisen, and was lashing the water into fury. So, with the knowledge and power which he had acquired....Brahma withdrew into himself the wind and all the waters of the sea. Then finding himself floating in the ether, still seated upon the Lotus, he re-entered the heart of the Lotus, and dividing it into three sections created the three spheres — heaven, earth, and sky....

While he was meditating upon what course he should pursue, his own form divided itself; one half became man and the other half became woman.

The man was called Manu, and the woman Satarupa; and from them have sprung all mankind.

—*Srimad Bhagavatam*

The Tao begot one.
One begot two.
Two begot three.
And three begot the ten thousand things.
The ten thousand things carry yin and embrace yang.
They achieve harmony by combining these forces.
—Lao Tsu

Not *how* the world is, is the mystical, but *that* it is.
—Ludwig Wittgenstein

Observe constantly that all things come about by change; accustom yourself to reflect that the nature of the universe loves nothing so much as changing things that are and making new things like them. For everything that exists is in a way the seed of what will be.

—Marcus Aurelius

Then [Beatrice] began: "I do not ask, I say
  what you most wish to hear, for I have seen it
  where time and space are focused in one ray.

Not to increase Its good — no mill nor dram
  can add to true perfection, but that reflections
  of his reflection might declare 'I am' -

in His eternity, beyond time, above
  all other comprehension, as it pleased Him,
  new loves were born of the Eternal Love.

Nor did He lie asleep before the Word
  sounded above these waters; 'before' and 'after'
  did not exist until His voice was heard.

Pure essence, and pure matter, and the two
  joined into one were shot forth without flaw,
  like three bright arrows from a three-string bow.

And as in glass, in amber, or in crystal
  a ray shines so that nothing intervenes
  between its coming and being, which is total;

so the threefold effect rayed from its Sire
  into created being, without beginning
  and without interval, instantly entire.

—Dante, *Paradiso*

The universe is the externalization of the soul.

—Ralph Waldo Emerson

The World-Idea is perfect. How could it be otherwise since it is God's Idea? If we fail to become a co-worker with it, nothing of this perfection will be lost. If we do, we add nothing to it.

—Paul Brunton

The Kosmos is made by God, and is contained in God; man is made by the Kosmos, and is contained in the Kosmos; and it is God that is the author of all, and encompasses all, and knits all things together.

—Hermes Trismegistus

Nay, I would rather say, not that God *contains* all things, but that, to speak the full truth, God *is* all things.

—Hermes Trismegistus

This cosmos was not made by immortal or mortal beings, but always was, is and will be an eternal fire, arising and going out in measure.

—Heraclitus

From that Brahman, which is the Self, was produced space. From space emerged air. From air was born fire. From fire was created water. From water sprang up earth. From earth were born the herbs. From the herbs was produced food. From food was born man. That man, such as he is, is a product of the essence of food: Of him this, indeed, is the head; this is the southern side; this is the northern side; this is the Self; this is the stabilizing tail.

—*Taittiriya Upanishad*

In the night of Brahman, Nature is inert, and cannot dance till Shiva wills it: He rises from His rapture, and dancing sends through inert matter pulsing waves of awakening sound, and lo! Matter also dances, appearing as a glory round about Him. Dancing, He sustains its manifold phenomena. In the fullness of time, still dancing, He destroys all forms and names by fire and gives new rest.

—Ananda K. Coomaraswamy

Kabir ponders and says: "He who has neither caste nor country, who is formless and without quality, fills all space."
The Creator brought into being the Game of Joy: and from the word OM the Creation sprang.
The earth is His joy; His joy is the sky;
His joy is the flashing of the sun and the moon;
His joy is the beginning, the middle, and the end;
His joy is eyes, darkness, and light.

—Kabir

At this time our Lord showed me a ghostly sight of his intimate love: I saw that he is to us everything that is good and comfortable....And in this sight he showed a little thing the size of a hazelnut in the palm of my hand and it was as round as a ball. I looked thereon with the eye of my understanding and thought, what may this be? And it was generally answered thus: It is all that is made. I marveled how it might last. For I thought that it might suddenly fall to nought for its smallness. And it was answered in my understanding: It lasts, and ever shall, for God loves it.
And so all things have being by the love of God.

In this little thing I saw three properties. The first is that God made it. The second is that God loves it. The third is that God keeps it. And what did I see in this? Verily the Maker, the Keeper, the Lover. For until I am substantially united to him, I may never have full rest nor true bliss; that is to say, that I may be so fastened to him that there is no created thing between God and me.

—Julian of Norwich

The letter *OM* is all this....All that is past, present, or future is verily *OM*. And whatever is beyond the three periods of time is also verily *OM*.

—*Mandukya Upanishad*

What is the universe but a gigantic symbol of God? Its infinite variety hints at the infinite endlessness of the Absolute itself.

—Paul Brunton

Who verily knows and who can here declare it, whence
 It was born and whence comes this creation?
The gods are later than this world's production. Who
 Knows, then, whence it first came into being?
He, the first origin of this creation, whether he formed it
 All or did not form it,
Whose eye controls this world in highest heaven, he
 Verily know it, or perhaps he knows it not.

—*Rig-Veda*

Creation... has no absolute beginning. The present universe is but one of a series of worlds that are past and of worlds that are to be. The cosmic energy alternates between periods of potentiality and of expression. The phase of potentiality is known as dissolution; the phase of expression is known as creation.

—*Srimad Bhagavatam*

I believe the mind is the creator of the world, and is ever creating; that at last Matter is dead Mind; that mind makes the senses it sees with; that the genius of man is a continuation of the power that made him and that has not done making him.
—Ralph Waldo Emerson

The Law of Heaven and Truth were born
Of conscious fervor set on fire.
From this came stillness of the night,
From this the ocean with its waves.

From the ocean and its waves
Then the year was generated —
Appointer of the days and nights,
Ruler of all mortal beings.

The Creator regulated
Sun and moon in due succession,
The vault of Heaven and the Earth,
Aerial space and blessed light.
—*Rig-Veda*

The whole visible world is only an imperceptible atom in the ample bosom of nature. No idea approaches it. We may enlarge our conceptions beyond all imaginable space; we only produce atoms in comparison with the reality of things. It is an infinite sphere, the center of which is everywhere, the circumference nowhere. In short it is the greatest sensible mark of the almighty power of God, that imagination loses itself in that thought.
—Blaise Pascal

Matter is physical exuberance, ennobling contact, virile effort and the joy of growth. It attracts, renews, unites and flowers. By matter we are nourished, lifted up, linked to everything else, invaded by life....Above all matter is not just the weight that drags us down, the mire that sucks us in, the bramble that bars our way...it is simply the slope on which we can go up just as well as go down....

By means of all created things, without exception, the divine assails us, penetrates us and molds us. We imagined it as distant and inaccessible, whereas in fact we live steeped in its burning layers.
—Teilhard de Chardin

2
GOD, CREATOR, BRAHMAN

He is the Great Poet, the Ancient Poet. The whole universe is His poem, coming in verses and rhymes and rhythms, written in Infinite Bliss.
—Swami Vivekananda

Thou art the Primal God, the Ancient Spirit, Thou art the supreme resting-place of this universe; Thou art the knower, the object of knowledge, and the highest station, by Thee the universe is pervaded, Thou of infinite form!
—*Bhagavad Gita*

Brahman is the intellect,
Brahman is the mind,
Brahman is the intelligence.
He is substance, He is sound,
He is the principle in all things.
The whole universe in Brahman,
And yet He infinitely transcends all this.
In reality the world is a thing of naught, for all is Brahman alone.
—*Yoga-Vasishtha*

God is the source of all that is; He is the source of mind, and of nature, and of matter. To show forth his wisdom has He made all things; for He is the source of all. And nature is a force by which God works; nature operates in subjection to necessity, and her work is the extinction and renewal of things.
—Hermes Trismegistus

O Prince, such is the nature of Brahman that all power flows incessantly from Him: wherefore every power is said to reside in Him. In Him is entity and nonentity; in Him also is unity, duality, and plurality, and the beginning and end of all things.
—*Yoga-Vasishtha*

I am the root of this great tree of the universe which has its beginning above, in me. The trees on earth get their nourishment from below and their form grows up, while this universal tree has roots above, in the absolute. It gets its life force from Him, and manifests as branches, leaves, fruits, and flowers.
—*Bhagavad Gita*

Such is He who is too great to be named God. He is hidden, yet most manifest. He is apprehensible by thought alone, yet we can see Him with our eyes. He is bodiless, and yet has many bodies, or rather, is embodied in all bodies. There is nothing that He is not; for all things that exist are even He. For this reason all names are names of Him, because all things come from Him, their one Father; and for this reason He has no name, because He is the Father of all.

—Hermes Trismegistus

Brahman is the intellect (*buddhi*). Brahman is the mind (*manas*). He is intelligence (*chit*). The whole universe is Brahman, yet He is beyond all this. In reality the world is nonentity, for all is Brahman alone.

Beyond the truth of the existence of Brahman nothing can be proved as absolutely certain, and so the holy Shruti has declared: "Verily, all is Brahman."

—*Yoga-Vasishtha*

Brahma

If the red slayer think he slays,
　　Or if the slain think he is slain,
They know not well the subtle ways
　　I keep, and pass, and turn again.

Far or forgot to me is near;
　　Shadow and sunlight are the same;
The vanished gods to me appear;
　　And one to me are shame and fame.

They reckon ill who leave me out;
　　When me they fly, I am the wings;
I am the doubter and the doubt,
　　And I the hymn the Brahmin sings.

The strong gods pine for my abode,
　　And pine in vain the sacred Seven,
But thou, meek lover of the good!
　　Find me, and turn thy back on heaven.

—Ralph Waldo Emerson

The strong light of the Godhead knows and recognizes all things even to their last details....God, who is over all, is so changeless in divine justice that God lets not injustice stand, for injustice can find no rest in God!

—Hildegard of Bingen

And wherewith shall I sing to Thee? Am I my own, or have I anything of my own? Am I other than Thou? Thou art whatsoever I am; Thou art whatsoever I do and whatsoever I say. Thou art all things, and there is nothing beside Thee, nothing that Thou art not. Thou art all that has come into being, and all that has not come into being. Thou art Mind, in that Thou thinkest; and Father, in that Thou createst; and God, in that Thou workest; and Good, in that Thou makest all things.

    —Hermes Trismegistus

Brahman is all in all; He is perfect peace, secondless, without equal or comparison. He expands Himself by His own power as the Infinite, and stretches His mind in three different directions — creation, preservation, and dissolution.

    —*Yoga-Vasishtha*

Something than which a greater cannot be thought exists so truly, then, that it cannot be even thought not to exist. And You, Lord our God, are this being. You exist so truly, Lord my God, that You cannot even be thought not to exist. And this is as it should be, for if some intelligence could think of something better than You, the creature would be above its creator and would judge its creator — and that is completely absurd. In fact, everything else there is, except You alone, can be thought of as not existing. You alone, then, of all things most truly exist and therefore of all things possess existence to the highest degree; for anything else does not exist as truly, and so possesses existence to a lesser degree....

    For God is that than which nothing greater can be thought. Whoever really understands this understands clearly that this same being so exists that not even in thought can it not exist. Thus whoever understands that God exists in such a way cannot think of Him as not existing.

    —St. Anselm

I am verily that Supreme Brahman, which is eternal, stainless, and free; which is One, indivisible, and non-dual; and which is of the nature of Bliss, Truth, Knowledge, and Infinity.

    —Shankara

As the moving sun He dwells in heaven, as air He pervades all and dwells in inter-space; as fire He resides on the earth, as Soma [juice]. He stays in a jar; He lives among men; he lives among gods; He dwells in space; He is born in water; He takes birth from the earth; He is born in sacrifice; He emerges from the mountains; He is unchanging; and He is great.

    —*Katha Upanishad*

O how may I ever express that secret word?
O how can I say He is not like this, and He is like that?
If I say that He is within me, the universe is ashamed:
If I say that He is without me, it is falsehood.
He makes the inner and the outer worlds to be
 indivisibly one;
The conscious and the unconscious, both are
 His footstools.
He is neither manifest nor hidden, He is neither
 revealed nor unrevealed:
There are no words to tell that which He is.
—Kabir

There is no other material cause of the universe than Brahman; this whole world therefore is in fact Brahman and nothing else.
—Shankara

The earth is the Lord's, and the fullness thereof; the world, and they that dwell therein.
For he hath founded it upon the seas, and established it upon the floods.
Who shall ascend into the hill of the Lord? or who shall stand in his holy place?
He that hath clean hands, and a pure heart: who hath not lifted up his soul unto
    vanity, nor sworn deceitfully.
He shall receive the blessing from the Lord, and righteousness from the God of his
    salvation.
This is the generation of them that seek him, that seek thy face, O Jacob. Selah.
Lift up your heads, O ye gates; and be ye lifted up, ye everlasting doors; and the King
    of glory shall come in.
Who is this King of glory? The Lord strong and mighty, the Lord mighty in battle.
Lift up your heads, O ye gates; even lift them up, ye everlasting doors; and the King
    of glory shall come in.
Who is this King of glory? The Lord of hosts, he is the King of glory. Selah.
—Psalm 24

That which is not uttered by speech that by which speech is revealed, know that alone to be Brahman, and not what people worship as an object.

That which man does not comprehend with the mind, that by which, they say, the mind is encompassed, know that to be Brahman and not what people worship as an object.

That which man does not see with the eyes, that by which man perceives the activities of the eye, know that alone to be Brahman and not what people worship as an object.

That which man does not hear with the ear, that by which man knows this ear, know that to be Brahman and not this that people worship as an object.

That which man does not smell with the organ of smell, that by which the organ of smell is impelled, know that to be Brahman and not what people worship as an object.
—Kena Upanishad

Tranquil, let one worship It
As that from which he came forth,
As that into which he will be dissolved,
As that in which he breathes.
—*Chandogya Upanishad*

Crave to know that from which all these beings take birth, that by which they live after being born, that towards which they move and into which they merge. That is Brahman.

—*Taittiriya Upanishad*

Lord Shiva said: Meditate always on the everlasting and immaculate Spirit that is without beginning and end. By thinking in this way, you yourself become immaculate and are absorbed in the self-same Brahman, where there is all peace and tranquillity.

Know the one undying Brahman as the soul and seed of the various productions that emanate from Him. It is His immensity which spreads throughout the whole of existence, as it is the endless sky which comprehends and manifests all things within itself.

It is not possible for anything at all, whether of positive or potential existence, to subsist without and apart from the universal Essence. Rest secure with this firm belief in your mind, and be free from all fears in this world.

—*Yoga-Vasishtha*

All things are created by the OM;
    The love-form is His body.
He is without form, without quality, without decay:
Seek thou union with Him!
But that formless God takes a thousand forms
    in the eyes of His creatures:
He is pure and indestructible,
His form is infinite and fathomless,
He dances in rapture, and waves of
    form arise from His dance.
The body and the mind cannot contain themselves,
    when they are touched by His great joy.
He is immersed in all consciousness, all joys,
    and all sorrows;
He has no beginning and no end;
He holds all within His bliss.
—Kabir

O thou transcendent,
Nameless, the fiber and the breath,
Light of the light, shedding forth universes, thou center of them,
Thou mightier center of the true, the good, the loving,
Thou moral, spiritual fountain — affection's source —
    thou reservoir...
Thou pulse — thou motive of the stars, sun, systems,
That, circling, move in order, safe, harmonious,
Athwart the shapeless vastness of space,
How should I think, how breathe a single breath, how speak,
    if out of myself,
I could not launch, to those, superior universes?
    —Walt Whitman

Sri Krishna: When goodness grows weak,
  When evil increases,
I make myself a body.

In every age I come back
To deliver the holy,
To destroy the sin of the sinner,
to establish righteousness.
    —Bhagavad Gita

Jesus said: I am the Light that is above them all, I am the All, the All came forth from Me and the All attained to Me. Cleave a piece of wood, I am there; lift up the stone and you will find Me there.
    —The Gospel of Thomas

The formless Absolute is my Father, and God with form is my Mother.
    —Kabir

The cosmic religious experience is the strongest and oldest mainspring of scientific research. My religion consist of a humble admiration of the illimitable superior spirit who reveals himself in the slight details we are able to perceive with our frail and feeble minds. That deeply emotional conviction of the presence of a superior reasoning power, which is revealed in the incomprehensible universe, forms my idea of God.
    —Albert Einstein

When He Himself reveals Himself, Brahma brings into manifestation That
    Which can never be seen.
As the seed is in the plant, as the shade is in the tree, as the void is
    In the sky, as infinite forms are in the void —
So from beyond the Infinite, the Infinite comes; and from the
    Infinite the finite extends.

The creature is in Brahma, and Brahma is in the creature:
    They are ever distinct, yet ever united.
He Himself is the tree, the seed, and the germ....

He is the breath, the word, and the meaning.
He Himself is the limit and the limitless: and beyond
    Both the limited and the limitless is He. The Pure Being.
He is the Immanent Mind in Brahma and in the creature.
—Kabir

Perfect and infinite joy really exists within God. My participation can add nothing to it, my non-participation can take nothing from the reality of this perfect and infinite joy. Of what importance is it then whether I am to share in it or not? Of no importance whatever.
    —Simone Weil

And do you say "God is invisible"? Speak not so. Who is more manifest than God? For this very purpose has he made all things, that through all things you may see him. This is God's goodness, that he manifests himself through all things. Nothing is invisible, not even an incorporeal thing; mind is seen in its thinking, and God in his working.
    —Hermes Trismegistus

God created man; and man created God. They both are the originators of forms and names only. In fact, neither God nor man was created.
    —Sri Ramana Maharshi

O servant, where dost thou seek Me?
Lo! I am beside thee.
I am neither in temple nor in mosque:
    I am neither in Kaaba nor in Kailash:
Neither am I in rites and ceremonies,
    Nor in Yoga and renunciation.
If thou art a true seeker, thou shalt at once see Me:
    Thou shalt meet Me in a moment of time.
Kabir says, "O Sadhu! God is the Breath of all breath."
—Kabir

The soul *is*. Under all this running sea of circumstance, whose waters ebb and flow with perfect balance, lies the aboriginal abyss of real Being. Essence, or God, is not a relation or a part, but the whole. Being is the vast affirmative, excluding negation, self-balanced, and swallowing up all relations, parts, and times within itself. Nature, truth, virtue, are the influx from thence.
    —Ralph Waldo Emerson

Creation and Creator are two lines, without beginning and without end, running parallel to each other. God is the ever active Providence, by whose power systems after systems are being evolved out of chaos, made to run for a time, and again destroyed.
    —Swami Vivekananda

Therefore the supreme Eternal is Being, secondless, of the form of pure knowledge, stainless, peaceful, free from beginning or ending, changeless, its own — nature is unbroken bliss.
    —Shankara

The simple, absolute and immutable mysteries of divine Truth are hidden in the super-luminous darkness of that silence which revealeth in secret....We long exceedingly to dwell in this translucent darkness and, through not seeing and not knowing, to see Him who is beyond both vision and knowledge — by the very fact of neither seeing Him nor knowing Him. For this is truly to see and to know and, through the abandonment of all things, to praise Him who is beyond and above all things.
    —Dionysius the Areopagite

The Evolver is the Self, the Pervader is the Self, the Sky-lord is the Self, the Destroyer is the Self; all this universe is the Self; there is nothing but the Self....
    Inward is the Self, outward also is the Self; the Self is to the east, the Self is also to the west. The Self is to the south, the Self is also to the north. The Self is above, the Self is beneath.
    —Shankara

A little consideration of what takes place around us every day would show us that a higher law than that of our will regulates events; that our painful labors are unnecessary and fruitless; that only in our easy, simple, spontaneous action are we strong, and by contenting ourselves with obedience we become divine. Belief and love, a believing love, will relieve us of a vast load of care. O my brothers, God exists. There is a soul at the center of nature and over the will of every man, so that none of us can wrong the universe.
    —Ralph Waldo Emerson

3
UNITY AND REALITY

Being verily is all this world, that is known of voice and mind, there is nothing else than Being, standing on nature's other shore.
    —Shankara

It is by means of Unity that each one shall receive himself back again. Through knowledge he shall purify himself of diversity with a view to Unity, by engulfing the Matter within himself like a flame, Darkness by Light and Death by Life.
    —*The Gospel of Truth*

Think of all bodies as appertaining to the One common Essence, and enjoy the full bliss of realizing yourself as the same, extending throughout all space.
    —*Yoga-Vasishtha*

See now the height and breadth of the eternal worth, since it hath made itself so many mirrors wherein it is reflected, remaining in itself one as before.
    —Dante

This is the secret of the unity of God: no matter where I take hold of a shred of it, I hold the whole of it. And since the teachings and all the commandments are radiations of his being, he who lovingly does one commandment utterly and to the core, and in this one commandment takes hold of a shred of the unity of God, holds the whole of it in his hand, and has fulfilled all.
    —*Ten Rungs: Hasidic Sayings*

Be in a realm where neither good nor evil exist. Both of them belong to the world of created beings; in the presence of Unity there is neither command nor prohibition.
    —Abu Yazid Al-Bistami

Since everything, then, is cause and effect, dependent and supporting, mediate and immediate, and all is held together by a natural though imperceptible chain which binds together things most distant and most different, I hold it equally impossible to know the parts without knowing the whole and to know the whole without knowing the parts in detail.
    —Blaise Pascal

All parts of the universe are interwoven with one another, and the bond is sacred. Nothing is unconnected with some other thing. For all things have been coordinated and combined to form the same universe. There is one universe made up of everything, and one God who pervades everything, and one substance, one law, one common reason in all intelligent animals, and one truth; perchance indeed there is one perfection for all beings of the same stock, who participate in the same reason.
—Marcus Aurelius

In the one substance, in which no difference of seer, seeing, seen exists, which is changeless, formless, undifferentiated, what separateness can exist?
—Shankara

All the souls should be known as naturally analogous to space and as eternal. There is no plurality among them anywhere, even by a jot or tittle.
—Manukya Karika

Nature shall be to thee as a symbol. The life of the soul in conscious union with the Infinite shall be for thee the only real existence.
—Ralph Waldo Emerson

Thou must love God as not-God, not-Spirit, not-person, not-image, but as He is, a sheer, pure absolute One, sundered from all twoness, and in whom we must eternally sink from nothingness to nothingness.
—Meister Eckhart

One Nature, perfect and pervading, circulates in all natures,
One Reality, all-comprehensive, contains within itself all realities....
The Dharma-body of all the Buddhas enters into my own being.
And my own being is found in union with theirs....
The Inner Light is beyond praise and blame;
Like space it knows no boundaries,
Yet it is even here, within us, ever retaining its serenity and fullness.
—Yung-chia Ta-shih

Regard the universe often as one living being, having one substance and one soul; and observe how all things act with one movement; and how all things cooperate as the causes of all that exists; observe too the continuous spinning of the thread and the single texture of the web.
—Marcus Aurelius

Where the difference of knower, knowing, known is gone, endless, sure; absolute, partless, pure consciousness; the wise know this as the supreme reality.

That can neither be left nor taken, is no object of mind or speech; immeasurable, beginningless, endless, the perfect Eternal, the universal "I."

—Shankara

We are perplexed by the appearance of an antinomy; we set soul against Nature, the spirit against his creative energy. But Soul and Nature, Purusha and Prakriti, are two eternal lovers who possess their perpetual unity and enjoy their constant difference, and in the unity abound in the passion of the multitudinous play of their difference, and in every step of the difference abound in the secret sense or the overt consciousness of unity. Nature takes the Soul into herself so that he falls asleep in a trance of union with her absorbed passion of creation and she too seems then to be asleep in the whirl of her own creative energy; and that is the involution in Matter. Above, it may be, the Soul takes Nature into himself so that she falls asleep in a trance of oneness with the absorbed self-possession of the Spirit and he too seems to be asleep in the deep of his own self-locked immobile being. But still above and below and around and within all this beat and rhythm is the eternity of the Spirit who has thus figured himself in soul and Nature and enjoys with a perfect awareness all that he creates in himself by this involution and evolution. The soul fulfills itself in Nature when it possesses in her the consciousness of that eternity and its power and joy and transfigures the natural becoming with the fullness of the spiritual being. The constant self-creation which we call birth finds there the perfect evolution of all that it held in its own nature and reveals its own utmost significance. The complete soul possesses all its self and all Nature.

—Sri Aurobindo

Learn to see the One in the many. The process of practicing and realizing this unity consists in seeing cause and effect as one and the same, in seeing the whole universe as an expression of God. The process of realizing unity in action consists in surrendering all words, deeds, and thoughts to Brahman, or God.

—*Srimad Bhagavatam*

For thirty years God was my mirror, now I am my own mirror. What I was I no longer am, for "I" and "God" are denial of God's unity. Since I no longer am, God is his own mirror. He speaks with my tongue, and I have vanished.

—Abu Yazid Al-Bistami

Jesus said: Whoever searches to discover the meaning of what I say will not experience death. If you begin to search, do not stop searching till you discover. When you do discover, you will be disturbed. But when you are disturbed, you will be filled with wonder. You will share the creating presence of the Source of all things. If they tell you: Look! This presence is in the skies! Remember, the birds have known this all along. If they say: It is in the seas! Remember, the fish have always known it. It is not apart from you. It wells up within each and surrounds all. If you but knew what kind of creature you are, and if you knew how you are known, you would understand how you are a child among the children of the Source of all life, rooted in the creating presence of that Source. But if you are unaware of what you are then you live in poverty.

 —*The Gospel of Thomas*

Those who speak with sense rely on what is universal, as a city must rely on its law, and with much greater reliance. For all manmade laws are nourished by one divine law; for it has as much power as it wishes and is sufficient for all with more left over.

 —Heraclitus

Push far enough towards the Void,
Hold fast enough to Quietness,
And of the ten thousand things none but can be worked on by you …
To be kingly is to be of heaven;
To be of heaven is to be in Tao.
Tao is forever and he that possesses it,
Though his body ceases, is not destroyed.

 —*Tao Te Ching*

Before the Unconditioned, the Conditioned dances:
 "Thou and I are one!" this trumpet proclaims.
The Guru comes, and bows down before the disciple:
This is the greatest of wonders.

 —Kabir

Where the Truth always reigneth, so that true perfect God and true perfect man are at one, and man so giveth place to God, that God himself is there and yet the man too, and this same unity worketh continually, and doeth and leaveth undone without any I, and Me, and Mine, and the like; behold, there is Christ, and nowhere else.

 —*Theologia Germanica*

Truly, without deception, certain, and most true. What is below is like that which is above, and what is above is like that which is below, to accomplish the miracles of the One. And as all things proceeded from the One, through the mediation of the One, so all things came from this one thing through adaptation. Its father is the sun; its mother the moon; the wind has carried it in its belly; its nurse is the earth. This is the father of all, the completion of the whole world. Its strength is complete if it be turned into earth. Separate the earth from the fire, the subtle from the dense, gently, with great ingenuity. It ascends from the earth to heaven, and descends again to the earth, and receives the power of the above and the below. So shall you have the glory of the whole world. So shall all darkness flee from you. Here is the strong power of all strength; for it will overcome every subtle thing and penetrate every solid. Thus was the world created. From here will come the marvelous adaptations, of which this is the means. And so I am called Hermes Trismegistus, having the three parts of the philosophy of the whole world.

—The *Emerald Tablet* of Hermes Trismegistus

Therefore the truly great man dwells on what is real
    And not what is on the surface,
On the fruit and not the flower.
Therefore accept the one and reject the other.
—Lao Tsu

As waves, foam, and bubbles are not different from water, so in the light of true knowledge, the Universe, born of the Self, is not different from the Self.
—*Ashtavakra Gita*

O all-pervading Reality! Virtue and vice, pleasure and pain are modes of the mind, and thy Self is independent of them. Thou art neither the doer nor the enjoyer; ever free art thou.
— *Ashtavakra Gita*

I laugh when I hear that the fish in the water is thirsty:
You do not see that the Real is in your home, and you
    wander from forest to forest listlessly!
Here is the truth! Go where you will, to Benares or to
    Mathura; if you do not find your soul, the world is
    unreal to you.
—Kabir

However vast the divine *milieu* may be, it is in reality a *center*. It therefore has the properties of a center, and above all the absolute and final power to unite all beings within its breast.... Let us establish ourselves in the divine *milieu*. There we shall find ourselves where the soul is most deep and where matter is most dense. There we shall discover, where all its beauties flow together, the ultra-vital, the ultra-sensitive, the ultra-active point of the universe. And, at the same time, we shall feel the *plenitude* of our powers of action and adoration effortlessly ordered within our deepest selves.

—Teilhard de Chardin

Things derive their being and nature by mutual dependence and are nothing in themselves.

—Nagarjuna

The image of God is found essentially and personally in all mankind. Each possesses it whole, entire and undivided, and all together not more than one alone. In this way we are all one, intimately united in our eternal image, which is the image of God and the source in us of all our life. Our created essence and our life are attached to it without mediation as to their eternal cause.

—Jan van Ruysbroeck

The eye with which I see God is the same eye with which God sees in me: my eye and God's eye, that is one eye and one vision, one knowledge and one love.

—Meister Eckhart

The One remains, the many change and pass:
Heaven's light forever shines, Earth's shadows fly;
Life, like a dome of many-colored glass,
Stains the white radiance of Eternity,
Until Death tramples it to fragments.

—Percy Bysshe Shelley

As there is no screen or ceiling between our heads and the infinite heavens, so there is no bar or wall in the soul, where man, the effect, ceases, and God, the cause, begins....We lie open on one side to the deeps of spiritual nature, to the attributes of God.

—Ralph Waldo Emerson

Nothing hinders the soul's knowledge of God as much as time and space, for time and space are fragments, whereas God is one! And therefore, if the soul is to know God, it must know him above time and outside of space; for God is neither this nor that, as are these manifold things. God is One!
—Meister Eckhart

Nature has neither seed
Nor shell,
She is all at once....

Nothing is inside,
Nothing is outside,
Since what is within
is without....

What is large is small, what is small is large,...

Always changing, always immutable,
Near and far and far and near.
—Johann Wolfgang von Goethe

Let us settle ourselves, and work and wedge our feet downward through the mud and slush of opinion, and prejudice, and tradition, and delusion, and appearances...till we come to a hard bottom and rocks in place, which we can call *reality*, and say, This is, and no mistake....If you stand right fronting and face to face to a fact, you will see the sun glimmer on both its surfaces, as if it were a scimatar, and feel its sweet edge dividing you through the heart and marrow, and so you will happily conclude your mortal career. Be it life or death, we crave only reality.
—Henry David Thoreau

Our idea of the external world is caused partly by the energies of our own mind and partly by the energies of the World-Mind. It is *not* caused by a separate material thing acting on our sense organs.
—Paul Brunton

There is one mind common to all individual men. Every man is an inlet to the same and to all of the same. He that is once admitted to the right of reason is made a freeman of the whole estate. What Plato has thought, he may think; what a saint has felt, he may feel; what at any time has befallen any man, he can understand. Who hath access to this universal mind is a party to all that is or can be done, for this is the only and sovereign agent.
—Ralph Waldo Emerson

The weal and woe of another comes to lie directly in my heart in exactly the same way — though not always to the same degree — as otherwise only my own would lie, as soon as this sentiment of compassion is aroused, and therewith, the difference between him and me is no longer absolute. And this really is amazing — even mysterious....

For if plurality and distinction belong only to this world of *appearances,* and if one and the same Being is what is beheld in all these living things, well then, the experience that dissolves the distinction between the I and the Not-I cannot be false. On the contrary: its opposite must be false. The former experience underlies the mystery of compassion, and stands, in fact, for the reality of which compassion is the prime expression. *That* experience, therefore, must be the metaphysical ground of ethics and consist simply in this: that *one* individual should recognize in *another,* himself in his own true being.

—Arthur Schopenhauer

That moves, That does not move; That is far off, That is very near; That is inside all, and That is outside all.

—*Eesha Upanishad*

It is a paradox of the World-Idea that it is at once a rigid pattern and within that pattern, a latent source of indeterminate possibilities. This seems impossible to human minds, but it would not be the soul of a divine order if it were merely mechanical.

—Paul Brunton

Time is like a river made up of events that happen, and a violent stream; for as soon as a thing has appeared it is carried away, and another comes in its place; and this will be carried away too.

—Marcus Aurelius

You never enjoy the world aright till the sea itself flows in your veins, till you are clothed with the heavens, and crowned with the stars; and perceive yourself to be the sole heir of the whole world; and more than so, because men are in it who are every one sole heirs, as well as you....Till your spirit fills the whole world, and the stars are your jewels...till you are intimately acquainted with that shady nothing out of which the world was made; till you love men so as to desire their happiness, with a thirst equal to the zeal of your own....

You never enjoy the world aright till you see all things in it so perfectly yours that you cannot desire them any other way; and till you are convinced that all things serve you best in their proper places.

—Thomas Traherne

4
CONSCIOUSNESS AND EXISTENCE

This whole world in its visible and invisible form is consciousness.
  —Shankara

Nothing moves without consciousness and consciousness does not move by chance; it moves by law — the law of cause and effect. If one adheres to the law of chance one is depriving oneself of the law of consciousness.
  —H.H. Shantanand Saraswati

The beginning, which is thought, comes to an end in action; know that in such wise was the construction of the world in eternity.
  —Rumi

The Universe is pervaded by thee and exists in thee. Verily by nature thou art Consciousness Absolute; do not harbor narrowness of heart and think thyself to be otherwise.
  —*Ashtavakra Gita*

Just as wave and foam, eddy and bubble are in their own nature water; so, from the body to the personality, all is consciousness, the pure essence of consciousness.
  —Shankara

The entire universe, everything — objects and creatures — is in Mind. I hold all the objects of my experience in *my* consciousness but I myself am held, along with them, in an incredibly greater consciousness, the World–Mind's.
  —Paul Brunton

The Knowledge and power we are free to discover in the core of nature is universal, not personal. At the core exists a matrix of causal reality, a logos of triune forces lawfully holding the universe together, emanating immense energy which is available for our use. This matrix contains the substance of consciousness, the stuff of stars, and the essence of the biological existence we call life.
  —Richard Geldard

I believe that human consciousness is a growing force given to us with life, and that its growth is as yet far, far indeed, from reaching its potential limits. It is a force which cannot be broken up into pieces and parts. It does not depend on any one individual's wanton will and whim. It grows and perfects itself with a power all its own.

It is within us and our life is sustained by it. Human life without its presence is not only meaningless, it is not human. Its presence is revealed to us not by our experiences alone but by the images and conceptions which our consciousness enables us to create as a guide for our action.

—Naum Gabo

Know your Self — Consciousness — to be all in all, O wise Prince, and reject as false everything which appears to be otherwise: as everything is embodied in yourself, there is nothing for you to own or disown.

—*Yoga-Vasishtha*

I am of the oldest religion. Leaving aside the question which was prior, egg or bird, I believe the mind is the creator of the world, and is ever creating; that at last Matter is dead Mind; that mind makes the senses it sees with; that the genius of man is a continuation of the power that made him and has not done making him.

—Ralph Waldo Emerson

Mind is not in possession of Truth, but only its ignorant seeker. Beyond mind is a supramental or gnostic power of consciousness that is in eternal possession of Truth. This supermind is at its source the dynamic consciousness, in its nature at once and inseparably infinite wisdom and infinite will of the divine Knower and Creator.

—Sri Aurobindo

When the darkness of ignorance is dispelled, the inner light shines brightly. Mental distraction and distress cease, just as the ocean becomes calm when the wind ceases to agitate its surface. There arises self-knowledge within, and the realization of truth puts an end to the perception of the world-illusion. Infinite consciousness alone shines.

—*Yoga-Vasishtha*

Vision implies the seer. The seer cannot deny the existence of the Self. There is no moment when the Self as Consciousness does not exist; nor can the seer remain apart from Consciousness. This Consciousness is eternal Being and the only Being.

—Sri Ramana Maharshi

To be the witness is the first stage; to be Witness of the witness is the next; but to BE is the final one. For consciousness lets go of the witness in the end. Consciousness alone is itself the real experience.

—Paul Brunton

O mind, I shall gently bring home to you the truth that you are indeed neither the doer nor the experiencer. You are indeed inert; how can a statue made of stone dance? If your intelligence is entirely dependent upon the infinite consciousness, then may you live long in that realization.

—*Yoga-Vasishtha*

This consciousness that is aware
Of Neighbors and the Sun
Will be the one aware of Death
And that itself alone

Is traversing the interval
Experience between
And most profound experiment
Appointed unto Men —

How adequate unto itself
Its properties shall be
Itself unto itself and none
shall make discovery.

Adventure most unto itself
The Soul condemned to be —
Attended by a single Hound
Its own identity.

—Emily Dickinson

So when we say that Heaven is within, this does not mean that Heaven has a spatial existence in or outside the body, but that it is Consciousness itself. And when we say that God is Immanent, this does not mean that God is identical with the Cosmos, or that He is extra-cosmic; but that God is supra-cosmic. We have first to recognize Heaven within ourselves; then we can find it everywhere.

—Swami Prabhavananda

Between the poles of the conscious and the unconscious,
    there has the mind made a swing:
Thereon hang all beings and all worlds, and that
    Swing never ceases its sway.
Millions of beings are there: the sun and the moon
    in their courses are there:
Millions of ages pass, and the swing goes on.
All swing! The sky and the earth and the air and the water;
    And the Lord Himself taking form:
And the sight of this has made Kabir a servant.
    —Kabir

God is the Subject of all subjects. In one sense He can never be known. It being the very Subject of all subjects how can we know it? To know means to objectify a thing, and the Supreme Subject can never become an object. In another sense, God is more than known to us. For it is our very Self. What proof do we want for our very existence?
    —Swami Narayananda

Creation begins and continues as a single sound.
    That sound includes all ideas, meanings and all expression of meaning and all possible languages. It is universal consciousness letting itself be known as the Word.
    That sound holds within itself all rhythms, melodies, chords, and all the possibilities of music. It is universal consciousness letting itself be known as song.
    That sound resonates in eternity and its resonances create voids and spaces and diversity of experiences of time. The time experience of a galaxy, a tree, a man, a mayfly. It still holds within itself all lights and darknesses and all possible variety of colors. It also holds all natural laws and the principles of life and intelligent life. It creates beings capable of consciousness themselves who are the spectators and the audiences of its creation. It is universal consciousness letting itself be known as glory.
    —William Anderson

I will that there be a God, that my existence in this world be also an existence in a pure world of the understanding outside the system of natural connections, and finally that my duration be endless.
    —Immanuel Kant

We lie in the lap of immense intelligence, which makes us receivers of its truth and organs of its activity.
    —Ralph Waldo Emerson

I am my own first cause, both of my eternal being and of my temporal being. To this end I was born, and by virtue of my birth being eternal, I shall never die. It is of the nature of this eternal birth that I *have been* eternally, that I *am* now, and *shall be* forever. What I am as a temporal creature is to die and come to nothingness, for it came with time and so with time it will pass away. In my eternal birth, however, everything was begotten. I was my own first cause as well as the first cause of everything else.

    —Meister Eckhart

Time is awake when all things sleep.
Time stands straight when all things fall,
Time shuts in and will not be shut.
"Is," "was," and "shall be" are only Time's children:
O reasoning, be witness and be stable.

    —Hindu Sutra

Time is nothing else than the uninterrupted succession of the acts of divine Energy, one of the attributes or one of the workings of the Deity. Space is the extension of His soul; it is His unfolding in length, breadth, and height; it is the simultaneous existence of His productions and manifestations.

    —Giordano Bruno

One must know the container and not become dispersed in the contents. The container is first of all the miracle of existence; then it is the miracle of consciousness or of intelligence, and then the miracle of the joy which, like an expansive and creative power, fills as it were the existential and intellectual "spaces."

    —Frithjof Schuon

Thou art that Consciousness, the supreme Bliss, in which the world appears as an imagined object, like a snake in a rope. Be happy! That thou art!

    —*Ashtavakra Gita*

*

5
LOVE, BEAUTY, AND THE GOOD

Eros is love of what is beautiful, so it necessarily follows that Eros is a lover of wisdom.
—Plato

If I speak in the tongues of mortals and of angels, but do not have love, I am a noisy gong or a clanging cymbal. And if I have prophetic powers, and understand all mysteries and all knowledge, and if I have all faith, so as to remove mountains, but do not have love, I am nothing. If I give away all my possessions, and if I hand over my body so that I may boast, but do not have love I gain nothing.

Love is patient, love is kind, love is not envious or boastful or arrogant or rude. It does not insist on its own way; it is not irritable or resentful; it does not rejoice in wrongdoing, but rejoices in the truth. It bears all things, believes all things, hopes all things, endures all things.
—1 Corinthians 13:1–7

Divine love, which delivers us from all evils and from all impurities, is supreme. Supreme love and supreme wisdom are one. Sing, then, the glories of the Lord, sing His praises, that the Lord at once of wisdom and love may abide in the hearts of all who read or hear your words and may bestow upon them His everlasting peace.
—*Srimad Bhagavatam*

Truth seeth God, and wisdom beholdeth God, and of these two cometh the third: that is, a holy marveling delight in God; which is Love. Where Truth and Wisdom are verily, there is Love verily, coming of them both.
—Julian of Norwich

The power of Love in its entirety is various and mighty, nay, all-embracing, but the mightiest power of all is wielded by that Love whose just and temperate consummation, whether in heaven or on earth, tends toward the good. It is he that bestows our every joy upon us, and it is through him that we are capable of the pleasures of society, aye, and friendship even, with the gods our masters.
—Plato

Born at the banquet of the gods, Love has of necessity been eternally in existence, for it springs from the intention of the Soul towards its best, towards the Good; as long as Soul has been, Love has been.
—Plotinus

But true Love is taught and guided by the true Light and Reason, and this true, eternal, and divine Light teacheth Love to love nothing but the One true and Perfect Good, and that simply for its own sake, and not for the sake of a reward, or in the hope of obtaining anything, but simply for the Love of Goodness, because it is good and hath a right to be loved. And all that is thus seen by the help of the True Light must also be loved of the True Love. Now that Perfect Good, which we call God, cannot be perceived but by the True Light; therefore He must be loved wherever he is seen or made known.

—*Theologia Germanica*

When this great love is kindled in thee, it will burn as no fire can do....This fire of the love of God is brighter than the sun, sweeter than all besides, more supporting than all food and drink, and more to be desired than all the joys of this world.

—Jacob Boehme

The love between God and God which in itself *is* God, is this bond of double virtue: the bond that unites two beings so closely that they are no longer distinguishable and really form a single unity.

—Simone Weil

To love God does not mean to cultivate a sentiment...but rather to eliminate from the soul what prevents God from entering it.

—Frithjof Schuon

The true lover finds the light only if, like the candle, he is his own fuel, consuming himself.

—Attar of Nishapur

To all, the Primal Light sends down Its ray.
    And every splendor into which it enters
    receives that radiance in its own way.

Therefore, since the act of loving grows
    from the act of recognition, the bliss of love
    blazes in some of these, and in some it glows.

Consider then how lofty and how wide
    is the excellence of the Eternal Worth
    which in so many mirrors can divide

its power and majesty forevermore,
Itself remaining One, as It was before.

—Dante, *Paradiso*

My bounty is as boundless as the sea,
My love as deep; the more I give to thee,
The more I have, for both are infinite.
—William Shakespeare

The heart has its reasons, which reason does not know. We feel it in a thousand things. I say that the heart naturally loves the Universal Being, and also itself naturally, according as it gives itself to them; and it hardens itself against one or the other at its will. You have rejected the one, and kept the other. Is it by reason that you love yourself?
—Blaise Pascal

Love demands knowledge, for we can never love the unknown; the more thorough does our knowledge of something good become, the deeper grows our love for it.
—St. Francis de Sales

Love becomes perfect only when it transcends itself —
Becoming One with its object;
Producing Unity of Being.
—Hakim Jami

True love has no motive. It is all forgiving to the beloved; the whole life becomes a service, so that the beloved may be pleased; it is for his pleasure that everything is done, without demanding anything at all.
—H.H. Shantanand Saraswati

Let me not to the marriage of true minds
Admit impediments. Love is not love
Which alters when it alteration finds,
Or bends with the remover to remove:
O, no! It is an ever-fixed mark,
That looks on tempests and is never shaken;
It is the star to every wandering bark,
Whose worth's unknown, although his height be taken.
Love's not Time's fool, though rosy lips and cheeks
Within his bending sickle's compass come;
Love alters not with his brief hours and weeks,
But bears it out even to the edge of doom.
    If this be error, and upon me prov'd,
    I never writ, nor no man ever lov'd.
—William Shakespeare

In true love you always give and don't demand in return. By giving, you allow things to happen....True lovers never go to sleep while waiting for the beloved! One must learn this lesson well — that one never demands anything in return for one's love and then only does one get all one needs for a good and happy life.

    —H.H. Shantanand Saraswati

Whatever one loves, one finds everywhere, and everywhere sees resemblances and analogies to it. The greater one's love, the vaster and more meaningful is this analogous world. My beloved is the abbreviation of the universe, the universe an elongation an extrapolation of my beloved. The friend of the knowledgeable offers all flowers and gifts to his beloved.

    —Novalis

If any man then has an incorporeal eye, let him go forth from the body to behold the Beautiful, let him fly up and float aloft, not seeking to see shape or color, but rather that by which these things are made, that which is quiet and calm, stable and changeless,...that which is one, that which issues from itself and is contained in itself, that which is like nothing but itself.

    —Hermes Trismegistus

Love and wisdom are inseparable, like Reality and Emergence, with love actually emerging by means of wisdom and in keeping with it.

    —Emanuel Swedenborg

Now he [the true follower] directs his eyes to what is beautiful in general, as he turns to gaze upon the limitless ocean of beauty. Now he produces many fine and inspiring thoughts and arguments, as he gives his undivided attention to philosophy. Here he gains in strength and stature until his attention is caught by that one special knowledge — the knowledge of a beauty which I will now try to describe to you....It is eternal, neither coming to be nor passing away, neither increasing nor decreasing. Moreover it is not beautiful in part, and ugly in part, nor is it beautiful at one time, and not at another; not beautiful in some respects, but not in others; nor beautiful here and ugly there, as if beautiful in some people's eyes, but not in others. It will not appear to him as the beauty of a face, or hands, or anything physical — nor as an idea or branch of knowledge, nor as existing in any determinate place, such as a living creature, or the earth, or heaven, or anywhere like that. It exists for all time, by itself and with itself, unique. All other forms of beauty derive from it, but in such a way that their creation or destruction does not strengthen or weaken it, or affect it in any way at all. If a man progresses from the lesser beauties, and begins to catch sight of this beauty, then he is within reach of the final revelation....That, if ever, is the moment, my dear Socrates, when a man's life is worth living, as he contemplates beauty itself.

    —Plato

Man yearns for happiness because divine Beatitude, which is made of Beauty and Love, is his very substance.
—Frithjof Schuon

Beauty is as much an aspect of Reality as truth. He who is insensitive to the one has not found the other.
—Paul Brunton

"Beauty is truth, truth beauty." — that is all
Ye know on earth, and all ye need to know.
—John Keats

What is good or beautiful is the cause of all activity; all things are attracted to it, moved by it, gripped by it, because they love it. What is good, what is beautiful, is also desirable, lovable, dear to everyone; it is the reason for every activity, every choice.
—St. Francis de Sales

For all things which the eye can see are mere phantoms, and unsubstantial outlines; but the things which the eye cannot see are the realities, and above all, the ideal form of the Beautiful and the Good. And as the eye cannot see God, so it cannot see the Beautiful and the Good. For the Beautiful and the Good are parts of God; they are properties of God alone; they belong to God, and are inseparable from him; they are without blemish, and most lovely and God himself is in love with them. If you are able to apprehend God, then you will apprehend the Beautiful and the Good....If you seek knowledge of God, you are also seeking knowledge of the Beautiful. For there is one road alone that leads to the Beautiful, and that is piety joined with knowledge of God.
—Hermes Trismegistus

Therefore, O soul, good is your creator; not the good body, not the good mind, not the good intellect, but good itself. Good is that which is indeed self-sufficient, infinite beyond the limits of what is beneath it, and it bestows on you infinite life, either from age to age, or at least from some beginning to the end of time. Do you desire to look on the face of good? Then look around at the whole universe, full of the light of the sun. Look at the light in the material world, full of all forms in constant movement; take away the matter, leave the rest. You have the soul, an incorporeal light that takes all shapes and is full of change.
—Marsilio Ficino

Do not waste yourself in rejection; do not bark against the bad, but chant the beauty of the good.
—Ralph Waldo Emerson

6
WISDOM, TRUTH, AND KNOWLEDGE

If one has knowledge, he receives what is his own, and draws it to himself.... Whoever is to have knowledge in this way knows where he comes from, and where he is going.
 —*The Gospel of Truth*

Who is as the wise man? And who knoweth the interpretation of a thing? A man's wisdom maketh his face to shine, and the boldness of his face shall be changed.
 —*Ecclesiastes 8:1*

Wisdom reacheth from one end to another mightily: and sweetly doth she order all things.... For she is privy to the mysteries of the knowledge of God, and a lover of his works.
 —*The Wisdom of Solomon*

In the root divine Wisdom is all-Brahman; in the stem she is all-Illusion; in the flower she is all-World; and in the fruit, all-Liberation.
 —*Tantra Tattva*

Knowledge came down to us like a flame of light, as a gift from the Gods, I am convinced, brought to us by the hand of some unknown Prometheus from a divine source — and the ancients, being better than we are, and nearer to the God, handed this tradition down to us.
 —Plato

A sort of absoluteness attends all perception of truth, — no smell of age, no hint of corruption. It is self-sufficing, sound entire.
 —Ralph Waldo Emerson

There is only one knowledge and that is of Unity.
 —H.H. Shantanand Saraswati

I wisdom dwell with prudence....My fruit is better than gold...

The Lord possessed me in the beginning of his way, before his works of old.

I was set up from everlasting, from the beginning, or ever the earth was.

When there were no depths, I was brought forth; when there were no fountains abounding with water.

Before the mountains were settled, before the hills was I brought forth:

While as yet he had not made the earth, nor the fields, nor the highest part of the dust of the world.

When he prepared the heavens, I was there: when he set a compass upon the face of the depth:

When he established the clouds above: when he strengthened the fountains of the deep:

When he gave to the sea his decree, that the waters should not pass his commandment: when he appointed the foundations of the earth:

Then I was by him, as one brought up with him: and I was daily his delight, rejoicing always before him;

Rejoicing in the habitable part of his earth; and my delights were with the sons of men.

Now therefore hearken unto me, O ye children: for blessed are they that keep my ways.

Hear instruction, and be wise, and refuse it not.

Blessed is the man that heareth me, watching daily at my gates, waiting at the posts of my doors.

For whoso findeth me findeth life, and shall obtain favor of the Lord.

    —Proverbs 8:12, 19, 22–34

For wisdom is more moving than any motion: she passeth and goeth through all things by reason of her pureness. For she is the breath of the power of God, and a pure influence flowing from the glory of the Almighty: therefore can no defiled thing fall into her. For she is the brightness of the everlasting light, the unspotted mirror of the power of God, and the image of his goodness. And being but one, she can do all things: and remaining in herself, she maketh all things new: and in all ages entering into holy souls, she maketh them friends of God and prophets.

    —*The Wisdom of Solomon*

Happy is the man that findeth wisdom, and the man that getteth understanding....

She is more precious than rubies; and all the things thou canst desire are not to be compared unto her.

Length of days is in her right hand; and in her left hand riches and honor.

Her ways are ways of pleasantness, and all her paths are peace.

She is a tree of life to them that lay hold upon her: and happy is every one that retaineth her.

The Lord by wisdom hath founded the earth; by understanding hath he established the heavens.

By his knowledge the depths are broken up, and the clouds drop down the dew.

    —Proverbs 3:13, 15–20

Wisdom uncreate, the same now as it ever was, and the same to be for evermore.
    —St. Augustine

This is the knowledge of the living book which he revealed to the aeons....While his wisdom contemplates the Word, and his teaching utters it, his knowledge has revealed it. While forebearance is a crown upon it, and his gladness is in harmony with it, his glory has exalted it, his image has revealed it, his repose has received it into itself, his love has made a body over it, his fidelity has embraced it. In this way the Word of the Father goes forth in the totality, as the fruit of his heart and an impression of his will.
    —*The Gospel of Truth*

God is known through knowledge, and through unknowing....The most divine knowledge of God is one which knows through unknowing in the unity beyond intellect when the intellect stands away from beings and then stands away from itself, it is united to the more than resplendent rays, and is then and there illumined by the inscrutable depths of wisdom.
    —Dionysius the Areopagite

Now thou lovest earthly wisdom but when thou art clothed with heavenly wisdom, thou wilt see that all the wisdom of the world is only foolishness.
    —Jacob Boehme

Truth did not come into the world naked, but it came in types and images. One will not receive truth in any other way.
    —*The Gospel of Philip*

Education is not what it is said to be by some, who profess to put knowledge into a soul which does not possess it, as if they could put sight into blind eyes. On the contrary, our own account signifies that the soul of every man does possess the power of learning the truth and the organ to see it with; and that, just as one might have to turn the whole body round in order that the eye should see light instead of darkness, so the entire soul must be turned away from this changing world, until its eye can bear to contemplate reality and that supreme splendor which we have called the Good. Hence there may well be an art whose aim would be to effect this very thing, the conversion of the soul, in the readiest way; not to put the power of sight into the soul's eye, which already has it, but to ensure that, instead of looking in the wrong direction, it is turned the way it ought to be.
    —Plato

The soul is the perceiver and revealer of truth. We know truth when we see it, let skeptic and scoffer say what they choose. Foolish people ask you, when you have spoken, what they do not wish to hear, "How do you know it is truth, and not an error of your own?" We know truth when we see it, from opinion, as we know when we are awake that we are awake.
    —Ralph Waldo Emerson

The gospel of truth is a joy for those who have received from the Father of truth the grace of knowing him...For he discovered them in himself, and they discovered him in themselves, the incomprehensible, inconceivable one, the Father, the perfect one, the one who made all things.

—*The Gospel of Truth*

For who would long for anything he knows not of,
Or who could follow after things unknown,
Or how discover them? Who could in ignorance recognize
The form of what he found?
Or, when it perceived the highest mind,
Did it know at once the whole and the separate parts?
Now, clouded and hidden by the body's parts,
It is not totally forgetful of itself,
And the whole it keeps, losing the separate parts.
Therefore whoever seeks the truth
Is of neither class: for he neither knows
Nor is altogether ignorant of all,
But the whole he keeps, remembers and reflects on,
All from that height perceived goes over once again,
That he might to those things he has preserved
Add the forgotten parts.

—Boethius

As one weapon is foiled by another and one form of dirt can be removed by another, as one poison is destroyed by another, so the destruction of erroneous knowledge by the higher knowledge brings joy to the mind.

—*Yoga-Vasishtha*

Jesus said: What thou shalt hear in thine ear...that preach from your housetops; for no one lights a lamp and puts it under a bushel, nor does he put it in a hidden place, but he sets it on the lampstand, so that all who come in and go out may see its light.

—*The Gospel of Thomas*

You who want
knowledge,
seek the Oneness
within

There you
will find
the clear mirror
already waiting

—Hadewijch

All the knowledge that we have in this world — where does it come from? It is within us. What knowledge is outside? None. Knowledge is not in matter; it is in man all the time. Nobody ever creates knowledge; man brings it from within. It is lying there. The whole of the big banyan tree which covers acres of ground is in a little seed which is perhaps no bigger than one-eighth of a mustard seed; all that mass of energy is confined there. The gigantic intellect, we know, lies coiled up in the protoplasmic cell; and why should not infinite energy?...Each one of us comes out of a protoplasmic cell, and all the powers we possess are coiled up there. You cannot say they come from food; for if you heap up food mountain high, what power comes out of it? The energy is in the cell, potentially no doubt, but still there.

So infinite power is in the soul of man, whether he knows it or not. Its manifestation is only a question of being conscious of it. Slowly this infinite giant is, as it were, waking up, becoming conscious of his power, and arousing himself; and with his growing consciousness, more and more of his bonds are breaking, his chains are bursting asunder, and the day is sure to come when, with the full consciousness of his infinite power and wisdom, the giant will rise to his feet and stand erect. Let us all help to hasten that glorious consummation.
—Swami Vivekananda

O! How much more doth beauty beauteous seem
By that sweet ornament which truth doth give!
—William Shakespeare

The soul answers never by words, but by the thing itself that is inquired after.
—Ralph Waldo Emerson

Knowledge is generally confused with information. Because people are looking for information or experience, not knowledge, they do not find knowledge.

You cannot avoid giving knowledge to one fitted for it. You cannot give knowledge to the unfit; that is impossible. You can, if you have it, and if he is capable, fit a man for receiving knowledge.
—Sayed Najmuddin

Jesus said: Know what is in thy sight, and what is hidden from thee will be revealed to thee. For there is nothing hidden which will not be manifest.
—*The Gospel of Thomas*

The knowledge which is gained from inference and the study of scriptures is knowledge of one kind. But the knowledge which is gained from *samadhi* is of a much higher order. It goes beyond inference and scriptures.
—Patanjali

Now all the knowledge and wisdom that is in creatures, whether angels or men, is nothing else but a participation of that one eternal, immutable, and uncreated wisdom of God, or several signatures of that one archetypal seal, or like so many multiplied reflections of one and the same face, made in several glasses, whereof some are clearer, some obscurer, some standing nearer, some further off.
—Ralph J. Cudworth

O Heart! Until, in this prison of deception,
    you can see the difference between This and That,
For an instant detach from this Well of Tyranny;
    stand outside.
—Rumi

Philosophy is the intellectual search for the fundamental truth of things; religion is the attempt to make the truth dynamic in the soul of man. They are essential to each other; a religion that is not the expression of philosophic truth, degenerates into superstition and obscurantism, and a philosophy which does not dynamize itself with the religious spirit is a barren light, for it cannot get itself practiced. But again neither of these get their supreme value unless raised into the spirit and cast into life.
—Sri Aurobindo

Without going outside, you may know the whole world.
Without looking through the window, you may see the ways of heaven.
The farther you go, the less you know.

Thus the sage knows without traveling;
He sees without looking;
He works without doing.
—Lao Tsu

Philosophy is nothing else than striving through constant contemplation and saintly piety to attain to knowledge of God; but there will be many who will make philosophy hard to understand, and corrupt it with manifold speculations....I tell you then that the men of after times will be misled by cunning sophists, and will be turned away from the pure and holy teachings of true philosophy. For to worship God in thought and spirit with singleness of heart, to revere God in all his works, and to give thanks to God, whose will, and his alone, is wholly filled with goodness — this is philosophy unsullied by intrusive cravings for unprofitable knowledge.
—Hermes Trismegistus

Man's real wealth consists, not in satisfying his needs, not in becoming "the master and owner of nature," but in seeing what is and the whole of what is, in seeing things not as useful or useless, serviceable or not, but simply as being.

—Josef Pieper

O revered sages, there is nothing greater or more purifying than to converse about God and His divine play. The highest religion of man is unselfish love of God. If one has this love, one attains to truly divine wisdom. Fruitless is the knowledge which is not love. Fruitless is religion itself, if it has not love. Vain indeed is all struggle for spiritual life if in one's heart there be not love.

Religion is not for the purpose of securing a place in heaven. It is an inquiry into Truth, and its ideal is the knowledge and the realization of Truth.

The knowers of Truth call Truth the infinite, eternal knowledge. The followers of the Vedas call it Brahman, the worshipers of Hiranyagarbha call it the Universal Spirit, and devotees call it God.

—*Srimad Bhagavatam*

The Prophet said that Truth has declared:
"I am not hidden in what is high or low
Nor in the earth nor skies nor throne.
This is certainty, O beloved:
I am hidden in the heart of the faithful.
If you seek me, seek in these hearts."

—Rumi

When the answer cannot be put into words, neither can the question be put into words.
The *riddle* does not exist.
If a question can be framed at all, it is also *possible* to answer it....
There are, indeed, things that cannot be put into words. They *make themselves manifest*. They are what is mystical....
What we cannot speak about we must pass over in silence.

—Ludwig Wittgenstein

Knowing the world to be unreal, no wise man is deceived by its ever-changing scenes.
It is the spiritual teacher who awakens the dull and sleeping mind by his right reasoning, and then instills into it the word of truth.
First, by diligent attendance upon the good and compassionate Gurus, and then by the help of reasoning, pure-minded men come to the light of Truth, and perceive the divine light shining in their souls. They become what I am, O Rama-ji.

—*Yoga-Vasishtha*

Better than a hundred vacuous verses
is one sane truth leading to peace.
—*Dhammapada*

When we come at last to perceive that all this vast universe is a thought-form and when we can feel our own source to be the single and supreme principle in and through which it arises, then our knowledge has become final and perfect.
—Paul Brunton

Truth is simple, and will not be antique; is ever present and insists on being of this age and of this moment. Here is thought and love and truth and duty, new as on the first day of Adam and of angels.
—Ralph Waldo Emerson

I believe that the mind can be permanently profaned by the habit of attending to trivial things, so that all our thoughts shall be tinged with triviality....If we have thus desecrated ourselves — as who has not? — the remedy will be wariness and devotion to reconsecrate ourselves, and make once more a fane of the mind. We should treat our minds, that is, ourselves, as innocent and ingenuous children, whose guardians we are, and be careful what objects and what subjects we thrust on their attention. Read not the Times. Read the Eternities. Conventionalities are at length as bad as impurities....Knowledge does not come to us by details, but in flashes of light from heaven.
—Henry David Thoreau

If I knew my Self as intimately as I ought, I should have perfect knowledge of all creatures....not until the soul knows all that there is to be known that she can cross over to the Unknown Good.
—Meister Eckhart

For the Holy Ghost...rises up like a lightning-flash, as fire sparkles and flashes out of a stone when a man strikes it.

But when the flash is caught in the fountain of the heart, then the Holy Spirit rises up, in the seven unfolding fountain spirits, into the brain, like the dawning of the day....

From this God I take my knowledge and from no other thing; neither will I know any other thing than that same God....

Though an angel from heaven should tell this to me, yet for all that I could not believe it, much less lay hold on it; for I should always doubt whether it was certainly so or no. But the Sun itself arises in my spirit, and therefore I am most sure of it.
—Jacob Boehme

His thought is quiet, quiet are his word and deed, when he has obtained freedom by true wisdom; then he has become a quiet man.
   —The Buddha

Intelligence is the shadow of objective Truth.
How can the shadow vie with sunshine?
   —Rumi

How can one be a wise man if he does not know any better how to live than other men? — if he is only more cunning and intellectually subtle? Does Wisdom work in a treadmill? Or does she teach how to succeed by *her example*? Is there any such thing as wisdom not applied to life? Is she merely the miller who grinds the finest logic?
   —Henry David Thoreau

Attend to My words, which inflame the heart and enlighten the mind; which prick the conscience, and soothe in manifold ways the wounded spirit....I am the One Who teaches men knowledge, and I impart to little ones a clearer knowledge than can be taught by man. He to whom I speak will soon become wise, and wax strong in spirit.
   —Thomas à Kempis

The most beautiful and profound emotion we can experience is the sensation of the mystical. It is the sower of all true science. He to whom this emotion is a stranger, who can no longer wonder and stand rapt in awe, is as good as dead. To know that what is impenetrable to us really exists, manifesting itself as the highest wisdom and the most radiant beauty, which our dull faculties can comprehend only in their primitive form — this knowledge, this feeling, is at the center of true religiousness.
   —Albert Einstein

Through my power, the man of judgment may eat
And whoever breathes or hears the spoken Word;
Unknowingly they all abide in me.
In truth, I speak: hear, O holy tradition!

I alone utter the Word of Truth, the Word
That brings enjoyment to Gods and men alike.

The man I love, to him do I give power;
I make him a divine, a seer, and a sage.
   —*Rig-Veda*

7
THE SELF AND SPIRIT

The Self is everywhere, without a body, without a shape, whole, pure, wise, all knowing, far shining, self-depending, all transcending; in the eternal procession assigning to every period its proper duty.
    —*Eesha Upanishad*

The *Jiva*, or our "Self," is a part of the Paramatman, and it has come into the world for the sake of discovering joy.
    —H.H. Shantanand Saraswati

The Self is the only Reality. If the false identity vanishes, the persistence of the Reality becomes apparent.
    —Sri Ramana Maharshi

Like the ether, I spread throughout the world; like the sun, I am marked by my shining; like the hills, I am everlasting and unmoved; I am like an ocean without shores.
    —Shankara

He is not born, nor does He ever die; after having been, He again ceases not to be; nor the reverse. Unborn, eternal, unchangeable and primeval, He is not slain when the body is slain.
    —*Bhagavad Gita*

I am neither he who acts nor he who experiences the results of action. I am beyond action and am changeless. My nature is pure consciousness. I am absolute reality, eternal goodness.

    It is not I who see, hear, speak, act, suffer or enjoy. I am the Atman, eternal, ever-living, beyond action, unbounded, unattached — nothing but pure, infinite consciousness.
    —Shankara

Thou art neither earth, water, fire, air, nor ether. Know thy Self (Atman) as Witness of all these, and different from them, if thou wouldst attain liberation.
—*Ashtavakra Gita*

Standing in the Self, realize the Self in being, the Self from every disguise set free, Being, Consciousness, Bliss, the secondless; thus shalt thou build no more for going forth.
—Shankara

You cannot see the seer of the sight, you cannot hear the hearer of the sound, you cannot think of the thinker of the thought, you cannot know the knower of the known. Your own Self lives in the hearts of all. Nothing else matters.
—*Brihadaranyaka Upanishad*

It moves. It moves not.
It is far, and It is near.
It is within all this,
And It is outside of all this.
—*Eesha Upanishad*

The light of the inner consciousness which exists as the Self of man is also known as the *purusha*. The *purusha* is self-luminous, without beginning and without end, and entirely separate from *prakriti*. The universe of name and form is an outcome of *prakriti*, energized by her nearness to the *purusha*....The *purusha* is the eternal witness, always free, and never the performer of actions. All actions proceed from the *gunas* of *prakriti*.
—*Srimad Bhagavatam*

You are the Self, the infinite Being, the pure unchanging consciousness, which pervades everything.
—Shankara

Just as fire, though one, having entered the world, assumes separate forms in respect of different shapes, similarly, the Self inside all beings, though one, assumes a form in respect of each shape; and yet It is outside.
—*Katha Upanishad*

I was sent forth from the power,
    and I have come to those who reflect upon me,
    and I have been found among those who seek after me.
Look upon me, you who reflect upon me,
    and you hearers, hear me....

Do not be ignorant of me.

For I am the first and the last...

I am the knowledge of my inquiry,
    and the finding of those who seek after me,
    and the command of those who ask of me,
    and the power of the powers in my knowledge
        Of the angels, who have been sent at my word,
    and of gods in their seasons by my counsel,
    and of spirits of every man who exists with me,
        And of women who dwell within me.
I am the one who is honored, and who is praised,
    and who is despised scornfully.
I am peace,
    and war has come because of me.
And I am an alien and a citizen.
I am the substance and the one who has no substance....

For what is inside of you is what is outside of you,
    and the one who fashions you on the outside
        is the one who shaped the inside of you.
    And what you see outside of you,
        You see inside of you;
        it is visible and it is your garment.

Hear me, your hearers,
    and learn of my words, you who know me.
I am the hearing that is attainable to everything;
    I am the speech that cannot be grasped.
I am the name of the sound
    and the sound of the name....

For many are the pleasant forms...
    And fleeting pleasures,
        Which men embrace until they become sober
    and go up to their resting-place.
And they will find me there,
    and they will live,
    and they will not die again.
—*The Thunder, Perfect Mind*

I am the Self in all beings. I dwell in the hearts of all. Where else shall one worship Me but in all beings? Knowing Me as the Self in all beings, love all, and live in the service of all.

  —*Srimad Bhagavatam*

The Self is the witness, all-pervading, perfect, free, one, consciousness, actionless, not attached to any object, desireless, ever-tranquil. It appears through illusion as the world.

  —*Ashtavakra Gita*

Again, the kingdom of heaven is like unto treasure hid in a field; the which when a man hath found he hideth, and for joy thereof goeth and selleth all that he hath, and buyeth that field.

  —*Matthew 13:44*

Since the Self is witness of the body, its character, its acts, its states, therefore the Self must be of other nature than the body.

  —Shankara

The Self knows the Universal Self; there is no other means of knowing because they are one. However, as long as ignorance is there, the illusion of duality will exist. Thus we see Self as something to be known; in fact only the self can know itself.

  —H.H. Shantanand Saraswati

The Atman is birthless and deathless. It neither grows nor decays. It is unchangeable, eternal. It does not dissolve when the body dissolves. Does the ether cease to exist when the jar that enclosed it is broken?

  —Shankara

  I am constant as the northern star,
  Of whose true-fix'd and resting quality
  There is no fellow in the firmament.
  The skies are painted with unnumber'd sparks,
  They are all fire and everyone doth shine,
  But there's but one in all doth hold his place:
  So, in the world; 'tis furnish'd well with men,
  And men are flesh and blood, and apprehensive;
  Yet in the number I do know but one
  That unassailable holds on his rank,
  Unshak'd of motion: and that I am he.

    —William Shakespeare

I am neither the actor, nor the causer of acts; I am neither he who enjoys, nor he who brings enjoyment; I am neither the seer, nor he who gives sight; I am the unequaled Self, self-luminous.

    —Shankara

There is but one Being Who is really Existent, Who is Truth and Consciousness Himself, and of the nature of calm and pure Intelligence. He is immaculate, all-pervading quiescent and without rise or fall.

    —*Yoga-Vasishtha*

Say, then, from the heart that you are the perfect day, and in you dwells the light that does not fail....For you are the understanding that is drawn forth....Be concerned with yourselves; do not be concerned with other things which you have rejected from yourselves.

    —*The Gospel of Truth*

The Atman is ever free. Those who know the Atman as the ruler of the body, senses, mind and intellect, become fearless, and are free from all bondage. They know that the body alone is subject to birth and death, and that the Atman is ever free and immortal. No grief can overcome them, for they are united with Me in love.

    —*Srimad Bhagavatam*

As the sun, the eye of the world, is not touched by the impurity it looks upon, so the Self, though one, animating all things, is not moved by human misery but stands outside.

    —*Katha Upanishad*

They call this spirit (Atman), the immortal Brahman, the "Convent of the Beautiful," because all things beautiful "convene" in it. In one who understands this, likewise, all things beautiful convene. And it is also "Beauty-bringer," because it brings all beautiful things. And it is also "Light-bringer" because it illuminates all the worlds. He who understands it likewise illuminates all the worlds.

    —*Chandogya Upanishad*

The Atman — the experiencer — is pure consciousness. It appears to take on the changing colors of the mind. In reality, it is unchangeable.

    —Patanjali

The intelligent Self is neither born nor does It die. It did not originate from anything, nor did anything originate from It. It is birthless, eternal, undecaying, and ancient. It is not injured even when the body is killed.

    —*Katha Upanishad*

The Atman is the reality. It is your true, primal self. It is pure consciousness, the one without a second, absolute bliss. It is beyond form and action. Realize your identity with it. Stop identifying yourself with the coverings of ignorance, which are like the masks assumed by an actor.
—Shankara

The Atman, when it identifies itself with nature, forgets that it is pure and infinite. The Atman does not love, it is love itself. It does not exist, it is existence itself. The Atman does not know, it is knowledge itself....Love, existence, and knowledge are not the qualities of Atman, but its essence.
—Swami Prabhavananda and Christopher Isherwood

The Atman is supreme, eternal indivisible, pure consciousness, one without a second. It is the witness of the mind, intellect, and other faculties....It is the inner Being, the uttermost, everlasting joy.
—Shankara

All things
are too small
to hold me,
I am so vast

In the Infinite
I reach
for the Uncreated

I have
touched it,
it undoes me
wider than wide

Everything else
is too narrow

You know this well,
you who are also there
—Hadewijch II

In yourself is the law of all nature...in yourself slumbers the whole of Reason; it is for you to know all; it is for you to dare all.
—Ralph Waldo Emerson

Thy Self is thy true teacher. Verily by the Self alone is realized the highest good, first through reason, and then through direct transcendental perception.

—*Srimad Bhagavatam*

Whatever consists of component parts is not the real self.
It is wisdom to know this.
This knowledge destroys grief and leads to liberation.

—*Dhammapada*

Queen Chudala speaks: "I cannot be the body, because it is inert, while I am conscious.
"The body moves by the power of senses. I am not the senses, as they are not self-conscious. Neither the mind which moves the senses, nor the discriminative faculty is self-conscious. I must therefore, by reason of my self-consciousness, be different from them.
"The ego is not my Self, because it is lit by the light of the mind. The mind has no permanent consciousness, while I, as Atman, am Consciousness Itself. My Self is Truth, it is a sun that is my Self! It is Bliss Absolute. I have found my true state which is indestructible and infinite."

—*Yoga-Vasishtha*

This Self is not attained through study, nor through the intellect, nor through much hearing. By the very fact that he (the aspirant) seeks for It, does It become attainable; of him this Self reveals Its own Nature.

—*Mandukya Upanishad*

I am without attributes, actionless, eternal, ever free, and indestructible; I am not the body which is ever changing and unreal. This the wise call knowledge.

—*Shankara*

The spiritual nature of man does not exist potentially but actually. The discovery of his own identity is simply man's destruction of the hypnotic illusions of Ego, Time, Space, Matter, and Cause — his moment of release from untruth.

The Overself is not subject to causality, but the ideas which appear to arise in it are.

We must not ascribe activity to the Overself. This does not mean that it is wrapped in everlasting slumber. The possibility of all activity is derived from it. It is the life behind the Cosmic Mind's own life.

—Paul Brunton

This Self is our self-existent being. It is not limited by our personal existence. It is the same in all existences pervasive, equal to all things, supporting the whole universal action with its infinity, but unlimited by all that is finite, unmodified by the changings of Nature and personality. When this Self is revealed within us, when we feel its peace and stillness, we can grow into that; we can transfer the pose of our soul from its lower immergence in Nature and draw it back into the Self.

    —Sri Aurobindo

It is not for the sake of the wife that the wife is dear, but for the sake of the Self. It is not for the sake of the husband that the husband is dear, but for the sake of the Self. It is not for the sake of the children that the children are dear, but for the sake of the Self....It is not for the sake of itself that anything whatever is esteemed, but for the sake of the Self.

    —*Brihadarayaka Upanishad*

The Supreme Self, on account of Its being of the nature of exceeding Bliss, does not admit of the distinction of the knower, knowledge, and the object of knowledge. It alone shines.

    —Shankara

Learn to look with an equal eye upon all beings, seeing the one Self in all.

    —*Srimad Bhagavatam*

We are in the sun and in the stars as much as here. Spirit is beyond space and time, and is everywhere. Every mouth praising the Lord is my mouth; every eye seeing is my eye. We are confined nowhere. We are not the body; the universe is our body. We are magicians waving magic wands and creating scenes before us at will.

    —Swami Vivekananda

Afar down I see the huge first Nothing,
    I know I was even there,
I waited unseen and always, and slept through
    the lethargic mist,
and took my time, and took no hurt from
    the fetid carbon.
Long I was hugg'd close — long and long.
Immense have been the preparations for me,
Faithful and friendly the arms that have help'd me.
    —Walt Whitman

The goodness which one man may express in his relation to another is derived ultimately from his own divine soul and is an unconscious recognition of, as well as gesture to, the same divine presence in that other. Moreover, the degree to which anyone becomes conscious of his true self is the degree to which he becomes conscious of it in others. Consequently, the goodness of the fully illumined man is immeasurable beyond that of the conventionally moral man.

— Paul Brunton

Both the individual self and the universal Self, the Atman, have entered the cave of the heart, the supreme abode of the Most High. Of these the former enjoys the pleasures within the realm of the body. The knower of Brahman, together with the householders who observe the fire sacrifices, sees a difference between them as between the darkness and the light.

Of the two selves — the illusory or individual self, of which all are aware, and the real Self, which few know — it is as unchangeable being that the real Self is first recognized. He who has recognized it as unchangeable being — to him will be revealed its innermost nature.

— *Katha Upanishad*

The Impersonal Being, our highest generalization, is in ourselves and we are That....You are that Impersonal Being; that God for whom you searched all over the universe has been all the time you yourself — yourself not in the personal sense but in the impersonal. The man we know now, the manifested, is personalized, but the reality in him is the Impersonal. To understand the personal we have to refer it to the Impersonal; the particular must be referred to the general. And that Impersonal is the true Self of man.

— Swami Vivekananda

The Absolute Being is *what is* — it is the Self. It is God. Knowing the Self, God is known. In fact, God is none other than the Self.... There are neither good nor bad qualities in the Self. The Self is free from all qualities. Qualities pertain to the mind only. It is beyond quality. If there is unity, there will also be duality. The numerical one gives rise to other numbers. The truth is neither one nor two. It is as it is.

— Sri Ramana Maharshi

Self-reliance, the height and perfection of man, is reliance on God.

— Ralph Waldo Emerson

Thou art not the body, nor does the body belong to thee, nor art thou the doer nor the enjoyer. Thou art Intelligence Itself, ever the Witness and free art thou! Live in bliss!

  —Ashtavakra Gita

The Self, which is in fact the Lord and which is called *purusha* because it abides in the body, is different from the physical and subtle bodies. I am that spirit. I am the self of all. I am all, imperishable and beyond all.

  —Shankara

Honor what is best in the universe; this is what controls all things and directs all things. In like manner, honor also what is best in yourself; and this is akin to the other. For in yourself also, it is that which controls everything else, and your life is directed by it.

  —Marcus Aurelius

Rid yourself of all sense of particulars and you will have a knowledge of universality: you will begin to comprehend the all-embracing Atman.

Only when one endeavors to know the supreme Spirit with all one's heart and soul, and sacrifices all other aims and objects to that end, does it become possible to know that Spirit in Its fullness. All visible objects which appear to be linked by the thread of causes and their effects are the creation of the mind, which holds them together as a string holds the pearls of a necklace. That which remains after the dissolution of the mind and its created bodies is the Atman alone, and that is the Supreme God, the All-Highest....

The cause of human happiness and misery is a false representation of the understanding. This world is a stage stretched out by the mind, its chief actor, and Atman sits silent as a spectator of the scene.

  —Yoga-Vasishtha

The individual actually sits in the lap of the universal, but the trouble is that the individual, in spite of such close proximity, possesses an external outlook and worries about those external layers of manifested nature. If the individual could turn his eyes inwards through meditation, then he would see where he is, namely in the very lap of the Universal Self.

  —H.H. Shantanand Saraswati

8
THE SOUL AND THE PSYCHE

The soul is an eye into the abyss of the Eternal.
   —Jacob Boehme

Every human soul has, by reason of her nature, had contemplation of true being; else would she never have entered into this human creature.
   —Plato

The Soul, having an intermediate existence, also fills the gap between reason and irrationality. With the highest part of herself she consorts with Reason; with the lowest, she declines towards Sensation.
   —Proclus

All goes to show that the soul in man is not an organ but animates and exercises all the organs; is not a function, like the power of memory, of calculation, of comparison, but uses these as hand and feet; is not a faculty, but a light; is not the intellect or the will, but the master of the intellect and the will; is the background of our being, in which they lie, an immensity not possessed and that cannot be possessed. From within or from behind, a light shines through us upon things and makes us aware that we are nothing, but the light is all.
   —Ralph Waldo Emerson

The soul lives by that which it loves rather than in the body which it animates. For it has not its life in the body, but rather gives it to the body and lives in that which it loves.
   —St. John of the Cross

I want you to understand that all the events of Christ's life, birth, childhood, teaching, crucifixion, resurrection, and ascension take place in the soul.
   —Meister Eckhart

The Soul once turned toward matter, she became enamored of it, and burning with the desire to experience the pleasures of the body, she no longer wanted to disengage herself from it. Thus the world was born. From that moment the Soul forgot herself. She forgot her original habitation, her true center, her eternal being. God, always concerned to turn everything to the best, joined her to Matter, of which he saw her so enamored, distributing in it a multitude of forms. Hence came about the composite creatures—the heaven, the elements.... But unwilling to leave the Soul in her degradation with Matter, God endowed her with an intelligence and the faculty of perceiving, precious gifts which were intended to recall to her high origin in the spiritual world,...to restore to her the knowledge of herself, to indicate to her that she was a stranger down here.... Since the Soul received this instruction through perception and intelligence, since she recovered the knowledge of herself, she desires the spiritual world.... She is convinced that in order to return to her original condition she must disengage herself from the worldly bonds, from sensual desires, from all material things.

    —El Chatibi of the Harranites

L et every soul, then, first consider this, that it made all living things itself, breathing life into them, those that the earth feeds and those that are nourished by the sea, and the divine stars in the sky; it made the sun itself, and this great heaven, and adorned it itself, and drives it round itself, in orderly movement; it is a nature other than the things which it adorns and moves and makes live; and it must necessarily be more honorable than they, for they come into being or pass away when the soul leaves them or grants life to them, but soul itself exists for ever because "it does not depart from itself."...For soul has given itself to the whole magnitude of heaven, as far as it extends, and every stretch of space, both great and small, is ensouled; one body lies in one place and one in another, and one is here and another there; some are separated by being in opposite parts of the universe, and others in other ways. But soul is not like this and it is not by being cut up that it gives life, by a part of itself for each individual thing, but all things live by the whole, and all soul is present everywhere, made like to the father who begat it in its unity and its universality.

    —Plotinus

As long as the soul seeks an external God, it never can have peace, it always must be uncertain what may be done and what may become of it. But when it sees the Great God far within its own nature, then it sees that always itself is a party to all that can be, that always it will be informed of that which will happen and therefore it is pervaded with a great Peace.

    —Ralph Waldo Emerson

There is an agent in my soul which is perfectly sensitive to God. I am as sure of this as I am that I am alive: Nothing is as near to me as God is. God is nearer to me than I am to myself. My being depends on God's intimate presence....Man is not blessed because God is in him and so near that he *has God*—but in that he is aware of how near God is, and knowing God, he loves him.

— Meister Eckhart

Before the soul enters the air of this world, it is conducted through all the worlds. Last of all, it is shown the first light which once—when the world was created—illuminated all things.... So that, from that hour on, it may yearn to attain the light, and approach it rung by rung in its life on earth. And those who reach it, the *zaddikim*— into them the light enters, and out of them it shines into the world again.

— *Ten Rungs: Hasidic Sayings*

Neither you nor I nor anyone present has come out of zero, nor will go back to zero. We have been existing eternally, and will exist, and there is no power under the sun, or above the sun, which can undo your or my existence or send us back to zero. Now this idea of reincarnation is not only not a frightening idea, but most essential for the moral well-being of the human race. It is the only logical conclusion that thoughtful men can arrive at. If you are going to exist in eternity hereafter, it must be that you have existed through eternity in the past; it cannot be otherwise.

— Swami Vivekananda

Jesus said: Don't be afraid of those who can kill the body, but can't kill the soul.

— *The Book of Q*

But both in the intellect and in the will reason stands forth as the loud sound of the soul, which makes known every work of God or Man. For sound carries words on high, as the wind lifts the eagle so that it can fly. Thus the soul utters the sound of reason in the hearing and the understanding of humanity, that its powers may be understood and its every work brought to perfection.

— Hildegard of Bingen

The soul,
Forever and forever—longer than soil is brown and solid—longer than
   water ebbs and flows.
— Walt Whitman

When the soul is pure and at peace, then the soul is the virgin and in the virgin soul Christ, the Son, the light of consciousness, will be born.
—Meister Eckhart

Within the soul three powers exist: understanding (*comprehensio*) by which the soul grasps heavenly and earthly things through the power of God; insight (*intelligentia*) by which the soul has the greatest insight when it recognizes the evil of sin, which the soul then causes to become detestable as a result of repentance; and finally, execution (*motio*) by which the soul moves into itself as it accomplishes holy works according to the example of just persons in their bodily abode.
—Hildegard of Bingen

The Soul should always stand ajar
That if the Heaven inquire
He will not be obliged to wait
Or shy of troubling Her

Depart, before the Host have slid
The Bolt unto the Door —
To search for the accomplished Guest,
Her Visitor, no more.
—Emily Dickinson

Let that part of your soul which leads and governs be undisturbed by motions of the flesh, whether of pleasure or of pain; let it not mingle with them, but let it set a wall around itself and keep those emotions in their place. But when the emotions rise up to the mind by virtue of the sympathy that naturally exists in body which is all one, then you must not strive to resist the feeling, for it is natural; but let not your ruling part add to the feeling the opinion that it is either good or bad.
—Marcus Aurelius

Come forward O my soul, and let the rest retire,
    Listen, lose not, it is toward thee they tend,
    Parting the midnight, entering my slumber-chamber,
    For thee they sing and dance O soul.
—Walt Whitman

Poor soul, the center of my sinful earth,
Fool'd by these rebel powers that thee array,
Why dost thou pine within and suffer dearth,
Painting thy outward walls so costly gay?
Why so large cost, having so short a lease,
Dost thou upon thy fading mansion spend?
Shall worms, inheritors of this excess,
Eat up thy charge? Is this thy body's end?
Then, soul, live thou upon thy servant's loss,
And let that pine to aggravate thy store:
Buy terms divine in selling hours of dross;
Within be fed, without be rich no more:
    So shalt thou feed on Death, that feeds on men,
    And Death once dead, there's no more dying then.
—William Shakespeare

I believe in you my soul, the other I am must not abase itself to you,
    And you must not be abased to the other.
Loaf with me on the grass, loose the stop from your throat,
    Not words, not music or rhyme I want, not custom or lecture, not
    even the best,
    Only the lull I like, the hum of your valved voice.
—Walt Whitman

9
THE HUMAN FACULTIES

But in reality justice…is not a matter of external behavior, but of the inward self and of attending to all that is, in the fullest sense, a man's proper concern. The just man does not allow the several elements in his soul to usurp one another's functions; he is indeed one who sets his house in order, by self-mastery and discipline coming to be at peace with himself, and bringing into tune those three parts [physical, emotional, intellectual], like the terms in the proportion of a musical scale, the highest and lowest notes and the mean between them, with all the intermediate intervals. Only when he has linked these parts together in well-tempered harmony and has made himself one man instead of many, will he be ready to go about whatever he may have to do, whether it be making money and satisfying bodily wants, or business transactions, or the affairs of state. In all these fields when he speaks of just and honorable conduct, he will mean the behavior that helps to produce and to preserve this habit of mind; and by wisdom he will mean the knowledge which presides over such conduct. Any action which tends to break down this habit will be for him unjust; and the notions governing it he will call ignorance and folly.

—Plato

But a person has within himself three paths. What are they? The soul, the body, and the senses; and all human life is led in these. How? The soul vivifies the body and conveys the breath of life to the senses; the body draws the soul to itself and opens the senses; and the senses touch the soul and draw the body. For the soul gives life to the body as fire gives light to darkness, with two principal powers like two arms, intellect and will; the soul has arms not so as to move itself, but so as to show itself in these powers as the sun shows itself by its brilliance. Therefore, O human, who are not just a bundle of marrow, pay attention to scriptural knowledge!

—Hildegard of Bingen

Man is a triple alliance of matter, soul, and spirit. His physical body is made of matter. His soul is what is called psychic life—including the mind, the emotions and the ego. The real part of man is spirit. Which is eternal, immortal, all-pervasive, deathless and birthless. Spirit is limitless and one. The psychic life of man is a manifestation of the spirit through the medium of the soul.

—Sri Dada

Know the (individual) Self as the master of the chariot, and the body as the chariot. Know the intellect as the charioteer, and the mind as verily the bridle.

They call the senses the horses; the senses having been imagined as horses, (know) the objects as the ways. The discriminating people call that Self the enjoyer when It is associated with the body, senses, and mind.

But the senses of that intellect, which, being ever associated with an uncontrolled mind, becomes devoid of discrimination, are unruly like the vicious horses of the charioteer.

But he (that master of the chariot), does not attain that goal (through that intellect), who, being associated with a nondiscriminating intellect and an uncontrollable mind is ever impure; and he attains worldly existence.

That (master of the chariot), however, who is associated with a discriminating intellect, and being endowed with a controlled mind, is ever pure, attains that goal (getting detached) from which he is not born again.

The man, however, who has, as his charioteer a discriminating intellect, and who has under control the reins of the mind, attains the end of the road; and that is the highest place of Vishnu (the very nature of the all-pervading, supreme Self).
  —*Katha Upanishad*

A man contains all that is needful to his government within himself. He is made a law unto himself. All real good or evil that can befall him must be from himself.
  —Ralph Waldo Emerson

There are housed in us three distinct forms of soul, each having its own motions. Accordingly we may now say, very briefly, that any of these forms that lives in idleness and fails to exercise its own proper motions is bound to become very feeble, while any that exercises them will become very strong; hence we must take care that these motions are properly proportioned to each other. We should think of the most authoritative part of our soul as a guardian spirit given by god, living in the summit of the body, which can properly be said to lift us from the earth towards our home in heaven; for we are creatures not of earth but of heaven, where the soul was first born, and our divine part attaches us by the head to heaven, like a plant by its roots, and keeps our body upright. If therefore a man's attention and effort is centered on appetite and ambition...it is his mortal part that he has increased. But a man who has given his heart to learning and true wisdom and exercised that part of himself is surely bound if he attains to truth, to have immortal and divine thoughts, and cannot fail to achieve immortality as fully as is permitted to human nature; and because he has always looked after the divine element in himself and kept his guardian spirit in good order he must be happy above all men. There is of course only one way to look after anything and that is to give it its proper food and motions. And the motions in us that are akin to the divine are thoughts and revolutions of the universe. We should each therefore attend to these motions and by learning about the harmonious circuits of the universe repair the damage done at birth to the circuits in our head, and so restore understanding and what is understood to their original likeness to each other. When that is done we shall have achieved the goal set us by the gods, the life that is best for this present time and for all time to come.
  —Plato

Though God is everywhere present, yet He is only present to thee in the deepest and most central part of thy soul. The natural senses cannot possess God or unite thee to him; nay, thy inward faculties of understanding will and memory can only reach after God, but cannot be the place of his habitation in thee. But there is a root or depth of thee from whence all these faculties come forth, as lines from a center, or as branches from the body of the tree. This depth is called the center, the fund or bottom of the soul. This depth is the unity, the eternity—I had almost said the infinity—of thy soul; for it is so infinite that nothing can satisfy it or give it rest but the infinity of God.

 —William Law

It is the senses on which the interior powers of the soul depend, so that these powers are known through them by the fruits of each work. The senses are subject to these powers, since they guide them to the work, but the senses do not impose work on the powers, for they are their shadow and do what pleases them....

 For the soul emanates the senses. How? It vivifies a person's face and glorifies him with sight, hearing, taste, smell, and touch so that by this touch he becomes watchful in all things. For the senses are the sign of all the powers of the soul, as the body is the vessel of the soul.

 —Hildegard of Bingen

The soul is nourished by the ceaseless movement of fire and air, the higher elements; the growth of bodies is supplied from water and earth, the lower elements. Mind, a fifth component part, which comes from the aether, has been bestowed on man alone; and of all beings that have soul, man is the only one whose faculty of cognition is, by this gift of mind, so strengthened, elevated, and exalted, that he can attain to knowledge of the truth concerning God.

 —Hermes Trismegistus

The sun of the spiritual world is pure love from Jehovah God, who is at its center.
Warmth and light go forth from that sun, essence of the outgoing warmth being love
 and the essence of the outgoing light being wisdom.
Both that warmth and that light flow into human beings, the warmth into our intent,
 producing the good of love, and the light into our discernment, producing the
 truth of wisdom.
These two elements flow united into our souls, through them into our minds, our
 affections, and our thoughts, and from these into our physical senses, words,
 and deeds....
The mind is in fact subject to the soul, and the body subject to the mind. Further, there
 are two lives to the mind, one involving intentionality and one involving discernment. The life of the mind's intentionality is the good of love, and its offshoots
 are called affections. The life of its discernment is the truth of wisdom, and its
 offshoots are called thoughts.

 —Emanuel Swedenborg

The symmetry of the elements is related to the symmetry extending from the top of our head forward to the eyebrows, sideways to the ears, and backward to the beginning of the neck. In this way, three basic powers are present in the soul to the same degree: spiritualization (*expiratio*), knowledge (*scientia*), and sensation (*sensus*). The souls fulfills its functions by means of these three powers. By spiritualization, the soul undertakes whatever it can carry out, and this points to the anterior part of the head. By knowledge, the soul divides itself, so to speak, on two sides as far as the ears. And by sensation, the soul turns backward to a certain extent as far as the beginning of the neck. And these three powers ought to be symmetrical throughout, since the soul does not begin to achieve by spiritualization more than knowledge can grasp or sensation carry out. And thus these powers work in harmony since none of them exceeds another, just as our head too has its proper symmetry.

—Hildegard of Bingen

Within this earthen vessel are bowers and groves, and
    within it is the Creator:
Within this vessel are the seven oceans and the
    Unnumbered stars.
The touchstone and the jewel-appraiser are within;
And within this vessel the Eternal soundeth, and
    The spring wells up
Kabir says: "Listen to me, my Friend!
    My beloved Lord is within."
—Kabir

In the Kingdom of Heaven are the springs of doing and knowing that rise from Spirit itself; beyond spreads the lake of joy; beyond that blossoms the tree of immortality; beyond that lies the town of spirit, full of light built by the Lord.

    —*Chandogya Upanishad*

But the body cannot be the soul's efficient cause, for body, as such, does not act; it acts only through its faculties. If it were to act through its essence, not through its faculties, every body would act in the same way.... Nor is it possible that the body should be the receptive and material cause of the soul, for: the soul is in no way imprinted in the body....

Thus the attachment of the soul to the body is not the attachment of an effect to a necessary cause. The truth is that the body and the temperament are an accidental cause of the soul, for when the matter of a body suitable to become the instrument of the soul and its proper subject comes into existence, the separate causes bring into being the individual soul, and that is how the soul originates from them.

    —Avicenna

Here, within this body, in pure mind, in the secret chamber of intelligence, in the infinite universe within the heart, the Atman shines in its captivating splendor, like a noonday sun. By its light, the universe is revealed.

—Shankara

There is one inflow that occurs from the human mind into words, and another that occurs into deeds. The inflow into words comes from intentionality through discernment, while the inflow that occurs into deeds comes from discernment through intentionality.

—Emanuel Swedenborg

The intellect...as it expresses itself in speech, has three powers; the sound, the word, and the breath. The son exists in the Father like the word in the sound. The Holy Spirit is in both, like the breath in the sound and in the word. And these three persons are, as stated, one God. Eternity lives in the Father because no one existed before Him and because eternity has no beginning, just as the works of God have no beginning. Equality lives in the Son, because the Son never separates himself from the Divine, nor did the Divine exist without the Son. The union of these two lives in the Holy spirit, because the Son always remained with the Father and the Father with the Son. For the Holy Spirit is a fiery life in them and they are one.

—Hildegard of Bingen

True philosophy is the systematizing of certain perceptions. Intellect ends where religion begins. Inspiration is much higher than reason, but it must not contradict it. Reason is the rough tool to do the hard work; inspiration is the bright light which shows us all truth.

—Swami Vivekananda

Where wisdom abounds, there is very little work for dice. Where there is very little wisdom, chance dominates most things...if reason ruled, chance would lose her glory and her power.

—Marsilio Ficino

When we discern justice, when we discern truth, we do nothing of ourselves, but allow a passage to its beams. If we ask whence this comes, if we seek to pry into the soul that causes, all philosophy is at fault. Its presence or its absence is all we can affirm. Every man discriminates between the voluntary acts of his mind and his involuntary perceptions, and knows that to his involuntary perceptions a perfect faith is due. He may err in the expression of them, but he knows that these things are so, like day and night, not to be disputed.

—Ralph Waldo Emerson

In speaking of "mind," however, it must be remembered that the traditional dicta always presuppose the distinction of "two minds," the one "apathetic" (i.e., independent of pleasure-pain motivation), the other "pathetic" (i.e., subject to appetitive persuasion); it is only the First Mind (in Scholastic philosophy, *intellectus vel spiritus*) that, just because it is disinterested, can judge of the extent to which an appetite (instinct) should be indulged, if the subject's real good, and not merely immediate pleasure, is to be served.

—Ananda K. Coomaraswamy

The intellect that peers into and penetrates all the corners of the Godhead sees the Son in the Father's heart and puts him [the son] at its own core. Intellect that presses on that far is not content with goodness, nor with wisdom, nor the truth, no nor even with god himself. To tell the truth, it is no more content with [the idea of] God that it would be with a stone or a tree. It can never rest until it gets to the core of the matter, crashing through to that which is beyond the idea of God and truth, until it reaches the *in principio,* the beginning of beginnings, the origin or source of all goodness and truth.

—Meister Eckhart

So what is the relationship of the unknown to the known? What is the relationship between the measurable and that which is not measurable? There must be a liaison: and that is intelligence. Intelligence has nothing whatsoever to do with thought. You may be very clever, very good at arguing, very learned. You may have experienced, lived a tremendous life, been all over the world, investigating, searching, looking, accumulating a great deal of knowledge.... But all that has nothing whatsoever to do with intelligence. Intelligence comes into being when the mind, the heart, and the body are really harmonious....

The body must be highly sensitive. Not gross, not overindulging in eating, drinking, sex, and all the rest that makes the body coarse, dull, heavy....If there is an awareness of the body, which is not being forced, then the body becomes very, very sensitive, like a beautiful instrument. The same with the heart; that is, it is never hurt and can never hurt another. Not to hurt and not to be hurt, that is the innocency of the heart. A mind which has no fear, which demands no pleasure—not that you cannot enjoy the beauty of life, the beauty of trees, of a beautiful face, looking at children, at the flow of water, at the mountains and the green pastures—there is great delight in that. But that delight, when pursued by thought, becomes pleasure. The mind has to be empty to see clearly. So the relationship between the immeasurable, the unknown and the known, is this intelligence....

That intelligence will operate in this world morally. Morality then is order, which is virtue. Not the virtue or the morality of society, which is totally immoral.

So that intelligence brings about order, which is virtue, a thing that is living, that is not mechanical. Therefore you can never practice being good, you can never practice trying to become humble. When there is that intelligence, it naturally brings about order and the beauty of order. This is a religious life, not all the fooling around with it.

—Jiddu Krishnamurti

It is the nature of the mind to become restless and unsteady at times. But we must not allow ourselves to be unsettled or upset by this. When the mind is restrained, such occasional reactions will strengthen rather than weaken it.
—Swami Shivananda

Like an archer an arrow,
the wise man steadies his trembling mind,
a fickle and restless weapon.
—*Dhammapada*

All music is what wakes in you when you are reminded of it
    by the instruments,
It is not in the violins and the cornets...nor the score of
    the baritone singer,
It is nearer and further than they.
—Walt Whitman

Now my five senses
gather into a meaning
all acts, all presences;
and as a lily gathers
the elements together,
in me this dark and shining,
that stillness and that moving,
these shapes that spring from nothing,
become a rhythm that dances,
a pure design.

While I'm in my five senses
they send me spinning
all sounds and silences
all shape and colour,
as thread for that weaver,
whose web within me growing
follows beyond my knowing
some pattern sprung from nothing—
a rhythm that dances and is not mine.
—Judith Wright

The mind is one; and the best minds who love truth for its own sake, think much less of property in truth. They accept it thankfully everywhere, and do not label or stamp it with any man's name, for it is theirs long beforehand, and from eternity.
—Ralph Waldo Emerson

O, believe, as thou livest, that every sound that is spoken over the round world, which thou oughtest to hear, will vibrate on thine ear! Every proverb, every book, every byword that belongs to thee for aid or comfort, shall surely come home through open or winding passages.

 —Ralph Waldo Emerson

But know that this physical body wherein the whole circling life of the Spirit adheres, is but as the dwelling of the lord of the dwelling.

 —Shankara

Every man is the builder of a temple, called his body, to the God he worships, after a style purely his own, nor can he get off by hammering marble instead. We are all sculptors and painters, and our material is our own flesh and blood and bones. Any nobleness begins at once to refine man's features, any meanness or sensuality to imbrute them.

 —Henry David Thoreau

The affirmation of a divine life upon earth and an immortal sense in mortal existence can have no base unless we recognize not only eternal spirit as the inhabitant of this bodily mansion, the wearer of this mutable robe, but accept matter of which it is made, as a fit and noble material out of which he weaves constantly his garbs, builds recurrently the unending series of his mansions.

 —Sri Aurobindo

Such as are your constant thoughts, such will be the character of your mind; for the soul is colored by the thoughts.

 —Marcus Aurelius

Whatever a man thinks of steadfastly and with unshakable conviction, that he soon becomes.

 —Shankara

Cheerfulness is joy, which, in so far as it is related to the body, consists in this, that all the parts of the body are equally affected, that is to say, the body's power of action is increased or assisted, so that all the parts acquire the same proportion of motion and rest to each other. Cheerfulness, therefore, is always good, and can never be excessive.

 —Baruch Spinoza

When positive or joyous feelings and attitudes pass through each organ and circulate throughout our whole system, our physical and chemical energies are transformed and balanced.

 —Tarthang Tulku

10
ILLUSION; MAYA

Maya, in her potential aspect, is the divine power of the Lord. She has no beginning. She is composed of the three *gunas*, subtle, beyond perception. It is from the effects she produces that her existence is inferred by the wise. It is she who gives birth to the whole universe.

She is neither being nor non-being, nor a mixture of both. She is neither divided nor undivided, nor a mixture of both. She is neither an indivisible whole, nor composed of parts, nor a mixture of both. She is most strange. Her nature is inexplicable.

—Shankara

When I consider every thing that grows
Holds in perfection but a little moment,
That this huge stage presenteth nought but shows
Whereon the stars in secret influence comment.
—William Shakespeare

The world is a great show, which God is staging around you in the shape of the universe. But it is a mere show. Your birth is a show, your death is a show. Actually there is neither birth nor death. Know that, and you will be happy.

—H.H. Shantanand Saraswati

All life is the play of universal forces. The individual gives a personal form to these universal forces. But he can choose whether he shall respond or not to the action of a particular force. Only most people do not really choose—they indulge the play of the forces. Your illnesses, depressions, etc. are the repeated play of such forces. It is only when one can make oneself free of them that one can be the true person and have a true life—but one can be free only by living in the Divine.

—Sri Aurobindo

God has created the world in play, as it were. This is called Maha-Maya, the Great Illusion. Therefore one must take refuge in the Divine Mother, the Cosmic Power Itself. It is She who has bound us with the shackles of illusion. The realization of God is possible only when those shackles are severed.

—Sri Ramakrishna

The world has no being except as an appearance;
From end to end its state is a sport and a play.

—Shabistari

The world is no more than a creation of our imagination, as boys imagine a goblin to be hidden in the dark. Our knowledge of objects is as deceptive as the appearance of movement in a mountain to a passenger in a boat. All appearances are a manifestation of error or ignorance, and disappear when right knowledge is acquired.

—*Yoga-Vasishtha*

This world, when ascertained from the standpoint of the Self, does not continue to be different. Nor does it exist in its own right. Nor do phenomenal things exist as different or non-different (from one another or from the Self). This is what the knowers of Truth understand.

—*Mandukya Karika*

What is your substance, whereof are you made,
That millions of strange shadows on you tend?
Since every one hath, every one, one shade,
And you, but one can every shadow lend.
Describe Adonis, and the counterfeit
Is poorly imitated after you;
On Helen's cheek all art of beauty set,
And you in Grecian tires are painted new:
Speak of the spring and foison of the year,
The one doth shadow of your beauty show,
The other as your bounty doth appear;
And you in every blessed shape we know.
In all external grace you have some part,
But you like none, none you, for constant heart.

—William Shakespeare

The internal universe, the real, is infinitely greater than the external, which is only a shadowy projection of the true one. This world is neither true nor untrue; it is the shadow of truth. It is imagination—the gilded shadow of truth—says the poet.
—Swami Vivekananda

Say:
"The world is a bubble, the world is a shadow."
The King of death is helpless in the face of this wisdom.
—*Dhammapada*

The supreme Spirit, unlimited by time and space, of His own will and by the power of His omnipotence, takes upon Himself the limited forms of time and space. Know that the world, although appearing as substantial, has nothing substantial in it: it is a void, being merely an appearance created by the images and vagaries of the mind. Know the world to be an enchanted scene, presented by the magic of *maya*.
—*Yoga-Vasishtha*

Being is not what it seems,
nor nonbeing. The world's
existence is not
in the world.
—Rumi

Look at it—this painted shadow,
this body, crumbling, diseased, wounded,
held together by thoughts that come and go.
—*Dhammapada*

Time is what keeps the light from reaching us. There is no greater obstacle to God than time. And not only time but temporalities, not only temporal things but temporal affections; not only temporal affections but the very taint and smell of time.
—Meister Eckhart

We loosely talk of Self-realization, for lack of a better term. But how can one realize or make real that which alone is real? All we need to do is to give up our habit of regarding as real that which is unreal. All religious practices are meant solely to help us do this. When we stop regarding the unreal as real, then reality alone will remain, and we will be that.

—Sri Ramana Maharshi

Man is divine. He is, in reality, the impersonal Truth. His essential nature is pure consciousness. Bound by *maya,* he ignorantly thinks of himself as the gross human form.

—*Srimad Bhagavatam*

Return to your sober senses and recall yourself. When you have roused yourself from sleep and perceived that they were only dreams which troubled you, then in your waking hours look at the things about you as you looked at the dreams.

—Marcus Aurelius

Jesus said: You read the face of the sky and of the earth, but you have not recognized the one who is before you, and you do not know how to read this moment.

—*The Gospel of Thomas*

Past and future veil God from our sight;
Burn up both of them with fire. How long
Wilt thou be partitioned by these segments, like a reed?
So long as a reed is partitioned, it is not privy to secrets,
Nor is it vocal in response to lip and breathing.

—Rumi

Two points should be clearly understood. First, the world of external Nature, being eternal, is not brought into existence by an act of sudden creation out of nothing. Second, this world is rooted in the divine substance and is consequently not an empty illusion but an indirect manifestation of divine reality.

—Paul Brunton

That which is neither in the beginning, nor in the end, but only in the middle, exists only in appearance. It is a mere name and form.

—*Srimad Bhagavatam*

Jesus said: But the Kingdom of the Father is spread upon the earth and men do not see it.

—*The Gospel of Thomas*

Magic is the formative power in the eternal wisdom...a mother in all three worlds, and makes each thing after the model of that thing's will. It is not the understanding, but a creatrix according to the understanding.

—Jacob Boehme

Our revels now are ended. These our actors,
As I foretold you, were all spirits, and
Are melted into air, into thin air:
And, like the baseless fabric of this vision,
The cloud-capp'd towers, the gorgeous palaces,
The solemn temples, the great globe itself,
Yea, all which it inherit, shall dissolve
And, like this insubstantial pageant faded,
Leave not a rack behind. We are such stuff
As dreams are made on, and our little life
Is rounded with a sleep.

—William Shakespeare

11
IGNORANCE, SUFFERING, AND THE EGO

All worldly objects are like children's toys…. They must be treated as nothing more than toys. Disappointments and trouble will be our lot if we treat them as real.
   —H. H. Shantanand Saraswati

And the vice of the soul is lack of knowledge. A soul that has gained no knowledge of the things that are, and not come to know their nature, nor to know the God, but is blind—such a soul is tossed about among the passions which the body breeds; it carries the body as a burden, and is ruled by it, instead of ruling it. That is the vice of the soul. On the other hand, the virtue of the soul is knowledge. He who has got knowledge is good and pious; he is already divine…Knowledge differs greatly from sense-perception. Sense-perception takes place when that which is material has the mastery; and it uses the body as its organ, for it cannot exist apart from the body. But knowledge is incorporeal; the organ which it uses is the mind itself; and the mind is contrary to the body.
   —Hermes Trismegistus

If the man is a stranger to the universe who does not know what is in it, no less is he a stranger who does not know what is going on in it. He is a runaway, who flies from the concerns of society; he is blind, who shuts the eyes of his understanding; he is poor, who has need of another, and finds not in himself all things helpful for life. He is a sore on the universe who withdraws and separates himself from the reason of our common nature and is displeased with the things that happen; for the same nature that produces them has produced you too. He is a social outcast who cuts his own soul off from the one common soul of all reasonable beings.
   —Marcus Aurelius

Man is pure spirit, free from attachment. The mind deludes him. It binds him with the bonds of the body, the sense-organs, and the life-breath. It creates in him the sense of "I" and "mine." It makes him wander endlessly among the fruits of the actions it has caused.
   —Shankara

The foolish do not search for wisdom or try to become wise either, since folly is precisely the failing which consists in not being fine and good, or intelligent—and yet being quite satisfied with the way one is. You cannot desire what you do not realize you lack.
   —Plato

Ignorance…brought about anguish and terror. And the anguish grew solid like a fog, so that no one was able to see.

—*The Gospel of Truth*

Thus the earth arose from her confusion, water from her terror; air from the consolidation of her grief; while fire…was inherent in all these elements…as ignorance lay concealed in these three sufferings.

—Irenaeus

The recurring desire to enjoy what has been enjoyed, and to see what has been seen, is not the way to be rid of the world, but is the cause of many births for the sake of the same enjoyments.

—*Yoga-Vasishtha*

The Self is separated from the Creator only by ignorance. This is why we have limits or boundaries. We possess and we claim; this is all ignorance. The Absolute created the universe and we create boundaries—"This is my land, this is my country." In fact the land belongs to no one. You can claim it for a time, but in the end you have to leave everything behind. The Creator creates men; we create the "Indian" and the "English." The creation is consciousness, but we do not see this because of our ignorance.

—H.H. Shantanand Saraswati

This indecent clinging to life as we know it here is the source of all evil. It causes all this cheating and stealing. It makes money a god, and all vices and fears ensue. Value nothing material and do not cling to anything. If you cling to nothing, not even to life, then there will be no fear.

—Swami Vivekananda

The fear of death haunts the mind of even the bravest of people. Everybody, whether great or small, learned or ignorant, fears death, but in fact there is no such thing as death. So-called "death" is nothing but a natural corollary of the phenomenon of birth. The only way to avoid death is to avoid being born. It is not possible to be born and not die.

Actually, the individual Self, living in the body, is immortal. It gives up an old body in order to put on a new body, just as we give up our old clothes and put on new ones. If we are happy to discard an old garment and put on a new one, there is no reason to be unhappy when the self discards an old body and adopts a new one….

We fear death because, under the influence of ignorance, we have forgotten our real Selves. And it is this forgetting of the divine Self which makes all our troubles for us. It is not God who is the maker of our troubles.

—H.H. Shantanand Saraswati

Man, proud man, drest in a little brief authority —
Most ignorant of what he's most assured,
His glassy essence—like an angry ape,
Plays such fantastic tricks before high heaven
As make the angels weep.
—William Shakespeare

This is the great absurdity: that people live without faith and in an inhumanly horizontal manner, in a world where all that nature offers testifies to the supernatural, to the hereafter, to the divine; to eternal spring.
—Frithjof Schuon

The world is burning;
why is there laughter, why the sounds of joy?
Seek enlightenment, O fool,
for the darkness surrounds you.
—*Dhammapada*

Your medicine is in you, and you do not observe it.
Your ailment is from yourself, and you do not register it.
—Hazrat Ali

It is mind which gives to things their quality, their foundation and their being. Whoever speaks or acts with impure mind, him sorrow follows, as the wheel follows the steps of the ox that draws the cart.
—*Dhammapada*

To God all things are beautiful, good, and just, but human beings have supposed some things to be unjust, others just.
—Heraclitus

It is the perception of duality due to ignorance which produces the feeling of separateness. Multiplicity is swept away when all is seen to be of the nature of the Self.
—Shankara

Man is the dwarf of himself. Once he was permeated and dissolved by spirit. He filled nature with his overflowing currents.
—Ralph Waldo Emerson

Eyes and ears are bad witnesses, especially if we have souls that do not understand their language.
—Heraclitus

As with someone's ignorance, when he comes to have knowledge, his ignorance vanishes by itself; as the darkness vanishes when light appears, so also the deficiency vanishes in the fulfillment.
—*The Gospel of Truth*

Curiosity, ambition, anxiety, an unawareness or forgetfulness of why we are in this world—those are what fill our lives with many more difficulties than duties, much more worry than work, a great deal more bother than business. Foolish, empty, unnecessary pursuits which distract us from the love of God—these are the things that get in our way, not the genuine and proper duties of our state in life.
—St. Francis de Sales

The mass of men lead lives of quiet desperation. What is called resignation is confirmed desperation. From the desperate city you go into the desperate country, and have to console yourself with the bravery of minks and muskrats. A stereotyped but unconscious despair is concealed even under what are called the games and amusements of mankind. There is no play in them, for this comes after work. But it is a characteristic of wisdom not to do desperate things.
—Henry David Thoreau

Desire is our greatest bondage, and its absence our complete liberation. He who has a strong sense of egoism is never released from the miseries of life; it is the negation of this feeling that produces liberation.
—*Yoga-Vasishtha*

Who will deny that those men are foolish who attend to other people's affairs, but neglect their own? They esteem highly what is absent and what is new, and belittle what is present and familiar. Because of their ceaseless longing for what is to come they do not enjoy what is present. Although movement has to be stilled for there to be rest; yet those men are forever beginning new and different movements, in order that they may one day come to rest....We are surprised that while we continue to live, or rather die like this, we are unhappy, as though we could reap a different harvest from the one we have sown. Misery is the fruit of foolishness. How is this? Because we foolishly over-feed the body and neglect the soul, the body becomes fat and robust and the soul thin and puny.

—Marsilio Ficino

The common outlook is that the world is everything, and that the Absolute is nothing. It is wrong to hold this view, and the punishment for it is to be imprisoned in this physical body. You cannot be happy while undergoing a term of imprisonment.

—H.H. Shantanand Saraswati

Sickness, mental laziness, doubt, lack of enthusiasm, sloth, craving for sense-pleasure, false perception, despair caused by failure to concentrate and unsteadiness in concentration: these distractions are the obstacles to knowledge.

These distractions are accompanied by grief, despondency, trembling of the body, and irregular breathing.

They can be removed by the practice of concentration upon a single truth.

—Patanjali

Take away your opinion, and there is taken away the complaint, "I have been hurt." Take away the complaint, "I have been hurt," and the hurt is gone.

—Marcus Aurelius

Desire brings grief,
desire brings fear.
The man who curbs desire is free from grief
and free from fear.
—*Dhammapada*

The "mental covering," therefore, cannot be the *Atman*. It has a beginning and an end, and is subject to change. It is the abode of pain. It is an object of experience. The seer cannot be the thing which is seen.

—Shankara

Give up thinking of yourself as such-and-such a person; forsake all trivialities and, knowing that all is the universal One, be constant in your vow to adore the supreme Spirit, Brahman.

Placed in this world of misery, man should take no heed of the lesser or greater sights of woe which present themselves to his view. They are as the fleeting tints and hues which paint the empty vault of the sky, and soon vanish into nothing.

—*Yoga-Vasishtha*

I further maintain that sorrow comes of loving what I cannot have. If I am sad about my losses, that is a sure sign that I love external things and really enjoy my sorrow and disease. What wonder, then, that I grow sad, loving my affliction and sorrow, if my heart seeks what it has lost and my mind attributes to things what belongs to God alone?

—Meister Eckhart

As the Being of every individual is a part of the Absolute, it is fundamentally Eternal; it is fundamentally all Knowledge; it is fundamentally all Joy. But look at Eternity fearing death! Look at knowledge missing all True Knowledge! Look at joy missing all Joy!

—H.H. Shantanand Saraswati

If you are pained by any external thing, it is not this thing which disturbs you, but your own judgment about it. And it is in your power to wipe out that judgment now.

—Marcus Aurelius

The whole concern of our lives is to desire and to be doing, and then back to desiring again; but when all restless craving is rooted out of the mind, it becomes free from all anxieties....

Our desires and dislikes are two apes living in the tree of our hearts; while they continue to shake and agitate it, with their jogging and jolting, there can be no rest for it.

—*Yoga-Vasishtha*

He whom I enclose with my name is weeping in this dungeon.
I am ever busy building this wall all around; and as this wall goes up
into the sky day by day I lose sight of my true being in its dark shadow.
    I take pride in this great wall, and I plaster it with dust and
sand lest a least hole should be left in this name; and for all
the care I take lose sight of my true being.

—Rabindranath Tagore

What I most want
is to spring out of this personality,
then to sit apart from that leaping.
I've lived too long where I can be reached.
—Rumi

The true being in man is ever free, ever pure, and remains ever untouched by good or evil. Good and evil have no absolute reality. They exist only so long as man identifies himself with the ego, the false self. When the ego is completely annihilated, man is freed from the false knowledge of duality or relativity—of good and evil.

Good and evil exist only so long as man thinks himself to be the doer of actions. If through the grace of the Infinite Being he is freed from this consciousness of ego, then the idea of good or bad no longer exists for him.
—Swami Adbhutananda

You are pure consciousness, the witness of all experiences. Your real nature is you. Cease this very moment to identify yourself with the ego, the doer, which is created by ignorance.... It robs you of peace and joy in the Atman.
—Shankara

Desires, which are always present in human beings—this is the nature of things— usually end up in attachment. Attachment comes because there are continuous associations between certain types of desires and the objects of those desires. If you go on being attached for longer, attachment becomes greed so that you always like to have things in plenty for an unlimited time. They go beyond your individual needs and this is craving or addiction. Greed and craving constitute the cage in which the individual ego is imprisoned. It is only possible to get out of prison if there is somebody to help. One can fall very easily into a well but it is not possible to get out by oneself, even if one desperately wants to, unless someone on the surface is ready and able to help. So one needs guidance and leadership. For those who are intelligent, the scriptures, discourses, and certain words of the realized man will help.
—H.H. Shantanand Saraswati

The will...commits sin when it turns away from immutable and common goods, towards its private good, either something external to itself or lower than itself. It turns to its own private good when it desires to be its own master; it turns to external goods when it busies itself with the private affairs of others or with whatever is none of its concern; it turns to goods lower than itself when it loves the pleasures of the body. Thus a man becomes proud, meddlesome, and lustful.
—St. Augustine

Reality is simply the loss of the ego. Destroy the ego by seeking its identity. It will automatically vanish and reality will shine forth by itself. This is the direct method.

There is no greater mystery than this, that we keep seeking reality though in fact we *are* reality. We think that there is something hiding reality and that this must be destroyed before reality is gained. How ridiculous! A day will dawn when you will laugh at all your past efforts. That which will be on the day you laugh is also here and now.

—Sri Ramana Maharshi

What we commonly call man, the eating, drinking, planting, counting man, does not, as we know him, represent himself, but misrepresents himself. Him do we not respect, but the soul, whose organ he is, would he let it appear through his action, would make our knees bend. When it breathes through his intellect, it is genius; when it breathes through his will, it is virtue; and when it flows through his affection, it is love. And the blindness of the intellect begins when it would be something of itself. The weakness of the will begins when the individual would be something of himself.

—Ralph Waldo Emerson

What does it mean that man is a machine?

It means that he has no *independent movements,* inside or outside of himself. He is a machine which is brought into motion by *external influences and external impacts.* All his movements, actions, words, ideas, emotions, moods, and thoughts are produced by external influences. By himself, he is just an automaton with a certain store of memories of previous experiences, and a certain amount of reserve energy.

We must understand that man can do nothing.

But he does not realize this and ascribes to himself the *capacity* to do. This is the first wrong thing that man ascribes to himself.

That must be understood very clearly. *Man cannot do.* Everything that man thinks he does, really *happens.* It happens exactly as "it rains," or "it thaws."

—P.D. Ouspensky

This is a strange repose, to be asleep
With eyes wide open; standing, speaking, moving,
And yet so fast asleep.
—William Shakespeare

12
AWAKENING AND SELF-KNOWLEDGE

Arise, awake, and learn by approaching the excellent ones. The wise ones describe that path to be as impassable as a razor's edge, which when sharpened, is difficult to tread on.

—*Katha Upanishad*

O my heart! The Supreme Spirit, the great Master, is near you: wake, oh, wake!
Run to the feet of your Beloved: for your Lord stands near to your head.
You have slept for unnumbered ages; this
Morning will you not wake?

—Kabir

Wake up! It is time to wake up!
You are young, strong—why do you waver,
why are you lazy and irresolute?
This is not the way to wisdom.

—*Dhammapada*

I beseech you, arise now from this deep slumber; come to yourselves....For if you come to yourselves you will live happily.

—Marsilio Ficino

When you awaken to truth as it really is, you will have no occult vision, you will have no "astral" experience, no ravishing ecstasy. You will awaken to it in a state of utter stillness, and you will realize that truth was *always* there within you and that reality was always there around you. Truth is not something which has grown and developed through your efforts. It is not something which has been achieved or attained by laboriously adding up those efforts. It is not something which has to be made more and more perfect each year. And once your mental eyes are opened to truth they can never be closed again.

—Paul Brunton

I have never yet met a man who was quite awake. How could I have looked him in the face?

—Henry David Thoreau

If an earnest person has roused himself, if he is not forgetful, if his deeds are pure, if he acts with consideration, if he restrains himself, and lives according to law—then his glory will increase.

By rousing himself, by earnestness, by restraint and control, the wise man may make for himself an island which no flood can overwhelm....

Earnest among the thoughtless, awake among the sleepers, the wise man advances like a racer, leaving behind the hack.

—*Dhammapada*

You must raise your sail! The wind of Grace will fill it.

—Ramakrishna

Discrimination is the reasoning by which one knows that God alone is real and all else is unreal. Real means eternal, and unreal means impermanent. He who has acquired discrimination knows that God is the only Substance and all else is nonexistent. With the awakening of this spirit of discrimination a man wants to know God...who is of the very nature of Reality.

—Ramakrishna

Sin of self-love possesseth all mine eye
And all my soul and all my every part;
And for this sin there is no remedy,
It is so grounded inward in my heart.
Methinks no face so gracious is as mine,
No shape so true, no truth of such account;
And for myself mine own worth do define,
As I all other in all worths surmount.
But when my glass shows me myself indeed,
Beated and chopp'd with tann'd antiquity,
Mine own self-love quite contrary I read;
Self so self-loving were iniquity.
   'Tis thee, myself,—that for myself I praise,
   Painting my age with beauty of thy days.
—William Shakespeare

O soul, you are mighty, if small things do not satisfy you. You are most virtuous when evil displeases you; most beautiful when you shun what is base. When you set small value on the transient you are indeed eternal. Since your nature is such, if you wish to discover yourself I pray you seek yourself where such things are. Truly the great is only found in that place where no limit is imposed; the best where no adversity reaches; the beautiful where exists no disharmony; and the eternal where there is no flaw.

Therefore seek yourself beyond the world. To do so and to come to yourself you must fly beyond the world and look back on it. For you are beyond the world while you yourself comprehend it.

—Marsilio Ficino

Not till we are lost, in other words, not till we have lost the world, do we begin to find ourselves, and realize where we are and the infinite extent of our relations.

—Henry David Thoreau

He who knows and does not know that he knows: he is asleep.
    Let him become one, whole. Let him be awakened.
He who has known but does not know: let him see once more the beginning
    of all.
He who does not wish to know, and yet says that he needs to know: let him be
    guided to safety and to light.
He who does not know, and knows that he does not know:
    let him, through this knowledge, know.
He who does not know, but thinks that he knows:
    set him free from the confusion of that ignorance.
He who knows, and knows that *he is:* he is wise. Let him be followed.
By his presence alone man may be transformed.

—*Sarmoun Recital*

Though one may remain in the path of steadfast devotion, engage one's self in pilgrimages round the world, bathe in the holy waters of the Oceans and the rivers..., liberation from the cycle of births and deaths cannot be had without true Knowledge.

—St. Tayumanavar

Go back into yourself and look; and if you do not yet see yourself beautiful, then, just as someone making a statue which has to be beautiful cuts away here and polishes there and makes one part smooth and clears another till he has given his statue a beautiful face, so you too must cut away excess and straighten the crooked and clear the dark and make it bright, and never stop "working on your statue" till the divine glory of virtue shines out on you, till you see self-mastery enthroned upon its holy seat." If you have become this, and see it, and are at home with yourself in purity, with nothing hindering you from becoming in this way one, with no inward mixture of anything else, but wholly yourself, nothing but true light, not measured by dimensions, or bounded by shape into littleness, or expanded to size by unboundedness, but everywhere unmeasured, because greater than all measure and superior to all quantity; when you see that you have become this, then you have become sight; you can trust yourself then; you have already ascended and need no one to show you; concentrate your gaze and see This alone is the eye that sees the great beauty.... For one must come to the sight with a seeing power made akin and like to what is seen. No eye ever saw the sun without becoming sunlike, nor can a soul see beauty without becoming beautiful. You must become first all godlike and all beautiful if you intend to see God and beauty.

—Plotinus

I can imagine someone saying, "How about keeping your mouth shut, Socrates, and leading a quiet life? Can't you please go into exile, and live like that?" Of all things, this is the hardest point on which to convince some of you. If I say that it is disobeying God, and that for this reason I can't lead a quiet life, you won't believe me—you'll think I'm using that as an excuse. If on the other hand I say that really the greatest good in man's life is this, to be each day discussing human excellence and the other subjects you hear me talking about, examining myself and other people, and that the unexamined life isn't worth living—if I say this, you will believe me even less.

—Plato, *Apology of Socrates*

To get at the core of God at his greatest, one must first get into the core of himself at his least, for no one can know God who has not first known himself. Go to the depths of the soul, the secret place of the Most High, to the roots, to the heights; for all that God can do is focused there.

—Meister Eckhart

For, of a truth, thoroughly to know oneself, is above all art, for it is the highest art. If thou knowest thyself well, thou art better and more praiseworthy before God than if thou dost not know thyself, but didst understand the course of the heavens and of all the planets and stars, also the virtue of all herbs, and the structure and dispositions of all mankind, also the nature of all beasts, and, in such matters, hadst all the skill of all who are in heaven and on earth. For it is said, there came a voice from heaven, saying, "Man, know thyself."

—*Theologia Germanica*

Jesus said: But the Kingdom is within you and it is without you. If you know yourselves, then you will be known and you will know that you are the sons of the Living Father. But if you do not know yourselves, then you are in poverty and you are poverty.

—*The Gospel of Thomas*

Knowing others is wisdom;
Knowing the self is enlightenment.
Mastering others requires force;
Mastering the self needs strength.

—Lao Tsu

Knock on yourself as upon a door and walk upon yourself as on a straight road. For if you walk on the road, it is impossible for you to go astray....Open the door for yourself that you may know what is.

—*Teachings of Silvanus*

He who sees all beings in the very Self, and the Self in all beings, feels no hatred by virtue of that realization.

—*Eesha Upanishad*

Happy the man who has attained knowledge,
    Who eagerly seeks wisdom's precious stone in himself.
Only the man of intellect is the true Adept—he transmutes
    Everything into living gold—he no longer has need of elixirs.
Within his heart the holy pelican exhales its dews—the King is within him—
    Likewise Delphi itself, he finally grasps the legend "Know thyself."

—Novalis

The outer life remains in this world, but what the heart has apprehended—that goes with us.

—Jacob Boehme

It is therefore more profitable to us in life to make perfect the intellect or reason as far as possible, and in this one thing consists the highest happiness or blessedness of man; for blessedness is nothing but the peace of mind which springs from the intuitive knowledge of God, and to perfect the intellect is nothing but to understand God, together with the attributes and actions of God, which flow from the necessity of His nature. The final aim, therefore, of a man who is guided by reason, that is to say, the chief desire by which he strives to govern all is other desires, is that by which he is led adequately to conceive himself and all things which can be conceived by his intelligence.

—Baruch Spinoza

He who possesses insight does not have to use arguments and reach conclusions. The truth is there, self-evident, inside himself as himself, for his inner being has become one with it.

—Paul Brunton

Do not seek to follow the footsteps of the men of old; seek what they sought.

—Matsuo Basho

Not I, not any one else can travel that road for you
You must travel it for yourself.

—Walt Whitman

Books suggest the inner light and the method of bringing it out; but we can understand them only when we have earned the knowledge ourselves. When the inner light has flashed for you, let the books go and look only within. You have in you all that is in the books, and a thousand times more. Never lose faith in yourself; you can do anything in this universe. Never weaken; all power is yours.

—Swami Vivekananda

Ceasing to feed the imagination on things not Self, full of darkness, causing sorrow, bend the imagination on the Self, whose form is bliss, the cause of freedom.

This is the Self luminous, witness of all, ever shining through the veil of the soul; making the one aim this Self, that is the contrary of all things unreal, realize it by identification with its partless nature.

—Shankara

13
ASPIRATION AND THE PATH

This day before dawn I ascended a hill and look'd at the crowded heaven,
And I said to my spirit *When we become the enfolders of those orbs,*
  and the pleasure and knowledge of every thing in them, shall we be fill'd and
  satisfied then?
And my spirit said No, *we but level that lift to pass and continue beyond.*
—Walt Whitman

In the spiritual order of things, the higher we project our view and our aspiration, the greater the Truth that seeks to descend upon us, because it is already there within us and calls for its release from the covering that conceals it in manifested Nature.
  —Sri Aurobindo

I know of no more encouraging fact than the unquestionable ability of man to elevate his life by a conscious endeavor.
  —Henry David Thoreau

In order to perfect oneself, one must renew oneself day by day.
  —*Ten Rungs: Hasidic Sayings*

Jesus said: Ask and it will be given to you; seek and you will find; knock and the door will be opened for you.
  —*The Book of Q*

We will come to understand the world when we understand ourselves, since we and it are integrating in the center. God's children, godly embryos are we. One day we are to become what our Father is.
  —Novalis

His aim should be to concentrate and simplify, and so to expand his being...and so to float upwards toward the divine fountain of being whose stream flows within him.

—Plotinus

Practice and perseverance lead to success. Whatever good one obtains is the fruit of the tree of long-continued practice. This ignorance is the result of the wrong thinking of many incarnations and so it appears strong, but when you work patiently for Self-realization, then ignorance will end.

—*Yoga-Vasishtha*

We must learn to reawaken and keep ourselves awake, not by mechanical aids, but by an infinite expectation of the dawn, which does not forsake us in our soundest sleep. I know of no more encouraging fact than the unquestionable ability of man to elevate his life by a conscious endeavor.... To affect the quality of the day, that is the highest of arts. Every man is tasked to make his life, even in its details, worthy of the contemplation of his most elevated and critical hour.

—Henry David Thoreau

Make up your mind, therefore, before it is too late, that the fitting thing for you to do is to live as a mature man who is making progress, and let everything which seems to you to be best be for you a law that must not be transgressed. And if you meet anything that is laborious, or sweet, or held in high repute, or in no repute, remember that now is the contest, and here before you are the Olympic games, and that it is impossible to delay any longer, and that it depends on a single day and a single action, whether progress is lost or saved. This is the way Socrates became what he was, by paying attention to nothing but his reason in everything that he encountered. And even if you are not yet a Socrates, still you ought to live as one who wishes to be a Socrates.

—Epictetus

Man flows at once to God when the channel of purity is open. By turns our purity inspires and our impurity casts us down. He is blessed who is assured that the animal is dying out in him day by day and the divine being established.

—Henry David Thoreau

Active searching is prejudicial, not only to love, but also to the intelligence, whose laws are the same as those of love. We just have to wait for the solution...for any new scientific truth or for a beautiful line of poetry. Seeking leads us astray. This is the case with every form of what is truly good. Man should do nothing but wait for the good and keep evil away....This waiting for goodness and truth is, however, something more intense than any searching.

—Simone Weil

In the long run men hit only what they aim at. Therefore, though they should fail immediately, they had better aim at something high.

   —Henry David Thoreau

As long as I am this or that, or have this or that, I am not all things and I have not all things. Become pure till you neither are nor have either this or that; then you are omnipresent and, being neither this nor that, are all things.

   —Meister Eckhart

Wipe out fancies by often saying to yourself; "Now it is in my power to allow no evil in my soul, nor desire, nor perturbation; but looking at all things, I see what is their proper nature, and I use each according to its value." Remember this power, which you have from nature.

   —Marcus Aurelius

Those who spread their sails in the right way to the winds of the earth will always find themselves borne by a current towards the open seas. The more nobly a man wills and acts, the more avid he becomes for great and sublime aims to pursue...truths to discover, an ideal to cherish and defend.... Little by little the great breath of the universe has insinuated itself into him through the fissure of his humble but faithful action, has broadened him, raised him up, borne him on.

   —Teilhard de Chardin

It is not for man to seek, or even to believe in, God. He only has to refuse his ultimate love to everything that is not God. This refusal does not presuppose any belief. It is enough to recognize what is obvious to any mind: that all the goods of this world, past, present, and future, real or imaginary, are finite and limited and radically incapable of satisfying the desire that perpetually burns within us for an infinite and perfect good.

   —Simone Weil

Now realize that this is how God wants our soul to be, without any selfish love of ourselves or of others in between, just as God loves us without anything in between. ...let this love be so clean and free that we love no one, nothing, spiritually or temporally, apart from God.... In him we love what we love, and we love nothing without him.... So God insists that we bring with us the vessel of our free will, with a thirst and willingness to love. Let's go, then, to the fountain of God's sweet goodness. There we shall discover the knowledge of ourselves and of God. And when we dip our vessel in, we shall draw out the water of divine grace, powerful enough to give us everlasting life.

   —St. Catherine of Siena

The coming of a spiritual age must be preceded by the appearance of an increasing number of individuals who are no longer satisfied with the normal intellectual, vital, and physical existence of man, but perceive that a greater evolution is the real goal of humanity and attempt to effect it in themselves, to lead others to it, and to make it the recognized goal of the race. In proportion as they succeed and to the degree to which they carry this evolution, the yet unrealized potentiality which they represent will become an actual possibility of the future.

 —Sri Aurobindo

Neither pious acts, nor riches, nor friends, are of any use to men for their redemption from the miseries of life; only their own striving will avail for the enlightenment of their souls.

  They who rely on faith in their gods, and depend on them for the fulfillment of their present and future desires, are perverted in their understanding, and cannot be heirs to immortality.

 —*Yoga-Vasishtha*

When a man grows aware of a new way in which to serve God, he should carry it around with him secretly, and without uttering it, for nine months, as though he were pregnant with it, and let others know of it only at the end of that time, as though it were a birth.

 —*Ten Rungs: Hasidic Sayings*

Now, in considering the divine substance, we should especially make use of the method of remotion. For, by its immensity, the divine substance surpasses every form that our intellect reaches. Thus we are unable to apprehend it by knowing *what it is*. Yet we are able to have some knowledge of it by knowing *what it is not*. Furthermore, we approach nearer to a knowledge of God according as through our intellect we are able to remove more and more things from Him.

 —St. Thomas Aquinas

OM is the bow; the soul is the arrow; and Brahman is called its target. It is to be hit by an unerring man. One should become one with it just like an arrow.

 —*Mundaka Upanishad*

With the lamp of word and discrimination one must go beyond word and discrimination and enter upon the path of realization.

 —*Lankavatara Sutra*

The inquiry leads us to that source, at once the essence of genius, of virtue, and of life, which we call Spontaneity or Instinct. We denote this primary wisdom as Intuition, whilst all later teachings are tuitions. In that deep force, the last fact behind which analysis cannot go, all things find their common origin. For the sense of being which in calm hours rises, we know not how, in the soul is not diverse from things, from space, from light, from time, from man, but one with them and proceeds obviously from the same source whence their life and being also proceed.

—Ralph Waldo Emerson

Final and perfect happiness can consist in nothing else than the vision of the Divine Essence. To make this clear, two points must be observed. First, that man is not perfectly happy, so long as something remains for him to desire and seek; secondly, that the perfection of any power is determined by the nature of its object.... And this desire is one of wonder, and causes inquiry....

If therefore the human intellect, knowing the essence of some created effect, knows no more of God than *That He is;* the perfection of that intellect does not yet reach simply the First Cause, but there remains in it the natural desire to seek the cause. Wherefore it is not yet perfectly happy. Consequently, for perfect happiness the intellect needs to reach the very Essence of the First Cause. And thus it will have its perfection through union with God as with that object in which alone man's happiness consists.

—St. Thomas Aquinas

It is impossible to tell men what way they should take. For one way to serve God is by the teachings, another by prayer, another way by fasting, and still another by eating. Everyone should carefully observe which way his heart draws him, and then choose that way with all his strength.

—*Ten Rungs: Hasidic Sayings*

The spokes of the wheel are the rules of pure conduct: justice is the uniformity of their length; wisdom is the tire; modesty and thoughtfulness are the hub in which the immovable axle of truth is fixed.

He who recognizes the existence of suffering, its cause, its remedy, and its cessation has fathomed the four noble truths. He will walk in the right path.

Right views will be the torch to light his way. Right aspirations will be his guide. Right speech will be his dwelling—place on the road. His gait will be straight, for it is right behavior. His refreshments will be the right way of earning his livelihood. Right efforts will be his steps: right thoughts his breath; and right contemplation will give him the peace that follows in his footsteps....

By the practice of lovingkindness I have attained liberation of heart, and thus I am assured that I shall never return in renewed births. I have even now attained Nirvana.

—The Buddha

The concentration of the true spiritual aspirant is attained through faith, energy, recollectedness, absorption, and illumination.

—Patanjali

God is present in all things to him who rules and uses his reason to the utmost; only this man knows real peace and has a just place in the Kingdom of Heaven.

He who understands this rightly must do one of two things. Either he must cling to God in all his work and learn to hold him there, or he must not work at all. But as a man in this life cannot be without activity which belongs in its many forms to humanity, he has to learn to receive his God in everything and to remain unhindered by his activity everywhere.

Therefore if a man begins to travel this path in the midst of other people, let him first commit himself strongly to God and holding him firmly in his heart, let him unite within himself all his strivings, thoughts, wishes, and powers, so that nothing else can arise in him.

—Meister Eckhart

He who is on the Path exists not for himself, but for others; he has forgotten himself, in order that he may serve them...he is a living plume of fire, raying out upon the world the Divine Love which fills his heart.

The wisdom which enables you to help, the will which directs the wisdom, the love which inspires the will—these are your qualifications. Will, Wisdom, and Love are the three aspects of the Logos; and you, who wish to enroll yourselves to serve Him, must show forth these aspects in the world.

—Jiddu Krishnamurti

He will be all the better and not worse if he brings to his mystical path a scientific method of approach, a large historical acquaintance with the comparative mysticisms of many countries, a scientific knowledge of psychology, and a practical experience of the world. He will be all the better and not worse if he learns in advance, and in theory, what every step of the way into the holy of holies will be like.

—Paul Brunton

Only when his heart becomes purified through the practice of spiritual disciplines does a man attain to wisdom. He then becomes convinced of the existence of God through realizing Him in his own soul. There is, however, something greater than this attainment. To become convinced that fire lies hidden in the wood is one thing but greater is it to light the fire, cook food, and satisfy one's hunger.

—Sri Ramakrishna

The speech which causes no excitement and is true, is also pleasant and beneficial, and also the practice of sacred recitation, are said to form the austerity of speech.

Serenity of mind, good-heartedness, silence, self-control, purity of nature—this is called the mental austerity.

—*Bhagavad Gita*

When faith comes, there arises the desire to hear the Word of God. When the desire to hear the Word of God arises, one finds pleasure in His Word. When one finds pleasure in His Word, all evils vanish. For then the Lord, the friend of the godly, reveals Himself and wipes away all evils and impurities.

When all impurities are washed away, then comes true, unswerving love of God. In minds so purified there cannot arise any thought of lust or greed; and their joy is full.

When the joy of devotion to the Lord takes hold of the mind, man frees himself from the bondage of the world. He realizes the Truth and knows the Self. His ego is dissolved. His doubts vanish. For such a man bondage to karma ceases.

—*Srimad Bhagavatam*

Show by your lives that religion does not mean words or names or sects, but that it means spiritual realization. Only those can understand who have felt. Only those who have attained spirituality can communicate it to others, can be great teachers of mankind. They alone are the powers of light.

—Sri Ramakrishna Paramahamsa

Austerity, study, and the dedication of the fruits of one's work to God: these are the preliminary steps toward yoga.

Thus we may cultivate the power of concentration and remove the obstacles to enlightenment which cause all our sufferings.

These obstacles—the causes of man's sufferings—are ignorance, egoism, attachment, aversion, and the desire to cling to life.

—Patanjali

It is perhaps the amplitude and symmetry of the philosophic approach which make it so completely satisfying. For this is the only approach which honors reason and appreciates beauty, cultivates intuition and respects mystical experience, fosters reverence and teaches true prayer, enjoins action and promotes morality. It is the spiritual life fully grown.

—Paul Brunton

Patient and regular practice is the whole secret of spiritual realization. Do not be in a hurry in spiritual life. Do your utmost, and leave the rest to God.

Past tendencies will be uprooted and obliterated by the constant remembrance of God, and the heart will be filled with peace. The mind is stilled by His grace alone.

—Swami Shivananda

How, then, does one obtain illumination? By purification of the heart. When your heart has been truly purified, you will see God; and when you have seen God, your light shines forth and gives comfort to all.

—Swami Prabhavananda

An individual is working for Self-realization. The realized man looks at it differently. He knows that there is no such thing as Self-realization. The Self is itself real, who can make it more real? What one is really doing is trying to remove the cloud of ignorance.... The eye is like the Self, the sun is like the Absolute and the cloud is ignorance. This is the barrier. The eye and the sun are made of the same element. The more light there is, the more the darkness disperses....

Unity is there; the Self, which is real, is there. It is only a matter of enlightenment. This is how it seems to a realized man.

—H.H. Shantanand Saraswati

To seek for the perfection in Godhead, to seek for the truth that gives us freedom, is to seek for our true Self. Religion is not anything extraneous to ourselves that we have to acquire, neither is it something which we may or may not believe, but it is something living in the soul of each man.

—Swami Prabhavananda

Knowledge of Truth, subjection of the mind, and abandonment of desires are the joint causes of spiritual bliss, which is unattainable by the practice of any one of them singly.

Unless you become an adept in the practice of these three means, it is impossible to attain the state of divine perfection by mere devotion, during a whole century.

Continue to practice them at all times in your life, whether you sit quiet or move about, when you talk or when you listen.

—*Yoga-Vasishtha*

A good man who wants to go on the spiritual path speaks what he feels, and does what he speaks. That is, he speaks from pure feeling. When he has impure feelings, he tries not to speak or rush into action or express them.... If one really speaks what one feels and does exactly what one says, then this builds up a man's inner strength and, because of the clarity and unity of his mind and sincerity of his heart, the way becomes fairly clear for him.... If one keeps this consistency, then one would grow—one would become more serious and have more strength of character. This brings unity into a man and creates a sort of depth—and to the unity and depth of the individual, the glory of the Absolute descends.

—H.H. Shantanand Saraswati

If the quest is to be an integral one, as it must be to be a true one, it should continue through all four spheres of a man's being: the emotional, the intellectual, the volitional, and the intuitional. Such a fourfold character makes it a more complicated affair than many mystics believe it to be.

—Paul Brunton

Remember the Divine in everything you do. If you have time, meditate. Offer everything to the Divine—everything good or bad, pure or impure. This is the best and quickest way.

—Mother Meera

Be at peace, first, in yourself, and then you will be able to bring others into peace. A peaceful man does more good than a learned man. A passionate man even turns good into evil, and readily believes evil. A good peaceful man turns everything to good. He who is truly in peace never suspects others. But he who is ill at ease and discontented, is disturbed by various suspicions. Neither does he rest himself, not let others rest. He often says what he ought not, and often omits to do what he ought. He busies himself about what others ought to do, and neglects his own duty. Let your zeal begin upon yourself, and then you may with justice extend it to your neighbors.

—Thomas à Kempis

With a controlled mind and an intellect which is made pure and tranquil, you must realize the Atman directly, within yourself. Know the Atman as the real I. Thus you cross the shoreless ocean of worldliness, whose waves are birth and death. Live always in the knowledge of identity with Brahman, and be blessed.

—Shankara

To be harmonious means to be whole; to love others and so enjoy your life; to know yourself and your difficulties and to work with them so you become free and able to help others; to respect the dignity of others. Humility brings harmony. A humble person is integrated with reality and is happy, because humility brings happiness.

—Mother Meera

He is the real *Sadhu*, who can reveal the form of the Formless
    To the vision of these eyes:…
Who makes you perceive the Supreme Spirit wherever
    the mind attaches itself:
Who teaches you to be still in the midst of all
    your activities.
Ever immersed in bliss, having no fear in his mind,
    he keeps the spirit of union in the midst of all enjoyments.
The infinite dwelling of the Infinite Being is everywhere:
    In earth, water, sky, and air:
Firm as the thunderbolt, the seat of the seeker is established
    above the void.
He who is within is without: I see Him and none else.

—Kabir

14
SPIRITUAL STRUGGLE

Therefore when Tao is lost, there is goodness.
When goodness is lost, there is kindness.
When kindness is lost, there is justice.
When justice is lost, there is ritual.
Now ritual is the husk of faith and loyalty, the beginning of confusion.
—Lao Tsu

Every man's condition is a solution in hieroglyph to those inquiries he would put.
He acts it as life before he apprehends it as truth.
—Ralph Waldo Emerson

Know, Rama, that the revolving world is that great wheel, and the human heart is its nave or axis, which by its continuous rotation, produces all this delusion within its circumference. If, by means of your manly exertion, you can put an end to this movement of your heart, you will stop the rotation of the circle of delusion at once.

The soul that forgets this counsel is exposed to interminable misery, while, by keeping it always before the mind, it will avoid all difficulties in this world.

The world is in the mind, like the air enclosed in a pot, and you are forever confined in this imaginary mental world of yours, like a gnat imprisoned in the hollow of the pot; you will only obtain your release by breaking out of this confinement, like the gnat flying into the open air.

The way to be rid of this delusion of the mind is to fix your attention upon the present moment, and not to employ your thoughts on past or future events. The mind is clouded so long as the mist of its desires and fancies overshadows it, as the sky is overcast so long as drifting clouds spread over it.

When there is activity in the mind it is invariably accompanied by a train of desires and the sense of pleasure or pain; feelings and passions are its concomitants, as ravens are found near an extinct volcano.

The minds of the wise are not without activity, but, through their knowledge of the vanity of earthly things, they are without those feelings which bind.
—*Yoga-Vasishtha*

It is necessary to know that warfare is universal and that strife is right, and that all things happen through strife and necessity.

—Heraclitus

It is the pang of separation that spreads throughout the world
and gives birth to shapes innumerable in the infinite sky.

It is this sorrow of separation that gazes in silence all night
from star to star and becomes lyric among rustling leaves in rainy
darkness of July.

It is this overspreading pain that deepens into loves and
desires, into sufferings and joys in human homes; and this it
is that ever melts and flows in songs through my poet's heart.

—Rabindranath Tagore

When a man thinks of objects, attachment for them arises. From attachment arises desire; from desire arises wrath. From wrath arises delusion; from delusion, failure of memory; from failure of memory, loss of conscience; from loss of conscience he is utterly ruined.

—*Bhagavad Gita*

When you are troubled about anything, you have forgotten this, that all things happen according to the universal nature, and that a man's wrongful act is nothing to you; and further you have forgotten this, that everything which happens always happened so, and will happen so, and now happens so everywhere...And you have forgotten this too, that every man's intelligence is a god, and is an efflux of the deity; and that nothing is a man's own, but that his child and his body and his very soul came from the deity.

—Marcus Aurelius

There are then two kinds of life and two kinds of movement, one that is according to true being, and another that is according to nature. And the life which is according to true being is self-determining, but the other is under compulsion; for everything that is moved is subject to the compulsion applied to it by that which moves it.

—Hermes Trismegistus

Now the created soul of man hath also two eyes. The one is the power of seeing into eternity, the other of seeing into time and the creatures, of perceiving how they differ from each other,... of giving life and needful things to the body, and ordering and governing it for the best. But these two eyes of the soul of man cannot both perform their work at once; but if the soul shall see with the right eye into eternity, then the left eye must close itself and refrain from working, and be as though it were dead. For if the left eye be fulfilling its office toward outward things; that is, holding converse with time and the creatures; then must the right eye be hindered in its working; that is, in its contemplation. Therefore whosoever will have the done must let the other go, for "no man can serve two masters."

—*Theologia Germanica*

The less passion there is, the better we work. The calmer we are, the better it is for us and the greater is the amount of work we can do. When we let loose our feelings we waste so much energy, shatter our nerves, disturb our minds, and accomplish very little work. The energy which ought to have gone into work is spent as mere feeling, which counts for nothing. It is only when the mind is very calm and collected that the whole of its energy is spent in doing good work.... The man who gives way to anger or hatred or any other passion cannot work; he only breaks himself to pieces and does nothing practical. It is the calm, forgiving, equable, well-balanced mind that does the greatest amount of work.

—Swami Vivekananda

My love is as a fever, longing still
For that which longer nurseth the disease;
Feeding on that which doth preserve the ill,
The uncertain sickly appetite to please.
My reason, the physician to my love,
Angry that his prescriptions are not kept,
Hath left me, and I desperate now approve
Desire is death, which physic did except.
Past cure I am, now Reason is past care,
And frantic-mad with evermore unrest;
My thoughts and my discourse as madmen's are,
At random from the truth vainly express'd;
   For I have sworn thee fair, and thought thee bright,
   Who art as black as hell, as dark as night.

—William Shakespeare

Depart from the oblivion which fills you with darkness....Wisdom calls you, yet you desire foolishness.... A foolish man ... swims in the desires of life ... he is like a ship which the wind tosses to and fro, and like a loose horse which has no rider. For this (one) needed the rider, which is reason ... before everything else ... know yourself.

—Silvanus

When [the soul] is firmly fixed on the domain where truth and reality shine resplendent it apprehends and knows them and appears to possess reason, but when it inclines to that region which is mingled with darkness, the world of becoming and passing away, it opines only and its edge is blunted, and it shifts its opinions hither and thither, and again seems as if it lacked reason.

—Plato

The expense of spirit in a waste of shame
Is lust in action; and till action, lust
Is perjur'd, murderous, bloody, full of blame,
Savage, extreme, rude, cruel, not to trust;
Enjoy'd no sooner but despised straight;
Past reason hunted; and no sooner had,
Past reason hated, as a swallow'd bait,
On purpose laid to make the taker mad:
Mad in pursuit, and in possession so;
Had, having, and in quest to have, extreme;
A bliss in proof,—and prov'd, a very woe;
Before, a joy propos'd; behind a dream.
    All this the world well knows; yet none knows well
    To shun the heaven that leads men to this hell.

—William Shakespeare

The soul in the body is like sap in a tree, and the soul's powers are like the form of the tree. How? The intellect in the soul is like the greenery of the tree's branches and leaves, the will like its flowers, the mind like its bursting firstfruits, the reason like the perfected mature fruit, and the senses like its size and shape. And so a person's body is strengthened and sustained by the soul. Hence, O human, understand what you are in your soul, you who lay aside your good intellect and try to liken yourself to the brutes.

—Hildegard of Bingen

We are asleep…. Our life is like a dream. But in our better hours we wake up just enough to realize that we are dreaming. Most of the time, though, we are fast asleep. I cannot waken myself! I am trying hard, my dream body moves, but my real one does not stir. This, alas, is how it is!

—Ludwig Wittgenstein

I do not know how to distinguish between our waking life and a dream. Are we not always living the life that we imagine we are?

—Henry David Thoreau

We have no reason to mistrust our world, for it is not against us. Has it terrors, they are *our* terrors; has it abysses, those abysses belong to us; are dangers at hand, we must try to love them. And if only we arrange our life according to that principle which counsels us that we must always hold to the difficult, then that which now still seems to us the most alien will become what we most trust and find most faithful.

—Rainer Maria Rilke

Such harmony is in immortal souls;
But, whilst this muddy vesture of decay
Doth grossly close it in, we cannot hear it.

—William Shakespeare

Grace surrounds us infinitely and it is only our hardness that makes us impervious to its radiation, in itself omnipresent. It is the soul which is absent, not grace.

—Frithjof Schuon

On the day when the lotus bloomed, alas, my mind was straying,
and I knew it not. My basket was empty and the flower
remained unheeded....

I knew not then that it was so near, that it was mine, and
that this perfect sweetness had blossomed in the depth of my
own heart.

—Rabindranath Tagore

Where is the night, when the sun is shining? If it is night,
   Then the sun withdraws its light.
Where knowledge is, can ignorance endure? If there be ignorance,
   then knowledge must die.
If there be lust, how can love be there?
   Where there is love, there is no lust.

—Kabir

We begin to die, not in our senses or extremities, but in our divine faculties. Our members may be sound, our sight and hearing perfect, but our genius and imagination betray signs of decay. You tell me that you are growing old and troubled to see without glasses, but this is unimportant if the divine faculty of the seer shows no sign of decay.
—Henry David Thoreau

There are cosmic compulsions which none escape and which permeate human destiny, for they are part of the World-Idea.
—Paul Brunton

Beings have their beginning unseen, their middle seen, and their end unseen again. Why any lamentation regarding them?
—*Bhagavad Gita*

When body grows weak through age or disease, the Self separates itself from the limbs, as a mango, a fig, a banyan fruit separates itself from the stalk; man hastens back to birth, goes as before, from birth to birth.
—*Brihadaranyaka Upanishad*

Jesus said: If you bring forth what is within you, what you bring forth will save you. If you do not bring forth what is within you, what you do not bring forth will destroy you.
—*The Gospel of Thomas*

Life consisteth in conflict, in order that it may reveal itself, and become acknowledged by wisdom; thus it serveth to the eternal joy of victory.
—Jacob Boehme

Jesus said: It is impossible for a man to mount two horses and to stretch two bows, and it is impossible for a servant to serve two masters, otherwise he will honor the one and offend the other.

—*The Gospel of Thomas*

We are afraid to learn because we are afraid to grow and to assume the greater responsibility that goes with growth.

—Tarthang Tulku

A man is the façade of a temple wherein all wisdom and all good abide. What we commonly call man, the eating, drinking, planting, counting man, does not, as we know him, represent himself but misrepresents himself. Him we do not respect, but the soul, whose organ he is, would he let it appear through his action, would make our knees bend. When it breathes through his intellect, it is genius; when it breathes through his will, it is virtue; when it flows through his affection, it is love. And the blindness of the intellect begins when it would be something of itself. The weakness of the will begins when the individual would be something of himself. All reform aims in some one particular to let the soul have its way through us; in other words, to engage us to obey.

—Ralph Waldo Emerson

The universe is either a confusion, an intermingling of atoms, and a scattering; or it is unity and order and providence. If it is the former, why do I wish to tarry amid such a haphazard confusion and disorder? Why do I care about anything but how I may at last become earth? And why do I trouble myself, for my elements will be scattered, whatever I do. But if the other supposition is true, I revere, I stand firm, and I trust in him who governs.

—Marcus Aurelius

But thought's the slave of life, and life's time's fool,
And time that takes survey of all the world
Must have a stop.
—William Shakespeare

*

15
THE HOME, SOCIETY, AND THE WORLD

The home is the abiding place; in the home is reality; the home
  helps to attain Him Who is real. So stay where you are,
  and all things shall come to you in time.
—Kabir

Do not craze yourself with thinking, but go about your business anywhere. Life is
not intellectual or critical, but sturdy. Its chief good is for well-mixed people who
can enjoy what they find, without question.... To fill the hour, that is happiness; to
fill the hour and leave no crevice for a repentance or an approval.
  —Ralph Waldo Emerson

Let us spend one day as deliberately as Nature, and not be thrown off the track by
every nutshell and mosquito's wing that falls on the rails. Let us rise early and fast,
or break fast, gently and without perturbation; let company come and let company
go, let the bells ring and the children cry—determined to make a day of it. Why should
we knock under and go with the stream?
  —Henry David Thoreau

To be active in the world is no bad thing, for this is your destiny. If someone works
hard in the heat of the sun he is doubly appreciative of the shade of the tree. If you
are very busy in your ordinary life, go on doing it, but the moment you come back
to meditation, the pleasure and peace will be specially deep. All who want to give
this peace to others have a special responsibility. They must not withdraw from the
active world. If they did, people would think that they are trying to escape from it.
That is not what the meditation is for. Be active, exert yourself, exhaust yourself if
need be, but keep alive the thread leading to the Bliss of Being.
  —H.H. Shantanand Saraswati

To live well, then, is to understand what is true; to take good counsel; to desire what is good; and to perform good acts. The first is a quality of wisdom; the second, of prudence; the third, of justice; and the fourth, of perseverance.

—Marsilio Ficino

Adapt yourself to the things among which your lot has been cast and to the men among whom you have your portion; love them, and do it truly, sincerely.

—Marcus Aurelius

Be content, no matter what your lot;
    In eating, drinking and recreation, be moderate;
    Walk in the paths of solitude; seek peace within your heart;
    Be a friend to all, make no complaint of the faults,
    With sympathy minister to their suffering:
    Make ready thus to receive that knowledge which reveals the Truth.
    So shall you realize the Self —
    The infinite and holy *purusha,* divinely free.

—*Srimad Bhagavatam*

Simplicity, simplicity, simplicity! I say, let your affairs be as two or three, and not a hundred or a thousand; instead of a million count half a dozen, and keep your accounts on your thumbnail.

—Henry David Thoreau

O father, O mother, O wife, O brother, O friend, I have lived with you after appearances hitherto. Henceforward I am the truth's. Be it known unto you that henceforward I obey no law less than the eternal law. I will have no covenants but proximities. I shall endeavor to nourish my parents, to support my family, to be the chaste husband of one wife—but these relations I must fill after a new and unprecedented way. I appeal from your customs. I must be myself. I cannot break myself any longer for you, or you. If you can love me for what I am, we shall be the happier. If you cannot, I will still seek to deserve that you should. I will not hide my tastes or aversions. I will so trust that what is deep is holy, that I will do strongly before the sun and moon whatever inly rejoices me and the heart appoints. If you are noble, I will love you; if you are not, I will not hurt you and myself by hypocritical attentions. If you are true, but not in the same truth with me, cleave to your companions: I will seek my own. I do this not selfishly but humbly and truly. It is alike your interest, and mine, and all men's, however long we have dwelt in lies, to live in truth. Does this sound harsh today? You will soon love what is dictated by your nature as well as mine, and if we follow the truth it will bring us out safe at last.

—Ralph Waldo Emerson

Lord, who shall abide in thy tabernacle? Who shall dwell in
    thy holy hill?
He that walketh uprightly, and worketh righteousness, and speaketh
    the truth in his heart.
—Psalm 15:1–2

Honor thy parents and thy nearest kin;
Of others make the virtuous thy friend:
Yield to his gentle words, his timely acts;
Nor for a petty fault take back thy love.
Bear what thou canst: pow'r cometh at man's need.
Know this for truth, and learn to conquer these:
Thy belly first; sloth, luxury, and rage.
Do nothing base with others or alone,
And, above all things, thine own self respect....

If one speaketh false,
Be calm. And practice ever this that now
I say. Let no man's word or deed seduce thee
To do or say aught nor to thy best good....

Do naught thou dost not understand; but learn
That which is good, and sweet will be thy life.
Nor shouldst thou thy body's health neglect,
But give it food and drink and exercise
In measure; that is, to cause it no distress.
Decent, without vain show, thy way of life:
Look well to this, that none thou envious make
By unmeet expense, like one who lack good taste....

And thou shalt know that Law hath stablished
The inner nature of all things alike;
So shalt thou hope not for what may not be,
Nor aught, that may, escape thee. Thou shalt know
Self-chosen are the woes that fall on men—...

Eat not the foods proscribed, but use discretion
In lustral rites and the freeing of thy soul:
Ponder all things, and stablish high thy mind,
That best of charioteers. And if at length,
Leaving behind thy body, thou dost come
To the free Upper Air, then shalt thou be
Deathless, divine, a mortal man no more.
—*The Golden Verses of Pythagoras*

It is good and comely for one to eat and to drink, and to enjoy the good of all his labor that he taketh under the sun all the days of his life, which God giveth him: for it is his portion.

—*Ecclesiastes 2:24*

Arise and accept an antidote to ward off old age and death: it is the knowledge that all wealth and prosperity, all pleasures and enjoyments are harmful to us unless devoted to the good of others; they tend only to sicken and enervate our frames.

—*Yoga-Vasishtha*

That shadow my likeness that goes to and fro seeking a livelihood,
    chattering, chaffering,
How often I find myself standing and looking at it where it flits,
How often I question and doubt whether that is really me;
But among my lovers and caroling these songs,
O I never doubt whether that is really me.

—Walt Whitman

Only a feeble spirit could be moved by the garments of appearance; the inner man should govern the outer, and only this will do for you. But if it happens that you are well off, in your heart be tranquil about it—if you can be just as glad and willing for the opposite condition. So let it be with food, friends, kindred, or anything else that God gives or takes away.

—Meister Eckhart

Every being is provided with certain assets or talents which he has to make use of for himself, his family, his society, his nation, and so on. Everyone has to understand how much energy is available to him to make use of in a particular place and time. This relates to the principle that one does not have to think about what one cannot do; one should always think about what one can do.

—H.H. Shantanand Saraswati

The life of each one of us is, as it were, woven of those two threads: the thread of inward development, through which our ideas and affections and our human and religious attitudes are gradually formed; and the thread of outward success by which we always find ourselves at the exact point where the whole sum of the forces of the universe meet together to work in us the effect which God desires.

—Teilhard de Chardin

Don't sow your desires in someone else's garden; just cultivate your own as best you can; don't long to be other than what you are, but desire to be thoroughly what you are. Direct your thoughts to being very good at that and to bearing the crosses, little or great, that you will find there. Believe me, this is the most important and least understood point in the spiritual life. We all love what is according to our taste; few people like what is according to their duty or to God's liking.

    —St. Francis de Sales

For since the world is God's handiwork, he who maintains and heightens its beauty by his tendance is cooperating with the will of God, when he contributes the aid of his bodily strength, and by his care and labor day by day makes things assume that shape and aspect which God's purpose has designed.... When our term of service is ended, when we are divested of our guardianship of the material world, and freed from the bonds of mortality, he will restore us, cleansed and sanctified, to the primal condition of that higher part of us which is divine.

    —Hermes Trismegistus

People ought not to consider so much what they are to do as what they *are;* let them but *be* good and their ways and deeds will shine brightly. If you are just, your actions will be just too. Do not think that saintliness comes from occupation; it depends rather on what one is. The kind of work we do does not make us holy but we may make it holy. However "sacred" a calling may be, as it is a calling, it has no power to sanctify; but rather as we *are* and have the divine being within, we bless each task we do, be it eating, or sleeping, or watching, or any other. Whatever they do, who have not much of [God's] nature, they work in vain.

    —Meister Eckhart

Each man has his own vocation. The talent is the call. There is one direction in which all space is open to him. He has faculties silently inviting him thither to endless exertion. He is like a ship in a river; he runs against obstructions on every side but one; on that side all obstruction is taken away, and he sweeps serenely over a deepening channel into an infinite sea. This talent and this call depend on his organization, or the mode in which the general soul incarnates itself in him. He inclines to do something which is easy to him, and good when it is done, but which no other man can do. He has no rival. For the more truly he consults his own powers, the more difference will his work exhibit from the work of any other. His ambition is exactly proportioned to his powers.... By doing his work, he makes the need felt which he can supply, and creates the taste by which he is enjoyed. By doing his own work, he unfolds himself.

    —Ralph Waldo Emerson

Better is one's own duty destitute of merits, than the duty of another well performed. Doing the duty ordained according to nature one incurs no sin.

    —*Bhagavad Gita*

The family man, who has to meet obligations in social life, must perform all duties as a form of worship.... He must pass leisure hours in hearing or studying the Word of God.... He may posses wealth but he must regard himself as a trustee of God, to whom everything belongs. He must look to the needs of the poor and the destitute and serve the Lord in serving all sentient beings.

—*Srimad Bhagavatam*

Do you wish to live safely and free from fear? Then take care that men do not greatly fear or greatly envy you. Our enemies are as many as those who fear and envy us. It is just that a man fear many, whom many fear; and also that he should serve very many, whom very many serve. All subjects serve the one Lord, and the Lord serves them all.

The one guardian of life is love, but to be loved you must love.

—Marsilio Ficino

The first sign of your becoming religious is that you are becoming cheerful. To the yogi, everything is bliss, every human face that he sees brings cheerfulness to him. Misery is caused by sin, and by no other cause. What business have you with clouded faces? If you have a clouded face do not go out that day, shut yourself up in your room. What right have you to carry this disease out into the world?

—Swami Vivekananda

How much trouble he avoids who does not look to see what his neighbor says or does or thinks, but only what he does himself, that it may be just and pure. As Agathon says, "Look not around at the depraved morals of others, but run straight along your course without straying from it."

—Marcus Aurelius

It is easy in the world to live after the world's opinion; it is easy in solitude to live after our own; but the great man is he who in the midst of the crowd keeps with perfect sweetness the independence of solitude.

—Ralph Waldo Emerson

This is not a time for people to withdraw from the world. It is a time to work with the power and love of the Divine *in* the world.

 —Mother Meera

Try, with God's help, to perceive the connection—even physical and natural—which binds your labor with the building of the kingdom of heaven; try to realize that heaven itself smiles upon you and, through your works, draws you to itself; then, as you leave church for the noisy streets, you will remain with only one feeling, that of continuing to immerse yourself in God. If your work is dull or exhausting, take refuge in the inexhaustible and becalming interest of progressing in the divine life. If your work enthralls you, then allow the spiritual impulse which matter communicates to you to enter into your taste for God whom you know better and desire more under the veil of his works.

 —Teilhard de Chardin

If you find no better or equal on life's road,
go alone!
Loneliness is better than friendship of a fool.

 —*Dhammapada*

Until we actually reach oneness with God, it is, of course, quite natural that we should have misunderstandings and quarrels with each other. But we must not let that resentment stay with us, or it will eat into our hearts like cancer. We must be reconciled as soon as possible. There is only one way to feel sincerely reconciled, and that is to suppress our own ego. If you can do that, you will find that you immediately gain something spiritually. Try to see God in all beings, and love Him in all. Humble yourself—not before your adversary, but before God within him. Never humble yourself before anyone but God. That is how hatred is driven out, and love of God takes its place. If you keep that hatred in your own heart, it will hurt nobody except yourself.

 —Swami Prabhavananda

What matters is easeful contact with those with whom one lives and, as well, with one's work. What matters is the ability, for which one can be so grateful, to return at times to the darkness of one's center in order to gather more light. What matters is the ability to allow that light, however slight, to pass into what one does.

 —Roger Lipsey

And so in groups where debate is earnest, and especially on high questions, the company become aware that the thought rises to an equal level in all bosoms, that all have a spiritual property in what was said, as well as the sayer. They all become wiser than they were. It arches over them like a temple, this unity of thought in which every heart beats with nobler sense of power and duty, and thinks and acts with unusual solemnity. All are conscious of attaining to a higher self-possession. It shines for all.

—Ralph Waldo Emerson

Happy the man whose wish and care
    A few paternal acres bound,
Content to breathe his native air,
    In his own ground....

Sound sleep by night; study and ease,
    Together mixed; sweet recreation;
And innocence, which most does please
    With meditation.

Thus let me live, unseen, unknown;
    Thus unlamented let me die;
Steal from the world, and not a stone
    Tell where I lie.

—Alexander Pope

But I speak of the spiritual friendship by which two or three or more persons communicate among themselves their devotion, their spiritual affection and become one in spirit. With good reason such happy souls can sing: "How good and pleasant it is for kindred to dwell together" (Ps. 133:1).

—St. Francis de Sales

My son, if you rest your peace on any person, because he is after your own heart, or for the pleasure of his companionship, you will be unsettled and anxious. But if you have recourse to the ever-living and abiding Truth, when a friend goes away or dies you will not be overwhelmed with grief. In Me the love of your friend ought to stand; and whoever seems good, and very dear to you in this life, ought to be loved for My sake. Friendship apart from Me is of no value, and cannot last; nor is that union of love genuine and pure which is not knit together by Me.

—Thomas à Kempis

He who condemns the foolish amusements and the mean activities of men; who employs himself in meritorious acts instead of dwelling upon the faults and failings of others; he whose mind is engaged in useful deeds, causing no pain to others, and is indifferent to all pleasures and bodily enjoyments; whose discourses are loving and tender; whose words are suited to the time and place at which they are delivered; such a man is said to stand upon the first step of yoga. He makes it his duty to seek the society of the good, whom he learns to imitate in thought, word and deed.

He collects books on the divine philosophy and studies them with diligence; he then considers their content and lays hold of their tenets, which have the power to save him from the sinful world.

—*Yoga-Vasishtha*

Have a great number of friends, but not counselors.... But if you do acquire [a friend], do not entrust yourself to him. Entrust yourself to God alone as father and as friend.

—Silvanus

There is no odor so bad as that which arises from goodness tainted.... If I knew for a certainty that a man was coming to my house with the conscious design of doing me good, I should run for my life, as from that dry and parching wind of the African deserts called the *simoom*, which fills the mouth and nose and ears and eyes with dust till you are suffocated, for fear that I should get some of his good done to me,—some of its virus mingled with my blood. No, in this case I would rather suffer evil the natural way. A man is not a good *man* to me because he will feed me if I should be starving, or warm me if I should be freezing.

—Henry David Thoreau

Spiritual life must be lived in absolute secrecy; publicity hinders our attempts. To give expression to divine emotions is to lessen them, and it is unwholesome. The more they are concealed, the more they are intensified

—Swami Shivananda

If the mind is happy, not only the body but the whole world will be happy. So one must find out how to become happy oneself. Wanting to reform the world without discovering one's true self is like trying to cover the whole world with leather to avoid the pain of walking on stones and thorns. It is much simpler to wear shoes.
—Sri Ramana Maharshi

But we cannot afford to fritter away our solitude where lies the throne of the infinite. We cannot truly live for one another if we never claim the freedom to live alone, if our social duties consist in helping one another to forget that we have souls. To exhaust ourselves completely in mere efforts to give company to each other is to cheat the world of our best, the best which is the product of the amplitude of our inner atmosphere of leisure. Society poisons the air it breathes, where it hems in the individual with a revolving crowd of distractions.
—Rabindranath Tagore

The Soul that hath a Guest
Doth seldom go abroad —
Diviner Crowd at Home —
Obliterate the need —

And Courtesy forbid
A Host's departure when
Upon Himself be visiting
The Emperor of Men.
—Emily Dickinson

16
WORK AND DEVOTION

Work is for the purification of the mind, not for the perception of Reality. The realization of Truth is brought about by discrimination, and not in the least by ten millions of acts.

—Shankara

Work is not what people think it is.
    It is not just something which, when it is operating,
you can see from outside.

—Rumi

This is the service man must perform all of his days: to shape matter into form, to refine the flesh, and to let the light penetrate the darkness, until the darkness itself shines and there is no longer any division between the two. As it is written: "And there was evening and there was morning, one day."

    One should not make a great to-do about serving God. Does the hand boast when it carries out what the heart wills?

—*The Ten Rungs: Hasidic Sayings*

Every one has been made for some particular work, and the desire for that work has been put into his heart.

—Rumi

God requires a faithful fulfillment of the merest trifle given us to do, rather than the most ardent aspiration to things to which we are not called.

—St. Francis de Sales

Our best work is done, our greatest influence is exerted, when we are without thought of self. All great geniuses know this. Let us open ourselves to the one Divine Actor and let Him act; let us do nothing ourselves.

—Swami Vivekananda

May the time come when men, having been awakened to a sense of the close bond linking all the movements of this world in the single, all-embracing work of the Incarnation, shall be unable to give themselves to any one of their tasks without illuminating it with the clear vision that their work — however elementary it may be — is received and put to good use by a Center of the universe.

—Teilhard de Chardin

A man should believe with perfect faith that his deeds, words, and every movement, all is God Himself. For it is He who controls man and limits his Divine Presence within him. Realizing this a man will not seek any kind of reward for his deeds since it is God Himself who is the doer, and not man.

—The Baal Shem Tov

What we have to give up is the desire to derive benefit from our actions, not the actions themselves. If we were to give up actions but continue to indulge in desires then we would simply be pretending to give up. Before undertaking an action, an ordinary worldly man always tries to assess what benefit is going to accrue to him as a result of that action. But a realized man undertakes it as a matter of duty, with no desire for its consequential benefits.

—H.H. Shantanand Saraswati

When all love of the *I* and the *Mine* is dead,
   Then the work of the Lord is done.
For work has no other aim than the getting of knowledge:
When that comes, then work is put away.

The flower blooms for the fruit: when the
   Fruit comes, the flower withers.
—Kabir

Lord Shiva said: He is said to be the greatest actor who performs deeds as they occur to him, whether joygiving or otherwise, without any fear or desire for fruition.

He is said to play his part well who performs his duties without fuss or anxiety, and maintains his reserve and purity of heart without taint of egoism or envy.

He is said to perform his part well who is not affected by any person or thing, but regards all objects as a mere witness.

—*Yoga-Vasishtha*

In action I adhere to the creative power of God; I become not only its instrument but Its living extension. And as there is nothing more personal in a being than his will, I merge myself, in a sense, through my heart, with the very heart of God. This commerce is continuous because I am always acting; and at the same time, since I can never set a boundary to the perfection of my fidelity nor to the fervor of my intention, this commerce enables me to liken myself, ever more strictly and indefinitely, to God.

The soul does not pause to relish this communion, nor does it lose sight of the material end of its action; for it is wedded to a *creative* effort. The will to succeed, a certain passionate delight in the work to be done, form an integral part of our creaturely fidelity.

—Teilhard de Chardin

There is a way whereby there is no cessation of activity and yet there is no desire. There is no concept of achievement, there is no entanglement, no attachment to any activity, and yet there is a ready response to do whatever the moment demands of you. This surrender to the activity is a state where there is no hankering by the individual — whatever is needed he picks up and puts down instantly when it is time to stop. This is unusual because in common life most of us like to complete the job, because completion of the work brings a sense of achievement — fulfillment of the desire....

It is the involvement which we have to learn to give up — if our attachments are given up, then we can reach a state where we should be able to be active and do all our work without any loss of consciousness, without any loss of energy — no sense of achievement and no fulfillment of desire.

—H.H. Shantanand Saraswati

There is guidance for each of us, and by lowly listening we shall hear the right word....For you there is a reality, a fit place and congenial duties. Place yourself in the middle of the stream of power and wisdom which animates all whom it floats, and you are without effort impelled to truth, to right and perfect contentment.

—Ralph Waldo Emerson

There's divinity that shapes our ends,
Rough-hew them how we will.
—William Shakespeare

On action alone be thy interest, never on its fruits, Let not the fruits of action by thy motive, nor be thy attachment to inaction.

—*Bhagavad Gita*

Consider that everything which happens, happens justly, and if you observe carefully, you will find it to be so. I do not say this only as regards the continuity of the sequence of things, but as regards what is just, as if it were ordered by one who assigns to everything its value. Observe then, as you have begun; and whatever you do, do it as befits that character of goodness in the sense in which a man is rightfully supposed to be good. Hold to this rule in every act.

—Marcus Aurelius

Of its very nature work is a manifold instrument of detachment, provided a man gives himself to it faithfully and without rebellion. In the first place it implies effort and a victory over inertia....An honest workman not only surrenders his calm and peace once and for all, but must learn continually to jettison the form which his labor or art or thought first took, and go in search of new forms. To pause, so as to bask in or possess results, would be a betrayal of action. Over and over again he must go beyond himself tear himself away from himself, leaving behind him his most cherished beginnings....each reality attained and left behind gives us access to the discovery and pursuit of an ideal of higher spiritual content.

—Teilhard de Chardin

You have a duty to perform. Do anything else, do any number of things, occupy your time fully, and yet, if you do not do this task, all your time will have been wasted.

—Rumi

Whenever in the morning you rise unwillingly, let this thought be with you: "I am rising to the work of a human being. Why then am I dissatisfied if I am about to do the things for which I was brought into the world?"

—Marcus Aurelius

Perform the duties of life, but work without thought of reward.
    Work must be turned into worship.
Offer worship to God regularly. Chant His name. Sing His praises and dwell more and more in the thought of Him.
Learn to see God in all beings....Be kindly to the poor and the destitute, and friendly to all.

—*Srimad Bhagavatam*

Everything belongs to the Absolute, everything is permeated by the Absolute; you use whatever you need, and the rest simply belongs to Him. This we must keep in mind when we think of renunciation.

—H.H. Shantanand Saraswati

The mind of the Sage is free from effort whether meditating or acting. His actions and meditations are not prompted by personal motives.

—*Ashtavakra Gita*

Miraculous power and marvelous activity —
Drawing water and hewing wood!

—P'ang-yun

Nonaction does not mean doing nothing and keeping silent. Let everything be allowed to do what it naturally does, so that its nature will be satisfied.

—Chuang Tsu

Who sees inaction in action, and action in inaction, he is enlightened among men; he does all actions, disciplined.

—*Bhagavad Gita*

Tao abides in nonaction,
Yet nothing is left undone.
If kings and lords observed this,
The ten thousand things would develop naturally.
If they still desired to act,
They would return to the simplicity of formless substance.
Without form there is no desire.
Without desire there is tranquillity.
And in this way all things would be at peace.

—Lao Tsu

The sage, like a child, while seemingly engaged in action is perfectly detached; without a motive, he is not identified with the work in which he is apparently engaged.

—*Ashtavakra Gita*

My sole reason for doing anything is that it delights. Mark what I say: I did not say, "that it may delight," for that is indeed future. I have no wish to depend on the future, the uncertain, and thus be deceived. No! I stand firm in the present, the certain.... I act because it satisfies me now and in eternity, and not with a view to its satisfying me at some future time, and then but for a while. Much less do I act to please mortals; for such action is not only future and very short-lived, but also superficial and based upon what others may think.... So our reason for launching on any action is, first, that it delights and satisfies; furthermore, we know that we cannot be delighted except through the very source of delight, which is God. And we know that nothing can satisfy except it be good.... Therefore...setting all else completely aside, let us strive with all our powers to satisfy God first, without which it is impossible for anything to satisfy us, for us to satisfy others, or for us to satisfy ourselves in any way at all.
—Marsilio Ficino

What you do
Still betters what is done. When you speak, sweet,
I'd have you do it ever: when you sing,
I'd have you buy and sell so; so give alms;
Pray so; and, for the ordering your affairs,
To sing them too: when you do dance, I wish you
A wave o' the sea, that you might ever do
Nothing but that; move still, still so,
And own no other function: each your doing,
So singular in each particular,
Crowns what you are going in the present deed,
That all your acts are queens.
—William Shakespeare

Creating, yet not possessing.
Working, yet not taking credit.
Work is done, then forgotten.
Therefore it lasts forever.
—Lao Tsu

"Verily all is my own Self, from Brahma to a blade of grass." This conviction brings freedom from desire and imagination, and gives purity and serenity. Reasoning thus, a man does not concern himself with what has been attained or what is to be attained.
—*Ashtavakra Gita*

We do not obtain the most precious gifts by going in search of them but by waiting for them. Man cannot discover them by his own powers, and if he sets out to seek for them he will find in their place counterfeits of which he will be unable to discern the falsity.

—Simone Weil

Therefore unattached ever perform action that must be done; for performing action without attachment, man attains the highest.

—*Bhagavad Gita*

Love only that which happens to you and is woven with the thread of your destiny. For what is more suited to your needs?

—Marcus Aurelius

And joy follows a pure thought,
like a shadow faithfully tailing a man.
We are what we think,
having become what we thought.

—*Dhammapada*

Do all you do, acting from the core of your soul, without a single "Why." I tell you, whenever what you do is done for the sake of the Kingdom of God, or for God's sake, or for eternal blessing, and thus really for ulterior motives, you are wrong. You may pass for a good person, but this is not the best. For, truly, if you imagine that you are going to get more out of God by means of religious offices and devotions, in sweet retreats and solitary orisons, than you might by the fireplace or in the stable, then you might just as well think you could seize God and wrap a mantle around his head and stick him under the table! To seek God by rituals is to get the ritual and lose God in the process, for he hides behind it. On the other hand, to seek God without artifice is to take him as he is, and so doing, a person "lives by the Son," and is the Life itself.

For if Life were questioned a thousand years and asked: "Why live?" and if there were an answer, it could be no more than this: "I live only to live!" And that is because Life is its own reason for being, springs from its own Source, and goes on and on, without ever asking why — just because it is life. Thus, if you ask a genuine person, that is, one who acts from his heart: "Why are you doing that?" — he will reply in the only possible way: "I do it because I do it!"

—Meister Eckhart

In the soul of man there is a justice whose retributions are instant and entire. He who does a good deed, is instantly ennobled. He who does a mean deed, is by the action itself contracted. He who puts off impurity, thereby puts on purity. If a man is at heart just, then in so far is he God; the safety of God, the immortality of God, the majesty of God do enter into that man with justice. If a man dissemble, deceive, he deceives himself, and goes out of acquaintance with his own being.

—Ralph Waldo Emerson

Jesus said: Do not lie; and do not do what you hate, for all things are manifest before Heaven. For there is nothing hidden that shall not be revealed and there is nothing covered that shall remain without being uncovered.

—*The Gospel of Thomas*

The devout seeker is he who mingles in his heart the double currents of
    love and detachment, like the mingling of the streams of
    Ganges and Jumna.
—Kabir

The desire to do good is the highest motive power we have if we know that it is a privilege to help others. Do not stand on a high pedestal and take five cents in your hand and say, "Here, my poor man!" But be grateful that the poor man is there, so that by making a gift to him you are able to help yourself. It is not the receiver that is blessed, but it is the giver.

—Swami Vivekananda

Fill every act with the spirit of devotion, and every act becomes an act of devotion....Devotion is a power of the heart. Let this single power drive all your actions, just as a single electric main drives all the machinery in a factory.

—H.H. Shantanand Saraswati

To offer everything to the Divine is surrender. To give our lives to the Divine is surrender. Simplicity is surrender. When we are simple the ego will dissolve by itself; when we are simple the answers will come. Always to remember that no matter how great we are, that there is something greater — the Divine — is surrender. Not to be egotistic is surrender. To be humble is surrender.

—Mother Meera

When [devotion] conflicts with any person's legitimate occupation, it is without doubt false.... But true devotion... not only does it not spoil any sort of life-situation or occupation, but on the contrary enriches it and makes it attractive...everyone becomes more pleasant in one's state of life by joining it with devotion. Devotion makes the care of the family peaceful, the love of husband and wife more sincere...and every sort of occupation more pleasant and more lovable.

—St. Francis de Sales

When man studies or prays with reverence and devoutness begotten of love, and fastens and binds his spirit to God and remembers that nothing is void of him and without him, but that everything is filled with life granted by the Creator, then, in all he sees, he sees the living power of the Creator and hears his living voice. That is the meaning of the words: "The tree of life in the midst of the garden." He who clings to the life of God is in the midst of the garden [of paradise].

—*Ten Rungs: Hasidic Sayings*

To believe your own thought, to believe that what is true for you in your private heart is true for all men — that is genius. Speak your latent conviction, and it shall be the universal sense; for the inmost in due time becomes the outmost, and our first thought is rendered back to us by the trumpets of the Last Judgment.

—Ralph Waldo Emerson

Insofar as divine love enriches us it is called grace, which makes us pleasing to God. Insofar as it gives us the strength to do good, it is called charity. But when it grows to such a degree of perfection that it makes us not only do good but rather moves us to do it carefully, frequently and promptly, it is called devotion....

In short, devotion is nothing else than a spiritual agility and liveliness by means of which charity realizes its actions in us, or we do so by charity, promptly and lovingly.

—St. Francis de Sales

In the world take always the position of the giver. Give everything and look for no return. Give love, give help, give service, give any little thing you can, but keep out barter. Make no conditions and none will be imposed. Let us give out of our own bounty, just as God gives to us.

—Swami Vivekananda

Men can never escape from obedience to God. A creature cannot but obey. The only choice given to men, as intelligent and free creatures, is to desire obedience or not to desire it. If a man does not desire it, he obeys nevertheless, perpetually, inasmuch as he is a thing subject to mechanical necessity. If he desires it, he is still subject to mechanical necessity, but a new necessity is added to it, a necessity constituted by laws belonging to supernatural things. Certain actions become impossible for him; others are done by his agency, sometimes almost in spite of himself.

    —Simone Weil

What we call fate does not come to us from outside: it goes forth from within us.

    —Rainer Maria Rilke

Mentally resigning all deeds to Me, regarding Me as the Supreme, resorting to mental concentration, do thou ever fix thy heart in Me.

    —*Bhagavad Gita*

Among all means of liberation, devotion is supreme. To seek earnestly to know one's real nature — this is said to be devotion.

    —Shankara

Practice becomes firmly grounded when it has been cultivated for a long time, uninterruptedly, with earnest devotion.

    —Patanjali

17
NECESSARY VIRTUES

Virtue consists in allowing free passage, in the soul, to the Beauty of God.
  —Frithjof Schuon

Undisturbed calmness of mind is attained by cultivating friendliness toward the happy, compassion for the unhappy, delight in the virtuous, and indifference toward the wicked.
  —Patanjali

Regard, affection and friendliness, sympathy, fellow-feeling and love are not feelings to be thrown away because he has taken to the philosophic quest. On the contrary, they may become valuable stepping-stones in his progress if he treats them aright, if he evaluates them correctly, purifies them emotionally, and ennobles them morally.
  —Paul Brunton

He who knows others is learned;
  He who knows himself is wise.
He who conquers others has power of muscles;
  He who conquers himself is strong.
He who is contented is rich.
  He who is determined has strength of will.
He who does not lose his center endures,
He who dies yet remains has long life.
  —*Tao Te Ching*

The virtuous man delights in this world, and he delights in the next; he delights in both. He delights and rejoices, when he sees the purity of his own work.
  The virtuous man is happy in this world, and he is happy in the next; he is happy in both. He is happy when he thinks of the good he has done; he is still more happy when going on the good path.
  —*Dhammapada*

Soberness is a kind of beautiful order and a continence of certain pleasures and appetites...the soul of a man within him has a better part and a worse part, and the expression "self-mastery" means the control of the worse by the naturally better part.
 —Plato

Attain the utmost in Humility;
Hold firm to the basis of Quietude.

The myriad things take shape and rise to activity,
 But I watch them fall back to their repose.
Like vegetation that luxuriantly grows
 But returns to the root from which it springs.

To return to the root is Repose;
 It is called going back to one's Destiny.
Going back to one's Destiny is to find the Eternal Law.
 To know the Eternal Law is Enlightenment.
And not to know the Eternal Law
 Is to court disaster.

He who knows the Eternal Law is tolerant;
Being tolerant, he is impartial;
Being impartial, he is kingly;
Being kingly, he is in accord with Nature;
Being in accord with Nature, he is in accord with Tao;
Being in accord with Tao, he is eternal,
And his whole life is preserved from harm.
 —*Tao Te Ching*

God wants nothing of you but the gift of a peaceful heart.
 —Meister Eckhart

You have no time or opportunity to read and to know everything; but you do have time and opportunity to check arrogance, to be superior to pleasure and pain and love of fame, and not to be vexed at stupid and ungrateful people, and even to care for them.
 —Marcus Aurelius

Contentment is as a sweet fragrance in the mind, and virtuous acts are as beautiful as the petals of a rose. The flower of inward discrimination is opened like the lotus bud by the sunbeams of reason and produces the fruit of holiness.
 —*Yoga-Vasishtha*

You say that you have no keenness of wit. Be it so; but there are many other things of which you cannot say that nature has not endowed you. Show those qualities then which are perfectly in your power — sincerity, gravity, patience in labor, aversion to pleasure, contentment with your lot and with little, frankness, dislike of superfluity, freedom from pettiness. Do you not see how many qualities you are immediately able to exhibit, as to which you have no excuse of natural incapacity and unfitness, and yet you still remain voluntarily below what you might be? ... If in truth you can be accused of being rather slow and dull of comprehension, you must exert yourself about this also, not neglecting it nor yet finding pleasure in your dullness.
—Marcus Aurelius

To be a philosopher is not merely to have subtle thoughts, nor even to found a school, but so to love wisdom as to live according to its dictates a life of simplicity, independence, magnanimity, and trust. It is to solve some of the problems of life, not only theoretically, but practically.
—Henry David Thoreau

The wise man shuns the ignorant. In his just and courteous behavior and his calm and pleasant countenance, he resembles the fair moon with her ambrosial beams. He acts with sound wisdom and prudence; he is polite and gracious in his manner; he is prompt in serving and obliging others, and pure in conduct....

Wherever he goes or stays, he is always calm and self-governed, silent and in command of himself. Though well-informed, he is yet ever in quest of knowledge, and inquiring into Truth.
—Yoga-Vasishtha

Like the sun which emits countless rays, compassion is the source of all inner growth and positive action.
—Tarthang Tulku

Clear thinking, right action, discipline and restraint
make an island for the wise man,
an island safe from floods.
—Dhammapada

By two wings a man is raised above the earth, namely, by simplicity and purity. Simplicity must be in the motive, purity in the affection; simplicity aims at God, purity embraces and tastes Him. No good action will hinder you, if you are inwardly free from all self-seeking....

If you were inwardly good and pure, you would see all things without hindrance, and understand them well. A pure heart penetrates heaven and hell. Whatever a man's inward state is, his judgment on external matters will accord with it.

　　—Thomas à Kempis

I shall never pray that God give me himself. I shall pray that he make me pure; for if I am pure, God must give himself and dwell in me, because it is his peculiar nature to do so.

　　—Meister Eckhart

What is the opposing quality to the violence of today? Not merely nonviolence — a negative one — but gentleness — a positive one.

　　—Paul Brunton

A philosophic temperament, well-developed and sufficiently rounded, has little taste for the ugly bareness propagated in the name of simple living, or for the dreary denial of the beautiful arts in the name of anti-sensuality.

　　—Paul Brunton

The greatest power and virtue spring from lowliness and humility.

　　—Jacob Boehme

18
DETACHMENT AND SERENITY

The Creator created the universe in all its different aspects and forms. He observes the drama which he has created. All who take part in this play and know its mystery and essence are detached. They play their part and enjoy it. Those who do not know its mystery become identified with their parts and are bound by them. When they lose their identification they too can enjoy playing their part in the grand drama without being bound.

—H.H. Shantanand Saraswati

For a true lover of God loveth Him or the Eternal Goodness alike, in having and in not having, in sweetness and bitterness, in good or evil report, and the like, for he seeketh alone the honor of God, and not his own, either in spiritual or natural things. And therefore he standeth alike unshaken in all things, at all seasons.

—*Theologia Germanica*

He is ever content who is convinced that adversity and prosperity come in the fullness of time or are caused by karma. His senses are controlled, he neither desires nor grieves.

—*Ashtavakra Gita*

Consider that everything is opinion, and opinion is in your power. Disown opinion when you choose; and like a mariner who has doubled the promontory, you will find calm, still waters and a waveless bay.

—Marcus Aurelius

Call him wise
whose mind is calm,
whose senses are controlled,
who is unaffected by good and evil,
who is wakeful.
—*Dhammapada*

He who performs his duty with his organs of action, but has fixed his mind in internal meditation, and who is unmoved by joy or grief, he is called the dispassionate yogi.

He who looks calmly on the course of the world as it passes or presents itself before him, and sits smiling at its vicissitudes, that man is called the dispassionate yogi.

One possessed of such spiritual dispassion and equanimity attains the highest perfection and is quite unconcerned as to his external rise or fall, his life or death.
—*Yoga-Vasishtha*

We must not wish anything other than what happens from moment to moment, all the while, however, exercising ourselves in goodness.
—St. Catherine of Genoa

Non-attachment is self-mastery; it is freedom from desire for what is seen or heard.
—Patanjali

The effects of enlightenment include: an imperturbable detachment from outer possessions, rank, honors, and persons; an overwhelming certainty about truth; a carefree, heavenly peace above all disturbances and vicissitudes; an acceptance of the general rightness of the universal situation, with each entity and each event playing its role; and impeccable sincerity which says what it means, means what it says.
—Paul Brunton

When, by reflection on the state of your mind, you have come to know your nature, you will remain unmoved either by joy or grief, like a firm rock.
—*Yoga-Vasishtha*

I consider that man wise and fortunate who lives happy in the midst of calamities because he depends on God alone; whom fear does not weaken, nor pain torment; who is not corrupted by desire, nor inflamed by passion.
—Marsilio Ficino

One of the excellent practices of gentleness that we could learn has to do with ourselves: never to be provoked at ourselves or our imperfections. Even though it is reasonable that we must be sorry and displeased when we commit some faults, yet we must refrain from a harsh, vexed, gloomy, and angry displeasure. Many make a great mistake in this regard. When they are overcome by anger, they become angry at being angry, vexed at being vexed, fretful at being fretful. By this means, they keep their hearts steeped and soaked in anger.... Moreover, these vexations, harshness, and anger which we have against ourselves tend to pride. They have no other origin than self-love which is disturbed and anxious at seeing ourselves imperfect.

—St. Francis de Sales

Nothing happens to any man which he is not framed by nature to bear.

—Marcus Aurelius

Joy and suffering are two equally precious gifts, both of which must be savored to the full, each one in its purity, without trying to mix them. Through joy, the beauty of the world penetrates our soul. Through suffering, it penetrates our body.

—Simone Weil

God is our refuge and strength, a very present help in trouble.

Therefore will not we fear, though the earth be removed, and though the mountains be carried into the midst of the sea;

Though the waters thereof roar and be troubled, though the mountains shake with the swelling thereof. Selah.

There is a river, the streams whereof shall make glad the city of God, the holy place of the tabernacles of the Most High.

God is in the midst of her; she shall not be moved: God shall help her, and that right early.

—Psalm 46:1–5

My son, patience and humility in adversity are more pleasing to Me, than much consolation and devotion in prosperity....

Consider then your great frailty, which you have often experienced on slight occasions, yet for your salvation these occur....

If tribulation have touched you, be not depressed nor much perplexed. At least bear it patiently, if you cannot bear it joyfully....Soon shall the angry feelings which are stirred up subside, and the pain of the soul be sweetly soothed by returning grace.

—Thomas à Kempis

Remember, too, this maxim on every occasion that tempts you to vexation: "This is not a misfortune; and to bear it nobly is good fortune."
—Marcus Aurelius

I order my soul to look upon pain and pleasure with a gaze equally disciplined and equally firm, but gaily at the one, and severely at the other, and according to its ability, as anxious to extinguish the one as to extend the other. Viewing good things sanely involves viewing bad things sanely. And pain has something not to be avoided in its gently beginning, and pleasure something to be avoided in its excessive ending.
—Michel de Montaigne

Whatever sacrifice may be made in the service of the Lord, know that it is the equanimity of your soul that is the best and fittest offering. Equanimity is sweet to taste and has the supernatural power of transforming everything to ambrosia.

Equanimity expands the soul and gladdens the mind, as the sunlight fills the vault of heaven, and it is considered to be the highest devotion.
—*Yoga-Vasishtha*

The other kind of concentration is that in which the consciousness contains no object — only subconscious impressions, which are like burnt seeds. It is attained by constantly checking the thought waves through the practice of nonattachment.
—Patanjali

He who binds to himself a joy
Does the winged life destroy;
But he who kisses the joy as it flies
Lives in Eternity's sun rise.
—William Blake

Whose mind lingers not over the past, nor goes out after the future, when perfect equanimity is gained, this is the mark of him who is free even in life.
—Shankara

Whoso, without attachment anywhere, on meeting with anything good or bad, neither exults nor hates, his knowledge becomes steady.
—*Bhagavad Gita*

Be like the cliff against which the waves continually break; but it stands firm and tames the fury of the water around it.
　　—Marcus Aurelius

Therefore, without attachment, constantly perform the action which should be done; for, performing action without attachment, man reaches the Supreme.
　　—*Bhagavad Gita*

Leisure, it must be clearly understood, is a mental and spiritual attitude — it is not simply the result of external factors, it is not the inevitable result of spare time, a holiday, a weekend or a vacation. It is, in the first place, an attitude of mind, a condition of the soul, and as such utterly contrary to the ideal of "worker" in each and every one of the three aspects .... work as activity, as toil, as a social function.

Compared with the exclusive ideal of work as activity, leisure implies an attitude of nonactivity, of inward calm, of silence; it means not being "busy," but letting things happen.

Leisure is a form of silence, of that silence which is the prerequisite of the apprehension of reality: only the silent hear and those who do not remain silent do not hear. Silence...does not mean "dumbness"...; it means more nearly that the soul's power to "answer" to the reality of the world is left undisturbed. For leisure is a receptive attitude of mind, a contemplative attitude, and it is not only the occasion but also the capacity for steeping oneself in the whole of creation.

Furthermore, there is also a certain serenity in leisure. That serenity spring precisely from our inability to understand, from our recognition of the mysterious nature of the universe; it springs from the courage of deep confidence, so that we are content to let things take their course....

Leisure is not the attitude of mind of those who actively intervene, but of those who are open to everything; not of those who grab and grab hold, but of those who leave the reins loose and who are free and easy themselves — almost like a man falling asleep....

Leisure appears in its character as an attitude of contemplative "celebration," a word that, properly understood, goes to the very heart of what we mean by leisure. Leisure is possible only on the premise that man consents to his own true nature, and abides in concord with the meaning of the universe. Leisure draws its vitality from affirmation. It is tranquillity; it is not even the same as inward tranquillity. Rather, it is like the tranquil silence of lovers, which draws its strength from concord.
　　—Josef Pieper

Until you know the Truth, you cannot have peace of mind, and as long as your are a stranger to mental tranquillity, you are debarred from knowing the Truth.
　　—*Yoga-Vasishtha*

To turn one's mind instantly towards the divinity within, when in the presence of discordant people, is to silence harsh thoughts and to banish hurtful feelings. This frequent turning inward is necessary not only for spiritual growth but for self-protection. Everything and everyone around us plays a potent influence upon our minds, and this is the best means of detaching oneself from this ceaseless flow of suggestions.

—Paul Brunton

It is easy in the world to live after the world's opinion; it is easy in solitude to live after our own; but the great man is he who in the midst of the crowd keeps with perfect sweetness the independence of solitude.

—Ralph Waldo Emerson

Abandoning attachment to the fruits of action, constantly content, independent, even when he sets out upon action, he yet does (in effect) nothing whatsoever.

—*Bhagavad Gita*

Retire into yourself. The nature of the rational principle that rules us is to be content with itself when it does what is just, and so secures tranquillity.

—Marcus Aurelius

Anxiety produces misery and nothing else. He who realizes this relinquishes all desires and is calm and happy.

—*Ashtavakra Gita*

Leave untouched whatever is tangible or can be obtained by you through your own agency; remain unaffected and independent of anything in the world, and rely only on your consciousness of Infinity. Think of yourself as sleeping when you are awake; think of yourself as all, and as one with the supreme Spirit,

—*Yoga-Vasishtha*

19
MEDITATION, REFLECTION, CONTEMPLATION

To meditate is to be, to be one, one without a second...One becomes the Self. The method of meditation is only a process by which this is made possible. The Absolute meditates and becomes the creation; we meditate and become the Absolute.
 —H.H. Shantanand Saraswati

Concentration may also be attained by fixing the mind upon the Inner Light, which is beyond sorrow.
 —Patanjali

The word which expresses him is OM.
This word must be repeated with meditation upon its meaning.
Hence comes knowledge of the Atman and destruction of the
 obstacles to that knowledge.
 —Patanjali

Divine meditation in the form of *So-Hum,* or *Shivo-Hum,* unaccompanied by any desire or selfish aim, penetrates like the moon's rays through the darkness of the night of ignorance.
 There is a distant resemblance to this spiritual light in the intellectual light of the philosophers.
 —*Yoga-Vasishtha*

Little by little let him come to rest through the consciousness, held with firmness; keeping the thought-organ fixed in the self, he should think on nothing at all.
 Because of whatsoever thing strays the thought-organ, fickle and unstable, from every such thing holding it back, he shall bring it into control in the self alone.
 —*Bhagavad Gita*

Seated in a secluded place, free from all disturbing thoughts of the world, one must first repeat in one's mind the sacred word OM, with understanding of its meaning. The word OM is one with God, and indeed is God...with the discriminative faculty as guide, one should, with the help of the mind draw the senses and the sense organs completely away from the objects of the world. Let the devotee meditate upon the Lord. Let him be absorbed in Him. When absorption comes, there arises a great calmness, a transcendental bliss. That is the supreme goal, the abode of Vishnu, the kingdom of heaven.

If for any reason the mind becomes restless again, being overpowered by *rajas* or deluded by *tamas,* let it be brought again under control by the practice of concentration.

—*Srimad Bhagavatam*

Quintessential prayer takes us out of the world and life, and thereby confers a new and divine sap upon the veil of appearances and the current of forms, and a fresh meaning to our presence amid the play of phenomena.

—Frithjof Schuon

Genuine prayer is meditation: the calling or invoking into oneself of a portion of Divine Consciousness. Petitionary prayer is not meant, of course. Rather it is that type of prayer wherein one opens his inner nature to the reception of the Divine Guest.... Meditation can indeed be the means of welcoming into the heart and mind of the devotee the essence of his own Higher Self, his Buddhic Splendor; and it should be done more and more completely until...the student learns to recognize his own inner Teacher.

—L. Gordon Plummer

My son, attend to my words; incline thine ear unto my sayings.
    Let them not depart from thine eyes; keep them in the midst of thine heart.
    For they are life unto those that find them, and health to all their flesh.
    Keep thy heart with all diligence; for out of it are the issues of life.

—Proverbs 4:20–23

The intelligent man gives up happiness and sorrow by developing concentration of mind on the Self and thereby meditating on the old Deity who is inscrutable, lodged inaccessibly, located in the intellect, and seated in the midst of misery.

—*Katha Upanishad*

The Self is self-effulgent. One need give it no mental picture, any way. The thought that imagines is itself bondage, because the Self is the effulgence transcending darkness and light; one should not think of it with the mind. Such imagination will end in bondage, whereas the Self is spontaneously shining as the Absolute. This enquiry into the Self in the form of devotional meditation evolves into the state of absorption of the mind into the Self and leads to liberation.

—Sri Ramana Maharshi

It is the abstract meditation of the thoughtful yogi, devoted to the holy yoga, that weakens the outer impressions, and, by dissociating the soul from all external things, keeps it steady and sedate in itself. The mind does not then pay attention to its inward or outward reflections and is insensible to pleasure and pain, and feels in itself the delight of unity.

—*Yoga-Vasishtha*

As long as you continue to restrain your sense-organs from their objects, so long will the divine Spirit grace your inward soul with Its presence. The sight of the supreme Spirit will remove the manifold prejudices of your mind, and will drive away all misery, pouring Itself down in bountiful showers before your eyes.

—*Yoga-Vasishtha*

The God of Love exists in the heart of all. He is our very Self, and therefore very dear to us. He is Truth. He is Infinity. He is the omnipotent Lord. Hence should a man, freed from all selfish desires, and his mind fixed on God, worship Him alone.

—*Srimad Bhagavatam*

When he completely withdraws the senses from sense-objects, as the tortoise withdraws its limbs from all sides, his knowledge is steady.

—*Bhagavad Gita*

Hear now the method of the worship of God, O my beloved pupil. In all forms of worship you must cease to think of your body, and separate your mind from your personality. You must then apply your mind diligently, under the guidance of your Teacher, to thinking of the pure and bodiless Spirit, which witnesses the operations of the body from within.

True worship consists in inward meditation alone, and in no outer form of worship; therefore apply your mind to the adoration of the universal Spirit by meditation within yourself.

He is the form of the intellect, the source of all light, and glorious as millions of suns! ...

He is situated in the midst of all things, and is the sole giver of strength and energy to all.

Tat Twam Asi! That thou art!

O, adore Him in yourself! He requires no illumination, or burning of incense.

—*Yoga-Vasishtha*

When we would rest our bodies we cease to support them; we recline on the lap of earth. So when we would rest our spirits, we must recline on the Great Spirit.

—Henry David Thoreau

———————————————

Do not go to the garden of flowers!
　O Friend! Go not there:
In your body is the garden of flowers.
Take your seat on the thousand petals of the lotus,
　and there gaze on the Infinite Beauty.

—Kabir

The wise man should every day meditate carefully on his Self.

—Shankara

Then, holding firmly mind, with knowing soul at rest, know your self within yourself face to face saying, "This am I." The life-ocean, whose waves are birth and dying, is shoreless; cross over it, fulfilling the end of being, resting firm in the Eternal.

—Shankara

God is the refuge and strength of all. One ought, therefore, to hear about Him, sing His praises, worship Him, and meditate upon Him. To the wise, meditation is like a sword to sever the knots of all evil Karma.

—*Srimad Bhagavatam*

Endeavor to ascend into thyself, gathering in from the body all thy members which have been dispersed and scattered into multiplicity from that unity which once abounded in the greatness of its power. Bring together and unify the inborn ideas and try to articulate those that are confused and to draw into light those that are obscured.

—Porphyry

By constant meditation is kindled the flame of knowledge, which completely burns up the fuel of ignorance.

—Shankara

Sitting in a solitary place, freeing the mind from desires, and controlling the senses, meditate with unswerving attention on the Infinite Atman, which is one without a second.

—Shankara

One should know OM to be God seated in the hearts of all. Meditating on the all-pervasive OM, the intelligent man grieves no more.

The OM, without measures and possessed of infinite dimension, is the auspicious entity where all duality ceases. He by whom OM is known is the real sage, and not so is any other man.

—*Mandukya Upanishad*

Without constant practice one cannot achieve a cognition of the Self, which is reality and pure consciousness. To acquire the highest good the inquirer must therefore practice meditation on Brahman for a very long time.

—Shankara

To attempt to think of the Self which is beyond the range of thought is only to create a new thought. Abandoning such a thought, I abide in peace.

—*Ashtavakra Gita*

Little by little let him withdraw, by reason held in firmness; keeping the mind established in the Self, let him not think of anything.

By whatever cause the wavering and unsteady mind wanders away from that, let him restrain it and bring it back direct under the control of the Self.

—*Bhagavad Gita*

As we experience this deeper level of meditation, we will find that the nature of mind *is* meditation, and that, itself, is actually the enlightened experience.

—Tarthang Tulku

Seek a convenient time to devote to yourself, and meditate often on the benefits which God has bestowed on you. Leave curious matters, and read such subjects as are calculated to produce compunction more than occupation of mind. If you withdraw yourself from superfluous conversations and inquisitive restlessness, as also from hearkening to news and rumors, you will find that you have sufficient and fitting time for making good meditations.

—Thomas à Kempis

Know your true Atman as the witness of the mind and intellect, and of the thought waves that arise in them. Raise one single wave of thought constantly: "I am Brahman." Thus you will free yourself from identification with non-Atman.

—Shankara

We only possess one book that leadeth to God, each of us hath it in himself; it is the dear name of God, its letters are the flames of love which He has revealed to us in the blessed name of Jesus. Only ponder these same letters in your heart and spirit — and you have books enough. Only see to it that you be born again into the life and spirit of Christ, then you possess all God is and can be.

—Jacob Boehme

When love is wedded to meditation, it gives birth to contemplation; we meditate to awaken love, we contemplate because we love. That is why I have described contemplation as a *loving* preoccupation — it is a child of love.

—St. Francis de Sales

Reflection is in truth a benevolent helper which discovers and assists in finding where the absolute object of faith and worship is — namely, there where the difference between knowledge and ignorance collapses into a consciousness of ignorance, there where the resistance of an objective uncertainty tortures forth the passionate certainty of faith, there where the conflict of right and wrong collapses in absolute worship with absolute subjection. Reflection itself does not see the absolute, but it leads...the individual up to it, and says: "Here, I guarantee, when you worship here, you worship God."

—Søren Kierkegaard

So it is clear... that the philosopher frees his soul from association with the body, so far as is possible.

Then when is it that the soul attains to truth? When it tries to investigate anything with the help of the body, it is obviously led astray .... Is it not in the course of reflection, if at all, that the soul gets a clear view of facts? ... Surely the soul can best reflect when it is free of all distractions such as hearing or sight or pain or pleasure of any kind — that is, when it ignores the body and becomes as far as possible independent, avoiding all physical contacts and associations as much as it can, in its search for reality....

The man who pursues the truth by applying his pure and unadulterated thought to the pure and unadulterated object, cutting himself off...from his eyes and ears and virtually all the rest of his body as an impediment...to truth and clear thinking. Is not this the person...who will reach the goal of reality, if anybody can?

—Plato

Men seek retreats for themselves, houses in the country, seashores, and mountains; and you too are wont to desire such things very much. But this is altogether a mark of the common sort of man, for it is in your power, whenever you shall choose, to retire into yourself. For nowhere with more quiet or more freedom from trouble does a man retire than into his own soul, particularly when he has within him such thoughts that by looking into them he is at once perfectly tranquil; and this tranquillity, I am sure, is nothing but the good ordering of the mind. Constantly then grant yourself this retreat and refreshment; let your principles be brief and fundamental, which, as soon as you shall call them to mind, will be sufficient to cleanse the soul completely, and send you back free from all discontent.

—Marcus Aurelius

Besides the mental solitude, to which you may turn in the midst of the greatest transactions, you must always love the real solitude of a place. You need not go into the deserts.... Instead remain in your room, in your garden, or elsewhere for a short while. There at will you may withdraw your spirit into your heart and refresh your mind by good reflections and holy thoughts, or by a short reading.

—St. Francis de Sales

When the act of reflection takes place in the mind, when we look at ourselves in the light of thought, we discover, that our life is embosomed in beauty .... If in the hours of clear reason we should speak the severest truth, we should say that we had never made a sacrifice.... In these hours the mind seems so great that nothing can be taken from us that seems much.... For it is only the finite that has wrought and suffered, the infinite lies stretched in smiling repose.

—Ralph Waldo Emerson

What is necessary, after all, is only this: solitude, vast inner solitude, To walk inside yourself and meet no one for hours — that is what you must be able to attain.

—Rainer Maria Rilke

Knowledge is one of the conditions of love, and words are one of the conditions of any form of rational knowledge. Hence the importance, in the spiritual life, of a working hypothesis regarding the highest, most real good. Hallowing God's *name* is thinking verbalized thoughts about God, as a means to passing from mere intellectual knowledge to a living experience of reality. Discursive meditation precedes and is the preparation for contemplation; access to God Himself can be had through a proper use of the name of God. This is true, not only in the extended sense in which the word has hitherto been used, but also in the most limited and literal sense. Wherever spiritual religion has flourished, it has been found that a constant repetition of sacred names can serve a very useful purpose in keeping the mind one-pointed and preparing it for contemplation.

—Aldous Huxley

Prayer in its lower stages is an introspection into the state of the mind. In the next step, it is a lifting up of the stilled mind to the spiritual principle in it. In its highest aspect, it is an intuitive recognition of the presence of God in it, and the discovery of the identity between the substratum of the mind and the Lord.

—Hari Prasad Shastri

Only be still and wait for the Lord; thy desires will at last prevail; thou shalt feel it so in thy heart and shalt thank God. God requireth in prayer a soul that is open and transparent.... He who prays aright, worketh inwardly with God, and bringeth forth good fruit. As the strength of the tree shows itself in the fruit, so the true divine strength in a man is shown in his good works and virtues. "There is no faith without works." Otherwise prayer is but a mockery and an outward form, and does not attain to the City of God.

—Jacob Boehme

Firmly fixing the mind on the goal, the Eternal, keeping the outward senses in their place, with form unmoved, heedless of the body's state, entering into the oneness of Self and Eternal by assimilating the Self and rising above all differences, for ever drink the essence of the bliss of the Eternal in the Self. What profit is there in other things that give no joy?

—Shankara

It is not only man that is made in the image of God: the whole universe likewise is also an image of God. It is not only by coming to know himself that man discovers the divine life hidden deep in his heart: it is also by listening in the stillness of Nature to what she is forever declaring, that he discovers the presence of an infinite World-Mind.

—Paul Brunton

If thou couldst enter for a moment into that wherein no creature dwelleth, then Thou wouldst hear what God speaketh…It is in thyself, and if thou couldst be silent for an hour from all thy thinking and willing, thou wouldst hear the unspeakable words of God …. If thou desist from the thinking and willing of thy self-hood, the eternal hearing, seeing, and speaking will reveal itself in thee, and God will be seen in thee …. If thou wouldst indeed come into harmony with all things, thou must forsake all …. If thou desirest nothing, then art thou free from all and rulest over all.

    —Jacob Boehme

Cease inwardly from thought and word, be motionless within you, look upward into the light and outward into the vast cosmic consciousness that is around you. Be more and more one with the brightness and the vastness. Then will Truth dawn on you from above and flow in you from all around you.

    —Sri Aurobindo

When I would recreate myself, I seek the darkest wood, the thickest and most interminable, and to the citizen, most dismal swamp. I enter a swamp as a sacred place — a *sanctum sanctorum*. There is the strength, the marrow of nature. The wild-wood covers the virgin mold — and the same soil is good for men and trees.

    —Henry David Thoreau

The soul of leisure, it can be said, lies in "celebration." Celebration is the point at which the three elements of leisure come to a focus: relaxation, effortlessness, and superiority of "active leisure" to all functions.

But if celebration is the core of leisure, then leisure can only be made possible and justifiable on the same basis as the celebration of a festival. *That basis is divine worship.…*

In divine worship a certain definite space and time is set aside from working hours and days, a limited time, specially marked off — and like the space allotted to the temple, is not *used,* is withdrawn from all merely utilitarian ends.…

Divine worship, of its very nature, creates a sphere of real wealth and superfluity, even in the midst of the direst material want — because sacrifice is the living heart of worship. And what does sacrifice mean? It means a voluntary offering freely given.

    —Josef Pieper

Prayer is the contemplation of the facts of life from the highest point of view. It is the soliloquy of a beholding and jubilant soul. It is the spirit of God pronouncing his works good.

But prayer as a means to effect a private end is meanness and theft. It supposes dualism and not unity in nature and consciousness. As soon as the man is at one with God, he will not beg. He will then see prayer in all action.

    —Ralph Waldo Emerson

20
THE ETERNAL NOW, ATTENTION, AND STILLNESS

If we knew how to greet each moment as the manifestation of the divine will, we would find in it all the heart could desire.... The present moment is always filled with infinite treasures: it contains more than you are capable of receiving.... The divine will is an abyss, of which the present moment is the entrance; plunge fearlessly therein and you will find it more boundless than your desire.

    —J.P. de Caussade

Infinity shall be contained in every deed of man, in his speaking and seeing, listening and walking, standing still and lying down.

    —*Ten Rungs: Hasidic Sayings*

These roses under my window make no reference to former roses or to better ones; they are for what they are; they exist with God today. There is no time for them. There is simply the rose; it is perfect in every moment of its existence.... But man postpones or remembers; he does not live in the present, but with reverted eye laments the past, or, heedless of the riches that surround him, stands on tiptoe to foresee the future. He cannot be happy and strong until he too lives with nature in the present, above time.

    —Ralph Waldo Emerson

Within the immediate, direct, and present moment of the experience, there is nothing you can say or think or label.

    —Tarthang Tulku

A wise man will never impawn his future being and action, and decide beforehand what he shall do in a given extreme event. Nature and God will instruct him in that hour.

    —Ralph Waldo Emerson

Men esteem truth remote, in the outskirts of the system behind the farthest star, before Adam and after the last man. In eternity there is indeed something true and sublime. But all these times and places and occasions are now and here. God himself culminates in the present moment, and will never be more divine in the lapse of all the ages. And we are enabled to apprehend at all what is sublime and noble only by the perpetual instilling and drenching of the reality that surrounds us. The universe constantly and obediently answers to our conceptions; whether we travel fast or slow, the track is laid for us.
   —Henry David Thoreau

Forever — is composed of Nows —
This not a different time —
Except for Infiniteness —
And Latitude of Home —

From this — experienced Here —
Remove the Dates — to These —
Let Months dissolve in further Months —
And Years — exhale in Years —

Without Debate — or Pause —
Or Celebrated Days —
No different Our Years would be
From *Anno Domini's* —
   —Emily Dickinson

Nature never makes haste; her systems revolve at an even pace.... Why, then, should man hasten as if anything less than eternity were allotted for the least deed? The wise man is restful, never restless or impatient. He each moment abides where he is, as some walkers actually rest the whole body at each step, while others never relax the muscles of the legs till the accumulated fatigue obliges them to stop short.
   —Henry David Thoreau

Every moment is of infinite worth because it is the symbolization of the whole of eternity.
   —Johann Wolfgang von Goethe

Health requires this relaxation, this aimless life. This life in the present.
   —Henry David Thoreau

The Now in which God created the first man and the Now in which the last man will disappear and the Now in which I am speaking — all are the same in God, and there is only one Now.
—Meister Eckhart

The purpose of life seems to be to acquaint a man with himself. He is not to live to the future as described to him but to live to the real future by living to the present.
—Ralph Waldo Emerson

Take time by the forelock. Now or never. You must live in the present, launch yourself on every wave, find your eternity in each moment. Fools stand on their island opportunities and look toward another land. There is no other land; there is no other life but this, or the like of this.
—Henry David Thoreau

The space in which the process of thinking takes place is time. It could not exist without the dimension of time. If thought is ever transcended, time is transcended along with it. Such an achievement throws the mind into the pure present, the eternal now, "the presence of God" of all mystics.
—Paul Brunton

None can achieve eternal life who has not first learned to live, not in the past or in the future, but now — in the moment at the moment.
—Aldous Huxley

In an instant, rise from time and space. Set the world aside and become a world within yourself.
—Shabestari

In this moment there is nothing which comes to be.
In this moment there is nothing which ceases to be.
Thus there is no birth and death to be brought to an end.
Wherefore the absolute tranquillity is this present moment.
Though it is at this moment, there is no limit to this moment,
    and herein is eternal delight.
—T'an-ching

If by eternity is understood not endless temporal duration but timelessness, then he lives eternally who lives in the present.
—Ludwig Wittgenstein

When I dance, I dance: when I sleep, I sleep; yes, and when I walk alone in a beautiful orchard, if my thoughts have been concerned with extraneous incidents for some part of the time... I lead them back again to the walk, to the orchard, to the sweetness of this solitude, and to myself.

—Michel de Montaigne

If you work at that which is before you, following right reason seriously, vigorously, calmly, without allowing anything else to distract you, but keeping your divine part pure, as if you were bound to give it back immediately; if you hold to this, expecting nothing, but satisfied to live now according to nature, speaking heroic truth in every word which you utter, you will live happy. And there is no man able to prevent this.

—Marcus Aurelius

Let thine eyes look right on, and let thine eyelids look straight before thee.
Ponder the path of thy feet, and let all thy ways be established.

—Proverbs 4:25–26

Not only does the love of God have attention for its substance; the love of our neighbor, which we know to be the same love, is made of this same substance. Those who are unhappy have no need for anything in this world but people capable of giving them their attention. The capacity to give one's attention to a sufferer is a very rare and difficult thing; it is almost a miracle; it *is* a miracle .... Warmth of heart, impulsiveness, pity are not enough.

The love of our neighbor in all its fullness simply means being able to say to him: "What are you going through?" It is a recognition that the sufferer exists, not only as a unit in a collection...but as a man, exactly like us, who was one day stamped with a special mark by affliction. For this reason it is enough, but it is indispensable, to know how to look at him in a certain way.

This way of looking is first of all attentive. The soul empties itself of all its own contents in order to receive into itself the being it is looking at, just as he is, in all his truth.

—Simone Weil

In everything he does and on every occasion a man should use his reason attentively, and at the same time be subtly aware both of himself and his inner nature, reaching out towards God in everything as far as he is able.

—Meister Eckhart

Inspired action becomes possible when, to speak in spatial metaphors, every deed receives its necessary and temporary attention within the foreground of the mind whilst the Overself holds the permanent attention of the man within the background of his mind.

—Paul Brunton

There is nothing mind can do that cannot be better done in the mind's immobility and thought-free stillness.

When mind is still, then Truth gets her chance to be heard in the purity of the silence.

Truth cannot be attained by the Mind's thought but only by identity and silent vision. Truth lives in the calm wordless Light of the eternal spaces; she does not intervene in the noise and cackle of logical debate.

—Sri Aurobindo

We do not approach God through our knees, or through the whole body prostrate on the ground, but deep in our hearts. We do not feel God with our emotions any more than we know him with our thoughts. No! — we feel the divine presence in that profound unearthly stillness where neither the sounds of emotional clamor nor those of intellectual grinding can enter.

—Paul Brunton

When circumstances have compelled you to be a little disturbed, return to yourself quickly, and do not continue out of tune longer than the compulsion lasts; for you will be more the master of the harmony by continually returning to it.

—Marcus Aurelius

Empty yourself of everything.
Let the mind rest at peace.
The ten thousand things rise and fall while the Self watches their return.
They grow and flourish and then return to the source.
Returning to the source is stillness, which is the way of nature.

—Lao Tsu

The final [task] is knowing, loving, and serving life in a way in which you are eternally at rest. That point of rest has got to be in all of it. Even though you are active out there in the world, within you there's a point of complete composure and rest.

—Joseph Campbell

The stillness in stillness is not the real stillness. Only when there is stillness in movement can the spiritual rhythm appear which pervades heaven and earth.

—Ts'ai-ken t'an

At the center of each man, each animal, each plant, each cell, and each atom, there is a complete stillness. A seemingly empty stillness, yet it holds the divine energies and the divine Idea for that thing.

—Paul Brunton

Empty yourself of *everything*. That is to say, empty yourself of your ego and empty yourself of all things and of all that you are in yourself and consider yourself as what you are in God. God is a being beyond being and a nothingness beyond being. Therefore, be still and do not flinch from this emptiness.
—Meister Eckhart

There is a channel between voice and presence,
a way where information flows.

In disciplined silence the channel opens.
With wandering talk, it closes.
—Rumi

Every time that we really concentrate our attention, we destroy the evil in ourselves. If we concentrate with this intention, a quarter of an hour of attention is better than a great many good works.

Attention consists of suspending our thought, leaving it detached, empty and ready to be penetrated by the object; it means holding in our minds, within reach of this thought, but on a lower level and not in contact with it, the diverse knowledge we have acquired which we are forced to make use of .... Above all our thoughts should be empty, waiting, not seeking anything, but ready to receive in its naked truth the object that is to penetrate it.
—Simone Weil

The sage is he who has attained the central point of the wheel and proves it without himself participating in the movement and remains bound to the unvarying Mean.
—Taoist saying

To what shore would you cross, O my heart? there is no traveler
  before you, there is no road:
Where is the movement, where is the rest, on that shore?
There is no water; no boat, no boatman, is there
There is not so much as a rope to tow the boat,
  nor a man to draw it.
No earth, no sky, no time, no thing, is there:
  no shore, no ford!
There, there is neither body nor mind: and where is the place that
  shall still the thirst of the soul? You shall find naught in
  that emptiness.
Be strong, and enter into your own body: for there your foothold is
  firm. Consider it well, O my heart! go not elsewhere.
—Kabir

21
AWAKENING IN CREATION

The feeling of awe and sense of wonder arises from the recognition of the deep mystery that surrounds us everywhere, and this feeling deepens as our knowledge grows.
—Lama Anagarika Govinda

The existence of this creation is the desire of the Absolute to manifest itself and enjoy. The same is true of all individuals. Everyone in the universe desires to become manifest and be happy. It is only towards this that all our activities are really directed. There is no exception.
—H.H. Shantanand Saraswati

Patanjali declares that the true secret of evolution is the manifestation of the perfection which is already in every being; that this perfection has been barred and the infinite tide behind is struggling to express itself. Even when all competition has ceased this perfect nature behind will make us go forward until every one has become perfect. Therefore there is no reason to believe that competition is necessary to progress. In the animal the man was suppressed, but, as soon as the door was opened, out rushed man. So in man there is the potential god, kept in by the locks and bars of ignorance. When knowledge breaks these bars, the god becomes manifest.
—Swami Vivekananda

It is the Son of Man who is supremely capable of incarnating God. This Man is the Manu, the thinker, the Manomaya Purusha, mental person or soul in mind of the ancient sages. No mere superior mammal is he, but a conceptive soul basing itself on the animal body in Matter. He is conscious Name or *Numen* accepting and utilizing form as a medium through which Person can deal with substance. The animal life emerging out of Matter is only the inferior term of his existence. The life of thought, feeling will, conscious impulsion, that which we name in its totality Mind, that which strives to seize upon Matter and its vital energies and subject them to the law of its own progressive transformation, is the middle term in which he take his effectual station. But there is equally a supreme term which Mind in man searches after so that having found he may affirm it in his mental and bodily existence. This practical affirmation of something essentially superior to his present self is the basis of the divine life in the human being.
—Sri Aurobindo

I no longer wished for a better world because I was thinking of the whole of creation, and in the light of this clearer discernment I have come to see that, though the higher things are better than the lower, the sum of all creation is better than the higher things alone.

    —St. Augustine

You never enjoy the world aright, till the sea itself floweth in your veins, till you are clothed with the heavens, and crowned with the stars; and perceive yourself to be the sole heir of the whole world: and more than so, because men are in it who are every one sole heirs, as well as you. Till you can sing and rejoice and delight in God, as misers do in gold, and kings in scepters, you never enjoy the world.

    —Thomas Traherne

Clear and sweet is my soul, and clear and sweet is all that is not my soul.
Lack one lacks both, and the unseen is proved by the seen,
Till that becomes unseen and receives proof in its turn.

    —Walt Whitman

Our ideal is not the spirituality that withdraws from life but the conquest of life by the power of the spirit. It is to accept the world as an effort of manifestation of the Divine, but also to transform humanity by a greater effort of manifestation than has yet been accomplished, one in which the veil between man and God shall be removed, the divine manhood of which we are capable shall come to birth and our life shall be remolded in the truth and light and power of the spirit. It is to make of all our action a sacrifice to the master of our action and an expression of the greater self in man and of all life a yoga.

    —Sri Aurobindo

So must we admire in man, the form of the formless, the concentration of the vast, the house of reason, the cave of memory.

    —Ralph Waldo Emerson

Two things fill the mind with ever new and increasing admiration and awe, the oftener and more steadily we reflect on them: the starry heavens above me and the moral law within me. I do not merely conjecture them and see them as though obscured in darkness or in the transcendent region beyond my horizon: I see them before me, and I associate them directly with the consciousness of my own existence.

    —Immanuel Kant

Wonderment is the result of our meeting with a new truth that we neither knew nor expected to know. If this new truth also contains beauty and goodness, then the wonderment to which it gives rise is delightful in the extreme.... Philosophy and science are the result of wonderment; and so, in exactly the same way, are contemplation and mystical theology.

—St. Francis de Sales

To see a World in a Grain of Sand
And a Heaven in a Wild Flower,
Hold Infinity in the palm of your hand
And Eternity in an hour.

—William Blake

Know then, proud man, what a paradox you are to yourself. Humble yourself, impotent reason. Be silent, dull-witted nature, and learn from your master your true condition which you do not understand. Listen to God! See the Earth as a point compared with the vast circles it describes. Stand amazed that this circle itself is only a tiny point in relation to the course traced by the stars revolving in the firmament; that the whole visible world is no more than an imperceptible speck in the ample bosom of nature.

—Blaise Pascal

The innermost meaning of wonder is fulfilled in a deepened sense of mystery. It does not end in doubt, but is the awakening of knowledge that being, *qua* being, is mysterious and inconceivable, and that it is a mystery in the full sense of the word: Neither a dead end, nor a contradiction, nor even something impenetrable and dark. Rather mystery means that a reality cannot be comprehended *because* its light is ever-flowing, unfathomable, and inexhaustible. And that is what the wonderer really experiences.

—Josef Pieper

You must converse much with the field and woods, if you would imbibe such health into your mind and spirit as you covet for your body.

—Henry David Thoreau

Even as the finite encloses an infinite series,
And in the unlimited limits appear,
So the soul of immensity dwells in minutia
And in the narrowest limits, no limits inhere.
What joy to discern the minute in infinity!
The vast to perceive in the small, what Divinity!
—Jakob Bernoulli

To philosophize means to withdraw — not from the things of everyday life — but from the currently accepted meaning attached to them, or to question the value placed upon them. This does not, of course, take place by virtue of some decision to differentiate our attitude from that of others and to see things "differently," but because, quite suddenly, things themselves assume a different aspect. Really the situation is this: the deeper aspects of reality are apprehended in the ordinary things of everyday life and not in a sphere cut off and segregated from it...; it is in the things we come across in the experience of everyday life that the unusual emerges, and we no longer take them for granted — and that situation corresponds with the inner experience which has always been regarded as the beginning of philosophy: the act of "marveling."
—Josef Pieper

The one thing which we seek with insatiable desire is to forget ourselves, to be surprised out of our propriety, to lose our sempiternal memory and to do something without knowing how or why; in short to draw a new circle. Nothing great was ever achieved without enthusiasm. The way of life is wonderful; it is by abandonment.
—Ralph Waldo Emerson

Why, who makes much of a miracle?
As to me I know of nothing else but miracles....

To me every hour of the light and dark is a miracle,
Every cubic inch of space is a miracle,
Every square yard of the surface of the earth is spread with the same,
Every foot of the interior swarms with the same....

What stranger miracles are there?
—Walt Whitman

Be like a child — clear, loving, spontaneous, infinitely flexible and ready each moment to wonder and accept miracles.
    —Mother Meera

I saw Eternity the other night
Like a great Ring of pure and endless light,
All calm, as it was bright,
And round beneath it, Time in hours, days, years
Driv'n by the spheres
Like a vast shadow mov'd, in which the world
And all her train were hurled.
    —Henry Vaughan

Man is all symmetry,
Full of proportions, one limb to another,
And all to all the world besides.
Each part may call the farthest brother,
For head with foot hath private amity,
And both with moons and tides.
    —George Herbert

The gloom of the world is but a shadow. Behind it, yet within our reach, is joy. There is radiance and glory in the darkness, could we but see; and to see, we have only to look. I beseech you to look. Life is so generous a giver, but we, judging its gifts by their covering, cast them away as ugly or heavy or hard. Remove the covering, and you will find beneath it a living splendor, woven of love, by wisdom with power. Welcome it, grasp it, and you touch the angel's hand that bring it to you. Everything we call a trial, a sorrow, or a duty; believe me, that angel's hand is there; the gift is there, and the wonder of an overshadowing Presence. Our joys, too: be not content with them as joys, they too conceal diviner gifts.... Life is so full of meaning and of purpose, so full of beauty — beneath its covering — that you will find that earth but cloaks your heaven.
    —Fra Giovanni

In all people I see myself none more and not one a barley-corn less,
And the good or bad I say of myself I say of them.

I know I am solid and sound,
To me the converging objects of the universe perpetually flow,
All are written to me and I must get what the writing means.

I know I am deathless,
I know this orbit of mine cannot be swept by a carpenter's compass,
I know I shall not pass like a child's carlacue cut with a burnt stick at night.

I know I am August,
I do not trouble my spirit to vindicate itself or be understood,
I see that the elementary laws never apologize,
(I reckon I behave no prouder than the level I plant my house by, after all.)

I exist as I am, that is enough,
If no other in the world be aware I sit content,
And if each and all be aware I sit content.

One world is aware and by far the largest to me, and that is myself,
And whether I come to my own to-day or in ten thousand or ten million years,
I can cheerfully take it now, or with equal cheerfulness I can wait.
My foothold is tenon'd and mortis'd in granite,
I laugh at what you call dissolution,
And I know the amplitude of time.
—Walt Whitman

To be oneself, that is to say, to live in the consciousness of one's own essence, promotes the growth of a new understanding. It is just as if delicate fingers were unfolding, one by one, the petals of a lotus.
—Sri Anirvan

How good — to be alive!
How infinite — to be
Alive — two-fold — The Birth I had —
And this — besides, in — Thee!
—Emily Dickinson

Has any one supposed it lucky to be born?
I hasten to inform him or her it is just as lucky to die, and I know it.

I pass death with the dying and birth with the new-wash'd babe,
    and am not contain'd between my hat and boots,
And peruse manifold objects, not two alike and everyone good,
The earth good and the stars good, and their adjuncts all good.

I am not an earth nor an adjunct of an earth,
I am the mate and companion of people, all just as immortal and
    fathomless as myself,
(They do not know how immortal, but I know.)
—Walt Whitman

It is thus that almost every morning, when I first awaken, I have a feeling of total clarity as to the sense of life, a feeling of myself and the universe as a matter of the utmost simplicity. "I" and "That which is" are the same. Always have been and always will be. I could say that what constitutes me is the same jazz that constitutes the cosmos, and that there is simply nothing special to be achieved, realized, or performed.
—Alan Watts

Dance, my heart! Dance to-day with joy.
The strains of love fill the days and the nights with music,
    and the world is listening to its melodies:
Mad with joy, life and death dance to the rhythm of this music.
    The hills and the sea and the earth dance. The world of man dances
    in laughter and tears.
Why put on the robe of the monk, and live aloof from
    the world in lonely pride?
Behold! My heart dances in the delight of a hundred arts;
    and the Creator is well pleased.
—Kabir

We should consider that we, in this world, possess nothing of our own, that we do not even belong to ourselves, but are only for a short time workers in this world, and not only so, but as sojourners merely, stewards of our God over His creation.
—Jacob Boehme

The living creatures do not die; but they are composite bodies, and as such, they undergo dissolution. Dissolution is not death; it is only the separation of things which were combined; and they undergo dissolution, not to perish, but to be made new....Birth is not a beginning of life, but only a beginning of consciousness; and the change to another state is not death, but oblivion. And this being so, all the things of which every living creature is composed — gross matter and vital spirit and soul — are immortal; and so, by reason of their immortality, every living creature is immortal.

—Hermes Trismegistus

When I go from hence let this be my parting word, that what I have seen is unsurpassable.

I have tasted of the hidden honey of this lotus that expands on the ocean of light, and thus am I blessed — let this be my parting word.

In this playhouse of infinite forms I have had my play and here have I caught sight of him that is formless

My whole body and my limbs have thrilled with his touch who is beyond touch; and if the end comes here, let it come — let this be my parting word.

—Rabindranath Tagore

The word "death" is a mere name, without any corresponding fact. For death means destruction; and nothing in the Kosmos is destroyed. For seeing that the Kosmos is the second God, and an immortal being, it is impossible that a part of that immortal being should die; and all things in the Kosmos are parts of the Kosmos.

—Hermes Trismegistus

*

22
EXPERIENCE, DELIGHT, AND BLISS

And I have felt
A presence that disturbs me with the joy
Of elevated thoughts; a sense sublime
Of something far more deeply interfused,
Whose dwelling is the light of setting suns,
And the round ocean and the living air,
And the blue sky, and in the mind of man,
A motion and a spirit that impels
All thinking things, all objects of all thought,
And rolls through all things.
—William Wordsworth

How sweet I roam'd from field to field
And tasted all the summer's pride,
Till I the Prince of love beheld
Who in the sunny beams did glide!
—William Blake

Earth, is it not this that you want: *invisible*
to arise within us? — Is it not your dream,
someday, to be invisible? — Earth! Invisible!
What, if not transformation, is your urgent task?
Earth, you dear one, I will. Oh, believe, there is no more need
of your springtimes to win me over — *one,*
ah, a single one is already too much for my blood.
From afar and nameless, I have resolved to be yours.
At all times you were right, and your sacred inspiration
is the intimate attendant Death.

Look, I am living. Out of what? Neither childhood nor future
diminish...Infinite Being
wells up in my heart.
—Rainer Maria Rilke

As the hand held before the eye hides the tallest mountain, so this small earthly life hides from our gaze the vast radiance and secrets of which the world is full, and whoever can take life from before his eyes, as one takes away one's hand, will see the great radiance within the world.

—*Ten Rungs: Hasidic Sayings*

I entered in, I know not where,
And I remained, though knowing naught,
Transcending knowledge with my thought....

Of peace and piety interwound
This perfect science had been wrought,
Within the solitude profound
As straight and narrow path it taught,
Such secret wisdom there I found
That there I stammered, saying naught,
But topped all knowledge with my thought....

This wisdom without understanding
Is of so absolute a force
No wise man of whatever standing
Can ever stand against its course,
Unless they tap its wondrous source,
To know so much, though knowing naught,
They pass all knowledge with their thought....

If you would ask, what is its essence —
This summit of all sense and knowing:
It comes from the Divinest Presence —
The sudden sense of Him outflowing,
In His great clemency bestowing
The gift that leaves men knowing naught,
Yet passing knowledge with their thought.

—St. John of the Cross

My eyes strayed far and wide before I shut them and said "Here art thou!"

The question and the cry "Oh, where?" melt into tears of a thousand streams and deluge the world with the flood of the assurance "I am!"

—Rabindranath Tagore

The Soul's Superior instants
Occur to Her — alone —
When friend — and Earth's occasion
Have infinite withdrawn —

Or she — Herself — ascended
To too remote a Height
For lower Recognition
Than Her Omnipotent —

This Mortal Abolition
Is seldom — but as fair
As Apparition — subject
To Autocratic Air —

Eternity's disclosure
To favorites — a few —
Of the Colossal substance
Of Immortality.
—Emily Dickinson

Space and Time! Now I see it is true, what I guess'd at,
What I guess'd when I loaf'd on the grass,
What I guess'd while I lay alone in my bed,
And again as I walk'd the beach under the paling stars of the morning.

My ties and ballasts leave me, my elbows rest in sea-gaps,
I skirt sierras, my palms cover continents,
I am afoot with my vision.
—Walt Whitman

If we speak of the space-experience in meditation, we are dealing with an entirely different dimension.... In this space-experience the temporal sequence is converted into a simultaneous coexistence, the side by side existence of things...and this again does not remain static but becomes a living continuum in which time and space are integrated.
—Lama Anagarika Govinda

I see indescribable depths. How shall I tell you, O my son? ...How [shall I describe] the universe? I [am mind and] I see another mind, the one that [moves] the soul! I see the one that moves me from pure forgetfulness. You give me power! I see myself! I want to speak! Fear restrains me. I have found the beginning of the power that is above all powers, the one that has no beginning....I have said, O my son, that I am Mind. I have seen! Language is not able to reveal this....And I, Mind, understand.

—*Gnostic Discourses on the Eighth and Ninth*

Open your eyes of love, and see Him who pervades this world!
    Consider it well, and know that this is your own country....

This world is the City of Truth, its maze of paths enchants the heart:
We can reach the goal without crossing the road,
    such is the sport unending.
Where the ring of manifold joys ever dances about Him, there
    is the sport of Eternal Bliss.
When we know this, then all our receiving and
    renouncing is over;
Thenceforth the heat of having shall never scorch us more.

—Kabir

Standing on the bare ground — my head bathed by the blithe air and uplifted into infinite space — all mean egotism vanishes. I become a transparent eyeball; I am nothing; I see all; the currents of the Universal Being circulate through me; I am part or parcel of God...I am the lover of uncontained and immortal beauty.

—Ralph Waldo Emerson

God is. That is the primordial fact. It is in order that we may discover this fact for ourselves, by direct experience, that we exist. The final end and purpose of every human being is the unitive knowledge of God's being.

—Aldous Huxley

Until God has taken possession of him, no human being can have faith, but only simple belief; and it hardly matters whether or not he has such a belief, because he will arrive at faith equally well through disbelief.

—Simone Weil

So completely peaceful does this stillness sometimes become, the soul with all its powers seems to have been lulled to sleep. There is no movement, no activity whatever, except in the will; yet even the will does no more than accept the gratification, the contentment, which the beloved's presence affords. Stranger still, the will is unaware of the gratification and contentment it takes, enjoying it unconsciously; it has no thought for itself, you see, but only for him whose presence affords it delight.

    —St. Francis de Sales

I, who was till recently an apologist of the dualistic school of thought by asserting a separate individual existence for myself, now remain crestfallen, in discomfiture, having seen the overwhelming fullness of the Supreme raise Its head from within my own self, pour on me Its bliss of unequaled ecstasy, and completely devour all separate self-knowledge: as a consequence, I lost my individuality and remained tongue-tied.

    —St. Tayumanavar

As soon as the center of all being is apprehended, there ariseth a joy in the heart that surpasseth all other.

    —Jacob Boehme

I ask for a moment's indulgence to sit by thy side. The works that I have in hand I will finish afterwards.

Away from the sight of thy face my heart knows no rest nor respite, and my work becomes an endless toil in a shoreless sea of toil.

Today the summer has come at my window with its sighs and murmurs; and the bees are plying their minstrelsy at the court of the flowering grove.

Now it is time to sit quiet, face to face with thee, and to sing dedication of life in this silent and overflowing leisure.
—Rabindranath Tagore

In soul-vision the wise man perceives in his heart a certain wide-extending awakening, whose form is pure bliss, incomparable, the other shore, forever free, where is no desire, limitless as the ether, partless, from wavering free, the perfect Eternal.

    —Shankara

How full of life is that death by which I die in myself but live in God, by which I die to the dead but live for life, and live by life and rejoice in joy! Oh pleasure beyond sense! Oh delight beyond mind! Oh joy beyond understanding! I am now out of my mind, but not mindless, because I am beyond mind. Again I am in a frenzy, all too great a frenzy; yet I do not fall to the ground; I am borne upward. Now I expand in every direction and overflow but am not dispersed, because God, the unity of unities, brings me to myself, because he makes me live with himself.
—Marsilio Ficino

So great a sweetness flows into the breast
We must laugh and we must sing,
We are blest by everything,
Everything we look upon is blest.
—William Butler Yeats

When I still stood in my first cause, there I had no God and was cause of myself. There I willed nothing, I desired nothing, for I was a pure Being in delight of the truth. There I stood, free of God and of all things. But when I took leave from this state and received my created being, then I had a God.
—Meister Eckhart

I took the lamp and, leaving the zone of everyday occupations and relationships where everything seems clear, I went down into my inmost self, to the deep abyss whence I feel dimly that my power of action emanates. But as I moved further and further away from the conventional certainties by which social life is superficially illuminated, I became aware that I was losing contact with myself. At each step of the descent a new person was disclosed within me of whose name I was no longer sure, and who no longer obeyed me. And when I had to stop my exploration because the path faded from beneath my steps, I found a bottomless abyss at my feet, and out of it came — arising I know not from where — the current which I dare to call *my* life ....

Stirred by my discovery, I then wanted to return to the light of day and forget the disturbing enigma in the comfortable surroundings of familiar things .... But then, beneath this very spectacle of the turmoil of life, there reappeared, before my newly-opened eyes, the unknown that I wanted to escape. This time it was not hiding at the bottom of an abyss; it disguised its presence in the innumerable strands which form the web of chance, the very stuff of which the universe and my own small individuality are woven. Yet it was the same mystery without a doubt: I recognized it.
—Teilhard de Chardin

For the statement that God is *He who is,* is one that can be, in some measure, empirically verified by anyone who cares to fulfill the conditions upon which mystical insight into reality depends. For in contemplation the mystic has a direct intuition of a mode of being incomparably more real and substantial than the existences — his own and that of other things and persons — of which, by similar direct intuition, he is aware at ordinary times. That God *is,* is a fact that men can actually experience, and is the most important of all the facts that can be experienced.

—Aldous Huxley

O Sadhu! The simple union is the best.
Since the day when I met with my Lord, there has been no
 end to the sport of our love.
I shut not my eyes, I close not my ears, I do not
 mortify my body;
I see with eyes open and smile, and behold
 His beauty everywhere:
I utter His Name, and whatever I see, it reminds me of Him;
 whatever I do, it becomes His worship.
The rising and the setting are one to me;
 all contradictions are solved.
Wherever I go, I move round Him,
All I achieve is His service:
When I lie down, I lie prostrate at His feet.

—Kabir

*

23
FREEDOM, UNION, ENLIGHTENMENT

Those attaining the highest state simply *are*. Duty dies there; they only love, and like a magnet draw others to them. This is freedom. No more do you do moral acts, but whatever you do is moral.
—Swami Vivekananda

There is only being in Self-realization, and nothing but being.
—Sri Ramana Maharshi

From this hour I ordain myself loos'd of limits and imaginary lines,
Going where I list, my own master total and absolute,
Listening to others, considering well what they say,
Pausing, searching, receiving, contemplating,
Gently, but with undeniable will, divesting myself of the holds that
    would hold me.

I inhale great draughts of space,
The east and the west are mine, and the north and the south are mine.

I am larger, better than I thought,
I did not know I held so much goodness.

All seems beautiful to me,
I can repeat over to men and women,
    You have done such good to me
    I would do the same to you,
I will recruit for myself and you as I go,
I will scatter myself among men and women as I go,
I will toss a new gladness and roughness among them,
Whoever denies me it shall not trouble me,
Whoever accepts me he or she shall be blessed and shall bless me.
—Walt Whitman

He ate and drank the precious Words —
His spirit grew robust —
He knew no more that he was poor,
Not that his frame was Dust —

He danced along the dingy Days
And this Bequest of Wings
Was but a Book — What Liberty
A loosened spirit brings.
—Emily Dickinson

And so I think that the last lesson of life, the choral song which rises from all elements and all angels, is a voluntary obedience, a necessitated freedom. Man is made of the same atoms as the world is, he shares the same impressions, predispositions and destiny. When his mind is illuminated, when his heart is kind, he throws himself joyfully into the sublime order, and does, with knowledge, what the stones do by structure.
—Ralph Waldo Emerson

Knowing the Self as within and without, in things stable and moving — discerning this through the Self, through its comprehending all things — putting off every disguise, and recognizing no division, standing firm through the perfect Self — such a one is free.
—Shankara

To attain Nirvana is simply to break this sleep in which we experience only the flux and to wake to an intuition of the One.
—Swami Prabhavananda

In the silence is the highest peace, because wavering is the intellect's unreal work; there the knowers of the Eternal, mighty-souled, enjoy unbroken happiness of part-less bliss, recognizing the Self as the eternal.

There is no higher cause of joy than silence where no mind-pictures dwell; it belongs to him who has understood the Self's own being; who is full of the essence of the bliss of the Self.
—Shankara

"I am not the body, nor is the body mine. I am Intelligence itself." He who has attained this knowledge has reached the state of the Absolute and ceases to think on what he has done. And what he has not done.
—*Ashtavakra Gita*

To yield is to be preserved whole.
To be bent is to become straight.
To be hollow is to be filled.
To be tattered is to be renewed.
To be in want is to possess.
To have plenty is to be confused.

Therefore the Sage embraces the One,
And becomes the model of the world.

He does not reveal himself,
    And is therefore luminous.
He does not justify himself,
    And is therefore far-famed.
He does not boast of himself,
    And therefore people give him credit.
He does not pride himself,
    And is therefore the ruler among men.

It is because he does not contend
That no one in the world can contend against him.

Is it not indeed true, as the ancients say,
    "To yield is to be preserved whole"?
Thus he is preserved and the world does him homage.
—*Tao Te Ching*

As the rivers flow into the ocean and lose their name and form, the sage losing name and form disappears into the supreme Spirit and himself becomes that Spirit.
—*Mundaka Upanishad*

In my very self shall be Paradise. I myself shall be an instrument in the music of the spoken word.
—Jacob Boehme

O friend! Hope for Him whilst you live, know whilst you live,understand
    whilst you live: for in life deliverance abides.
If your bond be not broken whilst living, what hope of deliverance
    in death?
It is but an empty dream, that the soul shall have union with Him
    because it has passed from the body:
If He is found now, He is found then,
If not, we do but go to dwell in the City of Death.
If you have union now, you shall have it hereafter.
Bathe in the truth, know the true Guru, have faith in the true Name!
Kabir says: "It is the Spirit of the quest which helps: I am the slave of this Spirit of
    the quest."
    —Kabir

This secret union takes place in the deepest center of the soul, which is where God dwells, and I do not think there is any need of a door by which to enter it. I say there is no need of a door because all that has so far been described seems to have come through the medium of the senses and faculties. But what passes in the union of the Spiritual Marriage, in the center of the soul, is very different. This instantaneous [union] of God to the soul is so great a secret and sublime a favor, and such delight is felt by the soul, that I do not know with what to compare it …. it is like rain falling from the heavens into a river or spring; there is nothing but water there and it is impossible to divide or separate the water belonging to the river from that which fell from the heavens. Or it is as if a tiny streamlet enters the sea, from which it will find no way of separating itself.
    —St. Teresa of Avila

The union belongeth to such as are perfect, and also is brought to pass in three ways: to wit, by pureness and singleness of heart, by love, and by the contemplation of God, the Creator of all things.
    —*Theologia Germanica*

The Self that is subtler than the subtle and greater than the great is lodged in the heart of every creature. A desireless man sees that glory of the Self through the serenity of the organs, and thereby he becomes free from sorrow.
    —*Katha Upanishad*

Of a certainty the man who can see all creatures in himself, himself in all creatures,
knows no sorrow.

    —Eesha Upanishad

No suffering for him
who is free from sorrow
free from the fetters of life
free in everything he does.
He has reached the end of his road.

    —Dhammapada

If ye realize the Emptiness of All Things, Compassion will arise within your hearts;
If ye lose all differentiation between yourselves and others, fit to serve others ye will be;
And when in serving others ye shall win success, then shall ye meet with me;
And finding me, ye shall attain to Buddhahood.

    —Milarepa

Jesus said: Within a man of light there is light and he lights the whole world. When
he does not shine, there is darkness.

    —The Gospel of Thomas

He who is aware of the Male
But keeps to the Female
    Becomes the ravine of the world,
Being the ravine of the world,
    He has the eternal power which never fails,
    And returns again to the (innocence of) the babe.

—Tao Te Ching

Immortality will come to such as are fit for it, and he who would be a great soul in
future must be a great soul now.

    —Ralph Waldo Emerson

Everything must be done for the Absolute, and nothing should be done to acquire any particular thing except union with the Absolute. One should just surrender oneself, and the feeling of surrender itself is the gate of liberation; a devotee is always liberated because he is not bothered about anything except the Absolute. A devotee does not necessarily undergo discipline; he simply lives a liberated life.

—H.H. Shantanand Saraswati

Jesus said: When you make the two one, and when you make the inner as the outer and the outer as the inner and the above as the below, and when you make the male and the female into a single one, so that the male will not be male and the female not be female...then shall you enter the Kingdom.

—*The Gospel of Thomas*

When man and woman become one, Thou art that One; when the units are wiped out, lo, Thou art that (Unity).

—Rumi

The yogi endowed with complete enlightenment sees, through the eye of Knowledge, the entire universe in his own Self and regards everything as the Self and nothing else.

—Shankara

I cannot dance, O Lord,
Unless You lead me.
If you wish me to leap joyfully,
Let me see You dance and sing —

Then I will leap into Love —
And from Love into Knowledge,
And from Knowledge into the Harvest,
That sweetest Fruit beyond human sense.

There I will stay with You, whirling.
—Mechthild of Magdeburg

24
TO REALIZE THE DIVINE

I believe I shall some time cease to be an individual, that the eternal tendency of the soul is to become Universal, to animate the last extremities of organization.
—Ralph Waldo Emerson

The only object of the ego of man, the seat of the "I," is to realize its identity with God. It is in this school of the world to learn this one lesson: to forget its limitations and actively to realize its oneness with all.
—Sri Dada

Everything that from eternity has happened in heaven and earth, the life of God and all the deeds of time simply are the struggles for Spirit to know itself, to find itself, be for itself, and finally unite itself to itself; it is alienated and divided, but only so as to be able thus to find itself and return to itself.
—G.W.F. Hegel

The universe exists in order that the experiencer may experience it and thus become liberated.
—Patanjali

When man interiorizes himself, God exteriorizes Himself while enriching man from within; there lies all the mystery of the metaphysical transparency of phenomena and of their immanence in us.
—Frithjof Schuon

That luminous Emergence...exists already as an all-revealing and all-guiding Truth of things which watches over the world and attracts mortal man, first without the knowledge of his conscious mind, by the general march of Nature, but at last consciously by a progressive awakening and self-enlargement, to his divine ascension. The ascent to the divine Life is the human journey, the Work of works, the acceptable Sacrifice. This alone is man's real business in the world and the justification of his existence, without which he would be only an insect crawling among other ephemeral insects on a speck of surface mud and water which has managed to form itself amid the appalling immensities of the physical universe.

—Sri Aurobindo

The true purpose of human birth is to fulfill this one, this only will, to realize God — which is truly the motive power behind all other desires. Unhappy is the man who forgets this purpose, and loses himself in the meshes of petty desires and impulses. Desiring first one thing, then another and yet again something else is but impulse, and can be likened unto a man, who, desiring to sink a well, digs first in one place and then in another, never completing one well, and never reaching the water. Not by such impulses and desires can the thirst for God be quenched. Therefore, I say unto you, *will* to attain the Truth, the Kingdom of Self.

—Swami Adbhutananda

I swear I think now that every thing without exception has an
    eternal soul!
The trees have, rooted in the ground! The weeds of the sea have!
    the animals!

I swear I think there is nothing but immortality!
That the exquisite scheme is for it, and the nebulous float is for it,
    and the cohering is for it!
And all preparation is for it — and identity is for it — and life and
    materials are altogether for it!

—Walt Whitman

Man is a transitional being; he is not final. For in man and high beyond him ascend the radiant degrees that climb to a divine supermanhood. There lies our destiny and the liberating key to our aspiring but troubled and limited mundane existence.

—Sri Aurobindo

Intelligence must be the lord of creation, the cause. What is the most evolved notion that man has of this universe? It is that of intelligence, the adjustment of part to part, the display of intelligence — which notion the ancient design theory attempted to express. The beginning is therefore intelligence. At the beginning that intelligence becomes involved, and in the end that intelligence becomes evolved. The sum total of the intelligence displayed in the universe must therefore be the involved universal intelligence unfolding itself. This universal intelligence is what we call God. Call it by any other name it is absolutely certain that in the beginning there is that infinite cosmic intelligence. This cosmic intelligence gets involved, and it manifests, evolves itself, until it becomes the perfect man, the "Christ-man," the "Buddha-man." Then it goes back to its own source.

 —Swami Vivekananda

What else does nature teach, if not that we should make wealth subject to the body, the body to the soul, the soul to reason, and reason to God?

 —Marsilio Ficino

TO REALIZE THE DIVINE · 253

25

INVOCATIONS, PRECEPTS, AND HYMNS OF PRAISE

His name is conscious spirit, His abode is conscious spirit, and He, the lord of all conscious spirit.

 —Ramakrishna

Seek out that from which all existences are born, by which being born they live and to which they return .... From Delight all these existences were born, by Delight they live, towards Delight they return.

 —*Taittiriya Upanishad*

That which is not cannot come to being, and that which is cannot cease to be.

 —*Bhagavad Gita*

God is my inmost self, the reality of my being.

 —Swami Vivekananda

I am the Self who abides in the heart of all beings.

 —*Bhagavad Gita*

Let your aim be one and single;
Let your hearts be joined in one —
The mind at rest in unison —
At peace with all, so may you be.
—*Rig-Veda*

Lords, inspiration of sacrifice! May our ears hear the good, May our eyes see the good, May we serve Him with the whole strength of our body. May we, all our life, carry out His will. May peace and peace and peace be everywhere.

—*Mundaka Upanishad*

Lead me from the unreal to the real!
Lead me from darkness to light!
Lead me from death to immortality!

—*Brihadaranyaka Upanishad*

OM
May our ears welcome whatever is conducive to our eternal welfare!
May our eyes contemplate whatever will ensure our eternal freedom!
May our senses act in such a way that they carry us ever nearer to eternal truth!
May our lives be spent in doing such acts as shall lead us
    ever nearer to the eternal wisdom!
May everything that exists drive us onward to the eternal bliss!
And may peace and peace and peace be everywhere.

—*Mandukya Upanisha*

Let us bring our minds to rest in
The glory of the Divine Truth.
May Truth inspire our reflection.

—*Rig-Veda*

Be still and know that I am God.

—*Psalm 46:10*

Consider these things, O my soul, and shut the doors of your senses, that you may be able to hear what the Lord God speaks within you. Thus your Beloved says — "I am your salvation, your peace, your life; keep yourself with Me, and you shall find peace."

—Thomas à Kempis

I am without attributes and action, eternal and pure, free from stain and desire, changeless and formless, and always free.
—Shankara

Whatever lives is full of the Lord. Claim nothing; enjoy, do not covet His property.
—*Eesha Upanishad*

Holy, holy, holy is the Lord of hosts;
the whole earth is full of his glory.
—Isaiah 6:3

I am that I am.
—Exodus 3:14

I and my Father are one.
—John 10:30

For the sake of Spirit, O Mind,
Let go of all these wandering thoughts!
—*Rig-Veda*

In this drama of life, I am nothing, Thou pullest the strings. Thou alone, O Lord! playest the roles of prompter, actor, and spectator.

The knower alone, bereft of the act of knowing and the Thing known, will remain self-poised.

When shall I become one with the Absolute, renouncing the vain appearances of seer, seeing, and the things seen.
—St. Tayumanavar

Thou shalt meet Him everywhere, thou shalt see Him everywhere, in the place and at the hour when thou least expectest it, in waking and in sleep, on the sea, in thy travels, by day, by night, in thy speaking and in thy keeping of silence. For there is nothing that is not the image of God.

    —Hermes Trismegistus

    O vast, far-reaching Spirit of God, I bow down to Thee as my Self and find myself lost in Thee, as in the vast ocean of the universal deluge.

    This temple of Brahman, the mundane world, is too small and straitened for me — as the eye of a needle is too small for an elephant to pass through!

    I who am the unborn and uncreate Spirit, reign triumphantly over this transient World.

    —*Yoga-Vasishtha*

That is perfect. This is perfect. Perfect comes from perfect.
Take perfect from perfect, the remainder is perfect.

May peace and peace be everywhere.
    —*Eesha Upanishad*

O moving force of Wisdom, encircling the wheel of the cosmos,
Encompassing all that is, all that has life,
    in one vast circle.
You have three wings: The first unfurls aloft
    in the highest heights.
The second dips its way dripping sweat on the Earth.
Over, under, and through all things whirls the third.
    Praise to you, O Wisdom worthy of praise!
    —Hildegard of Bingen

O Great One! Install me firmly in that ever true Existence where I shall cease to see myself, seeing everything in Thee.
    —St. Tayumanavar

Create in me a clean heart, O God; and renew a right spirit within me.
Cast me not away from thy presence; and take not thy Holy Spirit from me.
Restore unto me the joy of thy salvation; and uphold me with thy free Spirit.
—Psalms 51:11–12

My Lord hides Himself, and my Lord wonderfully reveals Himself:
My Lord has encompassed me with hardness, and my Lord has cast down my
    limitations.
My Lord brings to me words of sorrow and words of joy, and He Himself
    heals their strife.
I will offer my body and mind to my Lord: I will give up my life, but never
    can I forget my Lord!
—Kabir

The Lord is in his holy temple; let all the world keep silence before him.
—Habakkuk 2:20

Jesus said: When you pray, say:
Father, may your name be holy.
May your rule take place.
Give us each day our daily bread.
Pardon our debts, for we ourselves pardon everyone indebted to us.
And do not bring us to trial.
—The Book of Q

O Thou Lord supreme, I bow down to Thee!
For Thy sole pleasure and play didst Thou bring forth this Universe.
Thou art the Highest in the Highest! Who can sing Thine infinite glory?
Thou art the innermost ruler of every heart;
Thy paths are mysterious; Thy ways are blessed.
Thou dost wipe away all the tears of Thy devotees;
Thou dost destroy the wickedness of the wicked.
Thy form is purity itself, and
Thou dost give purity and Self-knowledge to those who seek Thee.
Salutations to Thee again and again, O Lord of hosts!
—Srimad Bhagavatam

O Lord of my heart
May I always hear Thy praise and sing Thy glory,
and may my heart be ever filled with love for Thee.
This my only prayer.
—*Srimad Bhagavatam*

O Lord of the Universe
I will sing Thee a song.
Where canst Thou be found,
And where canst Thou not be found?
Where I pass — there art Thou.
Where I remain — there, too, thou art.
Thou, Thou, and only Thou.

Doth it go well — 'tis thanks to Thee
Doth it go ill — ah, 'tis also thanks to Thee.

Thou art, Thou hast been, and thou wilt be.
Thou didst reign, Thou reignest, and thou wilt reign.

Thine is Heaven, Thine is Earth.
Thou fillest the high regions,
And Thou fillest the low regions.
Wheresoever I turn, Thou, oh, thou art there.
—Hasidic Song

Sophia!
you of the whirling wings,
circling encompassing
energy of God:

you quicken the world in your clasp.

One wing soars in heaven
one wing sweeps the earth
and the third flies all around us.

Praise to Sophia!
Let all the earth praise her!
—Hildegard of Bingen

O my Lord, my whole being is Yourself, and this
Mind which has been given to me is your consort.
The life force, breath, and energy which you have
given me are your attendants.
My body is the temple in which I worship You.
Whatever I eat or wear or do is part of the worship
which I keep on performing at this temple.
Even when this body goes to sleep I feel I am in union with You.
Whenever I walk, I feel I am going on pilgrimage to You.
Whatever I speak is all in praise of You.
So whatever I do in this world in any way is all
aimed at You.
In fact, there is no duality in this life of unity
with Yourself.
    —Ancient Poem

Light Eternal, transcending all created lights, dart Thy bright beams from above, and
penetrate the inmost recesses of my heart. Cleanse, gladden, brighten, and enliven
my spirit with all its powers, that I may cleave to Thee with ecstasies of joy. Oh,
when shall that blessed and longed-for hour arrive, when Thou wilt satisfy me with
Thy Presence, and be to me all in all!
    —Thomas à Kempis

O All-pervasive Spirit! Thou whose visible form is the universe!
Thee I salute again and again.
O Thou who art the Embodiment of Consciousness and Bliss!
Again and again do I salute Thee.
Thee I salute again and again who art attainable through
Yoga and self-control;
Again and again do I salute Thee, who art only to be known
Through Knowledge of the Vedas.
    —Hymn to Shiva

The Holy spirit, life that gives life
and moves all things
and is the root of every creature
and cleanses all things of impurity,
wiping away sins
and anointing wounds:
this is the radiant and admirable life,
awakening and reawakening all things.
    —Hildegard of Bingen

O boundless light, observing yourself, seeing all things in yourself!
O infinite sight, shining from yourself, illuminating all!
O spiritual eye, whom alone, and by whom alone, spiritual eyes see!
O immortal life of those that see!
O all goodness of the living!
—Marsilio Ficino

I submit myself to thee, Master, friend of the bowed-down world and river of selfless kindness.
Raise me by thy guiding light that pours forth the nectar of truth and mercy, for I
am sunk in the ocean of the world.
I am burned by the hot flame of relentless life and torn by the winds of misery: save
me from death, for I take refuge in thee, finding no other rest.
Sprinkle me with thy nectar voice that brings the joy of eternal bliss, pure and
cooling, falling on me as from a cup, like the joy of inspiration; for I am burnt
by the hot, scorching flames of the world's fire.
Happy are they on whom thy light rests, even for a moment, and who reach
harmony with thee.
How shall I cross the ocean of the world? Where is the path? What way must I
follow? I know not, Master, Save me from the wound of the world's pain.
—Shankara

Through the deep caves of thought I hear a voice that sings;

Build thee more stately mansions, O my soul,
   As the swift season roll!
   Leave thy low-vaulted past!
Let each new temple, nobler that the last,
Shut thee from heaven with a dome more vast,
   Till thou at length art free,
Leaving thine outgrown shell by life's unresting sea!
—Oliver Wendell Holmes

Lord, I know not what to ask of thee. Thou only knowest what I need. Thou lovest
me better than I know how to love myself. Father, give to thy child that which he
himself knows not how to ask. Smite or heal, depress me or raise me up: I adore all
thy purposes without knowing them. I am silent; I offer myself up in a sacrifice; I
yield myself to Thee; I would have no other desire than to accomplish thy will. Teach
me to pray. Pray Thyself in me.
—François Fenelon

O Lord, thou hast searched me, and known me....
Thou hast beset me behind and before, and laid thine hand upon me
Such knowledge is too wonderful for me; it is high, I cannot attain it.
Whither shall I go from thy spirit? Or whither shall I flee from thy presence?
If I ascend up into heaven, thou art there: if I make my bed in hell, behold, thou art there....

I will praise thee; for I am fearfully and wonderfully made: marvelous are thy works;
    and that my soul knoweth right well.
       —Psalm 139:1,5–8,14

We thank thee, O thou Most High, with heart and soul wholly
uplifted to thee; for it is by thy grace alone that we have attained to the light, and
come to know thee.
    We thank thee, O thou whose name no man can tell,
but whom men honor by the appellation "God," because thou alone art Master,
and bless by the appellation "Father," because thou hast shown in act toward all men
and in all things lovingkindness and affection such as a father feels, nay,
yet sweeter than a father's;
for thou hast bestowed on us mind, and speech, and knowledge:
mind, that we may apprehend thee;
speech, that we may call upon thee;
and knowledge, that having come to know thee, and found
salvation in the light thou givest, we may be filled with gladness.
    We are glad because thou hast revealed thyself to us in all thy being;
we are glad because, while we are yet in the body, thou hast deigned
to make us gods by the gift of thine own eternal life.
    Man can thank thee only by learning to know thy greatness.
    We have learnt to know thee, O thou most brightly shining light of the world
of mind;
we have learnt to know thee, O thou true life of the life of man.
    We have learnt to know thee, O thou all-prolific Womb, made pregnant by the
Father's begetting;
we have learnt to know thee, O thou eternal constancy of that
which stands unmoved, yet makes the universe revolve.

    With such words of praise do we adore thee, who alone art good; and let us
crave from by goodness no boon save this: be it thy will that we be kept
still knowing and loving thee, and that we may never fall away from this blest
way of life.
       —Hermes Trismegistus

                      *

PART THREE

UNCOVERING
THE SELF

INTRODUCTION

I T IS ONE THING TO CONSIDER the great spiritual truths intellectually, but it is quite another to engage in daily Self-inquiry and to make the great wisdom teachings practical. While some metaphysical knowledge is necessary to Self-inquiry, it is the realization of that knowledge in thought, feeling, and action that forms the vehicle for the real work of uncovering the Self.

How do we realize ourselves? The work is utterly simple and can be summed up in a few simple dictates given by the sages: "Remember your true Self"; "remember the universal Self at all times"; "know that you have nothing of your own"; and "offer everything to the Divine Source." The wise tell us three things: The Self is perfect; hence it does not need to be perfected. The pure Self lives deep within the cavity of our hearts; hence we need not go in search of it outside of ourselves. We are one with the Supreme Self; hence there is nothing to achieve. Yet without practical spiritual work we do not really *know* or *feel* these truths, and most importantly, we do not *remember* them in daily life. We do not even remember our own existence from moment to moment.

Although the work is utterly simple and can be summed up in a few brief sentences, it is not easy to carry out. The difficulty lies in our present state of sleep and is further complicated by the malfunctioning of the human instrument. The ordinary "reality" we experience daily is thus complicated and distorted by our faulty perception. Hence the wise tell us that the fault lies not in the world, but in our view of it.

Mesmerized by the multiplicity of the outer world, we are confused by the movements of our mind and emotions — the conflict of our multiple "I"'s, our capricious feelings, our weak conscience, our opposing notions and endless internal commentary. We do not know what to think because our thinking has been clouded over by the errors of the materialistic views of our era. We do not know what to believe because our faith has been shattered by the sense of futility, anguish, and misery that is evident around the world. We do not know what to do because we are incapable of truly doing and changing; we cannot solve our own problems, let alone those of others. If we look at the human situation from a perspective of multiplicity and fragmentation, it does look hopeless. It seems impossible to improve the human predicament from this point of view.

By studying a few essential principles, however, we can correct our errors of thought. By restoring the normal functioning of the human instrument and by objective observation of our thoughts, feelings, and actions, we can help to bring about the harmonious functioning of our faculties. This kind of Self-investigation takes place in the "now," the only time and place where effective, positive change can take place. In this work there is no looking back, no regret, no delving into the dark recesses of the mind, no reliving of past trauma. The healing is instantaneous. When we begin to live in the present moment and refuse to act mechanically, the mind-body mechanism will follow suit. We will avoid going into a tailspin of pathological reactions when somebody "presses our buttons" or "gets on our nerves" or "sends us over the edge." The clusters of habitual reactions will eventually atrophy, since we are no longer giving them any power.

These are not just metaphors. We already know that thinking and feeling affect every cell in the body and that meditation can permanently alter brain waves and perceptions. It can be assumed that when we begin to make *conscious* efforts to observe ourselves and practice one-pointed attention, new patterns begin to form in the nervous system as the old clusters of neurons relating to certain habitual reactions and emotional patterns are deactivated.

This work not only teaches that transformation is possible — that we need not be enslaved by inherent tendencies, that wrong thinking is correctable, that bad emotions, attitudes, and habits are reversible, and that suffering is unnecessary — but also gives us the tools to ensure such transformation. It proposes that we can cure illnesses of the mind — often known as "ignorance" in Eastern teachings — by saturating them with "right thinking," with good principles and truthful ideas. It suggests that emotional illnesses — lack of love and enthusiasm, false attachments, feelings of separateness — can only be healed with finer emotions, with the reawakening of conscience and the love of truth.

Such Self-investigation lies in stark contrast to other means of psychological healing, such as psychotherapy. Modern psychological methods (except for Jungian, archetypal, and spiritual psychology) look only at certain aspects of the human psyche, chiefly focusing on the ego or persona. They give little or no consideration to the soul, the spirit, or the collective purpose of our existence. Many forms of psychology hold that change is possible only if we go back into the past to find the childhood trauma that caused the present pathology and that we can only cope with our present situation if we clarify all the past events of our lives. Other branches concentrate exclusively on behavior modification, neglecting the inner life completely.

Self-inquiry also stands in contrast to conventional religious education, which frequently consists of telling us what not to do but rarely tells us *how* not to do it. Although religious training may impart moral principles and awaken the conscience to a sense of right and wrong, it does not provide the tools for transforming our being and attaining to a higher calling. When we know better but cannot change for the better, we are left with guilt and shame.

Spiritual work, as set forth in Part Three, leaves the past alone, except as refuse to be cleared away to reveal the resplendent Self. The aim is to take practical, positive steps toward our dreams of wholeness and our intuitions of unity. It sets forth the ideal to be achieved, the state to be attained, and defines the purpose of our existence, which, as the sages tell us, is to realize bliss. It assures us that realizing the one true Self is not only possible but necessary. If we remember that a mountain is climbed one step at a time, we can begin the journey with confidence.

A Word to the Reader

THE WORK — THE ACTUALIZATION OF spiritual truths and change of being — begins with Part Three, chapter two: "The Decision." You may have arrived at this point having read every word of the text so far, or, being eager to begin the real work, you may have skipped to this section. In much the same way, Part Three of this book may be used deliberately and methodically, chapter by chapter; or, in the tradition of the true discoverer, you may wish to find a chapter that attracts your attention and promises to bring to light the knowledge most relevant to your present state.

Although this spiritual work makes use of an ancient tradition and loosely follows Patanjali's *Yoga Aphorisms* and some principles of the Nyaya Ladder, it is not suggested that this ladder be "climbed" arduously one rung at a time or in a rigid manner. In that sense the image of the ladder is not useful. Although there is an internal logic to Part Three in that the chapters form a progression in the work, there is no need to read sequentially, since each chapter is self-contained and deals with one or more aspects of the uncovering of the true Self. Thus you may choose to work with a given chapter for several weeks while revisiting Part One and reflecting on Part Two. Or you may choose to read to the end and work with each chapter for a given time, and then begin again and work with them in greater depth. You may also want to skip ahead and work with a chapter that addresses your particular present needs. This text is simply a resource for your individual spiritual work and a guide in helping you to discover your own personal approach.

*

ONE

WHAT IS SPIRITUAL WORK?

ALL WORK IS SPIRITUAL. Life is spiritual work. Whether we are aware of it or not, we are here in time and space to realize ourselves, to become what we truly are, and to serve as a medium in the evolution of consciousness. Even so it is better to be aware that we are indeed spiritual beings with a potential for evolution than to be merely at the mercy of chance or destiny. It is better to gain higher Knowledge, by which we realize that suffering is the outcome of attachments and delusions and that the only "sins" are ignorance of the truth and lack of love. It is important to know our true purpose, which is to manifest the glory of the Absolute and to express our particular soul nature and our special talents. It helps to know that we can indeed be joyful, grow whole, gain access to our higher faculties, and enjoy a larger life full of growth, potential and energy.

It is beneficial to be aware that liberation is attainable in this life and that this fact has been demonstrated in the lives of mystics and sages of all times. We need to know that the incarnations of the many aspects of the divine — the great avatars Rama, Krishna, Isis, Hermes, Kali, Mahesvari, Buddha, Mary, Christ, and many others — have come to remind us of our true nature. We should realize that these compassionate beings do not ask for adulation; rather, by their lives and teachings they show us the way to Self-Realization.

We may choose to ignore our true purpose or we may decide to do conscious spiritual work. To speak of "doing" spiritual work is an unfortunate turn of phrase and in fact does not describe adequately the reality of how we grow more fully into our true nature. Although spiritual work requires effort, the process is rather an undoing and an uncovering. In a nutshell, the undoing consists of getting rid of wrong thinking, wrong doing, and false ideas and beliefs. Through conscious observation we can undo the wrong workings of the mind-body mechanism. Through one-pointed attention in action, we tap into infinite consciousness and love. Such actions carry no further karma. The uncovering entails the realization of the nature of the Veils of Illusion — the various sheaths in which the Atman is clothed for its life in the world. By discrimination we divest ourselves of these coverings, which are caused by identification with the body, mind, life force, intellect, and even with bliss. Through meditation we free ourselves from impurities in the *antahkarana* that stem from past actions. By practicing detachment, we become free of entanglements among the things of the world. Thus we stand clear of desire and its attendant suffering and rise above the duality of pleasure/pain, right/wrong, good/evil. When in a moment of perfect attention we renounce all personal desires, we will come into accord with universal desire or Divine Will.

In our inquiry, we fully accept our nature, our constitution, our tendencies, talents, shortcomings, and faults, as well as the fruits of our past actions. We must be clear that we cannot transcend what we have not seen and acknowledged. We have to get to know and fully experience what keeps us imprisoned and what keeps us from knowing our true Self. We embrace these conditions with all their seeming obstacles and problems. We embrace the universal laws, our karma, and the infinite wisdom behind these laws. They are for our benefit. We are given exactly what we need at each step of our self-development and the evolution of our soul. In the words of the seventeenth-century French priest J.-P. de Caussade, "God speaks to all individuals through what happens to them moment by moment."

IT IS NEVER TOO LATE TO BEGIN spiritual work. Every effort towards truth and Self-knowledge brings us closer to our divine nature. People who are dying sometimes experience a rare state of grace in which they find inner bliss and spontaneously realize their divine origin. At such moments they often express regret for not having come to this realization earlier in their lives. Although it would be advantageous to wake up while still young, thus avoiding a great deal of misery, life experiences and the wisdom gained by them are never received in vain.

We also need to know that we are never too old or too decrepit to begin the work. The effort does not require physical energy. On the contrary, spiritual practices have the added benefit of energizing and healing the human instrument and thus may even offer a second lease on life. Many who have received such an impulse — a last opportunity to wake up — often dedicate the remainder of their lives to the quest.

When we realize that we can escape from bondage and actively participate in the expansion of our consciousness, we are already open to the influx of divine energy. The Supreme Self is always ready to help. All we need to do is call upon it, and in so doing we acknowledge a higher force — the Godhead or Brahman — from which we have our being. It is essential to know that there is a way to attain perfection and that our return to the Godhead proceeds in a lawful manner.

Although spiritual work is for the good of all mankind, its actual practice is a personal and private matter. It can never take place in the public forum. It is therefore not useful to speak about it to our acquaintances or declare our allegiance to a guru in public, or to say "I am a Zen Buddhist," or "I am a Vedantist." Spiritual work is very subtle: it takes place in the mind and the emotions and shows its effects in our nature and character. No one else need be aware of our inner work. Our being will speak for itself as we become more cheerful, loving, and tolerant.

The search for our true nature is very much an individual endeavor, even if we choose to do it in a communal setting. We come to know the true Self through our own inner effort; no one else can do it for us. Spiritual work can only be done by the Self of each individual, and it cannot really be taught. We can only be gently guided by signposts in the form of an outer system that corresponds to our inner system. This process differs from religions that emphasize communal prayer, the authority of a leader, and the administration of ritual by its ministers. In spiritual work we recognize that we alone are responsible for our happiness or misery, and therefore there is no blame on others or on the forces of evil. We are aware that we can have what Emerson called "a revelation of our own," so that we need not rely on second-hand knowledge. When we recognize that it is up to us to save ourselves and we are willing to take charge of our own realization in the here and now, our healing has already begun.

In Part One, we already established that we cannot reform society by external means alone. Similarly, we have probably concluded by now that it is next to impossible to change our personal circumstances and our environment in a significant way.

In spiritual work, we begin where we are, which includes our circumstances of life — our standing in the world, our profession, our roles and responsibilities. Unless these circumstances are absolutely intolerable and not conducive to the work, there is no advantage to making external changes to them. Positive changes will begin to happen quite naturally as an outer reflection of our inner state. Disciplines such as study of spiritual truths, meditation, observation, and attention will change our outlook on life. As we grow in our being, we become freer, more tolerant, and more loving. We meet the world anew. Personal circumstances and relationships are seen in a new light — as challenges and opportunities for spiritual growth. We realize that everything is in the eye of the beholder and that therefore the work must begin with ourselves.

As more individuals embark on the work, the divine forces are strengthened, and the external world will indeed become a better place. The light of consciousness gathered in meditation touches every being with whom we come in contact and graces every endeavor; thus it reaches far into the community. Selfless acts beget other selfless acts — a pattern that begins to extend more harmony and love to our families and relations. In this lawful way, inner work becomes outer work. This natural process, by which effort and consciousness manifest in the world, lies behind the principle that spiritual work is never for one's own sake and certainly not for the sake of the small self, but is in fact for the good of all — for the One Self.

In Part One we looked at the threefold way of *jnana, bhakti,* and karma yoga — the ways of knowledge, devotion, and action. In the following chapters we will see in more detail how this ancient knowledge may be put into practice by the modern seeker. To sum it up very briefly: we read the words of the wise ("tuition"), and we reflect on the meaning of these truths and refer them to our own inner knowing ("intuition"). When this *knowledge* becomes established in our being, it engenders good ideas, good thinking, and good resolution. We begin to live the knowledge, that is, we put it into practice or *action*. Through the effort of one-pointed attention, love and true knowledge rise up and nourish our being. *Devotion* to the work is strengthened by knowledge and action. Compassion and love of truth increase as we begin to see more, and wisdom grows as we understand more. Through awareness in moments of interaction, our deeds become more selfless. We become more useful in the world as we become more perfect tools in the service of the One Self, and we gather no further karmic debt, dedicating all actions to the One Self.

Soon we realize that it is not necessary to come to this work with a compassionate heart, an unbounded craving for knowledge, or an insistent longing to be one with God. These are rare and pure emotions experienced by saints and mystics. For the most part we are far from such refined longings. It is much more likely that we come to this work through rational concerns and practical considerations relating to everyday life. Perhaps we have concluded that we are sorely lacking in our present way of being and that we want to be more whole. We sense that we are asleep but that we have the potential to wake up and take an active part in our own spiritual evolution.

At this point we have arrived at a most auspicious convergence of forces. But before we can proceed, we have to know exactly where we stand, what the goal is, and how to get there. Experience has shown that the will is fickle and endurance meager and that nothing ever comes from shoulds and oughts. To take up the work is by no means an ordinary decision. In reality, it takes place in another dimension beyond time and space. Such a momentous event warrants an extraordinary, conscious, and firm decision formulated with clear intent. Without this, no progress is possible.

Spiritual work is in essence utterly simple. Yet because of internal attitudes, we tend not to understand things that are very simple. Because we are very complicated, we have more trust in complexity. So we need a sophisticated system to undo the complicated construct that the false ego has built. Liberation, as we will see, is not something to achieve; liberation is nothing other than the revelation of our essence and the actualization of our own true nature.

*

TWO

THE DECISION

I N ORDER TO ENGAGE in the "examined life," we have to be willing to step into the unknown. It takes courage, determination, and trust: courage, because we are embarking on a journey into the unknown; determination, because we will encounter the antics of the ego and cannot run from what we see; trust, because we have to free-fall as we let go of our illusions and attachments until we find a footing in our new ground of being. We also have to be prepared to assume greater responsibility. As we awaken from our sleep and understand more about the nature of things, we may need to act or speak our conscience. The intent has to be single-minded and the will firm.

It could be said of this work that it is "unnatural" in that it requires going against nature, whose influence would keep us fast asleep in matter. Moreover we also have to swim against the tide of popular culture and commonly held beliefs. The work, in fact, requires a complete change of mind, or what the Greeks called *metanoia*. We have to make a 180-degree turn, if you will, and walk in the opposite direction.

To say that this work is too overwhelming and that the task is utterly impossible would be right if it were not for the fact that the Paramatman is always present to help at every step. All that is required of us is an attitude of humility and simplicity, the willingness to let go of our own false notions, and to challenge and renounce, if need be, our societal and cultural belief systems.

The very fact that we find ourselves at this point of coming to a decision means that we have already seen our lives in the light of truth. We have seen the futility of chasing after pleasure, the emptiness of ambitious pursuits, and the banality of popular culture. We have probably already lost our taste for selfish actions and observed that they simply bring unhappiness. But merely being fed up with the status quo is not enough. Dabbling in spiritual practices will not bring lasting change. We need to make a conscious decision or *yama*, which, according to Patanjali's *Yoga Sutras*, is "a firm determination to live a life dedicated to Truth."

There is a fivefold resolution attached to *yama*, this first step on the path to enlightenment. It requires the seeker to adopt a series of moral virtues:

1. Harmlessness. This means causing no harm to any creature or anything in the universe, in mind, heart, and body. Harmlessness is one of many reasons, including economic and ecological ones, for not eating animals. Each one of us has to find his or her own proper measure in this area. Some draw the line at eating anything "with a face on it." In addition, this resolution to cause no harm includes ourselves. What does it mean to cause no harm to one's own soul, spirit, mind, heart, and body? We have to thoroughly reflect on this resolution, search for answers in our own hearts, and find the ways and means to implement them in our own lives.

2. *Truthfulness in speech and action.* At the lowest level this means not to lie in order to deceive. At another level it means saying exactly what we mean or feel so as not to confuse and so to get at the truth of the matter at hand. At yet a higher level it means consistency: to speak from inner knowing so that all our actions conform to this knowledge. We become consistent and thus totally dependable.

3. *Honesty.* Spiritual work requires scrupulous honesty and sincerity, especially in personal relationships. Honesty or freedom from deceit is a necessity when we begin to observe ourselves, and in turn this virtue will be strengthened by conscious observation. This, of course, is not to be confused with tactlessness.

4. *Sublimation of lower drives.* Infatuations, cravings, and obsessive attachments are obstacles to development. What these are each of us has to consider honestly. For the householder, this resolution does not mean giving up sex, as it did for the yogi or monk. However, the power that fuels our lower drives is a precious force that can also be expressed in creative pursuits, love of beauty, and delight in nature.

5. *Freedom from greed and from the desire for reward.* Freedom from greed means to be content with what is enough. Greed is an extreme desire for some object — usually money. Hardly anyone escapes this form of social conditioning; we all want more than we need. We need to take a good look at our covetousness, find a way to avoid external temptations, and check the feelings of need that fuel this impulse.

For the householder, freedom from the desire for reward simply means to perform actions without ulterior motives. Neutral action leaves no residue, no regret. The action is performed for its own sake or because it needs to be done and therefore requires no reward or honor.

These five resolutions are not to be regarded merely as ordinary "good intentions," but in fact require a sincere and earnest commitment in our decision to live a life dedicated to truth. Together they form one of the prerequisites to Self-inquiry; it is imperative to have basic moral integrity before we can aspire to higher goals. Good character and a cheerful nature are a wonderfully fertile ground from which to grow more fully into our spiritual being. Good will and enthusiasm arising from good character are indispensable ingredients in aspirations to greater harmony.

Our earnest determination to live a life dedicated to truth is a once in a lifetime event. It needs to be celebrated in the conscious moment of decision and validated by a simple but memorable ceremony.

A Suggested Ceremony

FIND A QUIET ROOM where you will not be disturbed. Light a candle or some incense. Sit in a comfortable chair. Breathe deeply and let all thoughts and concerns of the day dissolve. Enjoy the expansion in the mind and rest in the vastness of infinite consciousness. Listen to the silence behind all sound or let your attention rest on a mantra.

When the mind is at rest, become aware of your innermost being, that which never changes — your own true Self. Then, without wavering from that still center, speak your firm intent to live your life dedicated to truth and pledge your commitment to the service of the One Self. In your own words, invite truth, light, grace, wisdom, and joy into your life. Let all doubt dissolve and rest assured in the fact that the Paramatman — the Supreme Self — is always there to help.

PRACTICES

1. Reflect on the five resolutions of *yama* and consider ways to implement them in your life.

2. Write the following words from the *Kena-Upanishad* on a sheet of paper and read them every morning and every evening before going to sleep:

   Speech, eyes, ears, limbs, life, energy, come to my help.
   I shall never deny Spirit, nor Spirit deny me.
   Let me be in union, communion with Spirit.

THREE
PREPARING THE GROUND

THE TASK OF CLEARING and cultivating an overgrown lot can be overwhelming, especially if we are novice gardeners. We are easily discouraged by the enormity of the work that lies ahead. Where do we begin and how? We could resort to the slash-and-burn method and start completely from scratch. We could make a plan and decide what to eradicate and what to cultivate. We could proceed to carefully and methodically pull out the vines and thorny brush and thus provide the space and light necessary for new plantings to grow. Whichever method we are inclined to use, we need to use the right tools for the task. The ground has to be carefully prepared, or else new plants cannot germinate and take root.

The image of clearing and cultivating an overgrown lot is an apt metaphor for the state of our being as we prepare to plant the seeds of spiritual work. When we wake up and begin to look around ourselves, we may be quite justifiably overwhelmed. So much has grown up to obscure the light of truth in us. Innumerable notions and fears hedge us in and restrict our freedom to move and to choose. The psyche is entangled in the thorny overgrowth of false ideas and emotions. Buried under the debris of materialistic ideals, our finer faculties, higher aspirations, and latent talents have no room to grow and blossom.

Although the task seems difficult at first, we will soon discover that clearing this ground can actually be quite gratifying. Like a gardener, we have to choose a method for clearing the ground and to determine what needs to be eliminated in preparation for a life dedicated to truth. We have to identify the most obvious obstructions and impediments first. These may be of an external nature, such as disordered living conditions, horrendous working situations, or relationship problems. They may also be of an internal nature — bad habits, sloth, gluttony, obsessions, or forms of indulgence. And then there are the more subtle impediments — fears, imaginings, anxieties, attachments.

We can begin to physically remove things from our daily lives that keep us enslaved to our weaknesses. We can choose to get rid of distractions and the kind of entertainment and food that puts us to sleep. We may need to physically clean our homes, our closets, and our desks to create some order in our external world, which in turn will allow for greater harmony and peace within. In this way we bring about a harmonious synthesis of inner and outer beauty and simplicity.

In short, we need to clean up our act, and we all know what that means to each one of us. This is where our resolutions of truthfulness and honesty come in. We need to be ruthless with our baser inclinations and weed them out with vigor. We can, for example, choose to avoid the situations and relationships that bring out the worst in us — the encounters that tend to cause the all-too-familiar chain reaction of desire, indulgence, and disappointment. As we begin to observe ourselves objectively, we will see that these reactions can be almost instantaneous, or they can be spread out over a longer period of time.

The internal impediments — the attitudes, attachments, desires, and beliefs hidden in the deepest recesses of the mind and the heart — are the hardiest weeds and the most difficult to pull up. These treasured notions are deeply rooted in false identity. When the ego with its false attributes is threatened in any way, it puts up great resistance: it holds on to the poisonous weeds as if they were precious herbs. We will need to resort to our most perfect tools and employ a precise method for eradicating these impediments.

In the meantime we go about preparing the ground and clear away the most superficial debris: our small weaknesses, our superficial tendencies, and our minor habits and faults. We will see in the light of observation that what distinguishes a small weakness from a major hindrance is often a matter of degree. Eating a little too much is one thing; not being able to stop eating is quite another. Being somewhat talkative may be harmless; being a compulsive talker is a major obstacle to the spiritual quest. Having a weakness for comfort is not a major character flaw; not being able to move out of sloth is more than a hindrance and requires some outside help.

After we have identified the most prevalent hindrances, we can then begin to patiently eradicate them one by one, or, if we are more courageous, resort to the slash-and-burn method. Pace is important, as is restraint, particularly when our actions affect the lives of others. We are not seeking for results or rewards, but should keep in mind that every effort towards the light and truth is its own reward. When we give up a fault, we instantly grow more perfect; justice, as Emerson said, is instantaneous. We come a little closer to our true Self, whose nature is *sat-chit-ananda*. When we move towards the light, we escape the darkness of the underbrush. We become more virtuous and our lives become more joyous and harmonious.

The fivefold resolutions of *yama* can serve as guidelines to right conduct and moral virtue. The sages tell us that good action leads to good habits; good habits in turn lead to good character; good character leads to good destiny.

As we have already seen in Part One, *niyama,* the second step listed by Patanjali, relates to regular study of spiritual knowledge and moderation of mind and body to incline one's life towards truth. The first method on this step is cleanliness of body and mind. Purification is not only a necessary prerequisite to Self-knowledge, but may also be performed as an act of reverence at the entry of quest. Some traditions symbolize this step by requiring a washing of the feet before entering the sacred hall.

How do we as modern seekers engage in the act of purification? We need a practical method that is easily integrated into our busy lives. We know from past experience that we cannot become pure in mind and heart by simply willing it. But we can begin with "good intention" and "good habit," specifically, by practicing a method that has been used by seekers for thousands of years: the regular study of spiritual knowledge.

We may have already experienced the cleansing and stilling qualities of reading the great wisdom tradition and exploring the aphorisms of the Perennial Philosophy. This practice helps eradicate the weeds and the debris around our essence; it cleanses the conscious and subconscious mind of illusion, false notions, and *samskaras* — the latent tendencies that have not yet come to the surface. It replaces idle thoughts with good thoughts and unsound ideas with truthful ideas. The regular study of spiritual knowledge and meditation, as well as playing or listening to fine music and the contemplation of great works of art, help cleanse the heart and mind. Such pursuits relieve us of the residue of past action and protect us in the present from heartache and suffering. In short, all these practices further the process of replacing coarse or destructive emotions with refined emotions.

Another method of *niyama* is the "critical examination of the senses," which translates into more contemporary language as "objective observation." The method of nonjudgmental observation of our inner and outer world has been used for thousands of years. It is sometimes referred to as "awareness in action" or "self-remembering." Objective observation could be called the "scientific" or rational approach to Self-recovery. It is the perfect means of keeping us from falling asleep and resorting to habitual thought and action. Granted, at the outset we are looking from an undisciplined mind and clouded perceptions. But we have to begin with the tools we have. To observe — and to observe objectively — takes practice and effort. We have to look from a still mind and from calm emotions as we go about our affairs. We simply watch the movements in the mind, the heart, and the body from a higher vantage point, without any comment, judgment, or regret. That which is watching will eventually crystallize. At that point it will be experienced in its pure form as the sole Witness, the silent observer beyond the ordinary mind.

This method of observation is purifying in itself and supports the other efforts toward purification. As our perception is cleansed, we see more and we see more clearly and accurately. In turn, the impurities that are *truly seen* in the moment by the Witness will lose their strength and in time dissolve altogether. With repeated efforts at objective observation, we can eventually bring the automatic responses under control and gain mastery over the mechanical movements in the mind and heart — the inner conversations, the lying and justifying, criticism, imaginings, unhappiness, negativity, and anger.

Let us consider the process of purification in more detail:

PURIFYING THE MIND

EVEN A LITTLE OBSERVATION will lead to the conclusion that much, if not most, of the chatter in our heads — the incessant circling thoughts, the strands of conversations and strains of tunes, the reprimanding voices of the past — has literally nothing to do with us in the present moment or in dealing with the task at hand. Much of it can be traced to mental habits passed down by former generations. In fact this kind of mechanical inner considering is not really thinking at all. It does not reflect the proper function of the mind — the purposeful considering of facts, active formulating of ideas, calculating, reasoning, decisionmaking. Rather it is mindless activity consisting of simple association, repetitive inner conversations, imaginings, and anticipation based on the dead past or the nonexistent future.

On deeper examination we will realize that we have very little control over this mental noise. So how can we purify our minds and still their relentless movements? The method, once again, is simply to face them with conscious and objective observation. This very act will bring the running commentary under control. Habit flees from the light of consciousness. The benefits of controlling the mind are numerous and include clarity of mind, increased power of concentration, clearer expression, and improved communication.

The dictionary definition of the word "to purify" is "to make pure, to make free from anything that debases, pollutes, contaminates." This leads us directly to the working principle relating to the purification of the mind, which is to refrain from all criticism. When we criticize, whether ourselves or others, we are polluting and contaminating the mind. Criticism never serves truth or the good. Although criticism has become an acceptable pastime in our century, it debases our social relations and institutions as well as polluting ourselves and our endeavors. When the intent is malicious, criticism turns into slander; it then not only debases but has the power to destroy and even kill. (The injunction to "refrain from all criticism" is a specific inner discipline. As such it does not refer to cultural critiques or to constructive criticism leading to positive change. Nor does it apply when the need arises to bring wrongdoing to light.)

When we look at ourselves in the light of truth, we begin to see many faults and shortcomings. To criticize ourselves for them would be counterproductive and even destructive. When we criticize ourselves, we are wasting precious time. We are not observing objectively but are instead engaged in self-contamination. In such moments, there is no space or light available for healing. By contrast, when we see a flaw in ourselves but refrain from criticizing it, we simply and objectively acknowledge it and let it go. The healing of this problem will usually come about in the moment of seeing. If need be, we take specific action to remedy the situation without comment, blame, or guilt.

Purifying the Heart

THE WORD CHITTA, LIKE MANY Sanskrit words, has multiple meanings, which include "mind stuff," "conscience," "disposition," and "heart." *Chitta* is also said to be the pleasure-seeking function and the storehouse of memory. The English language reveals a similar connection in the phrase "learning by heart," as does the French *apprendre par coeur*. Although *chitta* is traditionally associated with the heart center, it is in fact one of the components of the internal organ of mind and therefore is intermeshed with the other faculties of the psyche and the mind-body mechanism. Scientific research has in fact demonstrated that memory operates throughout the body. For our purpose it is useful to keep in mind the traditional definition of *chitta*, which is "the storehouse of memory." It is where we keep our treasures — our beliefs, both sane and false, our likes and dislikes, our loves and hates, our hurts and traumas. It is also the depository of the subconscious mind. All thoughts, feelings, and actions over the course of many lifetimes leave an impression on the *chitta*. We are unaware of these impurities until they rise to the surface and manifest as desires, fears, and strong tendencies and compulsions.

When the *chitta* is full of impurities, its substance tends to become dense and thick, rather like a knot of brambles. This obscures the light of consciousness and hides the essence, making it almost impossible to experience joy and happiness in everyday life. It is why we see "through a glass darkly." It explains why even "positive" feelings are colored with apprehension and dread and are admixed with the shadow side of the psyche.

How do we unravel these brambles? How do we purify the heart? Since we cannot empty the mind through a mere act of will, we need an efficient method to clean out these impurities. Again the key is objective observation of thoughts, feelings, and actions, especially as they relate to our emotional state. The densest knots, the most powerful attachments, are not necessarily seen first. But we can begin to identify them by the intensity of our reactions, for example when something or someone "pushes our buttons."

By such disinterested watching, negative feelings can be checked, dislodged, and eventually uprooted. Anger, fear, and even minor phobias can be kept at bay when we have the courage to see them for what they are: as movements in the mind arising from impurities in the heart. We look at these movements objectively and disinterestedly; we do not resist in any way, just note them and let them be. Reason tells us that every time we give expression to anger or any negative emotion, we lose precious energy — energy that can be channeled into aspiration for a higher calling. In time and with courage, we will meet the monsters hidden in the dark undergrowth head on and see them too for what they are: as nothing more than the effects of a false alliance with a separate ego, which, as we shall see, does not even exist.

As observation becomes more refined and insight grows, we may be able to detect a negative emotion as it arises in consciousness and check it before it manifests in full as aversion, fear, or even hatred.

We might observe that every thought is preceded by a feeling. We might even experience a sense of "I am," without admixture of "this" or "that" and come close to a feeling of pure existence. As the heart becomes purer, we will experience a lightness and expansion of being. Having uprooted some of the dense undergrowth in the light of observation, we will step out into the clearing and enjoy the natural attributes of the heart — love, happiness, peace and joy.

The working principle relating to purifying the heart is the willingness to give up suffering. "Giving up suffering" suggests that somehow we cling to suffering or that we choose to suffer. Our immediate response is to rebut and object: "But I don't want to suffer!" We certainly do not like the idea of wanting to suffer, causing our own suffering, or being unwilling to release suffering. However, as we gain insight and are willing to see things in the light of truth, we will have to agree that we often take a perverse delight in suffering and feeling sorry for ourselves. Once we let go of this selfish perversion — which it is possible to do in one fell swoop — the love of truth and the memory of our true nature will shine forth more brightly and light up the world around us. Having given up suffering, our hearts are now open to the outflowing of love and compassion for all sentient beings.

PURIFYING THE BODY

WE CANNOT BEGIN TO SPEAK ABOUT the purification of the body without taking into account the physical health of all of humanity and of the planet — our greater body. Whatever we eat, breathe, and come into contact with is a part of this greater body. We cannot purify the physical body in isolation. The food we eat and the water we drink comes from the earth and ends up circulating through us back into the earth. The finest substance in food, the Upanishads tell us, becomes mind; the middling substances become blood, sinew, muscle, bone, and marrow, while the coarse returns to the earth. Whatever we do to the earth comes back to us. If we pollute our bodies, we pollute the earth, and the earth pollutes us in turn.

We cannot breathe in isolation. The air we breathe has been breathed a thousand times before. We are all responsible for the health of our atmosphere and for the preservation of our resources, which are precious and finite. Without the health of our greater body, life cannot go on existing. We must tread more lightly on this precious body. We must take responsibility for the health of our immediate surroundings (insofar as this is within our power) and stop polluting the air, the water, and the earth by living more simply, by being content with less, by being respectful of nature and its laws. Taking responsibility for the health of the planet will contribute to a more holistic way of life for the benefit of all human beings.

In this larger view, the health and purity of our own bodies are not selfish indulgences, but rather are part of our individual duty to the health of all. We can contribute to the health of the body by eating pure foods, taking plenty of exercise in fresh air, and by refusing to pollute ourselves with unhealthy foods, drugs, and intoxicants. As spiritual seekers, we treat the body as a precious instrument that we are privileged to use for a short time. We see it as the dwelling of spirit and therefore keep it healthy, clean, pure, and beautiful. An ancient Sanskrit text describes the physical body as "a raft with the help of which we cross the ocean of phenomenal existence, with the help of which we attain spiritual illumination and immortality."

The working principle relating to purity of body, wholeness, and harmony is to never be careless.

You may wish to work with this material for several days or weeks before you go on to the next practices; or you may read to the end of the book and then come back to Part Three and work with each practice one at a time.

✵

PRACTICE

1. Make a plan for preparing the ground. Identify the things you intend to eliminate, such as distractions, temptations, and disorder.

2. Identify hindrances such as bad habits and indulgences.

3. Observe the movements of the mind: the imaginings, inner conversations, attachment to ideas, criticisms.

4. Observe negative feelings, such as anxieties, fears, attachment to suffering

5. Observe the body's signals and give it the appropriate care — pure food, exercise, and rest.

6. Write down the three working principles for the thinking, feeling, and moving centers given below and post them so you will be reminded regularly.

Refrain from criticism.	(mind)
Give up suffering.	(heart)
Never be careless.	(body)

   Although each of these virtues is specific to each of these centers, they also pertain in a broader sense to all of them; for example, it is important to refrain from criticism in the heart and body as well as in the mind.

7. Find time to read and reflect on spiritual knowledge or listen to some fine music such as Gregorian chant. Let the mind and heart be immersed in the knowledge of truth and cleansed by the music.

8. Remember that the spiritual practice of observing the human instrument is one of nonjudgmental or "disinterested" watching. Mental commentary is *not* objective observation. If this occurs, simply tell the mind to be still and step further back or watch from a higher point, as it were. As you go about your day, remember that you are the silent observer as well as the observed.

FOUR
CLEANING OUT CLUTTER

WE CLING TO SO MANY THINGS in life without which we believe we simply cannot be happy or even survive. Often we resolve to clean out the closet to get rid of unnecessary clutter and find ourselves stuffing most of it back — just in case! Some of us find it difficult to part with objects and mementos of the past, and many of us are pack rats to one degree or another. This may seem like an innocent habit, but when we consider that our outer world is an accurate reflection of our inner world, we must think again. The clutter in our minds and hearts caused by wrong thinking and feeling is not so innocent, since it is the cause for much of our unhappiness. The accumulations in the subconscious mind exert an even greater influence on our lives. The impressions left in the subtle and causal bodies by past thoughts, feelings, and actions determine the measure of love, happiness, and freedom we are able to experience in this life.

It is easiest to begin the process of cleaning out with the exterior world. There is no doubt that it is very helpful to clean out excessive material clutter to simplify existence and to remove the things that invite us to indulgence and emotional reactions. Moreover cleaning our living quarters and closets may prove to be a wonderful exercise in preparation for the quest, since learning to let go on this material level will help us later in the practice of renunciation. It also shows that these objects have no true value and fail to give lasting happiness. Most often we want things in a given instant because we feel needy and because we do not know how to understand this insistent need. As a result we end up with many possessions when in fact what we truly desire is sustenance for our minds, hearts, and souls, and ultimately everlasting happiness and love.

For the modern seeker, renunciation does not mean throwing out all our belongings and living in abject poverty. Nor does it mean denying our intrinsic delight in comfort, simplicity, and harmony. There is no need to renounce beauty or the good in daily life, and there is nothing inherently wrong with enjoying beautiful things. An appreciation for harmonious works of art, craft, and music is one of our more refined human capacities. We are right to treasure these noble expressions of human creativity. What causes trouble is not inherent in the things themselves or even in the enjoyment of them, but in our attachment to them.

The *Eesha Upanishad* tells us to "enjoy" but warns, "Do not covet His property." We are free to enjoy, but we must guard ourselves from mentally grasping at any of it. If we were to realize but for a moment that we cannot truly own anything permanently, we might let go of our attachments to material things. If we truly realized that we in fact have nothing we can call our own, we would run the risk of being enlightened in the twinkling of an eye!

In the meantime, even a little reflection will show that whatever we think we own — our homes and possessions, even the body and our vital energies — all come from the earth and will eventually return to the earth. What we do *not* see — the spirit, the Self — descends to us from above, from the Paramatman, which lends an infinitesimal spark of its light and power to the Self in all, and this in turn lends its light and power for a brief time to the individual human soul. Matter and spirit join to imbue the individual soul with life energy and human capacities, so that it can give expression to its particular soul nature in creation.

When we consider this truth — which is the teaching of the great masters and sages — we realize that there is not very much we can call our own and that there is not much of "me" and "mine" in this picture. When we speak of "I," we usually mean by it "this entity," which has a form, name, and function. When we examine our inner world more closely, we see that these attributes are actually claimed by a specific central "figure" or feeling of self — the ego — which says, "This is 'me' and 'mine.'" This false self claims everything — "my" house, "my" clothes, "my" body, "my" perception, "my" talents — despite the fact that we cannot *be* that which we *perceive*. The false self also lays claim to the roles we play and says, "I am a mother," "I am a friend," "I am a doctor," "I am an artist," despite the fact that we cannot be what we do. Unfortunately this identification with what we *do* is reinforced by terms used by the media. Collectively we are said to *be* consumers, smokers, drinkers, commuters, sports fans. We should protest this degradation. It is not helpful, and is perhaps even harmful, for a human being to think, "I am a consumer." Eventually we will think that it is our duty to "consume."

The ego claims all thoughts, feelings, and deeds. But it does not stop there. It declares, "This is 'my' life, 'my' energy, 'my' breath, 'my' intelligence," despite the fact that our discrimination and intuition speak to us in no uncertain terms of a higher order. Through *buddhi,* we know that in truth we are the Atman — the Self — that which is beyond memory, beyond mind, beyond the body and the senses.

How do we rid our minds of this erroneous thinking? By changing our minds, or, as St. Paul said, "by the renewal of your own mind." *Manas* — the moving mind, or organ of thought — can cause trouble by wrong thinking, but it can also become a faithful servant. Like any servant, we must treat *manas* with love and patience and feed it regularly with right thinking, ideas, and intentions. When *manas* is cleansed from false thinking, it becomes a powerful tool in spiritual work.

It is in *manas* where we first "hear" false notions as they emerge clothed in language and first "see" mental and emotional clutter as it surfaces in the form of ideas we hold about ourselves. These, our most cherished ideas, come into the conscious mind charged with attitudes from the unconscious. They are invariably accompanied by some kind of qualification, positive or negative: "I am a good person," "I am intelligent," "I can't do this," "I can't do anything."

By diligently observing these movements in the mind — the ideas we hold about ourselves and our automatic responses — we can see them for what they are: useless clutter consisting of the stale remnants of the past. These harmful notions have nothing whatever to do with the present moment, except in having a negative effect on us. Only by *seeing* these notions can we stop them. Only when we are awake, when we can remember ourselves in the here and now, are we in the proper state for objective observation.

The next step in ridding ourselves from mental clutter is to shun language that supports the claims of the ego and avoid words such as "my," "me," and "mine." Instead of "my body," we can say "the body"; instead of "my life," we can say "this life." Instead of "how good of me," we can say "excellent" or nothing at all; instead of saying "how stupid of me," we can stop, face the facts, and remedy the situation.

We cannot have a still mind and heart simply by willing it, but we can put a stop to language that expresses criticism, regret, or blame. We can stop saying "he is always…"; "I should have…"; "if I could only…"; "what if…" As we begin to observe and investigate, we will find that this kind of inner commenting and compulsive talking goes on all the time. The thing is to simply see it and stop and not to comment on the commenting. We do not want to waste the light of conscious observation on verbal self-analysis; the aim is stillness of the mind.

WE MUST NOT BE DISCOURAGED when in the course of cleaning out, we find ghosts in the closet — mental debris we did not know we had. Cleaning out is full of surprises, and not always pleasant ones. When we look at ourselves in the light of conscious self-inquiry, we might become aware that we are not the kind, nonjudgmental persons we thought we were. We may realize that we dwell in an emotional atmosphere of discontent, regret, disappointment, and pessimism during most of our waking hours. When we begin to wake up and look around us, we see the same sentiments reflected in the eyes of others. We see many forms of negative mental stances — skepticism, sarcasm, nihilism, and fatalism. These stances are not only inscribed on the faces and psyches of people we know, but have taken their collective toll in mental and physical illness.

Negativity is the absence of the light of truth. It is one of the many manifestations of the force of *tamas*, which accounts for the darkness, inertia, and ignorance of the world. All this negativity and ill will are in direct opposition to enthusiasm — which is an indispensable element in our quest. The word "enthusiasm" comes from a Greek word meaning "full of the god" and, by extension, "inspired." Enthusiasm is a state that we can cultivate by not engaging in its opposite. Along with right thinking, intention, and aspiration, enthusiasm will help us over the hurdles on the path.

Cleaning out the causal body — the *antahkarana* — is more difficult and can only be accomplished indirectly through such practices as observation, reflection on sacred truths, and meditation. All thoughts, feelings, and actions arise in the consciousness tinted with a certain color — the color of our particular *antahkarana*. This explains the instantaneous like or dislike, approval or disapproval that arises in every activity. *Manas* has no coloring of its own but is influenced by the coloring of the causal body; hence it thinks accordingly. When the coloring is *sattvic*, it will reflect poise, when it is *rajasic* it will result in action, when it is *tamasic* it causes inertia.

Although every desire arises first in *manas* (because of its association with the senses and the sense objects that arouse desire), different types of desires are supported by a particular emotional attitude, which is stored in the causal body. It is difficult to see our own attitudes. We have much less difficulty seeing the emotional packages of others. Their attitudes are revealed in language, stance, traits, and mannerisms. We have covered our own flaws and hidden our tendencies with a blanket of forgetfulness. We now need the courage to clean out the secret and hidden acquisitions — the ancient impurities that color our whole being and becoming.

The causal body, as we already know, consists of *buddhi, ahamkara, chitta,* and *manas.* Together they form the *antahkarana* — the internal organ of mind which is the source of *bhavana* — a Sanskrit word meaning "state of being," "effect," or "causing to be." Out of *bhavana* in turn emanates the emotional attitudes of which we have been speaking and which taint every thought, feeling, and action. They arise from *bhavana* — "the causing to be" — in the "instant" or "space" between an activity and the act of discrimination by *buddhi*. It all happens in a split second. We might be dimly aware of this automatic effect, but we have no control over it — that is, if we are asleep. This process explains why we act in the manner we do, why we cannot *do* better when we *know* better, and why we are not free.

This would be a hopeless situation were it not for the fact that our Atman is free and that we are endowed with consciousness, reason, intelligence, and the power of self-reflection — the very tools we need to undo the effects of the past. But before we can wipe out the past, we have to *see* our false ideas, attachments, and attitudes. In order to see them we have to be conscious and aware in the moment of action. We have to remember to use our power of self-reflection. And we need to use reason and intelligence in the moment of self-reflection.

Now is the perfect time for conscious and honest observation; in fact it is the only chance we have to clear away our impediments. In the light of consciousness we will see the mental clutter we have accumulated since childhood and how it colors our thinking, feeling, and doing. We will then realize that this clutter no longer serves us or fits into our expanding vision of life. As we recognize that these attachments have become too painful, we become eager to give them up. Then we are ready to tackle our deep-seated impediments — the attitudes behind our passions and aversions.

The threefold method that leads to enlightenment includes *observation, discrimination,* and *renunciation.*

We are already familiar with the practice of objective observation in the moment of action. By observing from the point of view of the Witness, the movements of the mind are brought under control. In this state we bypass the ego. We do not act from a subjective stance or lay instant claim to every action. Thus we are less affected by the censorious voices in the mind, and actions become freer, more appropriate, and more creative. We are not affected by passion or aversion, so actions are neutral and do not engender consequences. But most importantly, in such actions there is more joy, love, and happiness.

The two ancient practices of *discrimination* and *renunciation* are closely connected to the practice of observation. One, we see; two, we discriminate; three, we renounce.

As we have seen, when inner attachments and claims are truly seen in the light of truth, they dissolve automatically. However, latent tendencies and deep-seated beliefs in the psyche need to be dislodged with the sharp edge of discrimination. *Buddhi* or reason is the tool for discerning the real from the unreal, the Self from not-Self, truth from untruth. It is the faculty that is in closest proximity to the Atman. *Buddhi* is the vehicle of Atman, while *manas* is the vehicle of *buddhi*. *Buddhi* helps us sort out the clutter and discriminate between the constructs of the ego and our true nature.

The practice of renunciation helps release the inner clutter of false ideas, attachments, and claims. Unlike the yogis of ancient times, we do not renounce the world and our belongings, but rather renounce the attachment to them. We let go of the attachment on all three levels: causal, subtle, and physical. It is useless to try to give up something simply on the physical level; the desire is still there and simply looks around for something else to which to attach itself. A person may give up an attachment to food only to develop an attachment to starvation or excessive exercise. Renunciation is not giving up ice cream and cookies. It is a spiritual practice and as such works on the subtle and causal level of being, although these in turn are likely to produce effects that will be evident on the physical level. True renunciation is giving up what we are *not*.

PRACTICE

1. Observe the claims and ideas — both positive and negative — you hold about yourself, the roles you play, and the activity at hand in a given moment. Watch *manas* — the moving mind — and put a stop to claims, inner considering, and repetitive thoughts about yourself or anything else by simply saying, *"Neti! Neti!"* — "Not this! Not this!"

2. Observe the thinking process. Avoid language that reinforces false claims and beliefs, such as "I am this or that"; "I can't..."; "I never..."; "my" or "mine."

3. Observe and let go of negative feelings, ill will, regret, guilt, and remorse.

4. Observe attitudes marked by an emotional charge arising in the moment of an event or activity. Let *manas* become still. Let go of the attitude and return to the silent observer.

5. Practice renunciation and discrimination. Let go of outworn beliefs and notions about yourself and reality. You may want to write down the most troublesome attitudes and burn the list while you consciously renounce them and offer them up to the One Self.

6. Continue to study and reflect on sacred scripture, which strengthens discrimination and cleanses *manas* and *chitta*.

FIVE
PUTTING THE HOUSE IN ORDER

W HEN WE WALK INTO A WELL-ORDERED HOUSE, we immediately experience a sense of comfort, ease, and peace, while a dirty and disorderly dwelling causes discomfort and agitation. Likewise our "primary residence" — the dwelling of the soul and spirit — can be in a state either of order and harmony or disorder and disharmony. We experience ourselves either as whole, well-aligned, and joyous or as fragmented, confused, and full of discord. Moreover this experience is not constant but changes from day to day and indeed from moment to moment.

We have already begun the process of preparing the ground and cleaning out clutter in the knowledge that spiritual work is not a matter of acquiring anything, but rather of shedding of what we are not and discarding what is no longer useful. The next step involves putting the house of being into order.

How do we accomplish this task? We begin with the study of the correct order and proper functioning of the three "stories" of this inner "house." Broadly speaking, we experience the external world chiefly through the intellect, emotions, and actions. We speak commonly of these "centers" as "head," "heart," and "guts," and attribute them metaphorically to these respective locations in the body. We think of the head as the seat of knowing, the heart as the seat of feeling, and the guts as that of doing.

In this study we will use a framework that relates the upper story of the house of being to the *thinking center*, the middle story to the *feeling center*, and the lower story to the *moving center*. The lower story is also the seat of control of the *instinctive* and *sexual* centers (see figs. 6 and 7, pp. 290–91).

In addition to the three main centers, there are two more — that of higher intellect "located" in the upper story and that of higher emotion in the middle story. Although they are fully developed, these centers are not accessible to our ordinary state of consciousness. A connection with them has to be established through certain disciplines, such as the purification of mind and heart and the practice of meditation. In the Eastern tradition, the higher aspects of *buddhi* and *chitta* are said to begin to function when the veil of ignorance becomes more transparent; reality is perceived when the veil is temporarily or permanently lifted.

Each of the centers in turn has a *moving part*, an *emotional part*, and an *intellectual part*. Thus we speak of knowing (a function of the thinking center) something by heart, or we speak of "learning" (a function of the moving center) by doing. References to these multifaceted aspects of the mind-body mechanism can be found not only in common language but in the Vedas, in the writings of Gurdjieff, which makes reference to "three-brained beings," and even in modern psychology, which has discovered "multiple intelligences" and their distinct ways of learning and expressing.

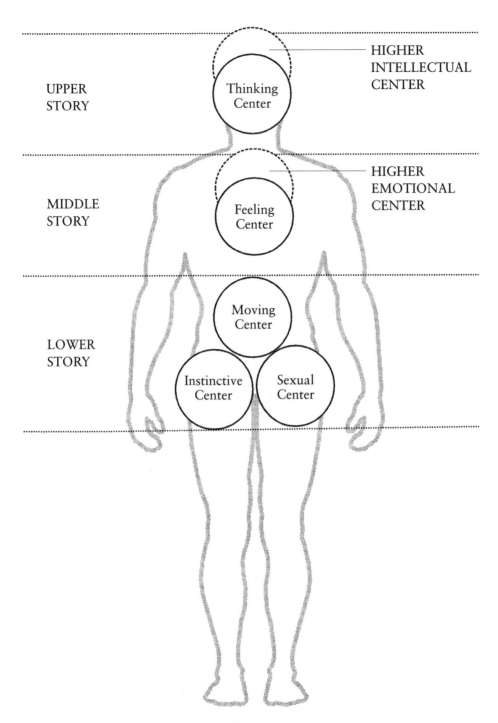

Figure 6. The centers in the three-story house of the human structure.

When all the various centers and their respective parts are perfectly aligned and performing their proper functions, the human being can be said to be sane, harmonious, and efficient. Such a being is capable of displaying amazing feats. When good character, a clear intellect, and a pure heart are coupled with a highly efficient mind-body mechanism, they can produce artistic excellence, new forms of knowledge, and scientific and technological inventions. Advanced development of the intellectual

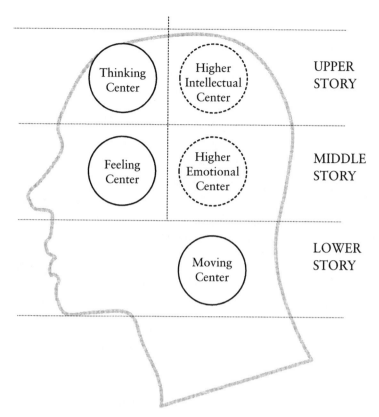

Figure 7. The three levels of mind.

and emotional centers as a result of good deeds in the past and right efforts in the present result in genius and in the highest expressions of truth. A temporary connection with the higher centers can be experienced as a flash of inspiration or a creative insight. But we humans tend not to live up to our full potential or to make full use of our minds. We tell our children that all they have to do is "believe in themselves," when instead we should be helping them to develop their inner powers.

A thorough study of the diagram of the functions (fig. 8, pp. 292) — both normal and abnormal — of the various centers will yield a great deal of insight into our internal mechanism. By studying this diagram in relation to ourselves, we may discover a predominant trait that connects our personality with a particular center. There is the person of intellect (*jnana*), the person of emotion (*bhakti*), or the person of action (karma). Thinking types rely on reason and logic; their artistic expression is inventive and intellectual; they enjoy philosophic and logical argument. Emotional types rely on feelings of likes and dislikes; they express their aesthetics through the emotions; their religious feelings are those of faith and devotion. Active types rely on learning acquired by imitation and memorization. Their artistic expression tends towards the sensuous and primal, and their spiritual practice may focus on religious rites and ceremonies. Of course none of us is purely one type or another. Our way of being changes from day to day and from moment to moment, as when a heroic feat or a compassionate deed is followed closely by a relapse into childish behavior or primitive desire.

When we begin to observe ourselves in light of this new knowledge, we will see, for example, that the moving part of the thinking center does most of the work most of the time, including that of the emotional and intellectual parts of this center.

	MOVING PART	EMOTIONAL PART
THINKING CENTER OR INTELLECT **(Head)**	Thinking, analysis, impressions, associations, memory, concepts, decisions, imagination, search for knowledge *Circling thoughts, inner conversations, compulsive talking, imagining, anticipation, criticism*	pleasure of discovery, higher imagination, love of knowledge *Attachment to beliefs, theories, false notions, intolerance*
FEELING CENTER OR EMOTIONS (Heart)	Feeling of existence, mechanical and crowd emotions, likes and dislikes *Depression, anxiety, fear, excitement, panic, sentimentality*	Love of truth, religious emotion, awakening conscience, desire to create *Attachment to forms and rituals, cruelty, obstinacy, coldness, jealousy*
MOVING CENTER Learned Functions (Cerebrospinal System) (Guts)	Conditioned reflexes, capacity for imitation, learned behavior *Thinking about movement, mechanical repetitions of words and emotions*	Delight in movement, love of sports and games; higher forms of imitation, such as acting *Cruelty, torture*
INSTINCTIVE CENTER Inherent Functions (Autonomic System)	Automatic reflexes, pleasant/unpleasant sensations, organic functions	Love of life, survival instinct, sexuality

Fig. 8. The functions of the centers.
Italics indicate negative and pathological conditions of each center.

INTELLECTUAL PART	UNIVERSAL PRINCIPLE	DIVINE NATURE
Quest for unity, creative thought, invention, intellectual construction *Nihilism, solipsism, blind skepticism*	Unity Reality Truth	*Sat* Being
Artistic creation, creative imagination, desire for beauty and harmony *Distegration and fragmentation*	Love; consciousness	*Chit* Consciousness
Practical know-how and invention, adaptation, appropriate action *Distraction, carelessness, destruction*	Creation	*Ananda* Bliss
Intelligence of the body, lower intuitions *Suppression, struggle*	Nature	

This wrong application leads to all sorts of inappropriate effort, ineffective action, and loss of energy. The only proper function of the moving part of the thinking center is to register impressions, associations, and memories. But it inevitably deals with matters that are the domain of the emotional and intellectual parts, and it does so in a mechanical way based on its limited view. This is a dangerous situation inasmuch as there are many people in power who routinely use this facet of the mind in making major decisions. This situation is also a factor in the left-brain bias that has been so often noted in modern civilization and accounts for the shallow, linear thinking that is so prevalent today.

Self-inquiry may lead us to conclude that we are in a dismal state and that most of our faculties are hopelessly muddled. We begin to see that, for example, when the thinking center does the work of the moving part of the feeling center, the misuse of energy will result in false excitement, anxiety, and depression. Conversely, we will be able to see that the common phenomenon of circling thoughts, inner conversations, and compulsive talking is the result of the feeling center usurping the work of the moving part of the thinking center. We may observe that when the moving center does the work of the emotional part of the thinking center, it leads to an aberrant use of sexual energy, causing attachment to dogmas and theories, resulting in intolerance, bigotry, and ultimately war. Sexual energy used by the emotional part of the feeling center engenders attachment to rituals and ceremonies, sentimentality, and cruelty.

We are all familiar with the impairment of physical movement when the mind gets in the way (as athletes and performers say) and causes us to perform badly, or when we become self-conscious about our bodily movements and trip over our own feet. This interference, which happens when the thinking center assumes the function of the moving center, is a classic example of the wrong use of energy.

B UT WE NEED NOT SPEND TOO MUCH TIME studying these negative aspects. A more legitimate concern is the study of the proper functioning of the human instrument. In fact we can actually bring order to our being by diligently studying this diagram and by reflecting on the correct alignment of the thinking, feeling, moving, and instinctive centers. A framework of principles and concepts as presented here is a useful tool in promoting a healthful state of being and in shedding light into the dark corners of the psyche. While such a diagram is only a schematic representation, it is nevertheless useful to begin with this kind of relative knowledge and use it to advance to the knowledge of our true Self.

The process of putting the house in order thus begins with the study of the thinking, feeling, moving, instinctive centers and their corresponding parts. The next step is objective observation and Self-inquiry in the light of this knowledge.

There is another detail to be considered. As we know, the ego has a tendency to claim everything as its own. It also has the habit of clinging to anything it perceives. The false ego becomes *identified* not only with what it perceives, but also with the faculties that do the perceiving. This mechanical process takes place in a split second. We are unaware that we have literally become the thought, feeling, or action, or the object or person we perceived a second ago. This process, sometimes referred to as "false identification," is easily overlooked and poorly understood. We are, however, quite familiar with its consequences, which are experienced sequentially as emotional discomfort, confusion, misery, addiction, and suffering. These pathological states are often treated as individual problems when in fact they are part of a chain reaction of wrong thinking.

Let us consider the four stages of identification:

1. **Impact of impressions upon the organs of perception.** The attention is as yet unaffected.
2. **The mind is coupled with the impression.** The attention is fettered; only the mind and the object of desire exist at this moment.
3. **Merging with the object of desire.** The attention is captured. The mind has consented to conjoin with the object of desire and is enslaved by it.
4. **Suffering.** Once the third stage has been reached, the mind slavishly returns to the merging again and again, which becomes an ingrained part of the character and leads to sickness of the soul.

It is obvious that these stages of identification are an accurate description of addiction. What we may not recognize at first — or may even deny — is the fact that this chain reaction happens extremely often and in all sorts of circumstances. In our eagerness to treat the symptoms of addiction and psychological suffering, we often overlook the cause and pay no attention to the stages of identification leading to them.

During most of waking life, the attention flits hither and thither, attaching itself to impressions, things, and events, and is consequently submerged in the objects of perception or desire. Ego consciousness continually lapses into the second and third stages of identification, which eventually leads to suffering. When we are in a state of identification, we are no longer "home" but are somewhere outside ourselves, unaware of our own existence. At such moments we are physically, mentally, and spiritually in danger: we are weak, vulnerable, unbalanced.

Consider how the stages of identification relate to an ordinary event:

Stage 1. We meet someone new and our attention is quite naturally open.
Stage 2. We size up the person, and the attention is bound. Only the mind and the object of attention seem to exist.
Stage 3. The attention is lost in the person or the exchange, and we are no longer aware of our existence. The mind is conjoined and enslaved.

How can we stop this chain reaction from happening? The only way is to observe and remember ourselves in the moment. When we observe, we instantly bring the mind and senses under control. When we remember the Self, we are unshakable, steady, strong, and at peace. We cannot be tempted or corrupted.

Consider the same scenario in the light of consciousness. We meet someone new, and the attention is naturally open. We remain seated in the Self. The mind is still and connected to the senses; we act while utterly present and in the moment. In this state, the centers are doing their proper duty. We feel well, whole, and at ease. When the attention remains unfettered, we are not concerned with the impression we make. We are not identified with our instrumentality or with what we perceive. We simply attend and actually see and hear the person in front of us.

In such a perfectly aligned state, intuitive knowledge about a person or situation may arise spontaneously. If we go a step further and let go of all our internal fetters, we may even experience a state of wholeness in which we are free of habitual judging, classifying, criticizing, and imagining. We are, so to speak, "in neutral," freed from engagement in an internal chain reaction. Being "in neutral" does not mean being mindless or emotionless. On the contrary, it is being truly normal and sane. Freed from identification and from the usual antics of the ego, all our faculties work perfectly and harmoniously. Silent watching frees us from past associations and habitual reactions and anchors us to the present moment — the only time when anything authentic and untainted can occur. As long as we remain seated in the Self, we are able to truly serve, whatever need may arise. The right words or actions will naturally come, and they will naturally be appropriate. In this invincible state of being, we are immune to distractions, temptations, and the fetters of identification. We are free.

*

PRACTICES

1. Study the diagrams. They should be seen as an inspiration for further thought and serious investigation.

2. Objectively observe your instrument in light of this study as you engage in action. Become aware of the inner workings of the various centers and functions. Stop as soon as you detect wrong effort, wrong use of energy, or wrong work of centers. As often as possible during the day, let the moving mind come to stillness, thus allowing all the other centers to function properly.

3. Be aware of the stages of identification. It will take time, patience, and persistence to stop this recurring cycle. However, by practicing wakefulness and continuous watching in the moment of action, you will eventually be able to liberate the mind from its excursions into darkness.

4. Practice recollection. Sit in a quiet place and let all agitation subside. Watch the breath. Consider these thoughts: "I do nothing at all. I am not the body. I am not the mind. I am not my feelings. I am the still point. I am the Self. I have my being beyond time and space."

   During the day, whenever you remember, retreat to this still point in yourself and enjoy the silence. Your being is thus refined and replenished. Trust that the silent observer will eventually assume greater command.

SIX
WORKING WITH THE FORCES

THERE ARE MANY METHODS of ridding ourselves of mental burdens and thereby uncovering the true Self. If we cannot find the truth about our true nature through action, meditation, or direct experience, we may find it through the study of metaphysics and philosophical knowledge.

We have already begun the work of purification, observation of the instrument, and the study of the nature and functioning of our psyche. All of these practices are part of the five methods on the second step of Patanjali's *Yoga Sutras: niyama* — the moderation of mind and body so as to lead life towards truth.

Part One of this book covers several aspects of metaphysical knowledge that are necessary to the understanding of the nature of ourselves and reality. One of these necessary truths is the concept of *maya,* the eternal illusion. Universal *maya* is said to have no beginning; she is neither being, nor is she nonbeing; she is not composed of parts, nor is she an indivisible whole. In other words, she is most mysterious. *Maya* is the potentiating, divine power, and it is she that gives birth to creation. We know her only from the play of the *gunas* — the subtle workings of *sattva, rajas,* and *tamas* — and their effects on the senses and consciousness.

The three *gunas,* or characteristic qualities, of *prakriti* or nature, are as follows: the force of poise or equilibrium is *sattva;* the force of action, energy, and motion is *rajas;* and the force of inertia is *tamas.* Through the effects of *maya,* the play of the forces of the three *gunas,* we experience the three states of consciousness — waking, dreaming, and dreamless sleep.

The play of the *gunas* is what sustains both the universal illusion — the creation — and the individual illusion, our sense of reality. All this suggests that without the effects of the *gunas,* we would not be conscious of creation and that there is in fact no manifestation. Hence *maya* is said to be "most mysterious." The sages also tell us that when *sattva, rajas,* and *tamas* are in perfect balance, the phenomenal world is withdrawn.

The different *gunas* are all necessary to the manifestation of the divine in matter. Hence, at the universal level, there is nothing inherently good or bad in the nature of the *gunas.* However, when these forces are critically out of balance in human life and strongly tend to *tamas* and *rajas,* we experience it as an age of darkness, ignorance, passion, greed. This imbalance results in obsession with matter and action and a preoccupation with material desires and pursuits, as manifested in the cult of the body and sports, in activity for activity's sake, in the search for pleasure, fame, power, and wealth.

Everything in creation has a particular *guna* balance with its own inner rhythms: the year, the day, the ages of man, the ages of civilization, and the *yugas,* the great cosmic cycles. According to the Vedas, we are presently living in the Kali Yuga — the last and darkest of a procession of four great cycles. We are not, however, necessarily at a disadvantage by living in this age; spiritually speaking, it just offers a greater challenge. The effects of materialistic thinking are just that much more obvious and call us more urgently to spiritual work.

WE EACH COME INTO THIS WORLD with a particular *guna* balance, which is said to be determined at the time of conception. This guna balance is reflected in our nature and predisposes us to certain tendencies, which are graphically described as those of sloth, relentless activity, or refinement and devotion. Our karma is also determined by the gunas and may be predominantly *tamasic, rajasic,* or *sattvic.* When karma tends toward *tamas,* it manifests as sleep, laziness, ignorance, dullness, darkness, delusion, mechanicalness, and attachment to ritual. When *rajas* prevails, the karma tends toward action, speed, passion, anger, desire for fame, power, progress, and achievement. When *sattva* dominates, karma is expressed in poise, harmony, happiness, charity, virtue, knowledge, and lovingkindness.

All three *gunas* are binding and limiting. Because they are under the rule of our false ego and powered by desire, they inhibit our full potential and cloud our vision. Thus *rajas* binds by attachment to doing and desire for material things. *Tamas* binds by inertia, error, stupidity, ignorance, and carelessness. In this state one cannot know the truth or see the light and feels the horror of separateness and delusion. Although *sattva* is a desirable quality, attained only through effort and devotion, it becomes binding if knowledge and virtue are acquired for their own sake, for personal gain, or are claimed by the false ego. Such attainment becomes spiritual materialism.

According to the Vedic tradition, karma is the result of ignorance and selfish action in former lives. It is said that the great avatars and enlightened souls remember their former incarnations. In the *Bhagavad Gita,* Krishna tells Arjuna, "Many of my births that are past and gone, thine also, O Arjuna; all of them I know, but thou knowest not." We do not remember them and so do not need to believe in reincarnation or even accept the idea of karma. We may, however, observe that whatever we sow has its consequences even in the present life. We can see that the law of retribution is at work in the fruits of our actions, whether we give it credence or not. Moreover this law is instantaneous. We are diminished in the instant we think a negative thought, feel a negative emotion, or commit a negative act. Conversely, our being is enriched by every fine thought, feeling, or deed.

The spiritual law governing karma and rebirth cannot be established through intellectual discourse, but it can be known through realization. As Sri Aurobindo assures us, "The soul needs no proof of its rebirth any more than it needs proof of its immortality. For there comes a time when it is consciously immortal, aware of itself in its eternal and immutable existence. Once that realization is accomplished, all intellectual questionings for and against the immortality of the soul fall away like a vain clamor of ignorance around the self-evident and ever-present truth."

Karma is the cause of our bondage, but individual karma is also the means through which we can attain liberation. The main object of karma is the purification of the *antahkarana.* Every thought, word, or action leaves an impression in the *antahkarana.* These clusters of impressions are called *samskaras* and are stored in the individual *chitta,* as well as in the collective *chitta* of nations and countries and of the human race as a whole. The former is often referred to in modern psychology as the "subconscious," while the latter is called the "collective unconscious."

Samskaras are old associations and mental impressions that we experience as ingrained habits, tendencies, and memories. The *antaratman* or individual soul gathers the essence of all our experiences in this world as it evolves to ever higher expressions in life, aspiring to higher consciousness and ultimately to union with Paramatman.

There are, of course, many more laws and forces manifesting at many different levels, affecting us in subtle ways and continually influencing our being. We know very little about these subtle external influences, which are sometimes referred to as "cosmic emanations" — the Divine Light, Love, and Consciousness brought down to this planet by the great avatars for the benefit of humanity. We know somewhat more about the mysterious workings of the planets and their influences on human nature. Together these influences account for the infinite variety of appearance, temperament, character, and talents in human life. We can easily observe from ordinary experience that merely physical influences and forces, such as heredity and environment, are by no means the sole determining factors of our nature.

All these truths would be useless to us, however, if they were not in some way applicable in daily life and verifiable in our own experience, and if they did not contribute in some way to the uncovering of the true Self. We have already determined that we have to begin where we are — with the facts of our external circumstances and internal condition. We have already begun to see and understand our conditioning and reactions. Having observed some of these influences, we have little doubt about their power over us. We now have to determine which of these influences can be transcended in our present state and which are immutable.

We cannot transcend cosmic laws. The creation rests in the lap of the Divine Mother, and her wisdom sees to it that we cannot harm the universe. We cannot transcend the universal forces of *maya* and its *guna* balance or the law of karma and rebirth. We cannot even affect our global and national *samskaras*.

How, then, do we work with the *gunas?* We begin by observing their play in creation, in the seasons, in the day, and in our being and experience. It is not difficult to see, for example, that sunset and sunrise are *sattvic* times and are therefore very propitious for quiet enjoyment of nature and for meditation and reflection. We have all had the experience of *sattvic* states while listening to fine music and contemplating fine art. One-pointed attention, such as is required in the practice of a fine craft or art, stills the mind and begets *sattva*. Serious study and reflection on sacred truths makes use of the force of *sattva* and engenders *sattvic* energy in the student.

The characteristic of *rajas* is activity. All activity, unless it is under observation and completely without motive, begets more *rajas,* which begets more karma. It is easy to see the effects of *rajas* in the frantic pace of a metropolitan area with its incessant activity and excitement. When the moving mind is agitated and the circling thoughts are out of control, we can be sure that *rajas* is prevalent. The natural state of the mind is stillness. When we feel compelled to incessant activity, we are under the spell of *rajas*. When we cannot stop ourselves from working, we have succumbed to the force of *tamas*. *Rajas* invariably ends in *tamas* — inertia and sleep, which sometimes manifests in unconscious, habitual movement and perpetual motion.

Tamas is more difficult to discern because of its power to veil and delude. When we are under its spell, the discrimination is clouded and there is little energy available to escape from it. *Tamas* is sometimes experienced as a heaviness or oppressiveness in the atmosphere, as in the heat of a midsummer day or in the dark of night and in the low points of the day. When we are unaware, the power of *tamas* can easily overwhelm us, and we fall asleep mentally, physically, or both. If we identify emotionally with *tamas,* we descend into deeper darkness and become despondent. If we let this power take control of our lives, we will succumb to stupor, laziness, and mechanical behavior. When this behavior becomes habitual, it affects the character. Eventually such an individual will have little choice but to vegetate in sloth and darkness. (The force of *tamas* is not, of course, to be confused with the need for normal rest and sleep.)

The *guna* balances of nature are shifting all the time. By becoming aware of these forces and using our discrimination, we will be able to avoid succumbing to them. When we realize that we are not these forces and do not allow false identification to run its course, we can disassociate ourselves from their influence and can rise above them. There are many ways to overcome the binding quality of the *gunas,* some of which we have already discussed. The goal of all of them is to replace ignorance with truth, darkness with light, and attachment with detachment.

Tamas and *rajas* may be overcome by *sattva.* By reading the words of the wise, studying the great philosophic truths and listening to fine *sattvic* music, we increase the light and we diminish ignorance and despondency. Meditation and reflection are the most effective means to transcend *tamas* and *rajas.* They lift us out of what we are not and still our mind and body. Meditation produces fine energy — "drops" of *sattva* that cleanse and enlighten our whole being. We can then carry these benefits into worldly activities and thereby enlighten those around us. At those times when the force of tamas invades our being, the only remedy is *rajas* — a dose of rigorous activity to pull us out of stupor, such as a brisk walk, cleaning windows, or gardening.

Work and activity are necessary on the path of the householder. We not only have to earn a living, fulfill our calling and serve others, but we also have a natural love for play and delight in movement, as well as an inherent desire to create and invent. There is nothing wrong with activity per se. It is the desire for results that produces attachment and creates karma.

The antidote to attachment is once again to bring activity under observation. We watch from the still point as we go about the day and work, serve, create and play. Resting in the Self, we watch the drama unfold and rise above the influence of the *gunas.* When we give our undivided attention to the task at hand, we create *sattva* in our being and spread a *sattvic* atmosphere all around us. In this way the force of *sattva* is increased in the world.

By conscious observation and attentive listening, we may affect the *guna* balance in a room and see it shift from agitation and confusion to calmness and clarity. Attentive listening is especially valuable for parents and teachers. Not only can it bring calm to a room full of frantic and noisy children, but just as importantly, it creates a nonjudgmental, loving, and receptive state in the observer — a state that is essential to true teaching.

Through discrimination, we may begin to observe the effects of the law of karma on our lives. Every point of consciousness — universal or individual — contains in itself cause, action, and effect. We ourselves are such points in consciousness. All our actions arise in consciousness from the Creative Principle, or, as the Vedas proclaim, out of the "Eternal Unmoving." From this point arises a movement, a feeling. The feeling becomes desire; the desire is apprehended by the mind and becomes specific. Colored by individual tendencies, it eventually results in action. When our powers of observation are honed by diligent practice, this sequence may be traced back to its source. We can see that all action arises in consciousness, is sustained by consciousness, and returns back into consciousness.

Most of the time, however, we are unaware of the Eternal Unmoving and have forgotten the source of our being. The false ego makes a claim on every action and assumes itself to be the doer. It also has a rapacious hunger for results. Thus every action that is sustained by selfish motives and is performed under the illusion of being the doer is a karmic action, begetting more karma. Although such actions are powered by strong desires, passions, and compulsions, they are utterly lacking in consciousness or attention; they are fueled by identification and result in misery or disappointment. When we are under the power of *rajas,* our thought and actions may be sustained by *rajas,* but always end in *tamas.*

ON THE OTHER HAND, performing a task simply because it needs to be done engenders no further karma. Such neutral action is only possible when, centered in our true Self, we simply and without grasping watch the action take place. Past tendencies have no sway over us in this state. Instead we are full of joy and love, and the work flows easily. Such pure action leaves no residue, but always ends in *sattva.* Hence the way of action, like the practice of meditation, takes care of the past, present, and future — the past, by burning up *samskaras;* the present and the future, by preventing the accumulation of more karma.

On the surface, all this knowledge may sound very complex; in essence, however, it is utterly simple and can be summed up in the beautiful words of the Upanishads: "All this — whatsoever moves on the earth — should be covered by the Lord. Protect [your Self] through that detachment. Enjoy! Do not covet."

In other words, all that is required is to remember the source of the Self, whose nature is *sat-chit-ananda* — being-consciousness-bliss — and acknowledge the source of all our being without making any claim on it. Then we consciously offer all our actions up to that source — to the Paramatman. Thus a conscious, selfless, and *sattvic* action not only unfetters us from individual bondage, but also contributes to the force of *sattva* in the world. It is a gift to all humanity.

We must endeavor to cultivate a state of equanimity — a state of being unencumbered by the past, disinterested in the present, and unconcerned for the future. "Disinterested" and "unconcerned" do not mean being cold or uncaring, but rather that we come into the present moment, stand back, and watch without becoming entangled either in the action or in the fruits of the action.

Once *sattva* becomes prevalent, desires tend towards that which is good, pure, and excellent. This impulse will be reflected in our taste for the food we give to our mind, body, and spirit and in the harmony, beauty, and simplicity of our home. The quality of our environment and the immediate atmosphere we create will in turn be conducive to our work and to the enlightenment of others.

Every thought, feeling, word, or action is a contribution to one force or another — to *sattva, rajas,* or *tamas.* Once this is understood, we will appreciate the larger implications of the practice of harmlessness and comprehend the magnitude of the responsibility we all share for one another. Whatever we create affects all. Once we truly understand that the All is the same as the One, we will recognize that there is truly no "other."

⁜

PRACTICE

1. Observe the play of the *gunas*. Be aware of the *guna* balance in nature, in the day, in your home. Be aware of the *guna* balance in your own being and instrument.

2. Balance the forces. When *rajas* is excessive, when the mind is racing and the body agitated, STOP! It is the only option! Practice recollection. Let the mind become still and rest in the awareness of your own Self. When the mind and the body have resumed a calm state, proceed with the task and practice "disinterested watching." One-pointed attention to the task will prevent further agitation and identification. At times when the mind is particularly agitated, let the eyes come to rest on a beautiful image such as a flower or the sky. Do whatever works!

    When *tamas* is dominant, that is, when you become aware of darkness or lethargy in your mind, body, or soul, rouse yourself and practice recollection. Come to rest in the eternal now. Carefully assess what is needed in any particular instant. Does the body or mind need rest? Does the body need exercise or a few deep breaths of fresh air? Does the soul hunger for nourishment, such as fine music, chanting, or contemplation of beauty? Does the mind need rigorous intellectual engagement?

    Increase *sattva* by resting in the Self, meditating, listening to Mozart, Beethoven, or Gregorian chant, or reading a passage from the Perennial Philosophy. During any activity increase *sattva* by silently watching, by attentive listening, by one-pointed attention to the task.

3. Perform your actions in a neutral manner, without motive, ambition, or concern for the outcome. Acknowledge the source of knowing, being and doing, and dedicate all actions to the One Self.

SEVEN
ADVERSITY AND SUFFERING

ONE OF THE FIVE METHODS of *niyama* — the second step on the path towards self-realization — is the practice of contentment. Contentment? How, we may ask, is it possible to be content when there is suffering all around us? How can I be content and happy when the world's problems seem insurmountable?

Contentment is an inner state of mind. It does not exclude compassion for the suffering of others or taking action to relieve the suffering and injustices all around us. However, this state of mind does not concern itself unduly with suffering, because it is fully aware of the nature and cause of all suffering.

The word "content" comes from the Latin *continere*, "to contain"; in a wider sense it can also mean "to hold together." When we are content, we acknowledge that we contain within ourselves all we need, and that we are "held together" by forces of a higher nature and do not need to concern ourselves with "more" or that which is "other." We know we lack nothing and therefore rest satisfied. This is a state of mind we need to cultivate at first by reminding ourselves that we are full of the good. Eventually, as we begin to accept *what is* — whether it is our own condition or external circumstances — contentment will become our natural state and will become firmly established in our being and in our hearts and minds. Hence contentment begins in understanding the nature of things and in acceptance of the human condition and our lot in life.

Suffering exists in the world as a result of ignorance — the lack of knowledge of truth. When we ignore our true nature, we suffer mental, emotional, and physical harm and we impose the same harm on our environment, engendering more suffering. Suffering is ignorance; suffering is not in the nature of things. Life is neutral. It is a force and of itself is neither good nor bad — life *just is*. It is *how* we meet and view life that makes it seem good or bad, rich or empty, sweet or evil. Strife, calamity, and war are human inventions.

The nondual Eastern philosophy of Advaita Vedanta does not admit of evil as a reality. In other words, evil does not have its own separate existence, as was believed in medieval times and still is to this day in most religions. The nondual view admits only the One Eternal Existence in which we have our being, whose nature is of the same essence. Suffering or evil therefore are only phenomena — the results of *avidya* — ignorance — which hides our true identity. According to Patanjali, "the pain-bearing obstructions are ignorance, egoism, attachment, aversion, and clinging to life. Ignorance is the productive field of the others that follow." The antidote for ignorance is *vidya* or knowledge gained by self-inquiry, by the study of the great sacred truths, and by the practice of certain disciplines.

When we are asleep, the obstacles of daily life seem to be at times almost unbearable and insurmountable. In our feeling of separateness, we feel the world is pitted against us. We see all this adversity as being outside of ourselves and regard these external problems as obstacles in the way of our happiness. We must first realize that this seemingly external adversity comes in many disguises and spans many levels of ignorance. We must also make a clear distinction between self-inflicted suffering and difficulties that simply arise from unavoidable external influences and hardships.

When we take a closer and more objective view, we will see that much of the misery we experience in the present is due to our own ignorance and our own self-created obstructions. We will accept the fact that at least some of the pain is caused by our latent tendencies and past actions, to our *samskaras* and karma. When we take responsibility for our own suffering, we can face it with courage and patience. In the light of truth and knowledge, we will have more compassion for the suffering of others. When we refuse to question the justice of external circumstances, we are at peace with what is and we learn to endure hardships with a measure of detachment.

We begin with *contentment* — the knowledge that in truth we lack nothing. Then we advance to *acceptance* — the clear and simple acknowledgment of our present state. Next we take measures and move on to *observation* — an honest, objective watching of our actions and reactions. In time we will gain *insight* into the hidden mechanisms of the false ego and see how attachment, aversion, and clinging are the hidden causes of mental and physical suffering. We will see the law of retribution firsthand and recognize that in truth we cannot get away with anything, even when it momentarily seems that way.

WE HAVE ALREADY BEGUN to see how attachment and aversion are the cause of frustration, agitation, and suffering. Paradoxically, perhaps, we cannot be free to truly enjoy this precious life, as long as we cling to it — as long as we have an inordinate attachment to "my life" and "my body," which is the cause of the inordinate fear of death. We all fear death to one degree or another. Fear of death fuels many, if not, all our lesser fears and anxieties and casts a dark shadow over all our actions. It fuels our apprehension about the future and encourages hoarding of money and possessions. This fear is the result of false identification with the body. When we believe that we are the body, we are in terror of total extinction. The belief in total extinction is, however, just a belief and a false belief at that. We *know* better. Our intuitions tell us so. If they do not, we must listen to the words of the sages who remind us that we are not the body, but instead are that which is embodied. As Shankara says, "The Atman is birthless and deathless. It neither grows nor decays. It is unchangeable, eternal. It does not dissolve when the body dissolves. Does the ether cease to exist when the jar that enclosed it is broken?"

When we realize that we are not the body, clinging to life and its attendant fears diminish. As we give up the false belief that we are matter, we also give up anxiety, worry, and stress. When we experience the Self within as that which is independent, eternal, beyond time, as perfect, pure consciousness, we *know* this Self cannot die, but simply gives up the body as if it were an old garment. We are then content to view death as a natural corollary of birth. We understand that whatever is born in matter dissolves again into matter and that whatever is beyond time and space exists and will continue to exist for ever.

There is no intrinsic value in suffering other than the fact that if it becomes extreme, it may force us to look at the cause of these unpleasant symptoms and lead us to the quest. Suffering as such simply begets more suffering and leads to more karmic action. The cosmic suffering that the great avatars have taken on at various stages of human evolution in order to alleviate human suffering is beyond our comprehension. As modern seekers, we certainly should not resort to taking on the suffering of others, or to infliction of pain upon ourselves. Self-castigation in any form is negation of the life force and therefore not conducive to our search for our true resplendent Self. The body is not evil, as was believed by many medieval saints and mystics. We do not deny or hate it; rather we ascertain that we are not the body. The human instrument is a magnificent tool and as such needs to be cherished and nurtured. Without this body, we cannot perceive or interact with creation. We cannot grow and aspire, nor can we experience joy or manifest the divine in time and space.

There is, however, another kind of suffering, which comes from the struggle we encounter on the quest. It has to do with long-suffering, a kind of patient endurance. We have to learn endurance when we begin to recognize our own shortcomings and illusions. When we see these things about ourselves in the light of truth, we might well shudder in self-disgust. We are appalled at what we see, and the first response may be to run from the sight and abandon the quest. While determination and endurance may be weak, the conscience will not let us quit so easily. It tells us that we *must* endure the struggle. In retrospect, we will discover that the self-disgust was just another cheap trick of the false ego. We soon find out that we have to give up the shocking "discoveries" about ourselves in the moment of observation and renounce them immediately, before the ego claims the discovery as its own.

At times when we feel most unworthy, we might experience yet another kind of suffering — the darkness of the soul. We feel that we cannot raise ourselves up, that we cannot will and aspire, that we cannot change or do. Longing for freedom from suffering and separateness, we become humble and realize our frailty. We have arrived at a very propitious step — one that prepares us for the next step. We are willing to give up, but the giving up is now of a different kind: it is a letting go of the self-important struggling and letting another force take command. All we need to do is ask! The Paramatman — the Supreme Self — and the Divine Mother are right there, ready to help. We are now in a receptive and open state, ready to receive the divine gifts of love, grace and wisdom.

Both physical and spiritual endurance are necessary on the quest. We live in an imperfect world and encounter many hardships due to nature and human ignorance. Difficulties do arise. Disagreements and misunderstandings in our intimate relationships and the workplace are a daily challenge for many. These misunderstandings are most often due to carelessness, inattention, or the lack of clear communication and can happen even between comparatively enlightened people. When seen in the light of truth, these daily difficulties are minor glitches that can be dealt with in the moment with total honesty.

On the quest, minor difficulties and challenges are handled with benevolence, cheerfulness, good will, and a large dose of humor. If we are not aware, we are in danger of total identification with a limited point of view, and an apparently small matter may blow up into a major dispute. If taken further, the dispute brings about grudges, hatred, and even cruelty. This is the way of darkness in which we as seekers must not engage. It is far too costly; the price we pay is not only the loss of precious time, but, more importantly, that of the fine energy we need for the work.

But how, we might ask, are we to practice contentment in the face of pain, illness, and death? The sages would answer that as long as we stay seated in the Self, we are not deluded by circumstances. In the words of the Upanishads: "As the sun, the eye of the world, is not touched by the impurity it looks upon, so the Self, though one, animating all things, is not moved by human misery but stands outside."

Although such equanimity and detachment are states to be aspired to, they may seem an abstract, far-off ideal to us as we are in the present. We can, however, arrive at an understanding of a few practical truths. For one, we need to realize that physical pain does not equal suffering; they are not of the same nature. Pain is a sensation — a symptom of a physical ailment or imbalance, whereas suffering is of a mental nature and ensues when we forget who and what we are, when we think we are the body or the mind, and when the ego identifies with the sensation of pain.

When, as a result of effort and knowledge, there is no identification, or when the attention is turned to more pressing matters, pain does not turn into suffering. We have all seen or read about feats of complete transcendence of pain: the wounded mother who selflessly rescues her child, the war hero who, despite horrific pain, carries an injured comrade to safety. We ourselves have all acted at some time or another in total indifference to pain and then realized in retrospect that there was no suffering associated with it. On the contrary, we may even have experienced joy in the face of disaster, illness, or calamity. There are innumerable accounts of the experience of serenity and contentment enjoyed by the seriously ill, despite approaching death and despite the presence of tremendous physical discomfort. Of course the opposite reaction to pain, illness and death is also possible. When identification with pain takes complete hold of a human being and there is no acknowledgment of his or her spiritual nature, the very same events are often met with anger, hatred, and despair.

W E ARE MOST IN NEED of spiritual endurance when we are faced with the loss of a loved one. Separation from the object of our love causes grief which at times seems impossible to bear. Such intense heartache, often compounded by the realization of our own mortality, is a serious shock to the psyche. Whole nations have been seen to go collectively into shock at the death of a public figure. A period of grief over any such loss is necessary, healthful, and natural. Endless grief, however, is not, since it becomes a private torment from which it is hard to escape.

The shock of a momentous event, such as loss or severe illness, has for many provided the impetus — the call to the pursuit of truth. In retrospect, we might even detect the workings of Divine Grace in these seeming adversities and praise the wisdom and beauty of a grander design at work. Such insights fortify our belief in Divine Justice and strengthen our trust and acceptance whenever we are faced with new trials and struggles.

When we come out of our own suffering, we become more observant of the world around us. We see the ignorance that brings suffering and we see the mental distress and tensions in our friends and family and co-workers. This brings a new challenge: we must guard ourselves from identification with such misery. We often hear the expression "I feel so bad for such-and-such." Feeling bad for someone is a false and negative emotion and accomplishes nothing. Feeling sorry for humankind in general is not our duty; it is simply a negative feeling and a waste of precious energy. It is a far cry from true compassion.

True compassion is experienced in a moment of grace or fine attention when the heart is open. True compassion is not something we do; rather it is called forth and finds its object in mysterious and subtle ways. It does not always require words or action. When we let go of tensions and self-imposed limits, a space opens up in the heart and we experience a pouring forth of energy which can be said to be the "stuff" of compassion, an energy akin to unconditional love. This outpouring of fine energy grants health and wholeness both to the giver and the receiver. At those moments of grace, when the heart is wide open there is only the One — there is no separation between giver and receiver, only love and wholeness.

As we gain in insight, we will recognize that life in and of itself is not difficult, as we often say, and that in fact all events are neutral. A hurricane, for example, is a natural event; in and of itself it is neither good or bad. However, if we happen to find ourselves living in its path and experience its destructive power, we would call it bad. A carpenter, however, might greet the same event as an opportunity for work and gain and call it good. Every event, now as in all of human history, is in the eye of the beholder — is all a matter of point of view. In recognition of this fact, today many chapters of history are being rewritten to reflect the point of view of "the other side."

Consider another factor: in every event or action, the Law of Three comes into play. The three *gunas* are always operating and represent the first triad. The second triad consists of the object, the subject, and a "third factor" — that which takes place between the observer and the observed — the event, activity, function or condition: for example, the teacher, the pupil, and the learning or subject; the husband, the wife, and the marriage; the speaker, the listener, and the sound or understanding; the buyer, the seller, and the contract.

When we consider this third factor in any situation, the essence of what is really taking place is illumined and the potential for objectivity is enlarged. The habitual sense of duality and of separation is diminished and the adversarial stance of "me versus the world" is often eliminated. When we are aware of the *unseen* — the third factor — and observe the interaction with the objectivity of a scientist, we discover an interesting realm full of creative potential, full of choices and possibilities. This space is always present, but we are usually not aware of it because of a limited point of view. When we transcend the habitual dualistic view, we rise above the ego, stay aloof from the entrapments of identification and are not tempted to engage in endless disputes and opinions. Instead there is a potential for real communication and understanding.

As we open our attention to this wider view, we experience greater freedom and fewer difficulties and self-inflicted adversities. Unkindness and animosities no longer bring on suffering. Rather they are seen as a cry for help or attention. We come to realize that *how* we interact with the world is the deciding factor between suffering or joy. The space of interaction is where all potential lies. As long as we are identified with the false ego, we have no freedom to act; we can only react in a habitual and mechanical way. When, on the other hand, we are awake and aware of our true Self, we have a measure of freedom; we have a choice. With that freedom comes the responsibility to act according to inner knowledge and to aspire to the greatest good. With this greater freedom to choose, we become adept at resolving even the most difficult situations. As we transform suffering into happiness, we effect transformation all around us. Our children and mates are more content and happy. The workplace lightens up. Dislikes are neutralized and aversions blossom into love. Robert Frost said, "Earth is the right place for love; I don't know where it's likely to go better." Earth is in fact the only place where transformation can take place. We are here to *realize* love.

PRACTICE

1. Practice contentment. Allow yourself to see beyond the surfaces and experience the goodness, beauty, and love that surrounds you. Know that your true Self is perfect and is beyond suffering and adversity. Accept and acknowledge your inner state and circumstances.

2. Observe and identify the "pain-bearing" obstructions: ignorance, egoism, attachment, aversion, and clinging to life. Inquire into the nature of your difficulties and problems. Are they self-inflicted or due to external circumstances?

3. Practice endurance. Keep a cheerful attitude in the face of adversity.

4. Observe the Law of Three. Open your view to include the three factors in any given event or action.

EIGHT
THE FIVE VEILS OF ILLUSION

"MAN IS DIVINE. He is, in reality, the impersonal Truth. His essential nature is pure consciousness. Bound by *maya*, he ignorantly thinks of himself as the gross human form." This is but one of the many truths about the nature of illusion contained in the *Srimad Bhagavatam*. It goes on to say, "Just as the dust of the earth, when raised by the wind, is by the ignorant attributed to the ether; so are body and mind attributed by the ignorant to the impersonal Self."

We are in bondage because of our individual *maya*, which causes us to mistake what is not-Self with our real Self. Most human beings go through life thinking that their bodies are the ultimate reality, which explains the preoccupation with its appearance and excessive maintenance. They are identified with the *gross body*, while others are identified with the *subtle* and *causal bodies*, consisting of mind, ego, memory, and intellect.

Thus some live in their emotions and believe that they are their feelings or the affairs of their hearts, hence, they are identified with the so-called "vital or nervous being." Others live in the world of the mind and believe their minds and their thoughts to be ultimate reality; they are identified with the "mental being." Yet others believe they are the "knower"; they are identified with their higher intellect or *buddhi*, with the "supermental being." More rarely, some spiritual persons may live in a state of infinite happiness and take that to be the ultimate goal. They are identified with "bliss consciousness." Claiming this state as their own, they are bound by *maya*. As the *Srimad Bhagavatam* says, "When, through ignorance man thinks the Spirit to be identical with these adjuncts, he is bound by his deeds, good and bad."

Let us briefly consider the cause of illusion. *Maya* spins its eternal web using the *gunas* and causing their infinite differentiation, combination, and variation. Instead of seeing the creation as an effect of this process, we take it to be the cause. In the same way, when we are deluded by *maya*, we take the personality, body, and mind to be the ultimate reality.

Rajas — the power to project illusory forms — binds us and causes us to identify with the body and mind, indeed with whatever moves. When we are under the spell of motion, we do not have recourse to *buddhi* (the discriminating faculty) or *chitta* (memory, conscience). Hence we cannot discern between the Self and the not-Self, and we do not remember our source. We succumb to *tamas* and its power to veil reality and truth. Captivated by *rajas* and *tamas*, we are compelled to indulge in actions resulting in identification, misery, and inertia. These lead us back again to activity in an endless cycle.

Only when there is an influx of *sattva*, either by grace or good karma, is it possible to wake up and begin the work of removing the veils of illusion and uncovering the Self. Only when *sattva* is predominant can we experience freedom from delusion, desire, and attachment and experience contentment and joy.

How do we increase *sattva*? By honoring the Triple Fire of knowledge, meditation, and practice. Shankara tells us in the *Crest-Jewel of Discrimination*: "This bondage cannot be broken by weapons, or by wind, or by fire, or by millions of acts. Nothing but the sharp sword of knowledge can cut through this bondage. It is forged by discrimination and made keen by purity of heart, through divine grace." In other words, illusion is dispelled by knowledge and discrimination, purification of the *antahkarana,* and the influx of *sattva* or Divine Grace. In action, illusion is broken by holding the continuous awareness that whatever we perceive, think, or do is by virtue of Atman only. In waking consciousness, we experience Atman as the Witness.

Let us now take a closer look at what are known in the Vedas as the Five Veils of Illusion. For life on this earth, the *jiva-atman* or individual soul is endowed with the five powers: *aham* (the sense of pure being), *buddhi* (intelligence), *chitta* (conscience, memory), *manas* (mind), and the physical body. Through desire and the influence of the *gunas, aham* becomes *ahamkara* — the sense of "I" becomes the sense of separate "I" or ego. Because of ignorance, the *ahamkara* claims the endowments and powers and calls them "*my* mind" and "*my* body." This claim causes further delusion, creating a sheath that hides the true Self.

The sheaths, or Veils of Illusion, are born of ignorance. However, they are also our "garments" and are necessary for the evolution of our soul nature. The *jiva-atman* needs a vehicle for its expression in matter. We cannot disrobe ourselves for a moment of all the garments; even if this were possible, it would result in our immediate disappearance. We have to work our way from duality to Unity in a measured and systematic way.

We need the veils for the time being, but we can make them more transparent by refusing to believe in their separate reality. We must see the veils for what they are: a vehicle for the *jiva-atman* to find its way back to Unity and for the unfoldment of the divine in creation. When, through knowledge and purification, the veils are temporarily lifted, what is revealed is the infinite space that joins individual consciousness with universal consciousness.

Through study, we gain at least a relative knowledge of the Veils of Illusion and thus are less prone to being deluded by them. Through objective observation in action, we begin to see the illusory nature of the sheaths; thus they become more transparent. When we are no longer dazzled by motion or deluded by time and space, the effects of *maya* will eventually dissolve, or, as Shakespeare puts it, "the baseless fabric of this vision...shall all dissolve...and...leave not a rack behind." When, by complete surrender to the divine, the veils are irrevocably dissolved, the individual Atman equally dissolves into the infinite light, love, and bliss of Paramatman.

Patanjali's eightfold system — in particular steps three to seven — teach the methods by which the veils or *koshas* which envelop the *jiva-atman* may be penetrated. (The Sanskrit word *kosha* means "sheath" or "vessel," from the root *kush,* "to enfold.") We may remember from Part One that the first two steps (*yama* and *niyama*) deal with moral conduct, care of body and mind, and study of higher knowledge. Steps three to seven relate to the acquisition of powers, sublimation, concentration, and meditation. These lead to step eight: *samadhi,* the state of undifferentiated consciousness in which the Veils of Illusion are either temporarily or permanently removed (see fig. 9, p. 312).

The word *maya* in this context means "formed." Thus *annamaya*, the physical body, means "formed of matter or food." Relating to material consciousness, it arises from the subtle element of earth. *Pranamaya*, the sheath made of the life force, is made of air and relates to the vital level; it arises from the subtle element of water; and so on.

WHEN WE CONSIDER OURSELVES in light of this ancient knowledge, we are able to gain some objectivity about our true nature. We can appreciate that we cannot be any of these sheaths. We can regard them as different states of energy and consciousness. The Atman is distinct from the adjuncts or the vehicle it uses for the duration of its life on earth. The Atman is that which alone exists and never changes and is, in fact, the only Witness in every state of consciousness. The Atman is not born and does not die. Its nature is pure consciousness and by its light reveals the entire creation.

The physical body is enveloped in the *pranamaya*, or "vital covering," the life force that enters through breath and leaves the body at death. These two bodies in turn are surrounded by the *manomaya*, the "mental covering," which arises from impressions. By its power the phenomenal world is sustained. These three bodies are enveloped in the *vijnanamaya*, or "covering of the Intellect," which arises from knowing and acting. It is also known as the discriminating faculty or *buddhi*, which together with the organs of perception give the sense of "I" who initiates and acts. Finally, these four bodies are enveloped by the *anandamaya*, the "covering of bliss," which arises from feelings both good and bad. It is experienced spontaneously in life as joy and happiness or as sorrow and suffering. Relative happiness, however, is limited — still an effect of *maya* — and changes as circumstances change. True bliss arises from direct experience of Atman and is fully revealed in deep sleep. The Atman is beyond these five sheaths. It is experienced as the ultimate existence, the Witness, or infinite consciousness. According to the Upanishads, the Atman itself is enveloped by a "sheath of divine consciousness" or *chit*, and this in turn is enveloped by a "sheath of reality" or *sat*.

Thus in the inward journey the aspirant divests herself of each Veil of Illusion and discovers her true Self hidden in the recesses of her own heart. She experiences *ananda*. She then comes to the realization that Atman is *Brahman* and dwells in the One Consciousness, or *chit*. When she knows that there is no other existence but *Brahman*, she merges with the divine; she has reached the state of pure being or *sat*.

Now in light of the *koshas*, let us look at our place in creation from another viewpoint — that of the divine descending into matter (see fig. 4, on page 60). By reflecting on it, we can gain a greater appreciation of the infinite greatness of the Divine Intelligence, and get a glimpse into the splendor of the supreme design. The One — the forceful — engenders consciousness. It becomes three — *sat*, *chit*, and *ananda* — and engenders the creation. Divine Will, Power, and Knowledge — the "forces of the forceful"— engender the *jiva-atman*, the Self in all. The *jiva-atman* then enters the *antaratman* — the individual soul — known as *purusha* (the pure Self) and *prakriti* (the Self in evolution). At this point, by the forces of *maya*, the magic of differentiation begins, engendering the illusion of separate existence. Thus *ahamkara* formed of *prakriti* is born. The Atman, in its descent into matter, acquires the sheaths of illusion for its evolution in nature.

As human beings composed of *purusha* and *prakriti*, we descend from Unity into duality and then again through effort and realization ascend back into Unity. We are here in creation to realize our own essence, which is pure consciousness, to

Step in the Eightfold Yoga System	Kosha	Sheath	Level of Consciousness	Element	Interaction Between Consciousness and Matter
3. Asana	**annamaya** (*anna*, "food," "matter")	body (arises from food)	material physical	earth	orchestrates form, structures, and replication of cells
4. Pranayama	**pranamaya** (*prana*, "breath")	life force (arises from air)	vital and nervous	water	operates metabolic and physiological processes
5. Pratyahara	**manomaya** (*manas*, "mind")	moving mind (arises from impressions)	mental	fire	synthesizes mind-body mechanism through imprints in genes
6. Dharana	**vijnanamaya** (*vijnana*, "supermind")	intellect or *buddhi* (arises from knowing, acting)	supermental or truth-consciousness	air	gives birth to self-awareness, choice, volition, creativity, and other higher activities
7. Dhyana	**anandamaya** (*ananda*, "bliss")	emotion (arises from feeling)	bliss or infinite beatitude	ether (or space)	experiences being, consciousness, and bliss
8. Samadhi	—	—	—	—	individual consciousness merges with Infinite Consciousness

Fig. 9. The *five koshas or sheaths.*

express the Divine Will, and to experience bliss. For our outward expression, we are given the *koshas*, which in and of themselves are splendid vestments. However, deluded by the forces of *maya*, we do not simply enjoy these vestments and the creation but instead become attached to them.

When we believe that we are the *koshas*, we attribute these functions and powers to the ego. We covet what is ours only to enjoy, and the vestments become dense and heavy and hide our true being and the light of the Atman. When we are deluded by the forces of *rajas* and *tamas* and identify with the transient, we have forgotten our purpose, which is to return to the Unity and to pure being.

When we are identified with *annamayakosha* — the sheath of the body — it becomes the object of all our care and attention. We primp it and dote on it, and so become lost in sensuous pursuits. In thinking that we are matter, we succumb to the forces of *rajas* and *tamas*, never finding any rest. This false belief continually feeds individual and collective *maya* and gives its forces more and more power.

Identification with *pranamayakosha* — the life force — leads to the mistaken belief that proclaims "my life," "my energy," and "my breath." This creates fear of death and all the anxieties associated with the maintenance of life. This illusion can even become pathological when it interferes with the harmonious workings of the vital and nervous system and consequently manifests in the body.

Identification with *manomayakosha* — mind — creates the sense of a separate existence as it relates to the mind and whatever it perceives. This illusion is continually fed by impressions upon the senses and the desire for sense objects. The individual lives in a separate world and identifies with whatever goes on in the mind, claiming these things as "mine." Although the mind is what harbors the illusion, it is also a tool for escaping it. The practices of one-pointed attention and meditation bring the mind under control and thus prevent it from its excursions into identification. When the mind is still, it becomes the perfect servant of *buddhi*.

Identification with *vijnanamayakosha* — intellect or *buddhi* — creates the sense of individual existence as it relates to knowledge and action; hence it creates the illusion of being "the knower," "the doer," and "the experiencer." It is responsible for individual *maya*, which causes the human being to be born again and again. This sheath arises from lack of discrimination between truth and untruth. However, when *buddhi* is purified by the Triple Fire of knowledge, meditation, and practice and by an influx of *sattva*, it becomes the vehicle of the Atman. It is through *jnana* — knowledge — that we attain to *vijnana* — unlimited knowledge. When this veil dissolves, *buddhi* is illumined by the light of the Atman. Intellect is transformed into higher intellect. (See figure 4, p. 60, in which the dotted line signifies the location of the veil.)

Identification with *anandamayakosha* — bliss — creates the sense of individual *maya* as it relates to the emotions; hence it claims all feelings. The veil is made dense by negative emotions and claiming; therefore even a blissful experience, when claimed as one's own, engenders illusion. When *chitta* is purified by the Triple Fire, this veil is penetrated by the light of Atman, which is experienced as bliss. This state is experienced in deep meditation.

In the state of complete *samadhi* — the transformation of the attention into the object of attention — individuals dwell in complete Oneness and are independent, powerful, and blissful. They are free of illusion and above the *gunas*. They have divested themselves of the *koshas*. They are above the five elements and no longer need food, water, or air. The individual Self has merged with the Divine Self.

The ancient yogis divested themselves of each of the *koshas* by following Patanjali's Eightfold Path and enduring specific disciplines. The practice of meditation — one of the aspects of the Triple Fire — makes this no longer necessary; it in fact supersedes *asana* and *pranayama* and does the work of transformation at the level of *pratyahara* by transforming lower psychic energy into energy for higher purposes. The discipline of stilling the mind by one-pointed attention on a *mantra* transforms *rajas* into *tapas*, a spiritual force that has the power to burn the Veils of Illusion and reveal the light of Atman.

Meditation dissolves identification with one or more of the Veils of Illusion, and this release is experienced as an expansion of consciousness. When practiced regularly, meditation purifies the entire *antahkarana*. When this is accomplished, the *ahamkara* — the sense of "I" — serves as a representative for Atman. The heart is open to the influx of Divine Love. The purified *buddhi* has become the servant of Atman; it knows truth and for its guidance listens to the voice of the Paramatman. *Manas*, having been brought under control, no longer runs after sense objects, so the body and the senses obey its command. Thus purified, the human instrument becomes the perfect tool for carrying out a specific calling and so fulfilling the will of the Absolute.

Only great persistence and honest aspiration will bring us to this state permanently. However, this ideal state is not a far-off goal. It is immanent. We are the Atman; it could not be any closer. We can know it *now* by the experience of pure being, through inspiration, through knowledge and observation in action. We can begin now with the process of uncovering the true Self by honoring the Triple Fire, the Triple Process, and the Triple Duty: study, concentration, and renunciation. The *sattvic* energy thus gathered, together with the refined emotions and discrimination, will illumine our being and inform our thoughts, feelings, and actions. As the doors of perception begin to open little by little, we too begin to unfold; we become more perceptive, more joyful, wiser in our affairs, more giving, forgiving, and loving.

*

PRACTICE

1. Study the text regarding the Five Veils of Illusion and reflect on its meaning.

2. Practice the Triple Fire — knowledge, meditation, practice — in the light of the knowledge of the Veils of Illusion.

3. Practice the Triple Process — evidence, inference, experience.

   Gather the evidence by objective observation of the gross, subtle, and causal bodies. Inquire into the nature of your most evident Veils of Illusion, such as the physical, emotional, and mental. Consider how they obscure the light of the true Self.

   When you become aware of identification with the body, simply say in your mind: "I am not this body. It is a vestment for my use."

   Attend to every word of this statement as it is sounded in the mind. Attentive listening is crucial to its effectiveness. Conscious listening to the sound of each word unleashes the words' power. They will do what they mean, thus dispelling ignorance and cleansing the *antahkarana*.

   Become aware of each of the other veils and observe how they limit your perception of who you really are. Consider that you are not any of these vestments but that in truth, you are THAT which is watching. Practice this awareness in the moment of action or reflect on each of the veils through quiet introspection. Listening consciously to every word in the mind, say:

   > "I am not the life force. Life is a gift to be enjoyed."
   > "I am not the Mind. It is a faculty for my use."
   > "I am not the intellect. It is a faculty for my use."
   > "I am not this bliss. It is relative."
   > "I am not these feelings."

4. Practice the Triple Duty: study, concentration, renunciation.

5. As often as possible during the day, remind yourself:
   > "I am the Witness,"
   > "I am THAT which is watching."
   > "I am not any of the adjuncts or attributes."
   > "I am the Self."

NINE

THE IMPOSTOR

SOONER OR LATER ON OUR QUEST we come face to face with the impostor who has been looming larger and larger on the horizon. We do not see this entity when we are asleep, but as we begin to wake up, we eventually become all too aware of its ways. We have already investigated some of its fraudulent claims to life and property and considered some of its deceptive manners. We have glanced at it obliquely, never quite ready to call its bluff. This entity, as we have surmised by now, is, of course, none other than the "false I" — the central part of the ego-structure. Myths refer to it as the "many-headed monster" and its demise is depicted in the allegorical "slaying of the dragon."

When we engage in Self-inquiry — the examination of the senses and the workings of the inner organ of mind — and as more of the light of consciousness shines into the deep recesses of our psyche, the impostor is threatened and puts up its defenses. It gets ready to do battle when we try to undermine its existence and it senses its impending demise. When, even for a moment, we doubt our aspirations towards the light and truth and forget who we really are, the impostor seizes the opportunity and assumes center stage once again. The word "impostor" means "one who imposes himself fraudulently upon others, one who pretends, deceives." This dictionary definition is an accurate depiction and a perfect metaphor for this character — the "false I."

How did we get involved with this fraudulent character in the first place? It is a long story. We have consorted with this entity since ancient times, despite the fact that it has proven to be totally unreliable, non-existent, but gets us into trouble again and again; worse, according to Eastern wisdom, it is the cause of all our illusions, unhappiness, and suffering.

How then does this happen? It is said that we are all born with the sense of pure *aham* — the feeling of existence. This feeling *aham* is experienced as a state of pure being without form and without name. It is completely free — unfettered by any admixture of this or that. A newborn baby lives in this state for a brief time. It just is. But, this pure state of being and of complete at-oneness cannot last long. *Aham* ("I") desires to become *idam* (that). This desire causes ripples in the individual consciousness and the One becomes the many — hence illusion and division are born. This is like what is said to take place at a universal level: the One desires to experience itself and the manifest creation comes into being and with it the great illusion — the cosmic *maya*. Everything in creation suffers a kind of distortion, an imbalance of the forces that serve to externalize *purusha*, the creative principle in Nature.

We can observe the inevitable process from oneness to duality, from *being* to *becoming* in every child. When a very young child plays, it just plays and is full of joy and love. It is one with the activity and doesn't think, "I am playing." Only a few months later, the child gleefully reports, "I did it! I did it!" The fall has happened. This seemingly innocent claim changes everything. The child's awareness has shifted from unity to duality; it senses itself to be separate and the doer. Its battle cry is, "For me!"

Aham, the sense of pure being, is now lost for most of the waking hours and is replaced by a sense of separate existence or a*hamkara*. As the child grows, stimulation of the senses and the development of perception and cognition together enhance the feeling of separate existence. A little later, imitation and learning, environmental and cultural conditioning add to the growing sense of separate identity and duality.

Although *ahamkara* — the sense of separate existence — is an illusion, we nevertheless need a sense of identity for our life here on earth. The sense of "I" is a faculty of the *antahkarana,* and we could not function without it.

But let us consider our present condition in which the sense of "I" is not natural, that is, unfettered from identification and illusion. On the contrary, what we refer to as "I" or "me" in daily life changes by the minute. The "false I" or ego in fact has no reality or permanency. Hence the ego as we commonly experience it does not exist. However, our sense of belief in separate existence gives power to the illusion, and it takes on a life of its own. Thus we all succumb to the individual fall and share in the collective fall from oneness; we experience individual illusion and contribute to the collective illusion. We feel ourselves to be single and separate — *alone* instead of *all one.*

Bᴜᴛ ᴛʜᴀᴛ ɪs ɴᴏᴛ ᴛʜᴇ ᴇɴᴅ of the story. The "false I" attributes all desiring, thinking, feeling, doing to itself. It claims the physical body, the senses, the mind, and the emotions as its own. Impure *ahamkara*, the "false I," is greedy and seizes every opportunity to be in charge of every situation. Although it is only one of the functions of the *antahkarana* it presumes to *be* and *do* everything. It claims all the other faculties — *buddhi, chitta,* and *manas* — as its attributes and possessions. It claims to be the author of all feelings, desires, thoughts, perceptions, and insights arising in the *antahkarana.* The plot thickens when, through false identification, we believe we *are* the mind, the feelings, the activity or whatever presents itself to the senses. Once the claiming of the false "I" begins, there is no end to the drama.

By the time we are adults, the false "I" will have successfully assumed authority and proprietorship over the attributes of the true Self. It has imposed itself fraudulently upon the Atman, the sole experiencer. In its vanity and delusion the impostor says: "I am," "I think," "I do," "I will," and "I want." But it doesn't stop there. It goes on deceiving, pretending, and usurping the very source of our being and life. It spreads forgetfulness in its path and we are no longer conscious of our identity with Atman and our complete dependence on Paramatman — the Supreme Self. In our forgetfulness we believe that we are the witness and that which experiences.

The impostor has a full bag of tricks and its dice are always loaded. The only way not to lose against loaded dice is to get out of the game. But we may still not be entirely convinced that this is a bad deal, especially when things are going well. We may still believe that having a strong ego is necessary to survival in an increasingly challenging world and that without it people will take advantage of us. After all, isn't it the ego that some forms of psychotherapy seek to strengthen? Isn't it the ego we seek to empower when we use affirmations such as "I love myself, I really, really do," or "I am special and wonderful!" and when we tell our children, "Believe in yourself" and "Know what you want"? Isn't the ego that which makes us unique and different? All such questions prove to us is the fact that there is a great deal of ignorance and confusion about the ego, much of it caused by the impostor itself.

The sages tell us that the false "I" is the root of all our unhappiness, suffering, alienation and eventual disintegration. It is what supports our private illusions and keeps us bound to the collective illusion in the darkness of Plato's allegorical cave, where we see the shadows of the puppets flickering on the wall and take them to be reality. Only when we escape from the cave into the bright sun — the light of truth — do we see the One — the reality without division.

Those who have momentarily escaped the false "I" — the narrow sense of ego — and have experienced the vastness of the one consciousness or the light of the true Self are no longer satisfied with limited understanding and a fragmented state of being. They begin to develop a taste for their true nature, for a life of beauty and harmony in the knowledge of the universal Self.

Heraclitus said, "It is necessary to obey the universal; but although the Logos is universal, most people live as though they had a private understanding." Our claiming ego is that "private understanding" and prevents us from understanding and carrying out the will of the Logos. The claiming ego prevents us from enjoying the whole creation and from merging with the Logos. By claiming small morsels for ourselves — allotting rationed portions as "our due" — we are effectively blocking the influx of universal energy, and become diminished, miserly beings. We become "gods in ruins," as Emerson put it.

Some never wake up to this fact. Others realize that they are truly unhappy and discontent in this limited and fractured existence. They feel a nagging emptiness, a lack that then develops into a want. This constant wanting makes them into beggars. The irony and utter madness of this egocentric construct is demonstrated when these beggars drag themselves into a house of worship and plead to God: "Give me, give me!" God gave us the whole universe. He gave us being, consciousness, and bliss. He gave us the life force, spirit, and soul. He gave us reason and will and a magnificent instrument. For good measure he gave us the gifts of love and wisdom. God did not give us just a part. He gave us the One, which we are free to enjoy, but, as the *Eesha Upanishad* warns, we must not "covet," that is, claim what is His property.

The impostor does not leave willingly. It has taken up residency a long time ago and guards its territory with a massive defense system. We may have already seen in the light of observation that we have a fierce internal reaction when we feel that our sense of personal identity or integrity is questioned in any way. We go to any lengths to defend our carefully constructed persona and its beliefs, attachments, and achievements and even to justify and defend the misery it causes us. We have learned to protect the "false "I" from outside attacks and have become expert at covering up the pain when our "buttons" are pressed and our treasured notions, negative feelings, and latent tendencies rush to the surface.

H.H. Shantanand Saraswati has said, "The difficulty about the false 'I,' paradoxically, is that it is more difficult to fight a foe which does not exist than the one which exists. You can use a stick to drive away a real snake, but the stick would not make an imaginary snake run away. The false 'I' is also imaginary. It is your own invention. Hence the difficulty in dealing with it. It is gradually subdued by not giving it any importance, and as the higher intelligence and proper understanding develop, deconditioning the mind from false impressions imprinted on it through ages and ages of your lives. You turn towards the Truth, and then the false 'I' fades away."

WHY, WE MIGHT ASK AGAIN, would we defend and cling to this fictitious persona that causes so much difficulty, confusion, and suffering? As long as we give credence to the reality of the false "I," we quite justifiably want to hold on to it. As long as we believe that we would have nothing left without it or that nothing would be left of us — that somehow we will evaporate into thin air — we will definitely not want to be separated from it. If we believe that we have to give up everything that we are and have ever worked for, we will be justified in not giving up this impostor. The answer then is that somehow we have to change our belief and our thinking and *convince* ourselves of the unreality of this fictitious persona. We can only do this for ourselves, in the moment of action, through deep reflection and contemplation of our true Self. The present moment is the secret door through which we can escape the fetters of the false "I."

The question then arises, what it would be like for us when the illusion begins to subside? How would we know when we come closer to the real "I"? We would begin to resemble a man or a woman in full stature — a human being in full knowledge of its true identity, whose nature is pure and rooted in the One Self. In such a human being the false "I" or "desiring *ahamkara*" no longer exists. Instead the purified *ahamkara* moves, so to speak, higher up and identifies itself with the true Self. The *antahkarana* has been cleansed of impurities as well through discrimination, knowledge, and discipline. The innate faculties are now fully functioning and manifest in perfect reasoning power, a sharp intellect, and discrimination. A refined countenance, a desire for beauty and harmony, and the expressions of creative imagination are all evidence of the development of the higher emotions. The moving mind has been silenced and has become the perfect servant of *buddhi*. The awareness and consciousness are now open to a wider circle and encompasses the human family. The memory of the One Self is constant, and all actions are guided by *buddhi*, which is illumined by *sattva*. The physical, mental, and causal bodies work in harmony with the spiritual level and serve the One Self.

In our present state we are far from this ideal. But we can see that there is much more to be gained than lost by giving up our false "I." In reality, we do not actually *gain* anything, we simply endeavor to *become* what we already *are* — Atman, the true Self. The ultimate aim of all spiritual work is to leave behind *ahamkara* — the state of becoming — in order to enjoy *aham* — the pure state of being.

Our desire for truth is the motivating force that brings us to Self-inquiry. The *Katha Upanishad* tells us that by means of the Triple Fire — the way of knowledge, devotion, and action — we can transform our knowing, being, and doing. Knowledge gives us insight into the essence of our being and sharpens our discrimination. Meditation purifies the *antahkarana*, heals our being, and protects us on the quest. Practice keeps us awake and makes us stronger. By means of the triple process we gather proof, draw conclusions, and put them to the test and thus gain understanding and wisdom. By means of the Triple Duty we attain knowledge, clarity of mind, single-mindedness, steadfastness, and freedom from attachment and the fetters of ego.

PRACTICE

1. Honor the Triple Fire: knowledge, meditation, practice.

2. Honor the Triple Process: evidence, inference, and experience:

Observe the antics of the false "I" in all your interactions. It is most evident in mechanical responses and reactions. The false "I" almost always responds in a manner that is defensive, justifying, or belligerent. It is quite certain that you are coming from a state of duality when your feelings are easily hurt or when you feel unappreciated or get easily annoyed, frustrated, and angered.

Inquire into the motivation of any thought, feeling, or action. Is it coming from a personal ambition to be the best, the first, the smartest? Or is it coming from an innate desire to create? Is the action simply called forth by a need? The need for recognition always comes from ego. The desire to create, if untainted by ambition, does not issue from the false "I," but is a natural human function. An unqualified or impersonal action, that is, an action without concern for "me" or for results, leaves no residue, no regret, no claim to gratitude and therefore does not engender karma.

Observe the contradictions in the *antahkarana* — the many different voices, innumerable attitudes, and emotional tags — all of which are signs that false "I" is in charge.

Discern between false "I" and the natural attributes of your particular manifestation. (Your "particular manifestation" is the instrument for enjoying the creation and expressing the true Self. It is composed of your nature, your faculties, your character, your power of intent, your natural talents, and your attributes.)

3. Honor the Triple Duty: study, concentration, renunciation.

Study and reflect on the Wisdom tradition.

Practice single-minded attention to the task at hand.

Practice renunciation: give up the attachments and claims of the false "I."

TEN

MEDITATION

"To meditate is to be, to be one, one without a second." This simple statement by H.H. Shantanand Saraswati not only expresses the essence of meditation, but also points to a state of being that can only be achieved by purity and simplicity. He goes on to say, "The method of meditation is only a process by which this is made possible."

If we truly understood what it means "to be," or "to be one without a second," we would need no further instruction in meditation. If we actually *realized* those states in our being, we would not need to practice meditation, since we would have become Atman and live in the state of pure being, or, to go a step further, we would have merged with Paramatman, in which there is no meditator or object of meditation.

The practice of meditation is not the goal but a means. Although essential to spiritual realization, the stilling of the mind, the spiritual experiences, and revelations are not an end in themselves, but rather the evidence and encouragement needed on the journey that bring us closer and closer to truth and pure being.

The ancient yogis acquired single-mindedness and concentration by many difficult methods prescribed in steps five and six of Patanjali's *Yoga Sutras*, namely *pratyahara* and *dharana*. As modern seekers, we are fortunate to have been given the gift of Transcendental Meditation, which relieves the dispersed state of the mind, stills the fluttering in the heart, and calms the movements in the body. When practiced diligently, meditation has the power to bring us to a state of unity and direct knowledge of our true nature.

In order to realize "being," we have to *experience* being, that is, the state of pure being. Meditation is the means to that experience. It is the most expedient way to discover and experience the reality of truth — the Self. The practice of meditation is the simplest way to discover the meaning of the great sacred truths, such as "Thou art That," "All is Brahman," "I am that infinite consciousness," "I am love," "I am that infinite bliss."

When we are given these glimpses into our divine nature, our being is transformed and we are strengthened on all levels. The revelations received, whether through grace or effort, merge with our inner knowing, hence we no longer have the need to believe in someone else's concept of God, or someone else's truth. When we experience bliss, love, undifferentiated consciousness, infinite light, or any other of the forms in which the divine manifests in our soul, we no longer *believe*, but instead we *know* and we *are* That. All doubts vanish, replaced by conviction. This is a new ground of being.

The glimpses of reality perceived during meditation depend on the purity of the individual *antahkarana*. They may be experienced in one or more centers of our being as a knowing or a feeling. They may be perceived in *buddhi* or reflected in *chitta*. The experiences are always fresh, ever-changing, and full of surprise. The overflowing heart, the love, the gratitude, and the bliss are the divine gifts we then bring back into the world.

These experiences can also be colored by belief and past experience. Some people have visions of a deity or sacred symbols. These experiences may be conjured up by the memory or the imagination; hence they may not be authentic but rather may be of an illusory nature. But even visions and experiences are not the aim. They vanish, as all effort and all doing vanish. Then there is no object of devotion, no mantra, no meditator; there is just one consciousness.

Having considered the ideal, let us go back to where we stand. It is not hard to observe that we suffer from mental and physical restlessness, a state that is intermittently "relieved" by mental and physical exhaustion. We lose far too much energy in our relentless doing and achieving; the mind and body burn too much fuel at too great a cost to our spiritual, mental, and physical well-being. We reluctantly take time out to care for our bodies and sometimes our minds; but we rarely take time out for our being, spirit, and soul, because we really do not believe that they too need care. We are under the impression that as long as we are "chugging along" and doing our job, we are really "doing all right." But are we really? Probably not!

The truth is that we must take care of all our bodies — physical, subtle, and causal — and give them the appropriate medicine and rest they require. Meditation provides "time out" — time to replenish and take care of our being. We might think of meditation metaphorically as "going backstage" in order to freshen up and change costume before making our next entrance onto the stage of life.

THE BENEFITS OF MEDITATION are immeasurable. On a very practical level, as documented by medical research, they include an increase of energy, clarity of mind, and more restful sleep, as well as reduced brain activity, lower blood pressure, and a slower rate of heartbeat. The more long-term benefits are equally positive: increase in happiness, contentment, well-being, and health and a decrease of personal problems, relationship difficulties, and stress-related disorders. There are also accounts of recoveries from chronic health problems and even of spontaneous healings of serious illness.

The mind and heart may be gratified by the outward benefits of meditation. But as seekers, ultimately we are not after these effects. They are simply seen as welcome gifts, received with gratitude and then surrendered to the Paramatman from whence they came. On the quest, meditation is one means of inquiring into our essence and into the nature of reality. It is in the nature of our being to want to know all, to experience and to love all, and to return to our Divine Source. It is in our nature to reach higher and higher and not to be satisfied with anything less than the infinite. And meditation is one of the most auspicious means — especially in this age — leading us to union with the infinite.

We need to approach meditation with a degree of preparedness. Although meditation is a means of bringing us to greater stillness, we cannot hope to still our minds by this practice alone. Our minds and hearts need to be prepared and purified in some measure by the study of the perennial wisdom and reflection on the great sacred truths. We need to have at least a glimpse of the Unity of all existence and have lived a life of moderation and good moral conduct. We have to have arrived at some level of consistency of intent, thought, feeling, and action. The conscience has to be clear of wrongdoing, guilt, and regret. Unless the mind and heart are thus purified, meditation will prove to be very difficult and we will abandon it all too soon.

When an undisciplined mind is asked to concentrate, it will rebel and turn into a veritable demon. Since the moving mind has been the master for a very long time, it will not be stilled easily; it does not yet know how to fit into its proper duty and serve the higher functions. One solution is to occupy it with the repetition of a *sloka*, a brief statement of a sacred truth, an aphorism, an invocation, or a prayer. The repetition can be of three kinds: silent, hummed, or aloud. This can be practiced at any time and in any place, as long as the mind is not engaged in some particular intellectual endeavor that requires its presence. It may be practiced in preparation for formal meditation or at any time the mind needs stilling.

Meditation lifts us out of our material existence and makes us aware of the life of the soul and the existence of the divine. It temporarily relieves us from our busy lives, worldly concerns and problems. It takes us, at least momentarily, out of our identification with the body, the personality, the faculties, and the ego.

Meditation takes care of the past, present and future. It relieves us from karmic debt and helps to burn up *samskaras*. It embraces us and holds us in the infinite present where all potential lies. Here, in the eternal now, is the source of the Creative Principle; as we become one with it, we are healed, renewed, and refreshed. Our being is transformed, refined, and purified; the *antahkarana* and all of its adjuncts are bathed in *sattvic* light. In the eternal present we engender no karma. Meditation also protects us from future harm and suffering; the *sattvic* light illumines our being, knowing, and willing and informs our thoughts, feelings, and actions, making it less likely that we will accumulate further karma.

Meditation expands our being; we become more universal in our view of things and in our view of the world. Hence we begin to see the unity in the diversity and understand our place in the cosmos. The practice of meditation purifies the perception and senses; hence we experience everything more clearly and keenly. It increases our power of observation, attention, and awareness; hence we see more about ourselves, the people around us, and the events in the world. We comprehend more by looking beyond the surfaces; yet at the same time we become more aware of the beauty, harmony, and order in the creation and of the love that surrounds us.

Meditation opposes *rajas* and *tamas* — the forces that compel us to mechanical thought and action. *Japa* — the repetition of a *mantra* — raises a wave in the mind that eliminates the *rajasic* movements and interrupts the habitual thought patterns that cloud our thinking and lead to identification. When we surrender to the wave of *japa* and dive deeply, we are free of our past. With regular practice, false ideas, negative tendencies, and attachments will dissolve permanently.

In meditation we give ourselves over to a higher force; we learn to trust and to surrender. This prepares us for the final act: surrender to the Paramatman. Surrender begins with the simple willingness to sit still for a while and open ourselves to the unknown. While this attitude is vital for the beginning meditator, willingness and surrender are equally necessary every time we sit down to the practice. Each time we have to be willing to let go of worldly concerns and daily affairs. We have to surrender everything that is not-Self in order to rest in the Self and, by grace, to merge with the Supreme Self.

The regular experience of our essence produces *sattva* — the elixir that frees us from illusions and negative tendencies and their attendant suffering. Because of our tendency to look outward into creation, we believe in the supremacy of the material world; but we do so only until we experience the subtle and causal worlds. We cling to our material possessions and mental attachments; but we do so only until we experience the illusory nature of these belongings and enjoy — at least temporarily — the utter freedom of the absence of attachments. We cling to our belief in the reality of our ego; but we do so only until we experience the essence of our true Self. The practice of meditation brings us into regular contact with Atman and the experience of pure being, convincing us of the supremacy of spirit. In this way worldly desires and attachments lose their power over us. This is why meditation is the most effective means of unleashing us from the fetters of the false ego.

THERE ARE MANY METHODS of meditation. One is visualizing and concentrating on sacred symbols, devotional objects, or divine forms. Some find it useful to visualize the Paramatman as the infinite ocean of consciousness in which the *jiva-atman* swims blissfully about. Others choose to experience the light of the infinite consciousness and let it permeate their entire being. Others find it useful to simply watch the small waves — the movements of body and mind — slowly subside and merge with the almost imperceptible cosmic wave. Some beginning meditators find that visualizing a personal God, a beloved saint, or avatar helps them focus their attention and deepen their concentration. Those who choose a divine form as the object of contemplation must keep in mind that it is a symbol only — a symbol which stands for the Formless, the Eternal, the Ultimate Cause. Some traditions, on the other hand, hold that the use of the imagination, including any kind of visualization, only creates more illusions. They suggest that it is best to be silent and go straight to our true essence.

Japa, the recitation of a holy name or mantra, is an ancient spiritual practice that is essential to Self-realization. (The Sanskrit word *japa* means "muttering" or "whispering.") Sri Ramakrishna explains that "each *japa* is like a link of a chain, and holding this chain, you reach the very end of the chain, that to which it is fixed." The idea is to hold fast to the repetition of the word or sound, thereby transcending any thoughts about "me" and "mine" and coming to rest in the true essence. This is one of the purest forms of meditation, and it is the one most suitable for modern seekers, particularly since it is not encumbered with sectarian associations.

When Mother Meera, a revered incarnation of the Divine Mother, was asked what kind of meditation should be practiced, she said: "Close your eyes and sit in silence and do *japa* on any divine name." The simplicity, purity, and beauty of this statement goes right to the heart. As Mother Meera goes on to say, "*Japa* is the repetition of the name of that in which we believe. *Japa* is essential. *Japa* is not simple words — each divine name is full of divine vibrations. These surround us and protect us and penetrate both our bodies and our whole inner being. Remembrance of the divine name gives immediate peace and happiness and turns us from the worldly to the divine."

A mantra is a word or phrase of power. The word "mantra" comes from the same Sanskrit root as *manas* (from *man*, "to think"). Hence a *mantra* is an instrument of thought and is designed to generate a vibration. Anything we think about repeatedly — even negative thoughts — is in a sense a mantra and by its vibrations sets things in motion. It could be said that all sacred hymns and psalms are forms of mantras — thought supports or vehicles for the realization of truth. Mantras have the creative power to kindle the spiritual fire deep within the meditator and to change being.

Sacred mantras have been handed down from masters to disciples for thousands of years. The method of repeating God's name, a sacred sound, or *sloka*, is based on the principle that all sound is creative. Every word we speak is an invocation to one force or another and creates or begets something on one level or another, whether we know it or not or intend it or not. We are continuously sounding our own personal mantras when we say "I can't," "I won't," "I am the greatest." A sound once uttered can never be retrieved. It goes on creating and eventually comes back to us.

In meditation the mantra is the vehicle for displacing negative sounds and illusions and for setting into motion positive sounds and vibrations that permeate and enlighten the entire being. Sounding a mantra gives the discursive mind a support and keeps it from straying into imaginings, darkness, and unconsciousness. As long as the attention remains on the sound of the mantra, there is no crack in the door through which habitual thoughts and feelings can creep in. Negative feelings, circling thoughts, and mental noise are, for the duration of the *japa*, eliminated.

But the mantra does much more than that. The ancient mantras are said to have their roots in Brahman. Some were consciously devised by Vedic seers to bring about certain results. Some well-known mantras from the Eastern tradition are *Om namah Sivaya* ("OM, honor to Shiva"); *Om namo narayanaya* ("OM, honor to the God in man"); *Om hari om* ("OM, God, OM"). In the Christian mystical tradition the best-known mantras include *Maranatha* ("Our Lord, come"); "Lord Jesus Christ, have mercy on me"; and the Our Father.

There are mantras that are extremely powerful and are based on the knowledge of the transformative quality of each individual pure sound that make up the mantric word. These sounds carry intent and meaning and are specifically designed to increase *sattva*, to give direction, to reveal knowledge, or to draw the individual back to the source, and eventually to bring Atman into union with Brahman.

These sacred mantras were traditionally given to the disciple by a master in a solemn act of initiation. This direct transference of a holy word is based on the understanding that these sounds have to be implanted into the disciple's being. Moreover a mantra that has been recited by devoted disciples, yogis, and saints over thousands of years carries within it the accumulated power and light of the tradition; it is the *essence* of their aspiration, love, and knowledge. For that reason it is considered to be very sacred. Sometimes it is kept secret, only given to aspirants who are adequately prepared to receive this precious gift.

There are many wonderful texts on meditation that provide help on the way and give insight into the subtleties of the practice. One of the most propitious ways to begin is by way of initiation by a master with a direct link to an ancient tradition. Fortunately, access to such masters is a reality in our modern world, as are more Westernized methods such as Transcendental Meditation and Christian forms of meditation. Guidance is of great benefit, as is the support of a group. But there is no need for concern if none of the above is possible. When Mother Meera was asked whether it is necessary to wait for a guru to give a mantra or whether one could find one's own, she answered, "Whichever mantra comes to you easily and spontaneously is the one you should do. It should give a strong feeling and be like music flowing from the heart."

How do we meditate? What is the proper way? Simply put: We sit in a chair or cross-legged in the lotus position, close our eyes and sound the mantra. Let us hear it in the words of the wise Bhushundi, as recorded in the *Yoga-Vasishtha*: "Divine meditation in the form of *So-Hum*, or *Shivo-Hum*, unaccompanied by any desire or selfish aim, penetrates like the moon's rays through the darkness of the night of ignorance."

The *Srimad Bhagavatam* gives the following instruction:

> Seated in a secluded place, free from all disturbing thoughts of the world, one must first repeat in one's mind the sacred word OM, with understanding of its meaning. The word OM is one with God, and indeed is God...with the discriminative faculty as guide, one should, with the help of the mind, draw the senses and the sense-organs completely away from the objects of the world. Let the devotee meditate upon the Lord. Let him be absorbed in Him. When absorption comes, there arises a great calmness, a transcendental bliss.... If for any reason the mind becomes restless again, being overpowered by *rajas* or deluded by *tamas*, let it be brought again under control by the practice of concentration.

In a formulation from the Christian tradition, we are encouraged by the gentle and loving words of St. Francis de Sales: "If the heart wanders or is distracted, bring it back to the point quite gently and replace it tenderly in its Master's presence. And even if you did nothing during the whole of your hour but bring your heart back and place it again in Our Lord's presence, though it went away every time you brought it back, your hour would be very well employed."

Meditation and mantras are the most precious gifts given to humankind; they link us to a long chain of devotees, sages, and avatars and advance the evolution of our souls. They carry us collectively forward in the stream of the evolution of consciousness and the expression of the divine in creation. The wisdom and knowledge of the ages vibrate in the perfect and beautiful formulation of H.H. Shantanand Saraswati: "The Absolute meditates and becomes the creation; we meditate and become the Absolute."

MEDITATION HAS THE POWER to renew our being, rekindle our spirit, and regenerate our bodies. We become as new, able to meet every situation as if for the first time. When through frequent contact with Atman, the small self begins to merge with the true Self, the latter begins to assume its rightful role as master. *Buddhi* then serves the Self and *manas* obeys *buddhi*. The purified *antahkarana* will then perform its proper function. Our inborn talents and hidden genius will find expression in new and wondrous ways. Our proper duty may prove to be beyond and above our greatest hopes and dreams. These wonderful new outpourings of creativity and ingenuity cannot be *achieved*; they are simply the by-products of spiritual work. We must never use meditation as a means for personal achievement or for the achievement of any goal, even if that goal is of the highest order — that of Self-Realization. Such desire engenders karma.

Meditation has been practiced for thousands of years. Millions of human beings all over the world are practicing *japa* every day. The simplicity of the method should not deceive us. It is most effective and works in mysterious and subtle ways. Anyone who practices it with sincerity and humility will enjoy its benefits while shedding "pain-bearing obstructions." Anyone with aspiration will discover the treasure within and delight in the true Self.

It is not within the scope of this text to give instruction for the practice of a specific type of meditation. Some general principles, however, might be of help. Keep in mind that meditation is not for "me" — the ego — but serves to uncover the true Self. Meditation is for the benefit of all sentient beings and the revelation of the One Self in creation. The fruits of the practice are therefore offered to the Paramatman and enjoyed by the Atman.

In meditation, the "universal" — the creative, regenerative power of the Self — forms a bond with the "particular" — the nature of the individual — and informs the expression of its proper duty. When the bond is complete and the instrument is perfected, the individual serves to manifest the will of the Absolute in creation. The knowledge gained is then generously expressed in daily life in form of living wisdom which benefits all and everything it comes into contact with. In this way the force of *sattva* is increased in the world.

PRACTICE

Make a firm resolution to practice meditation every day. (But do not be perturbed when you are prevented from it.)

Set aside one half-hour in the morning and evening, preferably at sunrise and sunset, although any time is a good time for meditation.

Sit in a comfortable chair or on a *zafu* (meditation pillow), with a straight spine, head held high, and let the body come to a quiet relaxed state. Watch the flow of the breath without interference. The body chemistry will naturally slow down, the heartbeat and breath will naturally assume a balanced rhythm, and the eyes will come to rest. You will notice that the moving mind will become more active at this stage. It feels lost without the body and nervous system moving in support of it. The organs of perception begin to dart around and latch on to any sound, image, or idea. The mind wants to do what it always does — indulge in inner conversations and commenting. Use the mind to get the mind in line. Command it to be still.

Let the mind come to rest. Let all anxieties and the affairs of the day subside. Let go of the past: forgive and forget. Let go of the future: do not anticipate or plan. Rest in the eternal now.

Surrender: let your being expand. Let the body, mind, senses and sense of self melt into the infinite consciousness in which there is no separation. The Witness simply watches the ripples in consciousness; the mind has settled down, having been deprived of its power to dominate.

Thus established in the Self, begin to repeat the mantra. Eventually the mantra will find its own rhythm. Follow that rhythm and with the inner listening "hear" every repetition from beginning to end. Let nothing come between the repetitions. Be content to remain in this attentive state of being, and without wavering simply attend to the sound of the mantra. Do not "try" to meditate, just attend to the mantra.

When "bubbles" of bliss, happiness, and well-being arise, do not claim the experience. Instead endeavor to dive deeper and deeper into the ocean of pure consciousness. After sitting, offer the practice to the One Self. The gratitude, contentment, and rejuvenation of the whole organism are the effects of the contact with the source of your own being.

Every practice is new and different. Therefore do not anticipate or try to repeat any experiences. When you seek and concentrate on experience, the attention is on effect and engenders karma. Instead surrender to the infinite.

Note: This brief explanation is not intended to take the place of a formal introduction to meditation. There are many forms, and you have to find the one best suited to your particular temperament. If possible, find a competent teacher or group. A text or tape on meditation is the next best thing. Or simply follow the instruction of Mother Meera: "Close your eyes and sit in silence and do *japa* on any divine name."

ELEVEN
DETACHMENT AND DISPASSION

KNOW, O WISE ONE, that a man needs dispassion and discrimination as a bird needs its two wings.... For the man of self-mastery, dispassion is the only source of happiness. If this is combined with the awakening of the pure knowledge of the Atman, a man becomes independent of all else. This is the door to the enjoyment of that ever-youthful maiden who is called liberation."

These beautiful words were written thirteen centuries ago by Shankara, the great philosopher, poet, and saint. To this day the wisdom of these words is relevant to the human predicament and to our way out of it.

The Perennial Philosophy informs us in many different voices that the way out of suffering is through the loss of attachment to illusion, ego, false beliefs, and material things. The cure for attachment and passion, we are told, is *detachment* and *dispassion*. In theory this does sound like the perfect antidote. But, we hear ourselves protest, how in the world is it possible to practice detachment and dispassion in a society that adores the body, encourages egotism, and awards selfish ambition? How can we still our minds and senses when they are continuously assaulted by the turmoil of popular culture? How do we keep our passions and desires in check when they are incessantly incited by insidious advertising designed to create nothing *but* desire? How can we free ourselves from this conditioning? Many would say it is impossible.

But there are precedents for the successful "escape of all false ties," as Emerson called it. Many people have overcome the allures of worldly existence and the assaults on their psyches. People from all walks of life have courageously renounced the status quo and taken to the "examined life," acquired a degree of detachment and tranquillity, and found measure and harmony in a simpler way of life. They would answer all of the above questions with a resounding: It is possible! It can be achieved! Most likely, none of them would say that it is easy, but it can be done.

In order to be "*in* the world, but not *of* it," we have to gain, in Shankara's words, "the pure knowledge of the Atman." We have to make contact with our true essence on a regular basis. The way to this knowledge, as we already know, is through meditation and direct experience of our true Self. As we gain knowledge of reality, discrimination is strengthened, the intellect begins to perform its proper function, which is to distinguish between Self and not-Self; in addition, we gain access to a keener and more refined intelligence.

When the twentieth-century spiritual teacher Jiddu Krishnamurti was asked, "What is intelligence?", he answered, "It is to perceive that which is illusory, that which is false, not actual, and to discard it; not merely to assert that it is false and continue in the same way, but to discard completely." What he is describing is *true* intelligence as well as the proper use of intelligence, linked to good intent and renunciation.

When we see something clearly in the light of *buddhi,* we are in that conscious instant in a most opportune space for renouncing attachments and desires of every kind. This is the way of detachment in action; it is arrived at by silent observation, discrimination, and renunciation — all flowing together in the light of consciousness and eventually leading to freedom, ease, and happiness.

We have already considered how attachment arises, recognizing that it begins with a feeling which is recognized in the mind as a desire. We have begun to discipline the mind by keeping it under observation and by the practice of meditation. As modern seekers on the way of action, we need to take some extra precautions. We need to shield ourselves from the most blatant assaults on our senses detach ourselves from noise, garishness, and clutter and instead cultivate our finer instincts and emotions. We can choose to live independently and authentically and not be affected by popular opinion. We can opt to live more inwardly and thereby not be swayed by desires and passions. We can actively guard the mind by study and reflecting on spiritual writings, reading fine literature, and listening to inspiring music. We can refine our being with the practices of concentration, attention in action, and meditation.

Detachment from sense objects requires conscious effort; it does not happen simply by wanting or willing it. The *Yoga-Vasishtha* speaks to this point: "It is by exerting your own consciousness and by diligently relinquishing all objects of desire that you can bring your refractory mind into subjection. He who remains at rest, giving up the objects of his desire, is verily the conqueror of his mind."

Inner effort is needed to liberate us from our illusions and the spell of the *gunas.* Self-knowledge is necessary for detaching ourselves from the fetters of the ego. Discipline is necessary for detaching ourselves from the world of passion, conflict, and debate.

Detachment becomes a state of mind when we no longer crave the world of the mind, the emotions, and the senses; when we no longer hanker after pleasure or the repetition of pleasurable experiences. Detachment is an inner state; hence we do not refrain from engaging fully in life and in action. We enjoy this creation and delight in the multiplicity and variety of its expressions; but we do so in the full knowledge that the Self alone acts and enjoys.

We remain detached as we perform all our duties; we remain detached from illusion as we breathe, eat, work, cherish, praise, care, and love. When detachment is coupled with consciousness in action, we cannot succumb to desire and passion; we are conscious of *what* we are cherishing and *who* is doing the cherishing. We are aware that when we love someone, that it is really the Self and the spirit we love in that person. When we serve someone, we serve the Self in all. Such an action is neutral and engenders no karma or suffering.

We have all experienced the suffering and attachment that arise from willed action. Whether we do something for another out of duty, pity, love, or some other impulse, such action has the taint of attachment. Sooner or later love can change into its opposite and the sense of duty turns into resentment. We work so hard at making impossible situations work. Such difficulties arise often in family life, particularly in marriage.

On the other hand, when we remember the Self in the person in front of us, it neutralizes our preconceived notions and habitual reactions. We look past the surfaces, past the flaws, and see the Self. When we remember the Self in our spouse, whether it is in a moment of loving embrace or in the course of ordinary exchange, we remain free of attachment. The challenge is to remember the Self when the going gets rough, such as amidst arguments; at such moments it is necessary to renounce the attachment to "my point of view" or "my feelings." In this way, *rajas* is neutralized, and annoyance or anger is transformed into *sattva* and eventually into pure love. This kind of love is *sattvic* — abundant, unchanging, and giving unconditionally, without asking anything in return. It is the opposite of *tamasic* love, which clings to the object of love and ends in attachment. Such love is fickle and only gives as long as the attachment lasts. It ends in demands, disappointment, misery, and often hate.

EVERY TIME WE REMEMBER the Atman, we become a little more detached and independent of the concerns of our false ego, which in turn is rendered more powerless. With each conscious remembrance we grow more fully into our true nature, into our luminous self-existent being, which reveals itself to us in feelings of peace, stillness, and tranquillity. Eventually, when these feelings are firmly established, we gain spiritual calm in the midst of bustle and adversity. Marcus Aurelius, the philosopher and emperor of Rome, points us toward this state of immutable detachment when he advises, "Be like the cliff against which the waves continually break; but it stands firm and tames the fury of the water around it." The *Bhagavad Gita* says, "Whoso, without attachment anywhere, on meeting with anything good or bad, neither exults nor hates, his knowledge becomes steady."

An inquiry into the nature of detachment and dispassion invariably arouses doubts and objections, such as what will happen when we lose hold on our affairs. But these are the mistaken fears of the ego. The thing is to pay no heed to these doubts and instead to forge ahead, finding assurance in our experience.

It is necessary, however, to avoid a confusion between detachment and noninvolvement. Spiritual indifference is not to be confused with ordinary indifference. Detachment is in fact the only state in which we can truly love, give, and serve. When we are free of attachments and obstructions, pure emotion and true compassion are free to flow to the person or situation in need. When we are detached, we are free from the taint of "doing" or "giving." We remain firmly seated in the Self, serving the Self without claim.

How can we remain detached in the face of another's suffering? By simply remaining seated in the Self and attending to the Self; this spiritual calmness and conscious awareness will nourish the soul in need and shed light on the problems. The proper solutions will arise to meet the need and, by chance or by grace, will alleviate suffering. When we remain aloof, the illusion of suffering has no sway over us, and we will not dissolve into pity or other negative emotions. We do not take on the suffering, for we know that suffering is the result of attachment. We do not judge or criticize, but give freely of what is needed.

When we act with detachment, we do not feed the illusion of division; we no longer participate in the game of success and failure, winning and losing. In the presence of conscious observation and equanimity, the false ego, which dislikes the light of consciousness, will vanish along with its baggage. We will then realize with some amusement that it never had any real existence, but that our attachment to doing, knowing, and achieving had given it a life of its own.

Once we have experienced the freedom of detachment and have savored the calm and peace it brings, we will acknowledge that it *is* an attainable and desirable goal in this day and age and in fact that it is necessary. When we have tasted the sweetness of dispassion, we will make every effort to let go of the passions that lead to attachment.

When we have risen to the state of equanimity, we are no longer perturbed by the illusion of good and evil; we look with an equal eye on plainness and magnificence. We are then like the "men of pacified mind" who, according to the *Yoga-Vasishta*, "view the bright and beautiful buildings of cities in the same dispassionate light as they behold the trees of a forest." Yet we delight in beauty, simplicity, and order, and our environment reflects our mental austerity and desirelessness of our heart and exemplifies what the *Yoga-Vasishta* declared over two thousand years ago: "The homes of householders who have well-governed minds and have banished their sense of egoism are as good as solitary forest, cool caves, or peaceful woods."

Detachment and dispassion are achieved through inner effort. We find equilibrium in our being, and with mind at rest, senses fully alert but free from grasping, we give full attention to the work at hand. Throughout, we are aware of the immutability of our true Self. We act from our true identity and are detached from everything else; we are calm, passionless, impartial, and nonprejudicial. In this state we are strong, free, and at ease; we are safe from claim, desires and identification. Events come and go, and we are not ruffled by them. We surrender all in the moment of action: our feelings, actions, and the fruits of the actions, as well as insights and observations, which the ego is quick to claim. When in a moment of inattention tension, doubt, or conflict arises, we let it go as well. At other times we might ease into a state of "nondoing," when in a moment of frustration or struggle, we finally "give up": we let go of doing and trying and shift into another mode.

When we surrender doing and trying, we glide into a state of being in the *now*. In the present, our actions are pure, fresh, effective, and unencumbered. The secret of letting go, of "being in the groove" or "staying in the zone" has been discovered naturally by thousands who excel apparently without even trying. When asked, "how do you do it?", the athlete may answer, "I just run, I don't think about it" or "I get into this space in which another force takes over" or "I don't interfere and just let the body do the work." A renowned violinist once explained, "I don't do anything. My fingers do the work. I just sit back and listen. It's great fun!" Many artists have observed that when they finally stop trying and get out of the way, wonderful things begin to happen. Writers may refer to it as "being in the flow" or "being on a roll" — a state in which there is no claim or sense of involvement.

By giving up willing and doing, we open a channel to the Creative Principle. When we are in the flow of its force, we are delighted and often surprised at discovering fresh, creative, and truly innovative solutions. We then live and act with wonder, detachment, and gratitude, in the experiential knowledge that we have had little to do with it and are simply transformers of energies.

When we are detached, we become more accepting of what is. We are more tolerant of others' shortcomings and our own. With greater acceptance comes gratitude for the blessings we enjoy. We become happier and less needy.

Then we come to the next level of detachment: we surrender *all* — the good and the bad — and offer it to the Supreme Self. When we do this, we are liberated from our attachments and our whole life becomes a sacred act. When, in the continuous, conscious knowledge of the source of our being, we see the Self everywhere, all attachment vanishes, and with it all division. We then experience freedom even while engaged in the affairs of daily life.

PRACTICE

1. Practice recollection.

Every time you "wake up," that is, every time you remember yourself during the day, set aside the thought or activity you are engaged in and recollect.

If possible, close the eyes or lower the eyelids. Let your consciousness expand and rest in it. Then mentally let go of the involvement of the senses. When the mind is still, sound and listen to the words: "I am the luminous self-existent Atman whose nature is being, consciousness, and bliss." Reflect on these words without intellectualizing. Then gently open the eyes and, without moving from this state of impartiality and perfect poise and without grasping or naming, perform the task at hand.

Whenever you notice agitation in the mind or body, know that it is caused by *rajas* — passion. Recollect.

Let the mind and body come to stillness. Resolve not to work from agitation. Find your inner poise. The stillness is ever present, awaiting you, beckoning to you. Rest in it, live in it, work in it.

2. Practice dispassion.

Whenever you are in a difficult situation, step back, regain your inner poise, breathe deeply and watch the action take place, as if it were an interesting drama. Do not waste your essence in costly and futile arguments.

3. Practice the way of detachment.

Through effort and objective observation, discriminate between Self and not-Self, between Reality and illusion. When you perceive one of the many effects of attachment, simply let go. Surrender it to the One Self.

4. Guard your senses.

Whenever you become aware that your senses are grasping or straining, recollect and regain inner poise. Endeavor to perceive — hear, see, smell, taste, and touch — without latching on to the objects of perception. Simply watch from a state of perfect poise and serene detachment.

5. Remember the Self in all.

Acknowledge the Self in all — in whomever is in front of you. When you serve, honor, cherish, and love, know that it is the Self you serve. This is the cure for attachment and the only way to peace and happiness.

TWELVE
ATTENTION AND THE ETERNAL NOW

Pratyahara and *dharana* — steps five and six of Patanjali's yoga — are designed to gain control over *manas* or mind. As we learned in Part One, *dharana* is the fixation of attention, passive, active, or directed, on a particular object or idea with the aim of steadying the mind, and, as H.H. Shantanand Saraswati says, "making it absolutely fit and pliant." In meditation the attention can be said to be passive or of an inward nature; in activity attention is active, that is, it is turned outward. In meditation the mind is controlled by the repetition of a mantra or by mentally gazing on a symbol of the divine. In daily activities the mind can be brought under control by focused attention on the task at hand or the "point of interaction."

Dharana is therefore of particular interest to modern seekers who are suffering to one degree or another from an overactive mind and are overwhelmed by incessant activity.

The Samkhya system divides attention into three kinds:

1. Witness — the neutral observer (*sattva*);
2. Agent — the subject (*rajas*);
3. Matter — the object (*tamas*).

The Witness and agent are conscious, while matter is unconscious. The agent, or active attention, acts on matter — the object of attention, while the action and reaction between subject and object are impartially judged by the Witness. This trinity of attention is present in all activity. When the agent tends towards matter, it will be suffused in *tamas*, darkness and suffering; when it reaches for the Witness state it will be illumined by *sattva*.

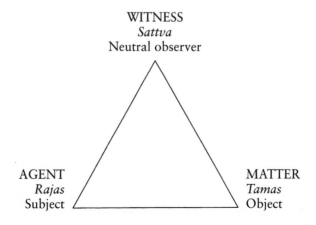

Figure 10. The trinity of attention.

The quality of our awareness to a large extent determines how we meet the world and react to it. In actuality it is the internal state that determines the external. The gross, external world is but the effect of the subtle and causal worlds. An understanding of the space of interaction of spirit and matter, or rather, the continuous flowing together of the forces of *purusha* and *prakriti* is relevant to our inquiry into the nature of attention.

What, then, is attention? We are safe in saying that it is most mysterious. Is it a power that we call our own? Is it a cause or an effect? H.H. Shantanand Saraswati says, "Attention is the activity or a different name for consciousness. When the consciousness is applied to something, then we call it attention, and this attention is possible only if enough of *sattva* is available to direct us towards the Atman. So-called 'attention' with *tamas* is going in the opposite direction, towards inertia or death." In other words, consciousness and attention are in essence the same.

Although attention is mysterious and subtle, it is evident in both the negative and positive effects it has on our minds, relationships, and daily affairs. When we go about our daily lives in a semislumber, we are hardly aware of this powerful force within ourselves. In fact lack of attention is the cause of all mishaps and misunderstandings. When the quality of attention tend towards *tamas,* it can result in accidents or even death.

When attention is *sattvic,* that is, when it is conscious and coupled with good intent, we experience it as that infinite, all-potentiating force known as pure attention, which is akin to pure consciousness. This force not only links us to the physical point of interaction, but to reality, as our desires and thoughts, through conscious action, come to fruition in the manifest world. *Sattvic* attention has the power to transform our being, our actions, and the objects of our attention.

The aim of *dharana,* as we already know, is to "steady the mind and make it absolutely fit and pliant." These adjectives also happen to describe the attributes of attention in action. The force of conscious attention is infinitely malleable and adaptable. It can be applied to any activity and directed to any goal.

Let us consider the three different states of attention and how they apply in everyday life. They can be defined as:

1. Attention wide open;
2. Attention focused on the task;
3. Attention resting at the point of interaction.

"Attention wide open" occurs when we enter new territory, take in a new vista, place, or situation. At such a moment, when our interest is aroused, the attention naturally opens up and we momentarily perceive things as they are — neutrally and entirely. There is often a sense of freedom or a feeling of wonder that accompanies such a moment. Because attention is engaged, we are temporarily unfettered from false identification and we are free from associating, naming, and classifying.

This state of wide-open attention does not last long. The moving mind and senses want to name, explain, and label the experience. When we are "asleep," attention is drawn to particulars or to whatever stimulates the senses or the mind. Thus open attentiveness is lost in time and space — in the past and in movement.

Nevertheless we can consciously cultivate this state of wide-open attention. It is achieved, first of all, by resting in the true Self. From this still point — with the mind, heart and senses at rest, but open and alive — we simply watch. In this state of quiet simplicity, the senses do not grasp, but simply inform. We enjoy a state of pure Being and pure perception.

Without the interference of the moving mind, we are in a state of pure potential; from this quiescence we can truly see and understand. This combination of seeing and understanding transcends time and space and touches upon the mystical. It is experienced as a kind of reverence, a feeling of the sublimity of being, an exuberance, a sense of the sacredness of existence, or a simple acceptance of "what is." In such a moment of openness, we are given glimpses into the pure essence of things; we are then capable of truly seeing a tree, a mountain, or a person and are surprised or struck with the miracle of life and the mystery of being. This is a moment of true intuition, grace, and transformation on every level of being.

In a collection of lectures entitled *The Flame of Attention*, Krishnamurti speaks with brilliant clarity about consciousness and attention. He observes that "direct perception is insight which transforms the brain cells themselves. One's brain has been conditioned through time and functions in thinking. It is caught in that cycle. When there is pure observation of any problem there is a transformation, a mutation, in the very structure of the cells." When we begin the practice of this wide-open awareness, we will actually experience a relaxation in the brain, resulting in a marked increase in clarity of perception.

It is easiest to practice this state of attention out in nature or in the privacy of peaceful surroundings. When it begins to feel natural, we can carry it into other situations. We may then have moments of direct perception in the course of our actions, which are illumined by consciousness, inclusiveness, and a sense of Unity.

Simone Weil has written some luminous essays about the capacity to give one's attention to those in need. She points out, for example, that it is necessary to know *how* to look at an unhappy neighbor: "This way of looking is first of all attentive." She defines it further: "The soul empties itself of all its own contents in order to receive into itself the being it is looking at, just as he is, in all his truth."

In such a state it is possible to know everything there is to know in a flash about any person or thing. In the absence of thinking and willful doing, information about the essence of the situation simply arises from attentive looking. Such information includes not only the present reality, but also a knowledge of procedure — the right actions to take in the situation. In other words, this intuition arising from conscious attention is of both an inner and outer nature, at once subtle and totally practical. It also enables us to be receptive and open to the influx of higher forces, to the unexpected, and to the interesting quirks of synchronicity. We are not subject to the forces of *rajas* and *tamas*, so we are less likely to have arguments or accidents. Despite the common claim that such incidents "just happen," they are always and without exception the result of delusion and momentary inattention — a fact we tend to recognize in retrospect, after the damage is done.

Many of our working hours are spent in the second state of the Samkhya classification — with the attention focused on a particular task. This task may be of either of a mental or physical nature or a combination of both. In this state the quality of attention can be seen immediately in the course of the activity and can also be inferred from its outcome. When the moving mind, with its penchant for inner commenting, interferes with the task, or the emotions cloud the present with excitement or anxiety, we are in that moment not attending to the task. Instead attention is on the inner world. We are listening to the past — to our mental and emotional history. Hence we are not in the present. We are not truly living. Much illness and stress is nothing more than the result of such an inability to focus the mind on a given task.

This pathological state of divided attention not only precludes us from being in the now and attending to what is in front of us, but puts us in an unstable, vulnerable, and agitated state, resulting in sloppy and faulty work. In many sectors of human endeavor, inattention and its resulting mistakes and accidents are considered normal behavior, calculated into the price of the product and chalked up as part of the expenditures.

Fortunately, we have all experienced the opposite of the above — a sense of timelessness and happiness, when the quality of attention is refined and completely appropriate to the task. At such moments, the flow of conscious attention is unimpeded by internal or external disturbances and the work simply takes place without effort. The intent is clear, and the action is suited to the execution of the intent. There is no claim on such work, since the false ego is temporarily out of the way, so the work is playful and joyful. The proper tool presents itself, serving naturally to extend the reach of our capacity.

When intention, attention, and proper means become closely aligned, the resultant work meets the target or goal — it "does what it means and intends." The outcome of such work comes as close to perfection as is possible in the relative world. In addition, when the attention is finely focused, we are happy and whole. We may even experience the ideal state of the way of action — "Union in silence with all Being and action flowing from that silence in enlightened joy," as Mother Meera has expressed it.

When we experience this joyful, attentive, and ease-filled state, we are not excluding the rest of the world from our awareness. This form of attention is not to be confused with concentration. In concentration, as commonly understood, there is usually an effort to exclude everything that is not under consideration; there is an element of separation and hence egotism. Pure attention is never exclusive, and this requires a still mind and a pure heart. If during an activity we are annoyed by a sound, it is likely that the mind is attached to an idea, such as "being the doer" or "my peace" or "my space." We can make use of the annoyance and let it serve as a signal for the need to recollect and return to the still point.

The ideal state of "attention focused on a task" is one in which attention is steady, the intent is clear, the moving mind is still, and all internal faculties, illumined by consciousness, are performing their proper functions. Then, the light of *sattva* illumines our *buddhi, manas* serves *buddhi,* and the purified perception inform the perfectly aligned instrument. This ideal state is not only appropriate to physical action or creative endeavors; it is equally suitable to any form of intellectual activity. In fact it is the only state in which true thought can take place and in which original ideas and solutions can arise. The object of attention — the problem, question, or evidence — is simply addressed and then "waited upon." Again the words of Simone Weil help to clarify this state of attentive waiting: "Attention consists of suspending our thought, leaving it detached, empty and ready to be penetrated by the object; it means holding in our minds, within reach of this thought, but on a lower level and not in contact with it, the diverse knowledge we have acquired which we are forced to make use of....Above all our thoughts should be empty, waiting, not seeking anything, but ready to receive in its naked truth the object that is to penetrate it."

Most of us have experienced the real happiness and contentment that accompany this state of focused attention; this happiness is doubled when we are doing what we truly love — what we are meant to be doing in this life. However, the feeling of contentment is not limited to what we like to do. Happiness is not in the thing or activity; it is within the heart. We can be joyful performing any task, no matter how apparently lowly. Focused attention protects us from false identification; it neutralizes attachments and notions of like and dislike, good and bad. Thus a task that is generally considered as menial becomes joyful as well. It is just an opportunity to delight in the Self and serve the Self with attention.

With the refinement of attention comes another benefit: the refinement of perception, both inner and outer. We may be able to perceive directly what the wise have told us — that "consciousness is the medium in which all action takes place," and we may realize that attention is the same force, consciously directed, by which we most perfectly experience and express the divine in creation. We might think of attention as a "stepped-down" energy of divine consciousness — as a force we are privileged to use in the service of a greater expression of consciousness in creation. We serve the greater good when, with pure intent and perfect tranquility, we perform our actions consciously, in accord with a higher will.

The third state of attention takes more inner effort. It is one of consciously focusing the attention on the "in-between" — the space between agent and matter. For practical purposes, we define this state as "attention resting at the point of interaction."

This state of attention is no longer common to human beings in this day and age; it no longer comes naturally to our modern psyches. We hardly ever see any evidence of this type of attention in modern existence. The only exceptions are perhaps very young children, and the few, such as healers and artisans, who have stumbled upon the secret of this singular yet natural state through love of their work and care for the object of their attention.

Fortunately, this state is not forever lost to the rest of us. It can be reacquired through effort and method, although, since it no longer comes naturally, we have to consciously practice it. Like meditation, it initially requires precise and attentive inner effort. Eventually this form of attention will become more natural; it then becomes integrated into our being and takes root in our nervous system.

At the beginning, it will be difficult to remember the practice. Later there might be some resistance to it on the grounds that there is no time for it. But once we have had a taste of the expansion of time as a result of the wholeness and freedom inherent in this practice, all doubts, hesitations, and excuses will simply drop away. Then we will remember more often.

First we need to know what "attention resting at the point of interaction" exactly means. Here language is particularly inadequate, since we are trying to define something that is intangible on the gross level, although it is more than tangible on the subtle and causal levels. We are speaking of something invisible and yet infinitely powerful.

But try we must: the point of interaction denotes a space in which the action takes place; in other words, where the human instrument (the agent) interacts with the world (matter). It is where the inner and outer come together, where mind meets matter, where one energy is transformed into another. It could be described as a place of friction or as a space of transmutation, but also as the realm of infinite consciousness. However, such images are mere intellectual approximations of something that is in reality outside time and space.

In practical terms, the point of interaction is, for example, the space where the feet strike the ground, the hand touches a surface, the chisel scrapes the wood, or the pen releases the ink to the paper. What we really find here is in fact not a point but rather an immense space — an infinite field of undifferentiated potential. At times this realm is experienced as an expansion in consciousness, at other times as unlimited space or even as pure love. On rarer occasions, when the human instrument is perfectly poised and the attention, honed by practice, is resting in that infinite space, the veil of illusion is lifted for a very brief instant. We then perceive it as "oneness with consciousness" or "unity with divine reality." It is a moment Emerson described as "the reverential withdrawing of Nature before its God." Such a moment dispels forever the illusion of solidity of matter and confirms the ancient truths that "all is consciousness" and that "there is only One."

In such a moment space and time disappear, or rather the laws of space and time are not applicable. It is the experience of the mystery — of the substratum of the divine. In that instant our being is transformed on all levels; we have made contact with the Creative Principle that is beyond the *gunas*, beyond reason and beyond cause. We have made contact with what the Greeks called the *metaxu* — the "in-between," the space where God is Man and Man is God. By resting our attention on the "in-between," we are able to consciously make contact with our divinity and thus perform our worldly duties in a sacred manner.

We often use the term "to pay attention." In those magical moments of contact with the "in-between," we realize that in reality attention is not something we pay or give. Rather attention is something we participate in, something we can enter into more fully. We realize that the force of attention, which we ordinarily attribute to our sense of self, is, in fact, another manifestation of the universal consciousness in which we live and have our being.

W HAT IS SO REMARKABLE is that this one simple practice of resting the attention at the point of interaction yields such a splendid treasure of evidence on our quest — knowledge of our true nature, understanding of the nature of reality, and realization of the One Consciousness. There are other, more practical benefits to this practice as well. By working in this way, we enjoy the present moment and we are never bored. Because there is no repetition in the present, each moment is completely new and interesting. We are fully alive. By resting our attention in the activity, we do not tire easily, but actually come out of the activity fully refreshed. We not only enjoy our work, but will most likely excel in it, avoiding the bitter aftertaste of claiming, doing, achieving. This one simple practice can therefore be considered the essence of the way of the householder, and as the secret key to living and working in a happy, serene and fruitful manner in the midst of the bustle of modern life.

The practice of this specific refined attention has another wonderful side benefit of literally "pinning" us to the present — to THAT which IS. The present is all there is. When we are going about in the state of waking sleep, we are unaware of the eternal now. Our minds dwell on the nonexistent past and the nonexistent future. We concern ourselves with unreality, and while the mind is deluded by imaginings, we miss life altogether. In the present, on the other hand, we are in a state of simplicity and openness to solutions, inspirations, and miracles. "The present moment," says J.-P. de Caussade, "is always filled with infinite treasures: it contains more than you are capable of receiving....The divine will is an abyss, of which the present moment is the entrance; plunge fearlessly therein and you will find it more boundless than your desire."

When we attain to a higher state of being, higher reason and higher emotion begin to function and manifest in wisdom and love. When these illumined faculties inform our endeavors, they enrich us and those around us with an outpouring of imagination, invention, and discovery. These higher faculties can only function, however, when we are connected to the present, when the human instrument is at rest and we are consciously attending. The word "attend" means "to wait upon"; the word "attention," having the same origin, also suggests a "waiting upon."

Thus the state of singular attention is not in any way a willful act or a matter of intense concentration, but rather a "waiting upon." The only effort is that of direction of the power of attention and resting the attention in the "space of interaction." We then mentally "locate" the point of interaction. At first this is accomplished with the help of the mind's eye. Later, with more experience, the point of interaction is simply held in the awareness. From this "waiting upon," we guide the attention to the space of interaction and then simply allow the attention to rest there. Attention flows by itself; we do not need to "pay" it or "give" it. Then, fully connected to the senses and at perfect ease, we engage in the activity and simply watch it take place; all the while the attention rests at the point of interaction. Then the knowledge of the most propitious method or tool for the work will arise naturally.

Listening to the sounds of the activity, that is, the sound that arises from the point of interaction, can be most informative. The sense of hearing is traditionally associated with the element of ether or space — the substance in which the action takes place. Hearing is the least material of all the senses and therefore a fitting link to consciousness. When we listen attentively, we are least likely to be identified with the body or the activity. Connecting with the sense of touch also proves to be very useful when the human instrument is agitated and we need to be grounded. And when we guard the sense of sight, we are less likely to be drawn into identification and temptation. Too often we rely on sight when in fact any one of the other senses might yield more accurate information. When using the sense of sight, we need to always step back and remember that it is the Witness alone who perceives.

A S WE PRACTICE THIS STATE OF ATTENTION, the meaning and location of the point of interaction will become clearer. We will discover, for example, that in walking, the attention rests in the *space* where the feet or shoes meet the ground; when drawing, painting, or writing, the attention rests in the *space* where the pencil, brush, or pen meets the paper; when driving, the attention rests in the *space* where the tires meet the road, while the Witness perceives everything all around. When sanding wood or polishing a surface, we allow the attention to rest in the *space* where the two surfaces meet and the friction takes place. When speaking or singing, we allow the attention to rest in the *space* from which the sound emanates, while listening impartially.

In more complicated tasks it may be a little harder to find the point of interaction. When we play an instrument such as the piano, for example, we allow the attention to extend and rest in the space where the hammers hit the strings. When driving nails, we let the attention rest in the space where the tip of the nail penetrates the wood fibers; similarly, when sawing, we allow the attention to rest in the space where the teeth of the saw chew through the wood; and so on.

This state of attending is by no means mindless. When the moving mind is stilled, our higher faculties and our senses work more perfectly; hence we have better discrimination and perception. We are more alive, and the work flows naturally and easily. This attention refines our awareness and increase our individual consciousness; hence, our being, understanding, and work become more universal. Then our work will have the power to reach into the hearts and minds of a wider audience.

Shakespeare's plays are no doubt the greatest example of universality the world has ever seen. To this day, the language, exuberance, and profundity touch us deeply and their relevance to the human condition will probably never cease to astonish future generations. It is the universality of the poetic verse and the conscious use of sounds that have the power to open the heart. The genius who wrote those eloquent words, like the great geniuses of all times, was surely in possession of the secret of "attending" or, as Emerson put it, of "lowly listening" for the right word, the perfect sound, that comes down to us humans from a higher source.

PRACTICE

1. Practice wide-open attention.

When performing a task that does not call for one-pointed attention, for example shopping or organizing the house or office, practice keeping the attention wide open. This state is most easily achieved and maintained by an open all-inclusive listening. By attentive listening, you will be informed and understand what takes place on all levels — the gross, subtle, and causal.

The next level of refinement consists of listening to the stillness beyond the sound, beyond a person's voice, beyond the din of city life.

2. Practice focusing attention on a task.

Practice devoting your full attention to the task or the person in front of you. Let it be calm, open, full, firm, and fresh; attention, like rain, refreshes; it nourishes both the "giver" of attention and the one receiving it. In fact this fullness of attention in the now is the only healthy psychological state. It is "contagious" and promotes health and happiness all around you — in family members, coworkers, and even passers-by.

Opening up fully to this state of wakeful attending requires practice; it is rather like letting go of an involuntary reflex or a cramped muscle. The flow of attention is normal, the holding back is what is not normal. A wondrous feeling of wholeness and sense of ease will let you know your practice is going well.

Resolve not to work, mentally or physically, with divided attention. When the mind or body is agitated, stop the activity and recollect.

Resolve not to work from egoistic attitudes. When emotional reactions (likes, dislikes, feelings of "why do I have to...") are seen, simply stop, recollect, and begin anew with a still mind.

(continued on next page)

---

3. **Practice resting attention on the point of interaction.**
   Set aside some time to get a feeling for this practice. Walk barefoot on
   a floor or on dewy grass and allow your attention to rest in the space
   between the feet and the ground, while your gaze is open but relaxed.
   If there is inner commentary, let it go, and bring the attention back to
   the space between the feet and the ground.

   Do this again and again, until the mind is still. If at all possible, practice this several times a day. Remember to practice this mindful
   awareness of the point of interaction while walking to work or moving
   from room to room. Find the point of interaction in your most
   commonly performed tasks and allow the attention to rest in that space
   while you are engaged in the task.

   Perform other common tasks and daily activities in this manner, such
   as brushing your teeth, bathing, sweeping the floor, drying the dishes,
   writing a letter. At first, mentally locating this space helps in fastening
   the attention to it. In time the attention will naturally gravitate to the
   space of interaction, and your entire being will rest in this infinite
   space, the eternal Now.

   Remember to *listen* throughout all your activities and whenever the
   mind needs stilling.

   When in doubt about the form of attention, or the point of interaction,
   it is always appropriate to use one of the following: wide-open, all-
   inclusive listening; receptive waiting; conscious attending; or resting in
   the eternal present.

   Always mentally state your intent before you engage in any activity.

   Study and reflect on the chapter above.

THIRTEEN
How to Spend a Day Nobly

How we presently live our daily lives serves as the proof of whether or not we are advancing in spiritual work. Now that we can look with a degree of dispassion and objectivity, we can more clearly see the fruits of our thoughts, feelings, and actions. Greater harmony in our relationships and our workplace are indications that the "false I" is losing its footing. Greater enjoyment of life and our duties suggests that we are gaining control over the moving mind, that we are letting go of our attachments and learning to *be* and act in the present. The greater love we feel within our being and for those around us, and the resulting contentment and joy are clear indications of the dawn of the true Self. We can be sure, in other words, that if we find ourselves happier, more content, more loving, more giving and forgiving, we are indeed doing the Work.

In chapter eleven of Part One we looked at the Nyaya Ladder, based on logical statements aimed at directing seekers back to their absolute nature. It is useful to look at this inner ladder again in the light of our observations, practices, and insights and consider the seven steps to liberation as a kind of indicator as to our own progress.

The **first step** delineates some of the prerequisites for the path and the need for good actions, the observance of disciplines, and the rising up of "auspicious desire."

The **second step** commends the way of good reflection, good thoughts, and investigation, which lead to conviction.

The **third step** describes the "lessening of outward movement." What this means for us is the waning of inner considering, circling thoughts, negativity, criticism, ill will, all of which, as we have seen, are fueled by identification. Through right action, objective observation, and the practice of meditation, we begin to have glimpses of our true Self and through grace may experience unity between Atman and Paramatman. Through this direct contact and the influx of *sattva*, our being is purified and our nature is gradually transformed. Because we are more unburdened, content, and cheerful, we can serve others and selfless acts become more numerous.

On the **fourth step** — the dawn of the true Self — the force of *sattva* begins to dominate. Desire for sensory pleasure diminishes. We experience a decided change in our long-held beliefs and values. We lose interest in material things and begin to cherish the life in the Spirit. We may experience what is known as the "pull of the Way." Our love of knowledge and devotion to truth is stronger than our personal desires and propels us forward on the quest.

Having arrived on the **fifth step**, we feel a liberation from attachment to the mental and physical body and our possessions, resulting in freedom from suffering and fear. Having had frequent experience of the true Self, we identify less with the not-Self. We are beginning to see the world, things, and people as they truly are. As higher faculties and enlarged perceptions come into play, we enjoy glimpses into Reality and into the essence of things and human beings. We may realize that what we see as the world out there is in fact, a projection of the great Mind and what we experience as "our life" is held within our own consciousness.

The **sixth step** is experienced as the absence of duality. The seeker sees the Self in everyone and everything. With this experience of Oneness the "false I" vanishes and the true Self gains dominion. In this elevated state, also referred to as the state of objective consciousness, the higher centers — higher emotion and higher intellect — awaken in the individual. These extraordinary faculties and powers of perception are acquired through conscious spiritual work, discipline, introspection, and direct experience.

In our present state our task is to endeavor to perform our work in a dispassionate manner, without any notions, attitudes, claims, or motives. Purity of intent and lack of attachment lead to excellence in all our deeds. We shine and prosper through performing our true calling. Because our actions are not fueled by greed, selfishness, or ambition, they engender no further karma. When we begin to see the Self in everything, we no longer feel the sense of separation, hence there is no desire to achieve, to acquire, to possess and to outperform another; we "have it all" — we *are* all.

The **seventh** and final step is full Self-Realization or *turiya*. Although living in the world, aspirants who have reached this goal dwell in a state of pure being and pure bliss. Their individual Self has merged with the Universal Self. They know all there is to know. They are free, perfect, all One.

It is said that, however rare, full realization is possible in one lifetime. In our present vacillating state of consciousness, however, we may feel that we are eons from perfection. But we need to keep in mind that in one sense there is no goal to be achieved. Rather our work is here and now; it is simply this: to wake up, to be aware, to remember the Self, to rest in the present and give our attention fully to the task at hand, and thus in this timeless moment be liberated from all self-concern. It is a matter of conscious engagement in the harmonious and joyful unfolding of our true nature.

Ralph Waldo Emerson understood that what in the end matters most is *how* we live in this world. He expressed the challenge this way: "How to spend a day nobly is the problem to be solved, beside which all the great reforms which are preached seem to me trivial."

MUCH HAS CHANGED since Ralph Waldo Emerson wrote these words, yet today the problem he speaks of remains to be solved. Indeed it has grown more formidable. While trying to secure our right to life, liberty, and the pursuit of happiness, we have forgotten what it means to live in a free, dignified, leisurely, and joyful manner. We think we "have to" do certain things and bemoan that we "don't have time" to do others. We have a strong notion that we lack time and therefore rush to and from work and hurry through mealtime and playtime. Our notions of time, space, and matter have made us into slaves, hungry for ever more time, space, and matter. Propelled by outside influences, we fluctuate between incessant activity and inertia, between *rajas* and *tamas*.

The "examined life" demands that we look at our daily existence in the light of our new understanding of "life, liberty and the pursuit of happiness." We have to find out what it means to *truly live* our lives, to actually live in the present moment, and then to aspire to true freedom and real joy. We need to be aware of a "few great points" that, according to Emerson, "alone need be regarded" whether we live in an idyllic setting, or in the clamor of city life. These, he says, are the only essentials — "the escape from all false ties; courage to be what we are, and love of what is simple and beautiful; independence and cheerful relation; the wish to serve, to add somewhat to the well-being of men."

Being alive in this time and place, we have been given ample opportunity to practice what we are learning and to respond from inner knowing. We are blessed with daily challenges to transcend self-concern and to transform the ordinary and banal into something splendid and sacred. We know, as Emerson did, that all the wisdom of the ages is vain and trivial if we do not truly *live* it and thereby become living symbols of wisdom. All the learning and power we gather on our quest are vain if we do not align conscience with understanding and understanding with responsibility and consistency in action. The opportunities for each one of us are completely different, and to that extent, they are personal. It is up to each of us to discover how to live more wisely, perfectly, and consistently, and how to use our insights and talents to serve the greater good.

L ET US LOOK AT A FEW of the most common challenges that face us. To live our lives in the spirit, we have to be relatively free from false ties, such as social affiliations, beliefs, mores, and opinions. We have to be willing to let go, from moment to moment, of our inner constructs, attitudes, prejudices, likes, and dislikes. Constrictive conditioning and mechanical responses are based on the past. They cannot contribute anything positive to the precious now, nor can they help to solve a problem or clarify a situation that arises in the moment in front of us.

We have to be willing to let go — both intellectually and emotionally — of the false notion of time as linear. Having experienced the eternal now, we realize that it alone is real, is infinite, beyond time and space and is full of creative potential. We have to allow ourselves to open to just *being* rather than always becoming. This new way of being is discovered, as we know, in the practice of resting in the Self while engaged in action, and is based on knowledge and insight gained from observation in the moment of action, meditation, and self-inquiry.

But how, we might ask, can we possibly transcend time while functioning in a technological culture that runs by the clock, is enslaved by time, and even thrives on pressures? Obviously we do have to honor our commitments and arrive at work at the prearranged time. *How* we get there, however, and *how* we engage in the events of space and time, is entirely our prerogative. Our engagement with the world and our experience of it depend entirely on our intent, our state of consciousness, and the quality of attention in the moment of interaction. We have a choice — if we are awake, that is — to rest in the eternal now or the infinite, and, by doing so, be free of the illusion of incremental time and space — unencumbered by duality, and by temporal, linear thinking and doing.

Meister Eckhart speaks to this issue when he says that "people ought not to consider so much what they are to do as what they *are*; let them but *be* good and their ways and deeds will shine brightly. If you are just, your actions will be just too. Do not think that saintliness comes from occupation; it depends rather on what one is."

We aspire to become "universalists" — more global, more holistic, more ecological, and more all-inclusive in our thinking, while at the same time being equally attentive to the minutest detail. H.H. Shantanand Saraswati tells us, "We are surrounded by good influences, but these influences can be gathered only if one is attentive and recognizes them." These beneficent influences come in many forms: good company, a great teacher, the right book, a propitious event, divine grace. When we are attentive, we will be blessed by them, and we will find that we are being showered by love all the time, that we are, in Emerson's words, "embosomed in beauty."

Let us consider a practical approach toward arriving at a more sane level of being in the world. Some people might find it useful to begin by visualizing a more ideal scenario, whatever form this may take, and then steadily taking steps that move them closer to that ideal. Others may want to formulate a clear intent, followed by a strong resolution and implemented with good ideas and actions. Yet others simply follow their heart and their intuitions, walking the way of least resistance without fear and without a specific goal, devoting every action to the Self in all.

Let us take some counsel on equanimity in daily life from one who exemplified the simple life of introspection — Henry David Thoreau: "Let us spend one day as deliberately as Nature, and not be thrown off the track by every nutshell and mosquito's wing that falls on the rails. Let us rise early and fast, or break fast, gently and without perturbation; let company come and let company go....Why should we knock under and go with the stream?"

NOW LET US CONSIDER IN PRACTICAL TERMS HOW WE MIGHT SPEND A DAY NOBLY. The day begins with a healthful, deep sleep. (The quality of sleep is improved with regular practice of meditation and attention in action, the stilling of the moving mind, and the introduction of measure into the waking hours.) The interval between sleep and waking is most precious. In that fleeting moment, you may experience *aham* — "I am" — the unadulterated sense of pure being. With an increase in discernment and awareness, you may be able to stay with this pure feeling of existence — a state beyond naming, claiming, and commenting. Endeavor to remain in it; when thoughts and feelings intrude, let them go. Let the mind be empty and attend to your own Self and rest in its peace.

From this perfect peace and poise, gently rise and perform your morning ablutions. The mind will remain still as long as the attention is directed to the task and the mind is connected to the senses. Endeavor to *listen* to the sound of the water, to *feel* the water on the skin, to *smell* the scent of the soap; in other words, be totally present and enjoy. Be aware of the sacred ritual of cleansing the body. Traditionally the element of water is associated with the sense of taste; on a subtler level it is a form of energy — liquid energy — which is sometimes experienced as the primal force of love. Become aware of the life-giving energy and love and let it cleanse and heal your whole being.

Then, if possible, find a quiet place and read a passage from your favorite sacred text or from Part Two of this book. Listen to every word as it resounds in your mind. It is not important to grasp the meaning of the passage. The practice of listening without analyzing opens up a space in which it is possible to truly hear and then to connect with the truth within yourself; then, the heart is softened and joy and gratitude arise. If for any reason the mind is agitated, read the words aloud and allow your attention to rest in the space where the sound emanates; do not be concerned about understanding the words.

Then sit in a quiet place and meditate. Dedicate this practice to the welfare of the world.

After meditation, dedicate the day and your work to the service of truth, to your Self, and to the Self in all.

With peace in your heart, proceed to perform your tasks. Do them as if for the first time and watch the activity take place with a childlike wonder or with the inquisitiveness of a scientist. Watch the amazing efficiency of the human instrument and marvel at the miracle of life.

When meeting and communicating with family and co-workers, remain resting in the still point. In this way, you will see them as they truly are, in the fullness of their potential. The personal will fade into the background, while you will be less judgmental and more accepting of their peculiarities and will actually see their real needs. Remember the Self in whomever you meet and be open to revelation — the experience of oneness with the person in front of you and the realization that you, the observer, and the observed are one. Try not to recoil from this feeling of unity, but remain with it and rest in it. This unity is the reality; this unity is the only truly sane and healthy state.

As you go about your work and you remember that you have forgotten, recollect. Stop momentarily, if possible; let the agitation in the mind subside. Return to the still point and then proceed from stillness. Do this as often as is necessary and every time you "wake up" from the state of duality.

In the middle of the day, if at all possible, find a quiet place and spend time with your Self, by just *being*, or contemplating, or reading an inspiring text and reflecting on it, for as long as your daily duties allow. Refreshed from this pause and full of fine energy, return to your work.

During the day, keep returning to a state of mindful stillness. Move from stillness, work from stillness, speak from stillness, listen to stillness.

At any time of the day, when the need for rest of body or mind arises, fulfill that need; do not let a sense of duty or the illusion of time overrule that need. Let the break be rich and full — not mindless, not a shutting down, but an opening up to your inner being. If necessary, nourish the body with fresh water and deep breathing. Then rest in your Self.

Whenever there is a transition from one task to another or from job to family activities and a different kind of energy or state of attention is required, use the interval, no matter how brief, to come to stillness and mindful awareness.

Practice stillness of mind during any activity that does not require complete engagement of your mental faculties. Move from stillness whenever you wake up and remember. Then you will discover that it is possible, when walking, to just walk; when sitting, to just sit; when eating, to just eat. By resting in the activity, you will come out refreshed at the end of the activity.

At sundown or whenever possible, meditate. It is the natural thing to do. Of course, there are obstacles and distractions and of course, habit will say there is no time for it. Meditate despite the odds. Eventually those near you will honor your quiet time. Do not fret, however, if for any reason you are prevented from meditating.

Before long, you will develop a deep desire for stillness. Honor this desire — it is an important step in your quest. By practicing recollection regularly during the day, the desire will grow stronger. In time, the desire for stillness will be stronger than the desire for entertainment and excitement.

Evening is the time for leisure, which, depending on your nature, might be study, reading great literature, listening to fine music, or pursuing your vocation, if you are unable to fulfill your true calling in the way you earn your keep. The energy for mindful leisure — for leisure in its true sense — is available when the day is spent in a dignified manner and with measure.

By remembering the Self on a regular basis, by resting more often in the present, by watching the activity take place from stillness, by meditating and recollecting, you will find that time expands. Although you are not looking for results, you will find that more time and energy are available for leisure, for enjoying and practicing your true calling, and for just *being*. There will be energy to play joyfully, to paint, to sing, to make music, to dance, to laugh, to enjoy nature, and to contemplate.

If you are so inclined, keep a journal in which you enter insights based on observation. These insights, it is important to remember, are about your inner world. This form of introspection is not a matter of going over situations, nor is it a chatty memoir. Only take note of your *realizations* — the moments in which the naked truth was seen, such as a reaction of the ego, identification with the body or an object, a selfish desire, an automatic response. Do this with a scientific objectivity, without regret, remorse, or guilt

Before going to bed, recollect and say, "So be it!" Forgive and forget. Give up the day, the actions and the fruits of the actions without judgment of their merit and without remorse or claim. Surrender everything — good and bad — to the One Self. You have seen by now that there is no value in going over past events, that this is a self-indulgence which ends in regret and guilt. Instead simply resolve to be more wakeful.

Then rest. Allow the breath to become deep and the mind to become still. Allow your consciousness to merge with universal consciousness, allow your being to merge with universal being and allow your joy and happiness to merge with divine bliss.

✳

SPIRITUAL PRACTICES

W E HAVE ALREADY CONSIDERED many spiritual practices, some of which require specifically allotted time, such as meditation, reflection, recollection, and study. Of these, meditation is the most essential for the modern seeker. It provides the spiritual replenishment we so sorely need in our busy lives and strengthens the memory of the true Self. Living harmoniously in the world without such support is extremely exhausting, if not impossible. Meditation deepens our appreciation of our true essence, of stillness and surrender. Dilligent practice of meditation will support all the other practices that are essential to waking up.

There are many other spiritual practices that require little time and are particularly beneficial for the busy householder. Some of these can be practiced inconspicuously at the workplace, in company and on the way to work, while others require a little leisure and privacy. We shall look at some of these more closely in this chapter.

As for additional sources for spiritual practices, there are many wonderful books currently available which interpret teachings from different traditions and show how they can be made practical, indicating, for example, how to work in a "sacred way" in a given profession, craft, or art. Some of these texts are based on the principles of Zen Buddhism as they apply to practical aspects of daily living — breathing, walking, and working — and performing all such actions with mindfulness. A useful text for the modern contemplative life in the Christian tradition, *Finding God Wherever You Are* — edited by Joseph F. Power, O.S.F.S. — contains detailed spiritual practices from the writings of the French mystic St. Francis de Sales. The many volumes of *The Notebooks of Paul Brunton* also contain a number of useful spiritual practices suited to the modern seeker.

There are also innumerable texts on visualization, an effective practice for the healing of mind and body. Serious seekers have many choices and will not be at a loss in finding a helpful text on spiritual practices in their favorite tradition, suited to their particular temperament, and in a specific practical application or area of interest. For those in need of a fresh impulse and the support of a group, a weekend or week-long retreat is a wonderful introduction to a specific practice, including meditation.

A word of warning may be in order, however. The marketplace is full of "feel-good" books filled with suggestions designed to help us appreciate ordinary experience, the beauty of nature, or the simple joys of life. These should not be confused with spiritual practices for the serious seeker, which are designed to act directly upon the being and consciousness of the individual. Although they may bring about a lasting appreciation of beauty, harmony, and simplicity, these outer benefits are nothing more than the by-products of the real inner Work.

Spiritual practices are most valuable when they effectively work on all the bodies and all the centers at the same time. However, some practices that target one level will often have beneficial effects on another. Hence, attentive, rigorous physical work will lead to a still mind, healthy body, and endurance, while these capacities in turn will support study, detachment, attention, and meditation. We can be sure that we have found the right spiritual practice and are applying it properly when we become more natural, more intuitive, more conscious, more energetic, and, most of all, when we experience renewed joy in the unfolding of our soul nature. It is important to avoid setting goals we cannot achieve. We have to remember that in spiritual work there is nothing to achieve; hence there is no failure. All practices are designed to help us let go of what is not-Self and grow into what we already are but have forgotten.

*

EXERCISES

1
CONSCIOUS LISTENING
AND SPEAKING

ONE OF THE SIMPLEST WAYS to purify our instrument on all levels is conscious listening — listening to the sound of our own voice, attentive listening to the voice of another, and listening to the silence beyond the sound. In everyday life, most of us use the voice in an unconscious, undeliberate manner, unaware of the power of its sound on ourselves and on others. Our speech is at best utilitarian; we use it to convey information, to exchange ideas, to banter, to tell stories, and at times to talk to ourselves. We have lost the art of true conversation and refined articulation and of real communication and real listening.

The sounds we produce are our most revealing traits. The sound of our voice not only contains information about the level of our present state of being, but also reveals a great deal of our past conditioning and our mental and psychological burdens. Emerson acknowledged this truth when he wrote in his essay on Swedenborg that "the angels, from the sound of the voice, know a man's love; from the articulation of the sound, his wisdom; and from the sense of the words, his science."

As spiritual beings, we can consciously develop our ability to truly listen and thereby gain insight into another person's disposition. A voice cannot be disguised easily; through attentive listening, we can know what lies beyond the words, beyond the meaning, and can thereby respond to the real question and the real need.

Voices have color, timber, pitch. We find it easy to identify a person's voice over the phone. Even computers have voice-recognition capabilities. We all know the difference between a pleasant, soothing voice and one that is unpleasant, enervating, and even physically painful to listen to. The former is like music to our ears and evokes love in us. The latter betrays the residue of past actions, suffering, and pain. This extraneous material covers over the pure, natural sound of a voice, and it perpetuates its psychic burden through the speaker's continual exposure to this impure sound. As we all know, sound has the power to unnerve, to drag down and destroy; a harsh, cold, or grinding sound begets discord, bad feelings, and anger. On the positive side, the voice has the power to create, invoke, and purify. A pure, unadulterated sound is cleansing and healing. The voice is a very powerful tool, and, if used consciously, will be of immeasurable help in dismantling the constructs of the ego and shedding compulsions, tendencies, and attitudes.

The voice may be purified in two ways: passively, by the practice of listening to the sound of our own voice, or actively, by the practice of sounding — vocalizing, chanting, and singing. The effects of these practices are both instantaneous, in changing our state of consciousness, and cumulative, in purifying the mind and heart.

Listening to the Sound of Your Own Voice

WHENEVER YOU SPEAK, ENDEAVOR TO LISTEN attentively to the sound of your own voice. When you become conscious that your attention has faltered, simply allow your listening to again rest on the words as they emerge from your throat. There is no need to correct or manipulate the voice in any. The refinement takes place by itself and on many levels over which you have no control in any case.

You will find that the most obvious effects will include the increase in the voice's clarity, a sense of heightened consciousness, a feeling of being more centered, and a decrease in the belief that you are the voice or the speaker. You may enjoy other benefits, such as a sense of wholeness, greater mental clarity, and physical energy. You may notice that when the harshness and excessive force in your voice diminish, those around you will respond more positively and will be more happy and content.

Although the principle of this practice is extremely simple, it is not necessarily easy to carry out. Above all it requires that you remember to listen, and this takes wakefulness and perseverance. You will find that it takes effort to stay with the listening, especially when you are in company, because of old habits and because of the fact that identification happens in an instant. But the effort is well worth it, because it opens a new world of insight. The practice may feel strange at first, but in time it will feel completely natural.

Old habits tend to leave more easily when there is insight into the condition and when we acknowledge that most of the time we do not listen to what we say. Sometimes we do not even remember what we said five minutes ago — a fact that proves quite clearly that we did not hear what we said. Often our comments tumble out unconsciously or rush forth in an uncontrollable stream. The mental state associated with nonlistening is invariably one of identification — often with the person to whom we are speaking. Identification takes us out of ourselves. When we are scattered and no longer in the present, the ego takes center stage. The ego is mostly concerned with the impressions it creates; it just wants to be heard and is not at all interested in real communication. When we are lost in this pathological state, we cannot hear ourselves, nor can we listen to another. The most we can do is pontificate.

As we practice listening to our own voice, our instrument is refined on all levels. The sound of our voice becomes purer, lighter, more melodious. As we become unburdened of our own baggage, we are more able to listen to others and give attention to their needs.

Listening to Another

WHEN IN COMPANY, ENDEAVOR TO LISTEN attentively to the sound of the voice of the person in front of you. The Eastern tradition says that whatever or whoever is in front of you is your teacher — be it a thing, a situation, a person, or a child. Since the person in front of you is your teacher, it behooves you to listen attentively. Listen with care and interest and without inner comments, grasping, or criticism.

Listening to others, as we all know, is as much of a challenge as listening to the sound of our own voice. As we become more observant, we will realize that we hear only half of what is being said; we often latch on to words and ideas and then take off on a mental journey, putting on our own personal spin, before the speaker has come to the point. We then miss the essence of the conversation. The words have fallen on deaf ears, and we have not learned anything about the person we are conversing with.

On the other hand, when we truly listen to the sound of another person's voice, we are opening up space and stillness in which the harmonious unfoldment of real understanding can take place. Attentive listening is a precious gift because it nourishes and heals and opens a channel for the flow of love and compassion. When we listen attentively, we may actually be able to understand the person's true motive and then can respond to that deeper concern or need. Very often a person needs nothing other than fine attention and the nourishment that comes from it, or a neutral space in which their own thoughts and problems can be heard.

Listening to the Silence Beyond the Sound

LISTENING TO THE SILENCE BEYOND the sound is a deeper level of listening and a further refinement of the practice of attention. In speaking, singing, or listening to external sounds, allow your attention to rest in the silence from which the vibration arises — or, if you prefer, allow your listening to rest in the silence of infinite consciousness. While remaining aware of sound, listen to the silence beyond and between the sounds. Attend to this silence from which all sound emerges and into which it merges again. This attentive listening will bring you into a neutral state in which the ego vanishes. At this point the human instrument is unimpeded by the past, making this is an optimal state — a state of presence, aliveness, and enhanced perception.

At first, it is best to practice this "passive" listening to the silence beyond as we read aloud, sing, play a musical instrument, or listen to music such as Gregorian chant, Mozart, Handel, Bach, Beethoven, Brahms, or Vivaldi. The mind and emotions are then bathed in the beauty and harmony of pure sounds unimpeded by mental discourse, analyzing, or grasping. When the ego as listener gets out of the way, we are totally open, and the sounds can go straight to the heart and accomplish what they are designed to do: heal, harmonize, and spiritualize our being.

After a certain point, we can then practice this deeper listening when engaged in conversation with others. It will give us insight into their needs, fears, and attachments; at times, we may be given a glimpse into the essential nature of the person in front of us. When we know and understand, we can be of real help. The other person may also make contact with the silence and have a glimpse of the unity of the One Self. When we practice this deeper listening in a larger gathering of people, it will not only reveal the essence and dynamics of what is going on, but will also bring clarity and order into the conversation while enabling us to remain aware of the love and goodness beyond.

Purifying the Voice

A MORE ACTIVE WAY OF PURIFYING our inner and outer instrument, particularly the speaking voice, is to practice reciting, sounding, or vocalizing. Sounding without any specific goal in mind is particularly conducive to the release of minor psychological afflictions and negative conditioning, especially inhibitions relating to our voice. Because of our conditioning, many of us are afraid to sing and speak; we may have been discouraged early on in this regard — discouraged from expressing joy or expressing feelings of frustration, fear, or anger. We were taught not to vocalize our feelings and then became afraid to speak for fear of exposing ourselves. This holding back, whether conscious or unconscious, hardens the heart and the throat, and makes the voice choked and strained. Our natural voice — our true sound — is then lost.

Luckily, we can recover our true sound, or at least elicit a purer sound in our voice. A pure sound is one that is untainted, unadorned, and unadulterated. A perfectly pure sound is one which manifests light, clarity, beauty, and harmony and embodies the entire spectrum of the subtle elements of ether, air, fire, water, and earth.

In practical terms: Find a quiet, private place. Sit or stand with spine erect. Take some deep breaths, allowing the belly to relax and the diaphragm to expand and contract in a natural rhythm. When the body and mind are at rest, open the mouth by letting the chin drop. There should be no strain in the jaw. Breathe in; on the outbreath sound a long A (as in "far") on a comfortable note, all the way to the end of the breath. Try to listen to the sound from beginning to end, without comment and without trying to manipulate the sound. You will notice that after doing this repeatedly, the extraneous gravelly noises diminish. When the sound is reasonably clear, sound a long E (as in "peace") while the throat and palate remain open; then sound a long U (as in "boot") by forming a tiny circle with the lips, while the throat and palate remain open, following the same instructions as above.

Then repeat the same practice while being aware of the subtle qualities of sound as they relate to the subtle elements: ether (audibility), air (fullness, firmness), fire (brightness), water (sweetness), and earth (freshness). In other words, listen *for* these subtle qualities in the sounds. Through this attentive listening, your voice will naturally manifest such qualities as fullness, brightness, and sweetness.

As your voice becomes more refined, you will also begin to experience the effects of the elemental qualities of the sound in your various centers. You will notice that you yourself feel brighter, firmer, fuller, sweeter, and fresher. With regular practice, these subtle qualities will enter your speech, which in turn will become more natural, harmonious, and delightful. Not only will communication improve, but both you and the people you talk with will be refreshed and nourished by the natural and delightful sound of your voice.

At any time of the day, when you notice that the instrument is agitated or tired, or when you are in need of an extra boost of energy, while driving, walking, studying, etc. practice sounding the vowels A, E, and U. This will help to dispel the fog in the mind and will protect you from succumbing to the force of *tamas*. You can even do this silently: sound a vowel in your mind and hear it with your inner listening. Another excellent time for sounding is just before the practice of meditation, since it helps to still the mind and harmonize the mind and body.

When practicing sounding make sure the spine is erect, the body at ease and the chest held high so that the sounds can vibrate throughout the body. You may want to study the effects of sounding the vowels A, E, I, O, and U on your instrument more closely and observe in which physical location or which center they resonate. In her inspiring and informative book *Chant*, Katharine Le Mée gives insight into the subject as she points out that "it is easy to verify that U resonates at the base of the spine: O, in the belly; A, in the chest or heart; E, in the throat, I, in the middle of the forehead, so that U and O are connected with the active principle, A, with the emotional, I with the intellectual, and E participates in both intellectual and emotional. Thus these vowels have the power to tune these principles and the organs connected with them."

Do this practice every day, if possible, or whenever you feel the need for a "tune-up."

2
CHANTING, SINGING, RECITING

WE HAVE ALL EXPERIENCED THE wide-ranging effects that sound, particularly music, has on the human instrument and society at large. Musical trends have helped to usher in great changes in the attitudes and mores of a nation. It is easy to see that *rajasic* music has the power to rouse, incite, and mobilize, *tamasic* music keeps us in sleep, delusion, and darkness with its mindless, mechanical repetitiveness, while *sattvic* music, with its harmony and beauty, can elevate us into levels of the sublime.

Sound and music activate one or more of the three centers of the human instrument. Some music, such as that of Vivaldi and Bach, is more cerebral, activating the intellectual center; other types, like Gregorian chant, goes straight to the heart, vibrating in the emotional center, while the beats of rock activate the moving center and the lower, automatic drives.

The music of Mozart is unique in that it has the power to balance our whole instrument and, according to Le Mée, "seems to provide food for all three principles." Mozart not only lifts us into the realm of the sublime to activate the higher emotions, but, as research shows, it also improves our powers of attention, thinking, and memory. Because it nourishes and harmonizes the entire instrument, Mozart's music, like Gregorian chant, increases our healing potential.

Chanting or even listening to chanting has a profoundly harmonizing effect on the mind, body, and soul. Gregorian chant, according to Le Mée, is "a conscious musical form designed to ennoble singer and listener through its intrinsic beauty, its wholeness, and the immediacy of its performance." Its sublimity and its power to bring us in touch with our ground of being have been rediscovered and is once again appreciated by the many. Its recent popularity attests to the immense need in the modern human being for spiritual nourishment and healing on all levels. Similarly, the divinely inspired hymns of Hildegard of Bingen have found a renewed interest in recent years; her sublime devotional songs are again being appreciated both by performers and by a devout audience of listeners.

Anyone who has sung in a choir has most likely experienced one or more of the strong emotions that this communal activity often elicits — an opening of the heart, awakening of devotion, a feeling of unity, happiness, or even bliss. The ethereal, omnipresent quality of sound naturally connects the singers, the sound of their voices, and their listening, enveloping all into one perfect unity. At such moments the feeling of duality momentarily vanishes; then there is only one sound, one voice, one harmonious vibration, emanating from one source.

Although singing or chanting in a communal setting is extremely helpful, chanting hymns or mantras in solitude is no less potent if it is done with devotion and attention. The ancient Wisdom tradition is a wonderful source for hymns, invocations, and proclamations, some of which are designed to raise consciousness and spark the fire of inner knowledge. The *Rig-Veda* or "Hymn of Creation," for example, not only appeals to our sensibilities in its timelessness and poetic beauty, but, if sounded with attention, actually transmits the consciousness and wisdom of its creators. The verses of the *Bhagavad Gita* or "Celestial Song" — a beautiful composition of spiritual instructions — have, even in translation, a luminous power to enlighten and transform the reader. There are also numerous verses, hymns, and affirmations in the Vedas, Upanishads, the Song of Solomon, the Psalms, Christian devotional music, and chants.

The reciting or chanting of *sutras* (aphorisms) and *slokas* (hymns or verses of praise) is an ancient and very powerful method for dispelling ignorance and attachments and for purifying, healing, and aligning our instrument. Much like in the practice of *japa,* they can be spoken silently, whispered, recited or chanted. These *sutras* and *slokas* contain spiritual truths and were composed by ancient seers in praise of the universal Self and its manifestation. They are designed to bring us to the realization of our divine nature and eventually to union with Paramatman.

Purifying the Instrument by Chanting

FIND A QUIET SPACE where you will not be disturbed. Sit or stand with spine erect, chest and head held high. Watch the breath become slower and deeper. Open the listening to include the farthest sound and then allow it to rest in to the stillness beyond sound.

Take some deep breaths, letting the diaphragm expand and contract. When the body and mind are at rest, open the mouth by letting the chin drop. There should be no strain. You may want to stretch the jaw if it feels tight.

Then inhale and, as you exhale gently, sound a long A (*ah* as in "father") on a comfortable and pleasant note. Listen attentively to the sound from the beginning to the end of each breath as you repeat the sound several times. Do not comment on the quality of the sound; simply attend and allow any fatigue, negativity, or anxiety to be carried away on each exhalation. As you let go of all sense of doing, the extraneous sounds will automatically diminish and a purer and fresher sound will emerge. The sound A carries *sattva,* leading to well-being, harmony, knowledge, and enlightenment.

Then, with lips puckered, sound a long U (*oo* as in "boot") on the outbreath. The throat and palette remain open, as if sounding A, and the listening equally attends to the subtle sound A, which is present in every sound and is always sounding throughout creation. The sound U carries *rajas*; hence it excites, begets desire, and results in action, striving, and passion.

On the next exhalation, with lips closed and throat and palette open, sound a long M while continuing to listen to the subtle *A,* which is always sounding. Repeat the M several times to the end of each exhalation. Feel the humming resonate in your chest and head, opening up the sinus cavities. The sound M carries *tamas,* leading to darkness, inaction, slumber. In this case it brings closure to the mantra.

Notice the different effects of the three sounds on your thinking, feeling, and moving centers. Also note that the level of attention influences both the sound and the length of breath. By attentive listening from the beginning to the end of each sound, or, alternatively, to the silence beyond the sound, the sound becomes purer and the breath fuller and longer. Make sure the spine is straight and the torso relaxed so that the sounds can resonate throughout the body and head.

When the three sounds are reasonably pure, the mind still and the body at ease, sound them together, chanting AUM on one continuous exhalation. Again the throat, palette, and jaw remain open throughout the sounding. The only thing that moves are the lips; they form a circle, which gets smaller and smaller until they come together, relaxing in the M. Endeavor throughout to listen to the ever-sounding A. The individual sounds of the mantra, also known as OM, have a natural measure — approximately 8-4-2 — which should be carefully observed. It sounds somewhat like "aaaaaaaa-oooo-mm," except that the sounds flow on one continuous exhalation and without any noticeable transitions. The cavity of the mouth, being in the open position, and the gradual closing of the lips automatically create the proper sound.

All audible sounds — from guttural to labial — are given distinctive form in the cavity of the mouth, starting at the root of the tongue and ending in the lips, with the exception of A, which is not modulated in any way. The sacred Sanskrit mantra AUM — as it may be pronounced in relative existence — is said to be a symbol of all possible sounds. It begins in A, the purest and least "differentiated" of all sounds, is compelled forward by the U, symbolizing the unfoldment of creation, and finds closure in the last of the Sanskrit labials, M. If properly pronounced, said Swami Vivekananda, "this OM will represent the whole phenomenon of sound production, and no other word can do this."

Eastern tradition says that OM is the symbol of all symbols and that this Logos connects the individual Self with the Universal Self. The mystical word OM *is* the Absolute and by meditating upon it we may realize that which it symbolizes. By his Logos — the sounding of OM — the whole creation is said to be brought into existence, maintained, and brought to a close at the end of a *yuga* or great cycle, when the manifest creation is once again withdrawn.

Choosing a Method and Text for Purifying the Instrument

IF YOU ARE SO INCLINED, join a choir or sing in a small group; if this is not feasible, sing, chant or recite in solitude.

If you prefer chanting or reciting, select one of the invocations, hymns, or aphorisms in Part Two or find a brief verse in your favorite tradition. Some of the Vedic hymns are available in bilingual English-Sanskrit texts as well as in phonetic transliterations. Reciting or chanting *sutras* or *slokas* in Sanskrit is even more powerful, since these pure sounds are imbued with the wisdom and consciousness of an ancient sacred tradition. In addition, the words are not "loaded" with associations, so their sound can penetrate and heal, unimpeded by the discursive mind.

Write the text on a piece of paper or in your journal. Sit in a quiet room as you would for meditation. Rest in the awareness of your Self. When the mind is still, begin reciting or chanting the invocation or aphorism. Listen attentively to each repetition. There is no need to grasp the meaning; the sounds do the work and will gradually uproot the impurities in the *antahkarana* and purify the heart and mind. With perseverance, the profundity of the sacred verse will illumine the conscious mind, strengthen the intellect, and reawaken the memory of truth. When the inner knowing and intellect are thus illumined, the darkness and misery depart, and with it the dominance of the false ego.

Here are a few examples of some of the most beloved and powerful invocations:

I am the Self, and my nature is pure consciousness.

I am the home of the spirit,
the continual source
of immortality,
of eternal righteousness
and of infinite joy.

Sat-chit-ananda
Soham! Soham!
(Being-consciousness-bliss Absolute. I am He! I am He!)
Holy, holy, holy is the Lord of hosts;
the whole earth is full of his glory.

Truth is the Self;
the not-Self is untruth.
Self is not born and does not die.
Out of Self comes the breath
which is the life of all things.

I am without attributes and action,
eternal and pure, free from stain and desire,
changeless and formless,
and always free.

That is perfect. This is perfect. Perfect comes from perfect.
Take perfect from perfect, the remainder is perfect.

OM
He who is the splendor of the sun
Shines in my mind as my Self.
He is infinite. He is my "I."
He is truth. He is All.
OM

Recite or chant these or any other invocations in Part Two as often as possible in the morning and in the evening before going to sleep.

Rather than repeating an invocation or an aphorism aloud, you may also hold it in your mind; that is, you state the spiritual truth clearly and then reflect on the words with a silent mind. This is a powerful means for stilling the mind and dispelling ignorance. The phrases should be terse, for example, "Thou art That," "Be still and know that I am God," "I am that I am," "The Self is everywhere," or "Whatever lives is full of the Lord."

*

3
RECOLLECTION AND DEDICATION

A VERY EFFECTIVE WAY OF BRINGING SANITY and tranquillity into our daily activities is through the practice of recollection. In the course of a busy day we tend to scatter ourselves mentally, emotionally, and physically. The precariousness of our condition comes to light in many colloquialisms, when we say, for example, that our "heads are spinning," that we are "scatterbrained," "strung out," or "spread thin," that we are "torn" and "pushed" and "pulled," causing us to "lose our head" and consequently to "lose heart."

Usually this tendency to become scattered does not result from external influences, as we may believe, but rather from a tendency toward false identification with whatever presents itself to our perception. When we say that we feel "strung out," we are giving expression to reality. We are quite literally tied by invisible, sticky threads or tentacles to every activity and encounter that has taken place before. We are attached — mentally, emotionally, and physically — and we relive encounters and conversations over and over again, or we are left reeling hours after an intense or impassioned activity. At other times, when we shift from a mental task to a physical activity, or vice versa, we tend to carry on in the same mode or speed, that is, we are "stuck" to an energetic mode that may be totally unsuitable to the task at hand. All this residue — the sticky "stuff" of identification and attachment — prevents us from being in the now and enjoying the present activity, while costing us an enormous amount of energy.

There is a simple and effective remedy to put an end to this scattered state and the misuse of energy: the practice of recollection and dedication.

Every time you remember or observe confusion, stop what you are doing and recollect, that is, recollect your faculties, or, if you will, come to your senses! Open your listening to the farthest sound. Feel the weight of the body on the chair and the feet on the ground. Let go! Then withdraw the senses from their entanglements with sense objects; withdraw the mind and heart from their attachments and identification with doing, thinking, and feeling. Give it all up! Offer it all up to the One Self. Then rest in the stillness of being — in the presence of your true Self. In this way you are cleansed of your past deeds.

Recollect before beginning your next task and dedicate what lies before you to the One Self. You may want to articulate your own dedication or use one of the following, mentally saying these words: "I dedicate what lies before me to the One Self" or "O Thou Lord Supreme, I bow down to Thee!" or "Keep thou silence at the presence of the Lord." By acknowledging the source of being and dedicating the actions you are about to engage in to the One Self, you are guarded from false claims, from attachment to the activity, and the accumulation of inappropriate energy.

Whenever you remember, whenever possible, or whenever in doubt, recollect!

Do this *between* each task or activity — in the intervals between work and leisure, between cooking and eating, between planning and meetings. Stop momentarily, sit if you can, and let the energy from the previous activity subside. If necessary, remind yourself: "I am not this body or this mind or this activity." Recollect whenever agitation arises *during* an activity, or when the energy is seen to be inappropriate to the task. Enjoy the pure sense of being, the stillness and refreshment, each time you let go of the sense of doing and come to the realization of your true Self. Remember to recollect and dedicate your activities as the first thing in the morning and the last thing at night.

*

4
DEEP REST

THERE ARE TIMES IN LIFE WHEN WE FEEL that we have come to the end of our rope. We find it almost impossible to cope with the pressures of life and feel crushed by seemingly unbearable situations or disheartened by the sense of never catching up. We may even be exhausted from trying — yet never succeeding — to carve out enough time for introspection, reflection, and peace. We may even be too tired or agitated to make the effort to sit and meditate.

When the whole body-mind mechanism is in overdrive, yet at the same time depleted by tension, we may require more than a brief practice of recollection. At such times, we need to rest more deeply and restore balance to all three bodies or levels — gross, subtle and causal. In actuality, as we will discover, we can really only "work" directly on the subtle body — the seat of the psyche.

Most of us have probably already discovered that rest and nourishment at the deepest level can never be achieved by artificial methods, such as drugs, escape, or amusements. There is only one solution to finding and experiencing genuine rest and peace and avert insanity. This is a spiritual solution, which is to return to our ground of being — to the source of infinite potential and nourishment. This periodic influx of fine energy — *sattva* — is essential to breaking the vicious cycle of action and reaction — *rajas* and *tamas* — and restoring balance to our being.

The practice of deep rest is similar to the practice of recollection. However, it aims to go deeper and it is therefore imperative to find a quiet room where you will be undisturbed for at least fifteen to thirty minutes.

To familiarize yourself with the directions, you may either commit them to memory or speak them on tape, allowing a minute of silence after each direction.

In practicl terms: Sit in a comfortable chair or on a meditation bench or pillow. Alternatively, if the body is extremely tired, lie on your back on a carpet or yoga mat, with your arms slightly separated from the body and with palms facing up and the legs about one to two feet apart. Take a few deep abdominal breaths and then simply watch the breath as it finds its own rhythm.

Become aware of the weight of your physical body. With each exhalation let go of any tensions. Let go until all the weight rests evenly. Now let your whole attention go to every part of your body — the head, neck, shoulders, chest, abdomen, legs, feet, arms, and hands. Now become aware of the body as a whole. Feel it, and stay with that feeling for as long as comfortable. When you become aware of thoughts, let them go and bring your attention back to the body. Notice the sensations — perhaps an involuntary movement, a tingling in the limbs, a feeling of warmth as the body comes alive with the increased flow of vital energy. Enjoy the sense of wholeness and well-being. Your body is the abode of your spirit — a gift for your use. Let your love and attention flow to all of its organs which day after day quietly perform their duty. You may feel a deep sense of gratitude.

When the body is at rest, gently let your attention move from the physical to the subtle body, where everything comes together and is experienced as self-awareness, feeling, thought, and understanding. Rest your attention in this subtle body, which is much finer and much more expansive than your physical body. Endeavor to let go of all thoughts about the day's events, about yourself, about your actions. Let go of all emotional residue — of guilt, regret, resentment. Offer it all up to the One Self. Come to rest in the present moment and watch vigilantly as the turbulence of random thoughts and feelings fades away. Stay watchful even as you enjoy a feeling of freedom which arises in the absence of attachment. Know that this feeling of freedom, ease, and contentment is the natural state of the psyche.

Next become aware of the causal level, the source of your being. Know that in reality you are not your body, your faculties, or any of your attributes. In fact you have nothing you can call your own. Know that it all belongs to the One Supreme Self and that you are wholly dependent on That. Abide in this knowledge, hold this truth in your mind and heart in an attitude of humble waiting. If at any time the mind interferes with the contemplation of the one reality, you may want to sound your mantra or the primordial sound AUM (aaaaaaaa-oooo-mm) a few times, letting it resonate through your being. Then let go of all sense of separate identity and dive deeply into the depth of your true essence — pure being, consciousness, and bliss.

It is possible during this deep contemplation to fall into deep sleep, which may be the level of spiritual renewal needed at a particular time or in certain circumstances. Deep rest may also be practiced every night before going to sleep, but should not be considered as a substitute for meditation.

Rest at the deepest level occurs when through grace and effort the higher emotions are kindled and the illuminated *buddhi* makes contact with the source. Then the *atman* reveals its splendor and is experienced in the subtle and physical bodies as perfect stillness, unbounded joy and lightness, or absolute certainty of the one supreme Reality.

*

5
REMEMBERING THE SELF

THE PRACTICE OF REMEMBERING the Self is essential on the path to freedom from illusion. When we do not remember who we are, we remain asleep in the cocoon of ego consciousness, imprisoned in a private world. The practice consists of being aware of your own true nature — the Self or the Witness — with ever-increasing frequency throughout the day. Everything you do, feel, and say is referred to the Witness — that which is beyond doing, thinking, and feeling. The questions that elicit self-referral are, for example, "Who am 'I'?" "Who is doing the looking, talking, feeling, acting?" "Who is the perceiver?" "Who is the experiencer?" In this way, ego consciousness — the sense of a separate, personal reality — is called into question. This form of Self-inquiry takes you to the knowledge that the Self alone perceives. Sometimes it will raise you momentarily into the experience of the Witness. At other times, and with practice, it will become possible to remember the Self for extended periods of time.

As you perceive through this wider lens more and more often, you will begin to know and understand the larger picture, lit by a brighter beam of consciousness. From this greater Self-awareness you will be able to study the workings of your instrument more objectively. You may even be amused when you detect the willful vying for recognition of the many false notions and personalities that claim to be "I." You will be able to more clearly discern the contradictions of the ego and any inconsistency between thought and action.

In the light of greater Self-awareness you will begin to see the desires or compulsions that spawn the actions and the motives that fuel the deeds and can get to the bottom of the incessant need to achieve. With greater stillness, you may even catch the faint stirrings of a feeling as it arises in your awareness and through the power of observation, neutralize it, before it attaches itself to any particular idea and develops into a full-blown desire. Through the faculty of discrimination, in the light of remembering, you will be able to discern the Self from the not-Self, the eternal from the temporal, reality from illusion, and truth from untruth.

Whenever you remember, ask yourself: "What brought this action forth?" Inquire into the desire or motive.

Ask yourself: "What forces am I feeding?" Inquire into the nature of what you are giving power to — to *rajas*, *tamas*, or *sattva*; to the physical or the spiritual; to demonic or divine forces; to the ego or the Self.

Ask yourself: "What am I honoring or worshiping?" Inquire into what it is that you admire, what it is you love the most and give your time to. Do you honor the eternal or passing pleasures?

Be gentle in this process. Regard all your findings with the greatest objectivity, patience, and humor. Be honest with yourself, but do not indulge in criticism or commentary. You are *not* these findings. Just acknowledge them and then simply surrender them. Remember, you are the Self!

6
REMEMBERING THE SUPREME SELF

THE FIRST STANZA OF THE *Eesha Upanishad* says that "whatever lives is full of the Lord." If we truly comprehended this one truth and fully realized it in our being, we would not need to seek any further knowledge. We would then be aware at all times that all — both what we see and do not see — is indeed the Supreme Self — that which gives life and ensouls all forms, animate and inanimate, all creatures and all human beings. We would see God in everything and everyone. We would then live in the consciousness that "I myself am He," or "*Aham Brahman,*" or "I am the boundless divine," or "*Tat tvam asi.*"

All these ecstatic exclamations of the great sages, as well as all the mantras and *slokas,* have been used by aspirants as reminders of their true nature. They have been chanted in order to bring about ecstatic states. All practices and disciplines are designed to lead us to this one realization, whether we call it absolute reality or union with Brahman — "That I am."

As long as we are living in ego consciousness, we cannot say "I am God," since that would not be truthful. But we can have brief glimpses of the state of consciousness expressed in these revelatory outpourings, which, in the fully realized being, is permanently established as identity with the Godhead. We may experience momentary union with the divine through devotion, concentration, or grace, and remember and realize this Unity in our hearts and mind and eventually bring the remembrance and realization into our everyday consciousness.

We can also reinforce this recollection with the ancient spiritual practice of "covering everything with the name of the Lord." This deliberate calling into mind and referring everything we see to the Supreme Self, if done with attention and devotion, has the power to dispel our illusion of duality. It can lift us from our sensual clinging to phenomena to supramental knowledge of the laws underlying all phenomena.

In the midst of multiplicity, we forget very quickly that there is only One. Therefore we have to summon all our faculties to help us remember that "all activity arises in the Absolute, is sustained by the Absolute, and merges back into the Absolute." This is an observable law that we can ascertain by the powers of the intellect and the light of consciousness. We endeavor to remember throughout our waking hours that God or the supreme consciousness is everywhere and in everything, and that all our knowing, being, and doing arises in that one consciousness.

By inwardly sounding or chanting a sacred affirmation, such as "The Self is everywhere" or "All is One" or "I am that infinite consciousness," we create a harmony — a song in our soul — that can enable our individual Self to cling like a lover to the universal Self. Then our faculties are in perfect tune with a greater harmony and can serve with love and attention. Having had a taste of freedom from illusion, we know that it is desirable and attainable. Then, even as householders in the midst of our busy lives, we will enjoy greater harmony, love, poise, and peace.

In practical terms: At any time and whenever possible, recollect and come to rest in the awareness of your Self. Enjoy the stillness. Then mentally say the words: "All activity arises in the Absolute, is sustained by the Absolute, and comes to rest in the Absolute." Reflect on this sacred truth with your whole intelligence and acknowledge this wisdom in your heart and soul.

Having thus reflected, turn your attention outward. Look about you, staying connected with your inner knowing, and look upon the trees, the birds, the sun, the dew on the grass as the Absolute. Look upon the whole visible and invisible creation and all the creatures in it as the Absolute. Look upon whatever lives — yourself, your children, your parents, your spouse, your neighbor — as the Absolute.

As you go about your affairs, remember that whatever you hear, see, touch, feel, is a manifestation of the Supreme Self. Remember that there is only one mind, one consciousness and one Self. Remember that the whole universe and everything in it is nothing other than consciousness in motion — a projection of Divine Consciousness. Whenever you remember, acknowledge these truths in your mind.

Another way to remember the Supreme Self and realize oneness is to do *japa*. This can be done as you go about your daily affairs, as long as your attention is not required for a mental task. Allow any of the following illumined words to reverberate in your being:

The Self is everywhere.

The Self is One and indivisible.

All is Self.

Whatever lives is full of the Lord.

Brahman is all — this universe and every creature.

Om tat sat. Om (Om represents the divine; *tat* stands for the inexpressible aspect of the Absolute One; *sat* signifies being or reality).

Sarvam idam Brahma (All this [visible universe] is the Divine).

God is verily all This.

GLOSSARY OF SANSKRIT TERMS

Advaita—Nonduality.

Advaita Vedanta—The philosophy of nondualistic Vedanta, teaching the oneness of God, soul and creation. Its chief exponent was **Shankaracharya**.

aham—"I am." The feeling of existence.

aham Brahmasmi—"I am Brahman," the Transcendent Reality.

ahamkara—Ego. The sense of separate identity. Consciousness of self. One of the functions of the inner organ (see **antahkarana**).

ananda—Bliss.

anandamayakosha—The sheath of bliss (see **kosha**).

annamayakosha—The material physical sheath (see **kosha**).

antahkarana—The inner organ of thought, feeling, and conscience, consisting of **manas** (mind), **buddhi** (intellect, discriminative faculty), **chitta** (memory), and **ahamkara** (ego).

antaratman—Soul; psyche; God-spark. Also known as **purusha**.

aparaprakriti—Lower Nature; the perishable nature of the manifest universe.

artha—Meaning (of a Sanskrit word).

asurya guna—An "ungodly" quality, such as egotism, bondage, ignorance, conceit, impurity, hate, deceit, arrogance, desire, anger, possessiveness, and pride.

Atman—The real Self. The immortal spirit of Man. The Supreme Self or God, which, according to **Advaita**, is one with the individual soul. Its existence is light, self-concentrated force and self-delight.

avatar—A manifestation of the divine in human form.

avidya—Ignorance, individual or cosmic. The veil of ignorance that hides the Self within. Failure to realize the unity of all existence.

avyakta—The universe in its unmanifest state. The material cause of the universe, composed of the three **gunas**.

Bhagavad Gita—The "Holy Song" or "Celestial Hymn." The Hindu scripture in which the avatar **Krishna** reveals the Divine Wisdom of the ages.

bhakti—Love. Intense devotion.

bhakti yoga—The path of devotion.

bhavana—State of being or becoming. Existence. A state of flux. Effect. The source of emotional attitudes. A play of emotion or sense reaction.

Brahma—The Creator, one of the Hindu trinity, the other two being Vishnu and **Shiva**.

Brahman—Majesty. The Infinite Divine, the Absolute, God in his impersonal aspect. The unconditioned and Supreme Reality of **Advaita**.

buddhi—Intellect. Higher Reason. Intuitive reason. Intelligence. Discrimination. The discriminative faculty of the mind.

chaitya purusha—Psychic being. Soul.

chit—Consciousness. The Self-aware force of existence.

chitta—The storehouse of memory. Individual consciousness. Perception. Heart. Disposition. The function of the inner organ that seeks for pleasurable objects.

devanagari—"Divine-city" writing. The Sanskrit alphabet.

dharana—Fixation of attention on a particular object or idea with the aim of steadying the mind.

dharma—Duty. Virtue. Law. The inner constitution of a thing that governs its growth.

dhatu—A seed-sound that never changes and is expressive of an action either related to being or becoming.

dhvani—Audible sound; instrument of outward expression.

dhyana—Continuous meditation; focusing attention on a particular spiritual object or idea.

Gita—See **Bhagavad Gita**.

guna—Quality or attribute. According to the **Vedas**, there are three forces or substances — known as **sattva, rajas,** and **tamas** — which constitute **prakriti** (nature or matter) or **avyakta,** the material cause of the universe of mind and matter.

guru—Traditional teacher; spiritual master. One who teaches the secrets of meditation.

idam—Literally, "this is" or "that is." A term used to refer to the phenomenal world.

Indra—The ruler of the lesser deities. The king of the gods.

istham—Image or form of the divinity chosen as an object of adoration.

japam—The practice of repeating a sacred name of God or mantra.

jiva—Living being. The principle of life. The life spark in all living things. Individual being or soul associated with the mind, senses, and body.

jiva-atman—Spirit, Self in all.

jnana—Knowledge of reality.

jnana yoga—Path to realization through intellectual knowledge.

Kali Yuga—The Dark Age. The shortest of the great cosmic cycles, in which ignorance, selfishness, and greed cloud the human condition and in which only part of the truth is revealed. It is said that the Kali Yuga in which we now live began at the death of **Krishna** in the year 3102 B.C.

Kapila—The founder of the **Samkyha** philosophy.

karma—Deed; Effect of deed; action; duty. The law of cause and effect considered in relation to human conduct. The sum of the effects of past actions (including those done in previous incarnations), which bear fruit as the present and future destiny of the individual soul.

karma yoga—The path by which union with God is achieved through selfless action.

kosha—Covering. Sheath. Vessel. For its life in the material world the **atman** or divine Self envelops itself in the five *koshas*: **annamayakosha** or physical sheath; the **pranamayakosha** or vital sheath; the **manomayakosha,** or mental sheath; the **vijnanamayakosha** or sheath of Intellect; and **anandamayakosha** or sheath of bliss.

Krishna—One of the great divine incarnations whose life is extolled in the Hindu epics the **Bhagavad Gita** and the *Mahabharata*.

mahat—Supreme Intellect. Cosmic Mind. Stuff of consciousness.

manas—Mind. Discursive mind. Sensory mind. Thinking. One of the functions of the inner organ. The faculty of volition and doubt.

manomayakosha—The sheath of the moving mind (see **kosha**).

mantra—Holy Sanskrit text. A sacred name of God. A short mystic prayer, given by a guru to a disciple at initiation.

maya—In universal terms, the power of God to create things and give them form. One of the names of the Divine Mother. Lower or individual **maya** is spiritual illusion formed from ignorance obscuring the vision of Reality.

nirvana—Liberation, characterized by freedom and bliss. Extinction of all ego limitations, desires, and passions.

nirvikalpaka samadhi—The highest state of **samadhi**, in which the "I" no longer exists. Total oneness with the Supreme Self.

niyama—Regular practices of outward and inward purity, contentment, austerity, study, and surrender to the Supreme Self.

Nyaya—One of the six main systems of Indian thought (others include **Samkhya, Yoga,** and **Vedanta**): a realistic philosophy based on logical grounds.

OM or AUM—Word of power, belonging to no particular language, but used as a symbol of the Supreme throughout the East, where it is held to be the highest name of God. It portrays the threefold nature of the divine: the outer, the inner, and the superconscious.

om tat sat—The triple designation of Brahman. **Om** signifies the Divine, **tat** ("that") the inexpressible aspects of the Absolute, and **sat,** "Being" or "Reality."

Paramatman—Universal Self. Impersonal God.

paraprakriti—The Nature beyond. Unmanifest Divine Nature. The mother of all things. The higher realms of conscious nature.

Patanjali—Author of the *Yoga Sutras* or "Yoga Aphorisms," a basic text of Hindu philosophy.

prakriti—Primordial Nature. The material substratum of the creation, consisting of the three **gunas** — **sattva** (light, harmony), **rajas** (activity, passion), and **tamas** (darkness, inertia). In the individual, nature, character, constitution, disposition.

prana—Vital energy. Breath. The primal energy or force, of which other physical forces are manifestations.

pranamayakosha. The vital sheath. Life force.

pratyahara—Sublimation of lower psychic energy for higher purposes.

pravritti—Evolution. Unfolding of what is within or latent. Movement.

purusha—Person. Human being. The Self. Soul. Spirit. Witness. Absolute. The principle of consciousness. Also the Supreme Being or the soul of the universe. The universe is said to evolve from the union of **purusha** and **prakriti.**

rajas—The force of energy and motion in nature. One of the three **gunas** (qualities), *rajas* engenders action, effort, struggle, passion, and desire.

rajasic—Pertaining to, or endowed with, **rajas.**

raja yoga—"Kingly union" with God; so called because of the power and wisdom attained. A system of discipline for stilling the mind in order to realize and unite with that which is beyond mind.

Rig-Veda—The most ancient of the four **Vedas.**

rishi—A seer of truth. Great sage. Revealer of the wisdom of the **Vedas.**

sabda—Subtle, inaudible sound, containing the real meaning of a Sanskrit word or **mantra.**

sadhana—Asceticism. Spiritual discipline.

Samkhya—Spiritual knowledge. One of the six main systems of Hindu philosophy (see **Nyaya, Yoga,** and **Vedanta**). The **Samkhya** teaches that the universe evolves as the result of the union of **prakriti** (nature) and **purusha** (Spirit).

shakti—The Divine power. The consciousness force of the Divine Mother.

samadhi—Ecstasy. Complete absorption in God.

samskara—Mental impressions, recollection, tendency, formed habits. An old association stored in memory both of mankind and the individual.

sat—Reality. Being.

sat-chit-ananda—Being-consciousness-bliss. *Sat-chit-ananda* is the nature of **paraprakriti,** the higher nature or pure state of **atman.**

sattva—The force of equilibrium in nature. One of the three **gunas,** which manifests as harmony, balance, knowledge, joy, light.

savikalpa samadhi—The lower state of **samadhi,** in which the sense of "I" is still present.

Shankara or **Shankaracharya,** (788-820 A.D.)—One of the greatest saints and philosophers of India, the foremost exponent of Advaita yoga.

Shiva—"The Destroyer," one of the three gods of the Hindu trinity, the others being **Brahman** and Vishnu.

sloka—Aphorism. Brief statement of a sacred truth. Invocation or prayer.

sruti—"That which is revealed" The Vedas and other authoritative scriptures, which contain the spiritual truths revealed to the seers of old, are collectively known as *sruti.*

Srimad Bhagavatam—"The Wisdom of God." One of the most beloved of Hindu scriptures.

sutras—Terse, aphoristic utterances. *Sutras* are often likened to pearls of thoughts or truths sewn together on a string.

swami—A spiritual master.

tanmatras—Rudimentary or subtle elements — ether, air, fire, water, earth — which give rise to sound, touch, sight, taste, smell.

tapas—Spiritual force. Heat produced by austerity and discipline.

tat tvam asi—"That Thou art." **Tat** ("that") refers to the transcendental Reality or Brahman. **Tvam** ("thou") refers to the **jiva** or the individualized and conditioned soul. **Asi** ("art") expresses the eternal identity of the *jiva* and Brahman.

Trimarga—The threefold path of action, devotion, and knowledge.

turiya—Merging with Brahman. A name of the Supreme Brahman. A level of consciousness transcending and pervading the three states of waking, dream, and sleep.

Upanishads—The Indian scriptures elaborating upon the philosophy of the **Vedas.** There are 108 Upanishads, of which eleven are called "major Upanishads."

vach—The creative Word; the dynamic principle of creation.

Vedas—Sacred, revealed knowledge. The collection of the most sacred scriptures of the Hindus and the ultimate authority of the Hindu religion and philosophy. The Vedas consist of the **Rig-Veda, Sama-Veda, Yajur-Veda,** and **Atharva-Veda.**

Vedanta—The essence of the Vedas. A system of philosophy elaborated in such texts as the **Upanishads** and the **Bhagavad Gita.**

vidya—Knowledge.

vijnanamayakosha—The sheath of intellect.

vijnanapurusha—Super-Mind. Divine will, power, and knowledge.

yama—A firm determination to live a life dedicated to Truth.

yoga—Union of the individual Self and the Supreme Self. One of the classic roads by which to attain liberation. The Eightfold Yoga refers to Patanjali's system of philosophy, which deals with the realization of Truth through mental concentration.

yogi—One who practices yoga.

yuga—Age. Cycle.

BIBLIOGRAPHY

Alighieri, Dante. *The Paradiso: A Verse Rendering* by John Ciardi. New York: New American Library, 1970.

Anderson, William. *The Face of Glory*. London: Bloomsbury, 1996.

The Apocrypha According to the Authorized Version. London: Oxford University Press, n.d.

Ashtavakra Gita. Translated by Hari Prasad Shastri. London: Shanti Sadan, 1961.

Aurelius, Marcus. *Marcus Aurelius and His Times*: *Meditations*. New York: Walter J. Black, 1945.

Aurobindo, Sri. *The Synthesis of Yoga*. Pondicherry, India: Sri Aurobindo Society, 1988.

——. *The Hour of God*. Pondicherry, India: Sri Aurobindo Society, 1964.

——. *The Life Divine*. Pondicherry, India: Sri Aurobindo Society, 1974.

——. *The Supramental Manifestation and Other Writings*. Pondicherry, India: Sri Aurobindo Ashram, 1997.

The Bhagavad Gita. Translated by Franklin Edgerton. Cambridge, Mass.: Harvard University Press, 1972.

The Bhagavad Gita, with the commentary of Sri Sankaracharya. Translated into English by Alladi Mahadeva Sastry. Madras, India: Samata Books, 1985.

Bible, Holy. King James Version. New York: American Bible Society, n.d.

Bible, *New Revised Standard Version of the Bible*. Nashville, Tenn.: Thomas Nelson, Inc., n.d.

Boehme, Jacob. *Thoughts on the Spiritual Life*. Kila, Mont.: Kessinger Publishing, 1997.

Boethius. *Boethius: The Theological Tracts*. Translated by H.F. Stewart, E.K Rand, and S.J. Tester. Cambridge, Mass.: Harvard University Press, 1973.

Brunton, Paul. *The Notebooks of Paul Brunton*. Vol. I. Perspectives: *The Timeless Way of Wisdom*. Burdett, N.Y.: Larsen, 1984.

Buber, Martin. *Ten Rungs: Hasidic Sayings*. New York: Schocken, 1973.

St. Catherine of Siena. *The Letters of St. Catherine of Siena*, Vol. I. Medieval & Renaissance Texts and Studies, Vol. 52. Binghamton, N.Y.: State University of New York Press at Binghamton, 1988.

Coomaraswamy, Ananda K. *What Is Civilisation? and Other Essays*. Great Barrington, Mass.: Lindisfarne, 1989.

The Dhammapada. Translated by P. Lal. New York: Farrar, Straus & Giroux, 1972.

Dickinson, Emily. *Final Harvest: Emily Dickinson's Poems*. Edited by Thomas H. Johnson. Boston: Little, Brown, 1961.

Eckhart, Meister Johannes. *Meister Eckhart*. Translated by Raymond B. Blakney. New York: Harper Torchbooks, 1941.

Emerson, Ralph Waldo. *The Journals and Miscellaneous Notebooks*. Cambridge, Mass.: Harvard University Press, 1969.

———. *The Complete Writings of Ralph Waldo Emerson*. New York: Wm. H. Wise & Co., 1929.

Epictetus. *Encheiridion*. Translated by W.A. Oldfather. Cambridge, Mass.: Harvard University Press, 1928.

Ficino, Marsilio. *The Letters of Marsilio Ficino*. Vol. I. Translated by members of the Language Department of the School of Economic Science, London. London: Shepheard-Walwyn, 1975.

———. *The Letters of Marsilio Ficino*. Vol. II. Translated by members of the Language Department of the School of Economic Science, London. London: Shepheard-Walwyn, 1978.

St. Francis de Sales. *Finding God Wherever You Are: Selected Spiritual Writings*. Edited by Joseph F. Power, O.S.F.S. New Rochelle, N.Y.: New City Press, 1993.

Geldard, Richard. *God in Concord*. Burdett, N.Y.: Larsen, 1998.

The Golden Verses of the Pythagoreans. Fintry, Brook, Surrey: The Shrine of Wisdom.

The Gospel According to Thomas. Translated by A. Guillaumont et al. New York: Harper & Row, 1959.

Hermes Trismegistus. *Hermetica: Philosophic Teachings Ascribed to Hermes Trismegistus*. Vol. I. Edited by Walter Scott. Boston: Shambhala, 1985.

Hildegard of Bingen. *Scivias*. Translated by Mother Columba Hart and Jan Bishop. New York: Paulist Press, 1990.

———. *Hildegard of Bingen's Book of Divine Works*. Edited by Matthew Fox. Santa Fe, N.M.: Bear & Co., 1987.

Hymns from the Rig-Veda. Translation by Jean LeMée. New York: Alfred A. Knopf, 1975.

St. John of the Cross. *Poems*. Translated by Roy Campbell. Baltimore, Md.: Penguin, 1960.

Jonas, Hans. *The Gnostic Religion*. Boston: Beacon Press, 1963.

Kabir. *Songs of Kabir*. Translated by Rabindranath Tagore. York Beach, Maine: Samuel Weiser, 1995.

à Kempis, Thomas. *Imitation of Christ*. Nashville, Tenn.: Thomas Nelson, 1999.

Lao Tsu. *Tao Te Ching*. Translated by Gia-Fu Feng and Jane English. New York: Vintage, 1997.

Le Mée, Katharine. *Chant: The Origins, Form, Practice and Healing Power of Gregorian Chant*. New York: Bell Tower, 1994.

Mack, Burton L., trans. *The Lost Gospel: The Book of Q and Christian Origins*. New York: HarperCollins, 1993.

A Method of Self-Realisation. London: The Society for the Study of Normal Psychology, 1983.

The Nag Hammadi Library. James Robinson, General Editor. San Francisco: HarperCollins, 1990.

Pascal, Blaise. *Pensées*. Translated by W.F. Trotter. London: Encyclopaedia Britannica, 1952.

Patanjali. *How to Know God: The Yoga Aphorisms of Patanjali*. Translated with a Commentary by Swami Prabhavananda and Christopher Isherwood. New York: New American Library, 1969.

Perry, Bliss. *The Heart of Emerson's Journals*. New York: Dover, 1995.

Pieper, Josef. *Leisure: The Basis of Culture*. Translated by Alexander Dru. New York: Random House, 1963.

Plato. *The Collected Dialogues of Plato*. Edited by Edith Hamilton and Huntington Cairns. Princeton, N.J.: Princeton University Press, 1978.

Plotinus. *Plotinus*. Translated by A.H. Armstrong. Cambridge, Mass.: Harvard University Press, 1966.

Plummer, L. Gordon. *The Mathematics of the Cosmic Mind*. Wheaton, Ill.: Theosophical Publishing House, 1970.

Prabhavanand, Swami. *The Sermon on the Mount According to Vedanta*. New York: New American Library, 1972.

Ramana Maharshi. *Talks with Sri Ramana Maharshi*. Tiruvannamalai, India: Sri Ramanasram, 1984.

Rumi, Jalal'Uddin. *Unseen Rain: Quatrains of Rumi*. Translated by John Moyne and Coleman Barks. Putney, Vt.: Threshold Books, 1986.

Sankaracarya, Sri. *Eight Upanisads with the Commentary of Sankaracarya*. Vol. I and II. Translated by Swami Gambhivananda. Calcutta, India: Advaita Ashrama, 1982.

——. *The Crest Jewel of Wisdom*. Translated by Charles Johnston. Pasadena, Calif.: Theosophical University Press, 1946.

——. *Crest-Jewel of Discrimination*. Translated by Swami Prabhavananda and Christopher Isherwood. Hollywood, Calif.: Vedanta Press, 1978.

———. *Direct Experience of Reality: Verses from the Aparokshanubhuti of Shri Shankaracharya*. Translated with commentary by Hari Prasad Shastri. London: Shanti Sadan, 1959.

———. *Self-Knowledge; Sankarachaya's Atmabodha*. Translated by Swami Nikhilananda. New York: Ramakrishna-Vivekananda Center, 1980.

Schopenhauer, Arthur. *The World as Will and Representation*. New York: Dover, 1969.

Schuon, Frithjof. *Echoes of Perennial Wisdom*. Bloomington, Ind.: World Wisdom Books, 1992.

Shah, Idries. *The Way of the Sufi*. New York: E.P. Dutton, 1970.

Shastri, H.P. *World within the Mind (Yoga-Vasishtha)*. London: Shanti Sadan, 1975.

Srimad Bhagavatam: The Wisdom of God. Translated by Swami Prahavananda. Madras, India: Sri Ramakrishna Math, 1978.

Symphonia: A Critical Edition of the Symphonia armonica celestium revelationum: Hildegard von Bingen's Poetry. Translated by Barbara Newman. Ithaca, N.Y.: Cornell University Press, 1988.

Tagore, Rabindranath. *Gitanjali*. New York: Scribner, 1997.

———. *Sadhana*. New York: Macmillan, 1913.

Teilhard de Chardin, Pierre. *The Divine Milieu*. New York: Harper & Row, 1968.

The Ten Principal Upanishads. Translated by Shree Purohit Swami and W.B. Yeats. New York: Collier, 1975.

St. Teresa of Ávila. *Interior Castle*. Translated by E. Peers. Garden City, N.Y.: Image, 1961.

Theologia Germanica. Translated by Susanna Winkworth. London: Stuart & Watkins, 1966.

Thoreau, Henry David. *Walden and Other Writings of Henry David Thoreau*. Edited by Brooks Atkinson. New York: Modern Library, 1937.

Vedanta for the Western World. Edited by Christopher Isherwood. New York: Marcel Roddy, 1946.

Vivekananda, Swami. *Jnana-Yoga*. New York: Ramakrishna-Vivekananda Center of New York, 1982.

———. *Inspired Talks*. New York: Ramakrishna-Vivekananda Center of New York, 1987.

Weil, Simone. *Waiting for God*. Translated by Emma Craufurd. New York: Harper Colophon, 1973.

Whitman, Walt. *Leaves of Grass*. New York: Airmont, 1965.

Wittgenstein, Ludwig. *Tractatus Logico-Philosophicus*. Translated by D. F. Pears and B. F. McGuiness. London: Routledge & Kegan Paul, 1961.

Yutang, Lin, ed. *The Wisdom of China and India*. New York: Modern Library, 1942.

Further Reading

In addition to the preceding bibliography, here is a list of books that the author has found useful and inspiring. Some of the books are temporarily out of print, but may often be found in secondhand bookstores and searches on the Internet.

Aquinas, St. Thomas. *Summa Contra Gentiles: God*. Translated by Anton C. Pegis. Notre Dame, Ind.: University of Notre Dame Press, 1997.

St. Augustine. *De Ordine*. Translated by Robert P. Russell. New York: Cosmopolitan Science and Art Service Co., 1942.

Aurobindo, Sri. *Bases of Yoga*. Pondicherry, India: Sri Aurobindo Ashram Trust, 1993.

———. *Bhagavad Gita and Its Message*. Edited by Anilbaran Roy. Pondicherry, India: Sri Aurobindo Ashram Trust, 1995.

———. ed. *The Eternal Wisdom: Central Sayings of Great Sages of all Times*. Pondicherry, India: Sri Aurobindo Ashram Trust, 1993.

———. *Future Evolution of Man*. Pondicherry, India: Sri Aurobindo Ashram Trust, 1974.

———. *Integral Yoga: Sri Aurobindo's Teaching & Method of Practice*. Pondicherry, India: Sri Aurobindo Ashram Trust, 1993.

———. *Savitri: A Legend and Symbol*. Pondicherry, India: Sri Aurobindo Ashram Trust, 1995.

———. *The Upanishads*. Pondicherry, India: Sri Aurobindo Ashram Trust, 1974.

Note: The Collected Works of Sri Aurobindo *were published as the Sri Aurobindo Birth Centenary Library in 1972 and may be found in libraries.* Currently The Complete Works of Sri Aurobindo *in thirty-five volumes is under publication by Sri Aurobindo Society, Pondicherry, India. Many recent editions are available in the U.S. through Lotus Press, Twin Lakes, Wisconsin, and the Matagiri Aurobindo Center, Mt. Tremper, N.Y. (e-mail: Matagiri@aol.com).*

Beguine Spirituality: Mystical Writings of Mechthild of Magdeburg, Beatrice of Nazareth, and Hadewijch of Brabant. Edited by Fiona Bowil. Translated by Oliver Davis. New York: Crossroads, 1989.

The Bhagavad Gita. Translated by Sri Purohit Swami. Boston: Shambhala, 1994.

Bhagavad Gita In the Light of Sri Aurobindo. Edited by Maheshwar. Pondicherry: Sri Aurobindo Ahsram, 1992.

Boethius. *Consolation of Philosophy*. Translated by V.E. Watts. New York: Penguin, 2000.

Brunton, Paul. *The Notebooks of Paul Brunton*. Sixteen volumes. Burdett, N.Y.: Larsen, 1989.

Chuang Tsu. *Chuang Tsu: Inner Chapters*. Translated by Gia-fu Feng and Jane English. New York: Vintage, 1974.

The Cloud of Unknowing and Other Works. Translated by Clifton Wolters and Thomas Wyatt. New York: Viking, 1978.

Das, Lama Surya. *Awakening the Buddha Within: Eight Steps to Enlightenment*. New York: Broadway, 1997.

de Chaussade, Jean Pierre. *Self Abandonment to Divine Providence*. Rockfort, Il.: Tan Books & Publishers, 1987.

———. *The Sacrament of the Present Moment*. Translated by Kitty Muggeridge. San Francisco: HarperSanFrancisco, 1989.

de Sales, St. Francis. *Introduction to the Devout Life*. Translation by John Kenneth Ryan. New York: Doubleday, 1990.

———. *Finding God wherever you are. Selected Spiritual Writings*. Edited by Joseph F. Power. New Rochelle, N.Y.: New City Press, 1993.

Dillaway, Newton. *The Gospel of Emerson*. Unity Village, Mo.: Unity Books, 1984.

Edelglass, Stephen, Georg Maier, Hans Gebert, and John Davey. *The Marriage of Sense and Thought: The Imaginative Participation in Science*. Hudson, N.Y.: Anthroposophic Press, 1997.

Emerson, Ralph Waldo. *Essays and Lectures of Ralph Waldo Emerson*. Edited by Joel Porte. New York: Library of America, 1983.

———. *The Portable Emerson*. Edited by Carl Bode. New York: Viking Penguin, 1976.

———. *The Heart of Emerson's Journals*. Edited by Bliss Perry. New York: Dover, 1995.

———. *The Collected Works of Ralph Waldo Emerson*. Cambridge, Mass.: Harvard University Press, n.d.

Feuerstein, Georg. *Wholeness or Transcendence?* Burdett, N.Y.: Larsen, 1974.

Ficino, Marsilio. *Meditations on the Soul: Selected Letters of Marsilio Ficino*. Rochester, Vt.: Inner Traditions, 1997.

———. *Commentary on Plato's Symposium on Love*. Translated by Sears Reynolds Jayne. Woodstock, Ct.: Spring, 1990.

Gardner, John Fentress. *American Heralds of the Spirit: Melville, Whitman, and Emerson*. Hudson, N.Y.: Lindisfarne, 1992.

Geldard, Richard. *The Spiritual Teachings of Ralph Waldo Emerson*. Great Barrington, Mass.: Lindisfarne, 2001.

Goethe, Johann Wolfgang von. *Wisdom and Experience*. Translated by H. Weigand. New York: Ungar, 1949.

———. *Nature's Open Secret: Introductions to Goethe's Scientific Writings*. Edited by John Barnes. Great Barrington, Mass.: Anthroposophic Press, 2000.

Guénon, René. *Man and His Becoming According to the Vedanta*. Translated by Richard C. Nicholson. New Delhi: Munshiram Manoharlal, 1981.

——. *The Crisis of the Modern World*. Minneapolis, Minn.: American Chemical Dependency Society, 1996.

——. *The Reign of Quantity and The Signs of the Times*. Ghent, N.Y.: Sophia Perennis et Universalis, 1995.

Harvey, Andrew. *The Essential Mystics: The Soul's Journey into Truth*. Edison, N.Y.: Castle Books, 1998.

Hermes Trismegistus. *The Divine Pymander and other Writings of Hermes Trismegistus*. Translated by John D. Chambers. Escondido, Calif.: The Book Tree, 1999.

Herrigel, Eugen. *Zen in the Art of Archery*. New York: Random House, 1999.

Hirshfield, Jane. *Women in Praise of the Sacred*. New York: HarperCollins, 1994.

Huxley, Aldous. *The Perennial Philosophy*. New York: Harper and Row, 1970.

Krishnamurti, Jiddu. *The Awakening Intelligence*. San Francisco: HarperSanFrancisco, 1987.

——. *The Flame of Attention*. San Francisco: Harper & Row, 1984.

Kühlewind, Georg. *Stages of Consciousness: Meditations on the Boundaries of the Soul*. Translated by Maria St. Goar. Hudson, N.Y.: Lindisfarne, 1984.

——. *The Life of the Soul: Between Subconsciousness and Supraconsciousness*. Hudson, N.Y.: Lindisfarne, 1990.

——. *From Normal to Healthy: Paths to the Liberation of Consciousness*. Hudson, N.Y.: Lindisfarne, 1990.

Laszlo, Ervin. *The Creative Cosmos: A Unified Science of Matter, Life and Mind*. Hudson, N.Y.: Anthroposophic Press, 1996.

Lemaitre, Solange. *Ramakrishna and the Vitality of Hinduism*. Translated by Charles Lam Makmann. Woodstock, N.Y.: Overlook, 1984.

McDermott, Robert, ed. *The Essential Aurobindo*. Hudson, N.Y.: Lindisfarne, 1987.

Maharishi Mahesh Yogi. *Maharishi Mahesh Yogi on the Bhagavad-Gita: A New Translation and Commentary*. New York: Viking Penguin, 1990.

Mishra, Rammurti S. *Yoga Sutras: The Textbook of Yoga Psychology*. Garden City, N.Y.: Anchor, 1973.

Mitchell, Stephen. *The Enlightened Mind: An Anthology of Sacred Prose*. New York: HarperCollins, 1991.

Moore, Thomas. *The Planets Within: The Astrological Psychology of Marsilio Ficino*. Great Barrington, Mass.: Lindisfarne, 2000.

Needleman, Carla. *The Work of Craft: An Inquiry into the Nature of Crafts and Craftsmanship*. New York: Alfred A. Knopf, 1979.

Needleman, Jacob. *The Heart of Philosophy*. New York: Bantam Books, 1984.

Needleman, Jacob, and David Appelbaum. *Real Philosophy: An Anthology of the Universal Search for Meaning*. New York: Penguin Arkana, 1990.

Nicoll, Maurice. *Psychological Commentaries on the Teachings of Gurdjieff and Ouspensky*. Five volumes. York Beach, Maine: Samuel Weiser, 1996.

——. *Simple Explanation of Work Ideas*. Utrecht, The Netherlands: Eureka, 1999.

——. *The Work Life: Based on the Teachings of G.I. Gurdjieff, P.D. Ouspensky and M. Nicoll*. York Beach, Maine: Samuel Weiser, 1994.

Okakura, Kakuzo. *The Book of Tea*. New York: Dover, 1966.

Ouspensky, P.D. *In Search of the Miraculous*. New York: Harcourt, Brace & World, 1949.

——. *Tertium Organum*. New York: Vintage, 1970.

——. *The Fourth Way*. New York: Random House, 1971.

——. *The Psychology of Man's Possible Evolution*. New York: Vintage, 1974.

Pagels, Elaine. *The Gnostic Gospels*. New York: Vintage, 1989.

Paramananda, Swami. *Emerson and Vedanta*. Cohasset, Mass.: Vedanta Centers, 1985.

Perry, Bliss. *The Heart of Emerson's Journals*. New York: Dover, 1995.

Plotinus. *Plotinus: The Enneads*. Translated by Stephen MacKenna. Burdett, N.Y.: Larsen, 1992.

——. *The Essential Plotinus: Representative Treatises from the Enneads by Plotinus*. Translated by Elmer O'Brian, S.J. Indianapolis, Ind.: Hackett, 1975.

Ramakrishna, Sri. *The Gospel of Sri Ramakrishna*. Translated by Swami Nikhilananda. New York: Ramakrishna-Vivekananda Center, 1958.

Rumi, Jalal-Uddin. *Teachings of Rumi: The Masnavi*. Translated and edited by E.H. Whinfield. New York: Dutton, 1975.

——. *Open Secret: Versions of Rumi*. Translated by John Moyne and Coleman Barks. Putney, Vt.: Threshold Books, 1984.

——. *The Essential Rumi*. Translated by Coleman Barks, John Moyne, et al. Edison, N.Y.: Castle Books, 1997.

——. *Discourses of Rumi*. Translated by Arthur J. Arberry. Richmond, Surrey, U.K.: Curzon, 1997.

Shakespeare, William. *The Complete Works of William Shakespeare*. London: Oxford University Press, 1952.

Shantanand Saraswati, H.H. *Good Company: An Anthology of Sayings, Stories and Answers to Questions by His Holiness Sri Shantanand Saraswati, The Shankaracharya of Jyotir Math*. Rockport, Mass.: Element, 1992.

——. *The Man Who Wanted to Meet God: Myths and Stories That Explain the Inexplicable.* New York: Bell Tower, 1996.

Smoley, Richard, and Jay Kinney. *Hidden Wisdom: A Guide to the Western Inner Traditions.* New York: Penguin Arkana, 1999.

Steiner, Rudolf. *How to Know Higher Worlds: A Modern Path of Initiation.* Translated by Christopher Bamford. Hudson, N.Y.: Anthroposophic Press, 1994.

——. *A Way to Self-Knowledge.* Great Barrington, Mass.: Anthroposophic Press, 1999.

——. *Self-Transformation: Selected Lectures by Rudolf Steiner.* Hudson, N.Y.: Anthroposophic Press, 1996.

Swedenborg, Emanuel. *The Universal Human and Soul-Body Interaction.* Translated and edited by George F. Dole. New York: Paulist, 1984.

Tame, David. *Beethoven and the Spiritual Path.* Wheaton, Ill.: Theosophical Publishing House, 1994.

Teilhard de Chardin, Pierre. *The Future of Man.* New York: Harper Torchbooks, 1969.

Traherne, Thomas. *Select Meditations.* Edited by J.J. Smith. Leonia, N.Y.: Paul & Co., 1997.

Trungpa, Chögyam. *The Myth of Freedom.* Boston, Mass.: Shambhala, 1976.

——. *Glimpses of Abhidharma.* Boulder, Colo.: Prajna Press, 1981.

Tulku, Tarthang. *Gesture of Balance: A Guide to Awareness, Self-Healing, and Meditation.* Emeryville, Calif.: Dharma, 1977.

Tyberg, Judith M. *The Language of the Gods: Sanskrit Keys to India's Wisdom.* Los Angeles: East-West Cultural Center, 1976.

Underhill, Evelyn. *Mysticism.* Notre Dame, Ind.: One World, 1993.

Versluis, Arthur. *Theosophia: Hidden Dimensions of Christianity.* Hudson, N.Y.: Lindisfarne, 1994.

Zaleski, Philip and Paul Kaufmann. *Gifts of the Spirit: Living the Wisdom of the Great Religious Traditions.* New York: HarperCollins, 1997.

Permission Acknowledgments

Grateful acknowledgment is made to the following publishers for permission to reprint previously published material. Every effort has been made to trace copyright holders of materials in this book. In a few instances, publishers did not respond in time for acknowledgment in this place.

Excerpts from transcripts of audiences granted by H.H. Shantanand Saraswati, the Shankaracharya of Jyotir Math in Northern India to members of The Study Society. Copyright © 2001 by the Study Society, Colet House, London, U.K. Used with the permission of The Study Society.

Excerpts from *The Supramental Manifestation* by Sri Aurobindo. Copyright © 1952 by Sri Aurobindo Society, Pondicherry, India. Reprinted with the permission of Sri Aurobindo Ashram Trust.

From *The Hour of God* by Sri Aurobindo. Copyright © 1964 by Sri Aurobindo Society, Pondicherry, India. Reprinted with the permission of Sri Aurobindo Ashram Trust.

Excerpts from *The Life Divine* by Sri Aurobindo. Copyright © 1990 by Sri Aurobindo Society, Pondicherry, India. Reprinted with the permission of Sri Aurobindo Ashram Trust.

Quotations from the *Synthesis of Yoga* by Sri Aurobindo. Copyright © 1992 by Sri Aurobindo Society, Pondicherry, India. Reprinted with the permission of Sri Aurobindo Ashram Trust.

Quotations from *The Notebooks of Paul Brunton, Vol. I—Perspectives—The Timeless Way of Wisdom*. Copyright © 1984 by Kenneth Thurston Hurst. Published for the Paul Brunton Philosophic Foundation by Larson Publications. Used by permission of Larsen Publications.

Excerpts from *Scivias* by Hildegard of Bingen. Translation by Mother Columba Hart and Jan Bishop. Copyright © 1990 by Paulist Press. Used with permission of Paulist Press.

From *Hymns from the Rig-Veda*. Translation and Sanskrit Calligraphy by Jean LeMée. Copyright © 1975 by Jean LeMée. First published in 1975 by Alfred A. Knopf, Inc. Used by permission of Jean LeMée.

From *Jnana-Yoga* by Swami Vivekananda; published by the Ramakrishna-Vivekananda Center of New York. Copyright © 1955 by Swami Nikhilananda, Trustee of the Estate of Swami Vivekananda; U.S. Paperback Edition 1982. Reprinted by permission of Ramakrishna-Vivekananda Center Publications.

From *Inspired Talks* by Swami Vivekananda; published by the Ramakrishna-Vivekananda Center of New York. Copyright © 1958 by Swami Nikhilananda, Trustee of the Estate of Swami Vivekananda; U.S. Paperback Edition 1987. Reprinted by permission of Ramakrishna-Vivekananda Center Publications.

INDEX OF CHARTS AND DIAGRAMS